Ents, Elves, and Eriador

Culture of the Land

A Series in the New Agrarianism

This series is devoted to the exploration and articulation of a new agrarianism that considers the health of habitats and human communities together. It is intended to demonstrate how agrarian insights and responsibilities can be worked out in diverse fields of learning and living: history, science, art, politics, economics, literature, philosophy, religion, urban planning, education, and public policy. Agrarianism is a comprehensive worldview that appreciates the intimate and practical connections which exist between humans and the earth. It stands as our most promising alternative to the unsustainable and destructive ways of current global, industrial, and consumer culture.

Series Editor
Norman Wirzba, Georgetown College, Kentucky

Advisory Board
Wendell Berry, Port Royal, Kentucky
Ellen Davis, Duke University, North Carolina
Patrick Holden, Soil Association, United Kingdom
Wes Jackson, Land Institute, Kansas
Gene Logsdon, Upper Sandusky, Ohio
Bill McKibben, Middlebury College, Vermont
David Orr, Oberlin College, Ohio
Michael Pollan, University of California at Berkeley, California
Jennifer Sahn, *Orion* magazine, Massachusetts
Vandana Shiva, Research Foundation for Science,
Technology and Ecology, India
William Vitek, Clarkson University, New York

Ents, Elves, and Eriador

The Environmental Vision of J. R. R. Tolkien

Matthew Dickerson
and Jonathan Evans

THE UNIVERSITY PRESS OF KENTUCKY

Publication of this volume was made possible in part by a grant
from the National Endowment for the Humanities.

Copyright © 2006 by The University Press of Kentucky

Scholarly publisher for the Commonwealth,
serving Bellarmine University, Berea College, Centre
College of Kentucky, Eastern Kentucky University,
The Filson Historical Society, Georgetown College,
Kentucky Historical Society, Kentucky State University,
Morehead State University, Murray State University,
Northern Kentucky University, Transylvania University,
University of Kentucky, University of Louisville,
and Western Kentucky University.
All rights reserved.

Editorial and Sales Offices: The University Press of Kentucky
663 South Limestone Street, Lexington, Kentucky 40508-4008
www.kentuckypress.com

06 07 08 09 10   5 4 3 2 1

Library of Congress Cataloging-in-Publication Data

Dickerson, Matthew T., 1963-
Ents, elves, and Eriador : the environmental vision of J.R.R. Tolkien /
Matthew Dickerson and Jonathan Evans.
p. cm. — (Culture of the land)
Includes bibliographical references and index.
ISBN-13: 978-0-8131-2418-6 (alk. paper)
ISBN-10: 0-8131-2418-2 (alk. paper)
1. Tolkien, J. R. R. (John Ronald Reuel), 1892-1973—
Knowledge—Environmental sciences. 2. Tolkien, J. R. R. (John Ronald Reuel),
1892-1973—Criticism and interpretation. 3. Ecology in literature.
4. Nature in literature. 5. Human ecology in literature.
6. Middle Earth (Imaginary place). 7. Environmentalism. 8. Ecocriticism.
9. Environmental literature—History and criticism.
I. Evans, Jonathan D.
(Jonathan Duane), 1954- II. Title.
PR6039.O32Z636 2006
823'.912—dc22
2006019174

This book is printed on acid-free recycled paper meeting
the requirements of the American National Standard
for Permanence in Paper for Printed Library Materials.

Manufactured in the United States of America.

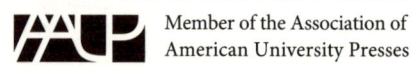

Member of the Association of
American University Presses

Yet it is not our part to master all the tides of the world, but to do what is in us for the succour of those years wherein we are set, uprooting the evil in the fields that we know, so that those who live after may have clean earth to till. What weather they shall have is not ours to rule.

—*Gandalf to the Captains of the West (V/ix)*

Contents

Foreword by John Elder   ix
Acknowledgments   xiii
Introduction   xv
Conventions and Abbreviations   xxv

Part I. "The Tides of the World": Gandalfian Stewardship and the Foundations of Tolkien's Vision

Chapter 1. Varda, Yavanna, and the Value of Creation   3

Chapter 2. Gandalf, Stewardship, and Tomorrow's Weather   37

Part II. "The Succour of Those Years Wherein We Are Set": A Complex Ecology of Agriculture, Horticulture, and Feraculture

Chapter 3. Hobbits and the Agrarian Society of the Shire   71

Chapter 4. Horticulture and the Aesthetic of the Elves   95

Chapter 5. Woods, Wildness, and the Feraculture of the Ents   119

Chapter 6. The Necessity of Margins in Middle-earth's Mingled Ecologies   145

Chapter 7. The Ecology of Ham, Niggle's Parish, and Wootton Major   163

Part III. "Uprooting the Evil in the Fields That We Know": Following the Vision, and the Consequences of Ignoring It

Chapter 8. Three Faces of Mordor   185

Chapter 9. Rousing the Shire   215

Chapter 10. Environmentalism, Transcendence, and Action   235
    Conclusion: Some Practical Matters   259

Afterword by Tom Shippey   269
Appendix: Further Reading   273
Notes   277
Index   299

Foreword

Over the past several decades, a form of literary scholarship has evolved that is now commonly referred to as ecocriticism. This approach to the dialogue between literature and the natural world seems, in retrospect, to have tracked fairly closely with certain phases in the environmental movement. It grew originally out of the study of "nature writing"—Thoreauvian nonfiction in which solitude amid wild landscapes was one central theme. Authors such as John Muir, Aldo Leopold, and Edward Abbey came to be prized not only because of their tangy voices but also because of their strong advocacy for preserving wilderness. The work of these writers and others like them strongly influenced the passage of the 1964 Wilderness Act. Readers of Rachel Carson were similarly influenced by her courage in decrying the toxicity in our manufacturing and agricultural practices and by the relevance of her writing to the formation of such regulatory agencies as the Environmental Protection Agency and to such legislation as the Clean Water and Clean Air acts. More recently, Native American writers like Leslie Marmon Silko and Joseph Bruchac have powerfully conveyed indigenous perspectives on nature to a broad audience. Their work has called into question some of the assumptions of the wilderness movement, as well as contributed to a growing emphasis on racial equity and environmental justice within the discourse of ecocriticism.

Beyond these key instances in which literature and activism have become intertwined, there are a couple of emerging developments that are well represented in *Ents, Elves, and Eriador*. Matthew Dickerson and Jonathan Evans's admirable study of J. R. R. Tolkien participates in an extension of the ecocritical inquiry to literature that has not been closely associated with the environmental movement and that may, in fact, have considerably predated it. Scholars are returning to such canonical authors as William Shakespeare, John Milton, Walt Whitman, Emily Dickinson, and Alfred, Lord Tennyson in poetry, and George Eliot and

Thomas Hardy in fiction, to investigate the natural themes and images that deepen the other meanings of their texts. They are comparing earlier twentieth-century writers like D. H. Lawrence, Virginia Woolf, William Faulkner, Robert Frost, Marianne Moore, and Wallace Stevens with such contemporaries as Gary Snyder and Mary Oliver, who are more overtly connected with environmental themes. They are investigating the ways in which classics from without the Anglo-American canon—including Dante, Cervantes, and such great non-Western writers as Basho and his followers in Japan's haiku tradition—can now illuminate the ecotone between nature and culture.

In focusing on the environmental vision of Tolkien, Dickerson and Evans identify promising terrain for such a project of mapping and reevaluation. Not only was Tolkien's *Lord of the Rings* trilogy one of the most widely read and best-loved works of the twentieth century, but Peter Jackson's celebrated film adaptation has done much to consolidate and extend that already vast audience. As Terry Eagleton argues in his books *Literary Theory* and *Beyond Theory*, we have arrived at a moment when criticism must speak directly to the larger challenges of social transformation. A literary study that articulates Tolkien's emphasis on restraining our individual appetites, defending beloved landscapes against the ethical and technological challenges symbolized by Mordor, and fostering sustainability in our communities can amplify that author's potential for exercising an impact on present-day values and practices.

This timely study also echoes a renewed emphasis, in ecocriticism and environmentalism alike, on the old-fashioned language of stewardship. It is a concept strongly associated with Tolkien's vision of the Shire. Raymond Williams and others have found nostalgia and sentimentality in this depiction—based on a Worcestershire village from Tolkien's boyhood that had long since been incorporated into the industrial sprawl around Birmingham. Indeed, if the landscape around Hobbiton were to be valued primarily for its thatched roofs and home-brewed beer, it might well be dismissed as no more than an appealing anachronism. But it is in fact presented as one distinctive region within a carefully graduated range of locales in Middle-earth. The rolling downs of Rohan, the deep woods of the Ents and Huorns, and the damaged but resilient gardens of Gondor offer the broader context in which to appreciate the specific importance of the Shire. As Dickerson and Evans show, the landscapes around Isengard that have been blighted by Saruman speak to the true value of the Hobbits' home country. In relation to their small, undramatic rural community, Tolkien evokes the old-fashioned value of stewardship—a concept that eventually comes to enclose the whole saga in its arc and to define the missions of both Gandalf and Aragorn.

Just as the Shire could be dismissed as provincial or sentimental by one not relating it to the broader framework of Tolkien's trilogy, so too the ideal of stewardship might be considered irrelevant because of its association with lordly structures of authority that are distant from our present democratic institutions. And in a figure like Denethor, the domineering steward of Gondor, all those aristocratic and authoritarian connotations are strongly sounded. But such an example is more than counterbalanced by the stewardship of the good gardener Sam Gamgee. His heroism grows from his youthful labors with hoe and trowel in the potato patch, and he returns to the Shire with a box of soil from Galadriel and sets to work repairing the ravaged groves and fields. For Sam—as for Frodo, Gandalf, and the other companions—stewardship is a matter of faithful and discerning action on behalf of a beloved landscape and community. It owes allegiance to the values that lie behind and ennoble both Gondor and the Grey Havens of the Elves, and it dedicates itself not only to one country of the heart but also to the health and harmony of all beautiful places. As Dickerson and Evans remark, the environmental movement is now looking beyond the dichotomy of wilderness preservation and the more utilitarian definitions of conservation that prevailed in environmental thinking throughout much of the twentieth century. In fact, maps of ecological and social health must encompass both these values, just as Tolkien's hand-drawn maps do. And stewardship, the knowledgeable and practical service of living communities, is called on to affirm and protect the full diversity of landscapes through which the members of the Fellowship pass.

A particularly powerful aspect of this book is its discussion of Saruman. Not only does he raze the forests, poison the waters, and denude the soil surrounding his Isengard stronghold, but in the guise of Sharkey he also brings the destructive impulse of Mordor back to the Shire itself, with devastating results for the hobbits who remain there. Although Middle-earth is different from our earth in many notable ways, Saruman's projects resonate with many of the destructive outcomes of political and commercial globalization today. From his biogenetic engineering of a new super race of Orcs, the Uruk-hai, to his liquidation of the forest and centralization of all resources at Isengard, Saruman sacrifices the values of permanence or sustainability for his grand scheme of domination and ownership. In Tolkien's epic, as in our world, however, a fundamentally different approach to globalization is possible, one in which a grand alliance of free peoples protects the world's health and integrity. This means upholding both the diversity of communities and landscapes and the beauty of the vast, unpeopled wilds that stretch between the settled realms.

The word alliance evokes the battles that are such a striking element in Tolkien's writing and are even more central to Jackson's films. But perhaps the most important distinction between a dominating vision of globalization and a whole-landscape vision of stewardship is the inclination of the latter to look for approaches other than warfare. Though the battles at the gates of Gondor and Mordor are indispensable to the victory of the Fellowship, even more essential is the patient, plodding trek of the hobbits and their uncanny guide up into the mountains, where they can relinquish power over the world. The fact that the trilogy concludes with Sam undertaking a long project of ecological and social restoration on behalf of his family, community, and land is also important. As William James famously said, in order to achieve authentic progress in the world, we must find an urgency and selflessness that constitute "the moral equivalent of war." Just as the skies over Mordor darkened and thickened in the climactic days of Tolkien's epic, our skies too are shadowed by the tide of carbon from the unrestrained burning of fossil fuels. But like faithful stewards we must meet such challenges on behalf of the values of ecological and social balance. And we may discover our hope, as did Frodo and Sam, not in the armories and pennants of Gondor but rather in the green shoots that continue to grow, even under the shadow of the monolith.

John Elder

Acknowledgments

This book is the product of a friendship that began long ago with the discovery of a mutual interest in and enthusiasm for the works of J. R. R. Tolkien. The writing process, which unfolded over more than two years, was genuinely collaborative. Matthew Dickerson, who originally proposed the project, wrote the first draft of the introduction and chapters 1, 2, 7, 8, 9, and 10; Jonathan Evans wrote the first draft of chapters 3, 4, 5, and 6, the conclusion, and the appendix. These initial drafts were exchanged and revised, and the working manuscript as a whole was revised again with much consultation, via e-mail and telephone and in person, to produce the final draft. The entire manuscript was revised in response to queries and suggestions by the press's anonymous readers and again after copyediting.

In retrospect, we liken our working relationship to that of the two main characters in Tolkien's "Leaf by Niggle," about whom the narrator says, "it is no use denying that at first they occasionally disagreed, especially when they got tired." Such moments were rare, however, and by and large the better picture is that of Niggle and Parish at the end of the story, who "walked about together, arm in arm," each tending to his respective portion of the garden and offering his own particular form of assistance to the other. (Those who know us both can make their own guesses about which one is the potato farmer.)

We are thankful to Steve Wrinn, Norman Wirzba, and the staff at the University Press of Kentucky for their vision and enthusiasm for this project, exhibiting both patience and efficiency in due measure and at appropriate times. We also express deep appreciation to Douglas Anderson and the University of Georgia Department of English for financial support for the graphics associated with this volume.

Jonathan Evans would like to thank Paul Mitchell for recommending Tolkien's books more than thirty years ago; Bill Mallonee for the social introduction that resulted in the friendship from which this book grew; and Matthew for initially proposing the project. He would also like to thank John Elder and the Environmental Studies Program at Middlebury College and Peter Hartel and the Environmental Ethics Certificate Program at the University of Georgia for providing lecture opportunities in Middlebury and Athens in March and October of 2004, respectively. Many of the ideas that appear here were developed in germinal form for those lectures. Thanks also are due to the University of Georgia's English department, whose faculty saw fit in 2005 to rescue "Environmental Literature" from the nebulous status of a special topics course and grant it independent status in the department's curriculum; to Cheryl Glotfelty for enthusiastic support and conversation; to Carl Rapp, Jim Kibler, and Simon Gatrell, colleagues at Georgia whose conversations over the years have helped sharpen Jonathan's critical instincts for the topics addressed in this book; to University of Georgia graduate student Matthew Lewis, who read an early draft and provided insightful comments; and to Jim Mitchell for timely corroboration of the Richard Foster reference.

Finally, Jonathan expresses his deepest gratitude to his wife, Susan, whose loving exercise of both encouragement and restraint helped preserve sanity and provide the personal matrix of affection without which academic and intellectual endeavors such as this have little value: *īdesa cyst eart þū, healsgebedda betst, līfes lūfu mīnes. Mulierem fortem quis inveniet? Procul et de ultimis finibus pretium eius.*

Matthew Dickerson also expresses his gratitude to John Elder, Tim McKenzie, Tom Shippey, and Norman Wirzba, all of whom read portions of early drafts of this book and provided valuable feedback and suggestions; to Devon Parish and everybody involved in the Tuesday lunch discussions on Christianity and the environment in the fall of 2004; to his colleagues in the Environmental Studies Program at Middlebury; and to Middlebury College, which provided some financial support for this project through the Faculty Professional Development Fund and the Ada Howe Kent Faculty Fellowship Program.

He also thanks his wife, Deborah, who is not only a model stigweard—a Gandalfian steward—but also a true ecologist: the *oikonomos agapêtê kai tês oikias hêmôn kai tôn musteriôn theou.*

Introduction

The modern environmental movement, like any significant large-scale social development, does not represent a single monolithic agenda or set of procedures; it is, rather, a varied collection of diverse subgroups. These subgroups often differ significantly not only in their means but also in the ends or goals toward which they are working. As such, they are often at odds; where there ought to be harmony and collaboration, we sometimes find disagreement and division. This is illustrated, for example, in the distinction between preservation and conservation, terms that describe two divergent extremes and two differing environmental agendas. Whereas conservationists may laud such efforts as sustainable forestry and agriculture, their preservationist counterparts sometimes act as if salvation of aboriginal wilderness was the *only* ideal worth pursuing. In its most extreme form, preservationism sees managed forests and timberlands as a poor and unacceptable substitute for native wildness. Often needlessly—but always wastefully—environmentalists who are battling the surrounding culture find themselves fighting battles within their own camp.

This division among environmentalists is a global problem that many environmental writers, scholars, and thinkers see as deeply regrettable. In his 2001 book *The Frog Run*, John Elder addresses the competing visions of conservation and preservation: the goals of maintaining the wildness of certain uncivilized areas of the landscape on the one hand, and of maintaining a sustainable system of agriculture or forestry on the other. Writing about his home state of Vermont, he comments that "sustainable forests feel less like a substitute for wilderness than a part, with it, of a balanced, nourishing, and varied landscape." Part of Elder's point is that conservationists and preservationists should be working together, guided by the realization that a complete environmental vision involves aspects of both groups' goals; neither is complete without the other. Of Vermont's forests and woodlands he writes, "While I strongly advocate the expansion of our system of wilderness, I also applaud the development of programs to encourage more sustainable approaches to logging elsewhere in our state." Elder goes on to write that "the challenge is to put all these elements together in an environmental vision with ecological depth." This is indeed a challenge, and Elder looks in part to literature to meet that challenge: to provide—imaginatively, or through imagery and literary example—a unifying vision that will successfully bring together disparate elements of this movement.[1]

This putting together of various elements to shape an ecologically deep environmental vision is one of the things that J. R. R. Tolkien accomplished supremely well more than half a century ago. In *The Lord of the Rings* especially, but more broadly in his Middle-earth legendarium[2]—the total corpus of his Middle-earth writings, including *The Hobbit, The Lord of the Rings, The Silmarillion,* a number of poems, and the numerous posthumously published volumes of histories and unfinished tales—as well as in various essays and even a small collection of short stories unrelated to Middle-earth, he provides a deep and complex ecological vision incorporating many elements and spanning a broad spectrum of approaches, including positions compatible with both conservation and preservation in modern environmentalism.

When we began writing this book, one of the titles we considered was the interrogative "J. R. R. Tolkien as Environmentalist?" The concluding question mark was the important point, because neither in purpose nor in result do we believe Tolkien's writings belong to the genre of "environmental literature" in the usual sense, nor do we think they ought to be classified in the related category of "nature writing." Indeed, upon hearing the great twentieth-century writer labeled an "environmentalist," students and scholars of literature or of the environment—including the most avid fans of Tolkien's works—might well raise their eyebrows and exclaim skeptically, "Tolkien an environmentalist?" Likewise, our own provisional posing of that question was not meant to be merely rhetorical. To the question, Was Tolkien an environmentalist? our answer is no. Nevertheless, we believe that all his writings—including his most famous work, *The Lord of the Rings*—convey a profound perspective on the natural world that constitutes an answer to Elder's call for "ecological depth" in literature with environmental vision. Tolkien's environmental vision has all of the following: a strong philosophical and theological basis, a comprehensive imaginative picture of what it might look like when worked out, a powerful reminder of what life looks like when that vision is rejected, and practical implications for day-to-day life for us all. This perspective is never explicitly stated as either a program for social change or a political agenda; that is, it is not an "environmental vision" per se such as we might find, for example, in the writings of Edward Abbey, Wendell Berry, Rachel Carson, Annie Dillard, John Elder, Wes Jackson, Barbara Kingsolver, or Aldo Leopold. But Tolkien's views concerning the natural world and environmental responsibility are nonetheless implicit throughout the body of his work.

Furthermore, what we call Tolkien's "environmental vision" should not be overlooked for at least two reasons. One is Tolkien's ongoing popularity and thus the potential for his views to influence the thinking of countless people, many of whom are drawn to his writing for reasons initially or ostensibly having nothing to do with the environment. *The Lord of the Rings* was among the most widely read works of the twentieth century, and its readership shows no sign of diminishing in the twenty-first. It is one of the most translated literary works in history, and Peter Jackson's phenomenally successful film adaptations, released from 2001 to 2003, brought Tolkien's writing to the attention of an even broader worldwide audience. The second reason that Tolkien's environmental vision should be given due consideration—and the more important one—is its breadth, its complexity, and its compelling importance, the elucidation of which is the purpose of this book. Although there are certainly numerous reasons behind the popularity of Tolkien's works, we believe that the depth and devotion of people's response to them are in part a recognition of the importance of some of the ideas shaping those works. We hope to explore these ideas and to illuminate how they have been expressed. In doing so, we hope to guide the response to those ideas—and to do so in a way in keeping with Tolkien's own ideas.

We acknowledge that the environmental vision we find in his works is only one part of what Tolkien accomplished. There are, of course, many other elements of equal or greater emphasis in his fiction besides environmental ones: philological ideas, philosophical and theological undercurrents, and, above all, simply the desire to tell a good story. This book does not address those elements, about which many books have already been written. Here, we explore the breadth and depth of Tolkien's environmental vision.

We are not the first to examine ecological aspects of Tolkien's writing. Although, in general, the academic world has been less responsive to Tolkien's books than the nonspecialist reading public has been, a small cadre of scholars has been working on Tolkien's ideas in a serious way for several decades, including his environmental concepts. Perhaps the first scholar to specifically equate Tolkien with the then-burgeoning environmental movement was Paul H. Kocher, who in 1972 said explicitly, "Tolkien was [an] ecologist."[3] Here, Kocher seems to express what a large number of Tolkien's readers intuited but had not explored or explained up to that time. Subsequently, scholars including Don Elgin, Patrick Curry, Christina Ljungberg Stücklin, and Verlyn Flieger called attention to the environmental perspective implicit in Tolkien's works and to some specific ways that this perspective is articulated in the Tolkien oeuvre.[4] What many of these scholars addressed in a more specific, even narrowly academic manner, we address on a broader and more thorough popular level, exploring the comprehensiveness of Tolkien's vision, how thoroughly it is integrated into his works, and how intimately tied it is to many other aspects of his writing. We show that Tolkien's environmental vision is connected to his underlying philosophical and theological perspective and even to his philology. In addition, his environmental vision has a significant impact on and is affected by the narrative aspects of his work that make him such a good storyteller.

Just as we acknowledge that a book devoted entirely to Tolkien's environmentalism must, of necessity, leave out many other important dimensions of his writing, we also acknowledge that the environmental aspects of Tolkien's works do not exhaust all the dimensions of environmentalism that modern readers can and should consider important. One charge we hope to avoid, however, is that we represent merely another special-interest group hoping to claim Tolkien for its own to achieve a specific ecological goal—that our work here is driven by our own environmental agenda. Although we are both personally committed to thinking and behaving in an environmentally responsible way, and although we are both faculty members in interdisciplinary environmental programs on our respective campuses, neither of us is trained as an environmentalist, and neither of us initially became interested in *The Lord of the Rings* in the course of professional scholarly study. In fact, we could claim that this project actually began when, as adolescents and first-time readers of *The Lord of the Rings*, we became fascinated with Middle-earth. Our perspectives on the world and our imaginations were shaped by Tolkien's, including the inherent environmental ideas in his books. It was only later that this fascination developed into the intellectual and scholarly preoccupations expressed in our teaching, research, and publications, and even later still that all the ecological and environmental implications were brought into focus. It might be said that we came to environmentalism through Tolkien, rather than the other way around. We hope that some readers, especially those whose interest in Tolkien was initially fostered by their moviegoing experiences, will follow a similar path.

We believe the ethical perspective on the natural world that is embedded in Tolkien's writing ought to be brought to the attention of general readers, not just to specialists in the fields of ecology and environmental studies or to specialists in medieval and fantasy literature—Tolkien's usual fan base. The average, intelligent reader who is appreciative of Tolkien's works and reasonably aware of environmental issues will readily understand the connection between the two and will recognize how these two interests can work hand in hand to expand environmental awareness. The phenomenal success of Peter Jackson's cinematic interpretation of *The Lord of the Rings* only adds to our sense that the time is right for an examination of Tolkien's environmental themes. Our hope is that these themes will gain acceptance among a new generation of readers and viewers who, in turn, will have a positive impact on our culture's evolving environmental ethos. We believe people ought to think strategically and creatively about environmental issues, and we believe J. R. R. Tolkien's works are both insightful and inspiring in this regard.

The first part of this book explores the foundations of Tolkien's ecology. Where there is a viewpoint, one can always find an underlying vision. Tolkien's vision is that of a responsible Catholic whose Christianity helped shape his fundamental perspectives on the Western intellectual tradition. Far from bearing most of the blame for environmental abuses—which some suggest is the case—ideas that are central to the Christian tradition deserve at least some credit for providing plausible and reasonable foundations for a responsible environmentalism. Chapter 1 examines how Tolkien embraced one of these ideas: the fundamentally positive value of the material world and the physical creation. He expressed this in several ways: by extolling the virtues of such simple pleasures as food and drink, music and song, the tilling of the soil, and the good work of one's hands; by ascribing great inherent mythic importance to the primordial trees Laurelin and Telperion, two of the most important objects in the history of Middle-earth; and by giving us the character of Tom Bombadil, whose selfless knowledge and love of the created world are independent of any power or advantage they might afford. We uncover the essence of Tolkien's environmental model not as an economic one but as one rooted in a belief in the goodness of the earth as the handiwork of its creator, Eru Ilúvatar.

We continue exploring these foundations in chapter 2, where we show that Tolkien's model can best be described by the phrase *Christian stewardship*. Here, we use the term *stewardship* strictly to mean the benevolent, selfless custodial care of the environment rather than as a "cover term" justifying the exploitation of our natural resources for commercial, corporate, or personal gain. In our sense, a steward is not one who owns property or is the lord over a domain but one who is responsible for the care of something placed in his or her custody. In *The Lord of the Rings*, according to Gandalf, we are not granted the freedom to decide *whether* to discharge our stewardship responsibilities; rather, we are required to decide *how* we will do so. We must choose whether to act destructively or constructively toward an environment that we do not own, and this decision must be made within the purview of our function as custodians of the world during the brief time we are in it. We are stewards of this earth whether we like it or not. In this respect, we share much in common with environmentalists of many faiths and those of no faith in particular who perceive our stewardship responsibilities as duties owed to something or someone higher than ourselves. Gandalf suggests that we must simply do our best to ensure that those who follow will have good soil to till. In Tolkien's trilogy, we see Gandalf passing on this model of stewardship to Faramir and Frodo, two of his disciples, as well as to Aragorn, whose kingship he helps to secure. We also see Tolkien passing it on to his readers, who are enjoined, to paraphrase the title of a recent book, to "follow Gandalf."[5]

The second, central, and longest part of this book looks at the comprehensive picture: in the history and in the peoples of Middle-earth, and in some of Tolkien's short fairy tales, the realization of what this picture looks like. In Middle-earth, it is worked out as a threefold vision that involves the sustainable agriculture of the agrarian society of the Shire, the home of the Hobbits (chapter 3); the horticulture of the Elves, along with the Entwives' preservation and nurturance of the ordered natural world (chapter 4); and the Ents' conservation of wilderness (chapter 5), which we call *feraculture,* a neologism welding the Latin *ferus* or *fera* (meaning "wild") with culture (see chapter 1 for a fuller explanation). Chapter 6 examines the subtle dynamics of the boundaries between these three ecological domains—often called *ecotones*—showing how they overlap and interact and how each one is part of a total environment that must be perceived as such. Chapter 7 explores how all these aspects can also be seen in three of Tolkien's short fairy tales unrelated to the Middle-earth legendarium: "Farmer Giles of Ham," "Leaf by Niggle," and "Smith of Wootton Major."

Although it is rarely allegorical in the strict literary sense, Tolkien always meant his work to be applicable to real-world situations. Thus, the final part of our book explores practical implications for us today, including a look at the potential hazards of ignoring the stewardship responsibilities outlined in earlier chapters. In chapter 8, we look at environmentally destructive acts: in their most extreme form, in Mordor; in a more rational and industrialized form, in Isengard; and finally in "our own backyard," as it were, in the Shire. In chapter 9, we examine how the characters in Middle-earth—centrally, the Hobbits—are roused to action and confront the sources of environmental damage perpetrated on the Shire. We end with chapter 10, addressing how we can respond in practical ways to the works of "Mordor" in our own contemporary world.

Throughout all the chapters of this book, the following features of J. R .R. Tolkien's environmental vision can be seen:

1. It is complex: at least three distinct ecological domains can be identified, with three corresponding environmental positions among the characters and character groups he created.
2. It is comprehensive, including whole landscapes, races, and civilizations in communion with one another.
3. It is in part his personal response to events in his own early life and includes his love for his early childhood home, his love of language, and his love for the beauties of nature—especially trees.

4. It is connected to linguistic matters and is part of the process of mythopoeia—the making of a myth.

5. It is transcendent, based on objective values that transcend any one particular personal or cultural value system.

The last feature is probably the most important. Tolkien's environmental ethic was firmly rooted in a deeply Christian, Catholic understanding of the world and its creator. This tradition sees the necessity of right relationships between the creator and humankind and between humankind and the rest of creation. Thus the religiously skeptical reader—an environmentalist, perhaps—should find in Tolkien's Christianity not a view at odds with a modern environmental consciousness but instead an allied perspective corroborating many doctrines and a priori assumptions of modern environmentalism. The person of faith—perhaps a Christian—reading this book should see in Tolkien's understanding of the biblical worldview a powerful argument—and, we hope, a compelling motivation—for a deep and meaningful environmentalism often ignored in some circles of Christendom.[6] At its best, the Christian faith, it might be said, is "green."

It should be noted that Tolkien wrote as a Christian before modern environmentalism was constituted as a movement and thus before the modern attacks on Christianity that have come from some quarters of that movement. Environmental concerns did not arise, and could not have arisen, in Tolkien's works as a response to charges brought against Christianity in the late twentieth century; rather, Tolkien simply understood these concerns as an important part of any serious Christian understanding of the world. The breadth and depth of Tolkien's vision anticipate rather than respond to later antagonisms. Put more broadly, many of the works we cite in this book were written in the three decades after Tolkien's death in 1973; they belong to the corpus of respected modern environmental literature. The point in citing these writers obviously is not to imply that they influenced Tolkien. Rather, we hope to show that what modern, well-respected writers and thinkers now address as serious and important ecological concerns arose in Tolkien's work more than half a century ago; they arose as elements consistent with his view of the world. Tolkien wrote in an era long before modern environmentalism had been conceived as a body of intellectual and political ideas, making his approach to some of the most important environmental issues of our day all the more remarkable.

The same principle holds true of various modern Protestant writers addressing environmental concerns from their faith perspective. In citing some of these writers, we hope to show that Tolkien was addressing important concerns shared not only by Catholics but also by a broad spectrum of his fellow Christians.

One final warning is necessary, and it applies primarily to the last two chapters. Although we sometimes quote from Tolkien's letters and nonfiction works, we are addressing primarily his fiction. To emphasize an earlier point, these are works of myth, fantasy, and fairy tale and are intended to be understood as such by the author, not as ecological tracts. In drawing implications for our world, we need to be careful to preserve Tolkien's fiction as fiction and to avoid treating it as a set of intellectual propositions. Tolkien was interested primarily in writing good stories, and like all good art, good stories must succeed imaginatively, not as propaganda. Our goal is to elucidate Tolkien's vision, not to reduce that vision to a set of environmental principles or Christian doctrines.

At the same time, however, Tolkien ardently defended the applicability of myth and fantasy, as well as its foundation in religious and moral truth. We believe that there are environmental principles to be drawn from Tolkien's fiction as well as from the underlying doctrines on which those principles are based. Thus, while we want to avoid reducing Tolkien's vision to a mere list of principles or propositions, we hope to point out to readers what some of these might be: Tolkien's brilliance lies not only in capturing our imaginations, but—and perhaps more importantly—in what he reveals after we have been caught.

Conventions and Abbreviations

As might be expected, this book contains frequent references to the works of J. R. R. Tolkien. For these, we use parenthetical references to indicate the work cited when this is not evident from the context. We use the following abbreviations for titles, following a slightly simplified version of the citation conventions used in *The J. R. R. Tolkien Encyclopedia: Scholarship and Critical Assessment,* to be published by Routledge in 2007.

App X	Appendix to *The Lord of the Rings* (where X represents A, B, C, D, E, or F). Boston: Houghton Mifflin, 1954.
H	*The Annotated Hobbit,* 2nd ed. Edited by Douglas A. Anderson. Boston: Houghton Mifflin, 2002.
Letters	*The Letters of J. R. R. Tolkien,* 1st ed. Edited by Humphrey Carpenter, with the assistance of Christopher Tolkien. Boston: Houghton Mifflin, 1981.
MC	"*Beowulf:* The Monsters and the Critics." In *The Monsters and the Critics and Other Essays.* Boston: Houghton Mifflin, 1984.
MR	*Morgoth's Ring: The Later Silmarillion.* Edited by Christopher Tolkien. Boston: Houghton Mifflin, 1993.
Pro	"Prologue to the 2nd Edition" of *The Lord of the Rings.* Boston: Houghton Mifflin, 1954.
Shadow	*The Return of the Shadow.* Edited by Christopher Tolkien. Boston: Houghton Mifflin, 1988.
Silm	*The Silmarillion,* 1st ed. Edited by Christopher Tolkien. Boston: Houghton Mifflin, 1977.
TL	*Tree and Leaf* (includes "On Fairy-stories," "Leaf by Niggle," and "Mythopoeia"). London: HarperCollins, 2001.

UT   *Unfinished Tales of Númenor and Middle-Earth.* Edited by Christopher Tolkien. Boston: Houghton Mifflin, 1980.

WMFG   *Smith of Wootton Major and Farmer Giles of Ham* (includes "Smith of Wootton Major" and "Farmer Giles of Ham"). New York: Ballantine, 1967.

Because there are many editions of *The Lord of the Rings*, with different paginations, we do not give page numbers for references to *The Fellowship of the Ring*, *The Two Towers*, *The Return of the King*, the Appendixes, or the Prologue. Instead, following the convention of T. A. Shippey (*J. R. R. Tolkien: Author of the Century*), we give book number and chapter number in uppercase and lowercase roman numerals. Thus the citation "(IV/ii)" represents the second chapter of the fourth book, a chapter titled "The Passage of the Marshes" in *The Two Towers*.

For all other sources—anything not written by J. R. R. Tolkien—we use endnotes. In these notes, we use the abbreviation OE for Old English and ON for Old Norse.

The decision of whether to capitalize the names of races in Middle-earth (Hobbit, Elf, Dwarf, Man, Orc, Ent, and so on) was not an easy one. Even Tolkien was not consistent. We made an effort to capitalize these words only when used collectively or in reference to a race as a race (for example, Treebeard is an Ent) and to lowercase them when speaking of individuals of a race (for example, the four hobbits left the Shire). Even so, we may not have been completely consistent with this distinction. Finally, we followed Tolkien's usage of the word *Man* or *Men* to represent the race in Middle-earth. To make the distinction clear and to strive for gender neutrality, when speaking of our own species, we preferred *human, humankind, human race,* or *humanity*. We use *people* as Tolkien did, as a generic term for the sentient beings of Middle-earth—the Children of Ilúvatar—including Elves, Dwarves (by adoption), Men, and (related to the latter) Hobbits.

Part I

"The Tides of the World"

❦

Gandalfian Stewardship and the Foundations of Tolkien's Vision

Chapter 1
Varda, Yavanna, and the Value of Creation

In setting out to explore the legendarium of J. R. R. Tolkien's Middle-earth and to comprehend his imaginative vision, environmental or otherwise, the first thing one must realize is that Tolkien communicates through myth and story, not primarily through a set of abstract propositions. His ideas are expressed mythically, mythologically, and mythopoeically. He works mythopoeically because artistically he creates narratives meant to be understood as myths within his fictional world (the word *mythopoeia* means "the making of myths"). He works mythologically because his created myths are modeled, at least partially, on mythologies that already exist in our own world: Greek, Roman, Norse, Finnish, Celtic, and biblical. And he works mythically because—like the mythologies of our world—Tolkien's created myths communicate not through the discursive impartation of factual propositions but through narratives. Traditionally, myths articulate the primordial, elemental, and foundational truths by which a culture defines reality and its origin and place within it, and they do so in story form. Environmental concerns represent one facet of the larger body of truths illustrated by Tolkien's myths.

Tolkien's Mythic Methodology

Although we are trying to describe objectively a set of abstract principles, ultimately the fact that Tolkien offers them to us in the highly subjective form of stories founded on myths is not a liability but an advantage. In their introduction to "Part III: Art and Creation Consciousness," the editors of the essay collection *Cry of the Environment* make a strong statement about the profound need for imagination and art in the formation of an environmental vision:

> The present ecological crisis we are facing is due in part to an impoverishment of imagination—creative solutions to admittedly complex ecological difficulties are rarely proposed and even more rarely taken seriously as "realistic."
>
> Artistic resources must be an integral part in the development of genuine creation consciousness. Art works—in every medium—can symbolize for us our deepest concerns: they can be documents of what is and is not meaningful in human existence. When we are *engaged* by a work of art, we begin to participate in a new vision of the world. . . . They help us to *see* our world—and our place in it—in a new way.[1]

These editors point to a factor that is often not acknowledged in our response to the ecological crisis: the importance of art and of our engagement with art in ways that transform and shape our consciousness. Our imagination must not only be put to use; it must also be hallowed and shaped. In his introduction to *The Art of the Commonplace: The Agrarian Essays of Wendell Berry*, Norman Wirzba makes a complementary point when he addresses current environmental problems, including competition between the perspectives of commercial industrialism and preindustrial agrarianism:

> First, we must recognize that an agrarian transformation of contemporary culture will require the work of the imagination. We need to be able to envision a future that is markedly different from today's world, and be creative in the implementation of economic, political, religious, and educational reforms.[2]

Here Wirzba echoes the sentiments of John Elder quoted in our introduction. Before any reforms can be initiated and implemented, the imagination of our culture must be reached, and this is best done through art and literature—especially through myth. In his legendarium, as well as in various shorter fairy tales, Tolkien provides just the sort of highly engaging work of imagination required, one that may play an important role in the transformation of contemporary culture. Although Tolkien wrote his stories half a century ago and set them in a far older mythical past, in Wirzba's terms, he enables us "to envision a future that is markedly different" from the present. Such a vision is itself mythic in import.

Where does that mythic vision begin? One of the most famous passages in *The Lord of the Rings* appears toward the end of *The Two Towers* when, on the verge of plunging into Mordor, Frodo and Sam pause to reflect on the narrative significance of their quest. Sam observes, rather acutely, that they are part of the same story as Beren and Lúthien, the famous characters of ancient legend whose tale, by the end of the Third Age, has acquired all the characteristics of myth:

> "But that's a long tale, of course, and goes on past the happiness and into grief and beyond it—and the Silmaril went on and came to Eärendil. And why, sir, I never thought of that before! We've—you've got some of the light of it in that star-glass that the Lady gave you! Why, to think of it, we're in the same tale still! It's going on. Don't the great tales never end?" (IV/iv)

The answer, of course, is no, the great tales "don't never end," as Sam colloquially puts it. In fact, the connection between Sam and Frodo and the mythic figures of the *Silmarillion* is closer than the inhabitants of Middle-earth or most of Tolkien's readers may realize. By the end of the Third Age, the name Eärendil is to most Hobbits simply the name of the Morning Star. In the mythology of Middle-earth, however, this star is a bright jewel, one of the three jewels known as the Silmarils, which are represented in the mythological text of the *Quenta Silmarillion* as the greatest treasures of the First Age of Middle-earth. Eärendil is the hero who carries a Silmaril through the heavens on the prow of his great ship *Vingilot*. He is also the grandson-in-law of Beren and Lúthien, who recover a Silmaril from the crown of the enemy Morgoth. And he is the father of Elrond, who plays such a significant a role in Sam and Frodo's quest for Mount Doom. All this is told in full in *The Silmarillion*, Tolkien's masterpiece recounting the creation of Middle-earth and its First Age. As is well known, Tolkien tried, ultimately without success, to have the book published simultaneously with *The Lord of the Rings* in a mammoth single-volume edition. In the end, he was able to secure publication of the trilogy, but *The Silmarillion* remained unpublished until

1977, four years after his death. Nevertheless, *The Silmarillion* provides the mythic background for *The Lord of the Rings* and is crucial to its full comprehension; Clyde S. Kilby notes that *The Lord of the Rings* has more than 600 references to the history of the First and Second ages of Middle-earth.[3] To get to the heart of Tolkien's vision, we have to begin with an examination of some of its mythic symbols.

The Two Trees of Valinor

Near the beginning of the first chapter of *The Silmarillion*, there is a description of the birth of two trees, which come to be known as the Two Trees of Valinor:

> And when Valinor was full-wrought and the mansions of the Valar were established, in the midst of the plain beyond the mountains they built their city, Valmar of the many bells. Before its western gate there was a green mound, Ezellohar, that is named also Corollairë; and Yavanna hallowed it, and she sat there long upon the green grass and sang a song of power, in which was set all her thought of things that grow in the earth. But Nienna thought in silence, and watered the mound with tears. In that time the Valar were gathered together to hear the song of Yavanna. . . .
>
> And as they watched, upon the mound there came forth two slender shoots; and silence was over all the world in that hour, nor was there any other sound save the chanting of Yavanna. Under her song the saplings grew and became fair and tall, and came to flower; and thus there awoke in the world the Two Trees of Valinor. Of all things which Yavanna made they have most renown, and about their fate all the tales of the Elder Days are woven. (*Silm*, 38)

One of the first things we must note is the mythic significance of this event, which is implied by the fact that all of the Valar—the most powerful beings of Middle-earth[4]—devote their full attention to this event, and "silence was over all the world in that hour." This significance is also made explicit in the closing line of the paragraph: woven about the fate of these two trees are "all the tales of the Elder Days." This might seem to be a surprising statement to make about a pair of trees. However, these trees not only have a central place in the *physical* layout of the undying city of Valmar, the capital of Valinor; they are also central to the early *chronology* of events in the mythic Elder Days of Middle-earth. It is a quest for the famed Silmarils, made from the light of the Two Trees, that drives the High Elves out of Valinor to return in exile to Middle-earth. This exile eventually results in the establishment of the Elvish kingdoms of western Middle-earth that remain in the Third Age—chiefly Lothlórien and Rivendell, but others as well—and, later, the founding of the kingdoms of Men in Gondor and Arnor. The famed White Tree of Gondor, replanted by Aragorn when he becomes king at the end of *The Return of the King*, is a descendent of the Two Trees of Valinor, and Aragorn's planting of it evokes the memory of Yavanna's primeval planting in the long-past mythic period. It is the light of the Two Trees of Valinor that lives in the star of Eärendil as well as in the Phial of Galadriel—the "star-glass" borne by Frodo.

As a philologist, Tolkien was interested in the sources and significance of names, and in his own works he showed the importance of people, places, objects, and other things by the patterns of their naming. "It gives me great pleasure, a good name," Tolkien said in a 1971 BBC radio interview. "I always in writing start with a name. Give me a name and it produces a story, not the other way about normally." In Tolkien's works, the most important things usually have many names. Gandalf, for example, is given the names Mithrandir, Tharkûn, Olórin, Incánus, and others. Some things are of such universal significance—and, by virtue of the number of people and races to whom they are significant, so multifaceted in meaning and nuance—that many names are required. This is the case with the Two Trees. "Telperion the one was called in Valinor, and Silpion, and Ninquelótë, and many other names; but Laurelin the other was, and Malinalda, and Culúrien, and many names in song beside" (*Silm*, 38). Even the hillock on which the trees grow has two names, Ezellohar and Corollairë, both of which mean in Elvish "The Green Mound"; Galadriel's realm of Lothlórien is also named Laurelindórenan after the younger of the two trees. All these names are evidence of the historic importance and of the deeper mythic qualities associated with the things they describe. Arguably, the Two Trees are the most mythically significant symbols in all of Tolkien's writings about Middle-earth.

This leads us to the issue of what these two trees are, what they represent, and why they are so prominent in the history and mythology of Middle-earth and in the environmental themes explored in this book. In Tolkien's ecology, the living world is not the only aspect of creation that is important. Mountains and rivers, seas and islands, the winds and skies, and the stars and stones are all part of nature. For this reason, the Valar—the godlike ruling powers—have their different identities bound up with different aspects of nature and with care for its various components. One might say that the Valar are *stewards* of Arda,[5] or of various aspects of its substance. Manwë, the king of the Valar, is associated with the winds of Middle-earth, Varda with the stars, Aulë with the material substance of the earth, and Ulmo with the waters. Living things, however, have a special role and a special importance—partly because man, the mythmaker, is a living being, and partly because the author himself was a man.[6] Among the Valar, Yavanna is the one most concerned with living things. She is called the "Giver of Fruits"; she is "the lover of all things that grow in the earth, and all their countless forms she holds in her mind, from the trees like towers in forests long ago to the moss upon stones or the small and secret things in the mould" (*Silm*, 27). To Yavanna, living beings in the biosphere can be divided into two groups, which she calls *olvar* (plants) and *kelvar* (animals). As illustrated by the earlier quotation, Yavanna pours "all her thought of things that grow in the earth" into the making of the Two Trees. It can be said, then, that these trees embody all living things in Arda at that time, a time so early in the cosmic history of Middle-earth that Men and Elves have not yet been brought into being. The timing here makes a great deal of difference, for—read in this light—the trees must be said to embody the living essence of the biosphere, the natural world *apart from Men*.

In this regard, it is interesting to note Tolkien's language. Although the event is one in which Yavanna makes or creates the trees, the narrator also describes the trees as *awakening*—as if to imply that they had a life already, prior to Yavanna's song of creation, which her singing simply arouses from dormancy. Even the very mound on which the trees grow is said to be "hallowed"—that is, made holy—by their presence. This mound is covered, we are told, with "green grass," and in Tolkien's writing, references to green, to grass, and especially to green grass suggest—like trees—important mythic symbolism.[7] Even the color green alone is powerful; in the first chapter of the *Quenta Silmarillion*, for example, we read that "the new-made green was yet a marvel in the eyes of the makers; and they were long content" (*Silm*, 36). The mythic importance of green grass carries over into *The Lord of the Rings*. When he first meets the figure of Aragorn crossing the plains of Rohan, Éomer exclaims in surprise, "Dreams and legends spring to life out of the grass." He later asks, "Do we walk in legends or on the green earth in daylight?" to which Aragorn replies, "The green earth, say you? That is a mighty matter of legend though you tread it under the light of day!" (III/ii).

In addition to the description of the trees as "fair," meaning "beautiful to the eye," subsequent paragraphs depict them in greater detail. Two of the most striking features of the trees are the color of their leaves and flowers and the fact that they emit a light or radiance of their own. Telperion has leaves of silver and gives off a "dew of silver light" ever falling from its countless flowers. Laurelin has leaves whose edges are "glittering gold," whose flowers are like "clusters of yellow flame" spilling "a gold rain upon the ground," giving forth "warmth and great light." We read:

> In seven hours the glory of each tree waxed to full and waned again to naught; and each awoke once more to life an hour before the other ceased to shine. Thus in Valinor twice every day there came a gentle hour of softer light when both trees were faint and their gold and silver beams were mingled. Telperion was the elder ... and that first hour in which he shone [was named] the Opening Hour, and [the Valar] counted from it the ages of their reign in Valinor. ...
>
> But the light that was spilled from the trees endured long, ere it was taken up into the airs or sank down into the earth; and the dews of Telperion and the rain that fell from Laurelin Varda hoarded in great vats like shining lakes, that were to all the land of the Valar as wells of water and of light. Thus began the Days of the Bliss of Valinor; and thus began also the Count of Time. (*Silm*, 38–39)

The overall imagery is fourfold: warmth, light, beauty, and—from the comparison to gold and silver, as well as their prominent place in Valinor—great worth or value. The word used by Tolkien here to capture all this is "glory," with which the Bliss of Valinor is closely associated.

After Laurelin and Telperion are created, but before they are destroyed, the Noldorin jewel-smith Fëanor ponders "how the light of the Trees, the glory of the Blessed Realm, might be preserved imperishable." Working in secret, summoning all his power, Fëanor creates out of crystal stronger than adamant the three great jewels known as the Silmarils. He encases in these jewels "the blended light of the Trees of Valinor, which lives in them yet, though the Trees have long withered and shine no more. Therefore even in the darkness of the deepest treasury the Silmarils of their own radiance shone like the stars of Varda; and yet, as were they indeed living things, they rejoiced in light and received it and gave it back in hues more marvelous than before." Varda hallows the Silmarils, and it is foretold that "the fates of Arda, earth, sea, and air, lay locked within them" (*Silm*, 67). Two of these jewels are ultimately lost, but the one that remains becomes the beacon of Eärendil, the Morning Star.

The moment when the trees are destroyed by the giant spider Ungoliant—a figure of darkness or *un*light whose name means "weaver of gloom"—is one of immeasurable grief and mourning for the Valar, a grief that "neither power nor wisdom" can assuage (*Silm*, 98). Yet this is not the end of the trees' light; it lives on not only in the Silmarils but also in the light of the Sun and the Moon. Before the trees die and their lifeless stems are left to stand forever in Valinor as "a memory of vanished joy," Yavanna coaxes from the failing life of Telperion "one great flower of silver" and from Laurelin one final "single fruit of gold." All the Valar then labor together and form the Moon and the Sun from this last silver leaf and golden fruit; Yavanna's spouse Aulë, the mythic smith, forges vessels for them that Manwë, their king, hallows. Finally, Varda, the queen of the Valar and the one most revered by the Elves, puts the Moon and the Sun into the heavens to light the earth and thwart the works of Melkor done in darkness. "Isil the Sheen the [Elves] of old named the Moon, flower of Telperion in Valinor; and Anar the Fire-golden, fruit of Laurelin they named the Sun." There they remain as "lamps of heaven, outshining the ancient stars" (*Silm*, 99). Forever after, anyone on Middle-earth who looks into the sky and sees the sun and moon looks upon the ancient light of the Two Trees, and anyone who looks to the Morning Star as a symbol of hope sees their blended light shining from the surviving Silmaril.

Thus, just as the Days of Bliss of Valinor are counted by the light of the trees, so too are the months in Middle-earth counted by the light of Telperion, now dwelling in the Moon, and the days are counted according to the movement of the Sun, the last remaining fruit of Laurelin. This may be the most significant indication of the importance of the Two Trees. Moreover, even in the mind of Yavanna, who gives birth to her, Laurelin is somehow representative of all nature. She now becomes a source of nourishment for all the *olvar,* the plant life of the world, on which the *kelvar,* including Elves and Men, physically depend.

Environmentally, there is much that can be made of this. It is worth noting in summary that (1) *The Silmarillion* begins with these powerful images of nature, (2) the glory and bliss of Valinor are closely associated with these trees, and (3) the Two Trees are closely associated with all of life itself. But as we noted earlier, it is particularly noteworthy that the Children of Ilúvatar—the name given collectively to Men and Elves—have not yet appeared in Middle-earth. Thus, in Tolkien's mythology, the beauty and value of Yavanna's works of creation are independent of any practical or utilitarian purposes they may have for Men or Elves. Their importance inheres in nature for its own sake. Even if the Children of Ilúvatar had never appeared, the trees would be seen—by the Valar, the Ainur, and Ilúvatar—as things of value, beauty, goodness, and glory, and upon their passing, even the fact of their existence would have been seen as good.

Food, Cheer, Song, and Well-Tilled Earth

The idea that nature has an inherent goodness is affirmed not only in the lofty mythological passages of the *Silmarillion.* It is apparent also in the more homely world of *The Hobbit* and in the opening passages of *The Lord of the Rings.* Turning for a moment from the distant and mythic realm of Valinor to the more familiar farms and fields of the Shire, we can see Tolkien's ideas further developed in the earthiness of the Hobbits and the simplicity of their lifestyle. Hobbits in general, and particularly those who are central to *The Hobbit* and *The Lord of the Rings,* show us that the common stuff of life—including, perhaps especially, the material things of this world—should be valued and appreciated for what they are in and of themselves.

The first two paragraphs of *The Hobbit* afford several valuable insights. The first thing we learn about Bilbo is that he lives in a hole in the ground. As a now famous anecdote tells us, it was this seemingly accidental sentence that Tolkien wrote on a blank piece of paper while marking examinations one day in the 1930s that led to the book's being written in the first place: "In a hole in the ground there lived a hobbit." A philologist both by trade and by passion, Tolkien immediately wondered, "What is a hobbit?" and "Why do they live in the ground?" *The Hobbit* and *The Lord of the Rings* may be seen as something of an exploration on his part into the possible answers to these questions.[8] It is not until Appendix F—written in 1955, after the trilogy had been completed and the first two volumes had reached print—that the reader finally learns the answer to these questions from a pair of Old English words: *hol* ("hole" or "hollow") and *bytla* ("built structure, building, or dwelling"). There, on the last page of the book preceding the indexes, Tolkien explains that he used Old English to represent the language of the Rohirrim and that the word *hobbit* is "a worn-down form of *hol-bytla,* if that name had occurred in our own ancient language," for the original Westron term *kûd-dûkan,* or "hole-dweller."

Still in the first two paragraphs of *The Hobbit*, we can also discern something from a comment about the layout of Bilbo's dwelling on the Hill: "The best rooms were all on the left-hand side (going in), for these were the only ones to have windows, deep-set round windows looking over his garden, and meadows beyond, sloping down to the river." There is a subtle suggestion here about the value Hobbits place on nature: their "best rooms" are not the ones with the most conveniences, the best paintings, the largest beds, or even (tellingly) the most food—they are the ones with the clearest views of the landscape. Their best rooms look out not only on gardens—that is, nature in cultivated form—but also on meadows and the river, natural features that, though by no means truly wild, are less domesticated or cultivated.

Reading more deeply, we might also reflect on the fact that windows let in natural light. That is, they provide access to the light of the Two Trees that lives on in the Moon, the Sun, and the Silmaril of Eärendil, the Morning Star. Thus, however indirectly or unknowingly, in their preference for rooms with ample windows, what Hobbits appreciate is actually the glory of the Two Trees of Valinor.[9]

In any case, their dwelling in the ground is fundamental to the nature of Hobbits, and although in Buckland and in Bree some live in houses aboveground, Hobbits of the Shire consider this aboveground life to be unnatural. Hobbits are close to the earth, and they are closely associated with the material substance of the soil. They wear no shoes, and their walking around barefoot keeps them in direct physical contact with the earth. This literally down-to-earth image is extended further when we learn in the fourth paragraph of *The Hobbit* of their uncanny ability to blend in with nature: "There is little or no magic about them, except the ordinary everyday sort which helps them to disappear quietly and quickly when large stupid folk like you and me come blundering along"—a point repeated at the start of the Prologue to *The Lord of the Rings*.

Likewise, the Hobbits' love of growing things can be seen throughout *The Hobbit* and *The Lord of the Rings*. Bilbo's love of nature and gardens is evident in the fact that, though there is no mention of a housekeeper or a cook, he has a paid gardener. We see it in the names that Hobbits give to their children; little girls are most often named after flowers: Rose, Elanor, Daisy, Primrose, Marigold. More generally, we see their appreciation for the simple pleasures of life in the songs they sing and the things they choose to take delight in: a bath at the end of the day, a mug of beer with friends, good food, a quiet walk in the woods and meadows, and—again, from the opening scene of *The Hobbit*—simply standing on the front step enjoying a pipe and some sunshine. They value these things over machines and technological contrivances, which do not make an appearance in their songs. When the four hobbits are imprisoned by the Barrow-wights and Tom Bombadil rescues them, he sends them running naked over the grass, thereby restoring their contact with the earth (I/viii). After hearing Merry and Pippin describe Hobbits, Treebeard comments about their earthiness, "So you live in holes, eh? It sounds very right and proper" (III/iv).

In the BBC radio interview quoted earlier, Tolkien associates the Shire with the English countryside of the central Midlands and its "good water, stones and elm trees and small quiet rivers and so on." Hobbits, and especially *our* hobbits, are able to take delight in these simple things for their own sake, and not merely as means to an end or as excuses for achieving power. This is one reason—perhaps the most important reason—that they are able to resist the seductive influence of the Ring for so long: they are not fundamentally concerned with the manipulations of power, so they are able to take things for what they are.[10]

The Value of Simplicity

Perhaps the most important overall picture we get of Hobbits and their lifestyle is one of simplicity. They are simple people with simple tastes, and they are fond of the simple comforts of modest living. As the narrator of *The Hobbit* tells us in the book's second sentence, Bilbo's home "was a hobbit-hole, and that means comfort." At certain points in the novel, the narrator seems critical of the Hobbits' *extreme* love of comfort, suggesting that at times it can manifest itself as something other than virtue. However, there is much that is good about the Hobbits' values. Even the particular types of comforts they prefer are associated not with modern gadgets and machinery but rather with living simply. To be sure, they are not averse to the ownership of possessions, but the Hobbits derive pleasure principally from good food, friendship, and an unhurried lifestyle that is made more leisurely not through the use of modern technology by the absence of it.

This idea runs counter to the modern orthodoxy of "bigger, better, more, faster" that lies at the heart of the relentless pursuit of technical and mechanical innovation in advanced societies. It has been pointed out that modern life can be characterized by, among other things, its frenetic pace. Colin Gunton, for example, calls "the paradox of modernity" the fact that technological advances have brought less, not more, leisure time: "The modern is less at home in the actual time and space of daily living than peoples less touched by [technological] changes.... The paradox is that there is to be found more genuine leisure in 'undeveloped' societies than in those dedicated to the creation of leisure."[11] Gunton cites E. F. Schumacher's 1973 *Small Is Beautiful,* a classic of its time that had widespread social impact and, among other things, helped inspire the "Green" movement of environmental activism. Schumacher wrote, "The pressure and strain of living is very much less in, say, Burma, than it is in the United States, in spite of the fact that the amount of labour-saving machinery used in the former country is only a minute fraction of the amount used in the latter."[12]

Schumacher was a cultural forerunner in popularizing an alternative orthodoxy of simplicity that could seemingly offer people greater satisfaction in their lives.[13] The title of Schumacher's book became a catchphrase for an enduring theme in popular culture, championed recently in Joseph Pearce's *Small Is Still Beautiful.*[14] It is interesting—

though perhaps not surprising—that Pearce also has written about J. R. R. Tolkien and sees environmental implications in Tolkien's portrayal of Hobbits. In an essay entitled "Tolkien as Hobbit," Pearce discusses Tolkien's anti-industrialism in connection with Schumacher's, seeing both writers as participants in "a long tradition of opposition to the evils of the industrial age."[15]

Similarly, in his book *Celebration of Discipline*, Richard Foster writes about the "discipline of simplicity," which in his opinion requires both an internal spirit and an external application. Perhaps the most important application of simplicity is in the lifestyle we live and its effect on both world ecology and those who suffer most from degradation of the environment. Discussing the lack of simplicity in modern society and in most modern lifestyles, he writes: "We must clearly understand that the lust for affluence in contemporary society is psychotic. It is psychotic because it has completely lost touch with reality. We crave things we neither need nor enjoy.... Covetousness we call ambition. Hoarding we call prudence. Greed we call industry."[16]

By contrast, simplicity is one of the defining features of the Shire. Rather than craving things they do not need, Hobbits enjoy what they have. They do not hoard but give freely, an attitude reflected in the habit of giving (rather than receiving) gifts on one's birthday. Thus they practice the third of Foster's ten principles of simplicity: "Develop a habit of giving things away." They also do well on the fourth: "Refuse to be propagandized by the custodians of modern gadgetry."[17] Unlike many of us, Hobbits are not collectors of gadgets.[18] Foster's sixth principle is "develop a deeper appreciation for the creation." He says, "Get close to the earth. Walk whenever you can. Listen to the birds . . . enjoy the texture of grass and leaves."[19] Foster, Schumacher, and other advocates of simpler living might have derived this principle directly from studying Tolkien's Hobbits. An overarching principle, and one that Foster suggests separates the positive virtue of simplicity from the negative one of asceticism, is that "the creation is good and to be enjoyed."[20]

The values of the Hobbits are seen most sharply when they come into contrast with those of others around them. Hoarding tendencies are most clearly exhibited by dragons, particularly the dragon Smaug, who is the archvillain of *The Hobbit*. But Tolkien also shows this hoarding tendency and its sad result in Dwarves, who appear frequently in connection with dragons. This connection seems to have been a commonplace of early medieval culture. A seminal source for Tolkien—both professionally and creatively—can be found in the Old Norse *Völsunga Saga*, where the dwarf Andvari has a golden treasure and a magic ring that are seized by Fáfnir, a man transformed into a dragon by the curse of greed, the curse of the hoard, or both.[21] One of the most moving scenes in *The Hobbit* is the death of the Dwarf king Thorin, whose dying words to Bilbo are, "If more of us valued food and cheer and song above hoarded gold, it would be a merrier world" (*H*, 348). As Thorin acknowledges only moments earlier, the specter of impending death—of going to "the halls of waiting to sit beside my fathers"—forces a clearer vision and a reevaluation of what is really important. Thorin repents of his earlier unkind words to Bilbo, contrasting the traditional values of the Hobbits, which are vindicated throughout the story, with those of the Dwarves, which have brought such trouble.

Wendell Berry might take the principle of Thorin's dying words a step further, seeing *hoarding*, a problem addressed by Foster as well, as the central problem to be corrected. Among other things, the hoarder cannot fully appreciate what he or she is hoarding. Tolkien certainly makes this point with respect to the dragon Smaug, who appreciates the monetary value of objects but not the objects themselves—their beauty or inherent worth. More significantly, perhaps, land itself cannot be appreciated or cared for properly when it is made the object of possessive accumulation: "It is well understood that ownership is an incentive to care. But there is a limit to how much land can be owned before an owner is unable to take proper care of it. The need for attention increases with the intensity of use. But the quality of attention decreases as acreage increases."[22] This idea is stated in many of Berry's essays as a contrast between small family farms and the agricultural empires of agribusiness. For the former, success is defined in terms of producing good crops, in an environmentally sustainable manner, for the consumption of the farmer and his family, the surplus being made available for the needs of neighbors. For people involved in agribusiness, success is defined in terms of the money economy; the agribusinessman must accumulate larger tracts of land, more equipment, and larger storage capacity to survive in the agricultural market, creating an endless cycle of acquisition and dependency. Hoarding fits the goals of agribusiness; by means of hoarding, there are "corporations that have bought cheap and sold high the products that, as a result of this agenda, have been increasingly expensive for farmers to produce."²³ Thus hoarding is sometimes a good way to make money, but it is always a bad way to live life.

An even greater contrast can be seen between Hobbits and Orcs. When we first meet Orcs—called Goblins in *The Hobbit*—we learn a good deal about their values, and they are not entirely without what one might call virtues. Although "they make no beautiful things," they at least "make many clever ones." Cleverness or ingenuity might be seen as having the positive value of problem solving. Mechanical solutions to the problems of the physical world often bring problems of their own, however, and the Goblins are said to have invented "some of the machines that have since troubled the world," ingenious devices that make use of "wheels and engines and explosions." Like us, Orcs are interested in saving labor, but they are described as "not working with their own hands more than they could help," suggesting not a pursuit of efficiency to liberate them from tedium for the sake of higher interests but rather lethargy or slothfulness. Their slothfulness has a particularly sinister side, too: whatever labor cannot be done by machines, the Orcs avoid by using slaves, who "have to work till they die for want of air and light." Tolkien's narrator passes judgment on the Orcs' badly applied value system, calling them "wicked and bad-hearted" (*H*, 108–9). The implications for modern life in the real world should not be lost. People in technologically advanced, consumer-oriented societies often find themselves enslaved to the very machines meant to free them from toil—machines that contribute in no small way to pollution of the soil, water, and air and thus to the general endangerment of life and health.

By contrast, Hobbits not only love beautiful things but also love to work with their hands. They particularly like good earth and well-farmed countryside. Though they are "skilful with tools," they dislike and do not understand any machines "more complicated than a forge-bellows, a water-mill, or a handloom" (Pro). We will postpone lengthier remarks on the agrarian nature of Hobbit society until chapter 3, but for now we want to connect this with several earlier points. The first is that the Hobbits' appreciation for the simple pleasures of good food, singing, hot baths, and the like is related to the value they place on nature: the grass, the brown earth beneath their feet, the river in the meadow, the blue sky overhead. The second is that they turn away from the sort of power over others—enslavement and war making—that technology affords: the kind of technology devised by Saruman and employed by Orcs. Instead, Hobbits prefer the work of their own hands and closer connections to the things of the earth they love.

Here it must be noted with some concern that neither of the Bagginses—neither Bilbo nor Frodo, the primary heroes of *The Hobbit* and *The Lord of the Rings*—do any such work themselves. As far as the reader is informed, Bilbo and Frodo never actually get their own hands dirty in their gardens; instead, they pay the Gamgees to do it for them. However, there are four important observations to make with respect to this fact. The first is that although the Bagginses are not farmers or even gardeners, their personal sympathies seem wholly consistent with those of their surrounding culture. Early in *The Lord of the Rings*, the fellow hobbits with whom the Bagginses are most closely and even affectionately related—Sam Gamgee, Hamfast "the Gaffer" Gamgee, Farmer Cotton, and Farmer Maggot, for example—*do* perform such work. Pippin is also from a farming family. Second, and more important, the narrator (at least in *The Hobbit*) seems critical of the Bagginses precisely because they are becoming too much like the snobby upper class: people who say the opposite of what they mean and make others do their work for them. As Tom Shippey points out, Gandalf is trying to rescue Bilbo from being a member of the bourgeoisie—a simple, selfish materialist like his relatives the Sackville-Bagginses, whom the narrator is clearly critical of. Bilbo is not there yet, but he is "heading that way."[24] Third, upon the return of the four heroes in *The Lord of the Rings*, the reconstruction of the Shire is clearly supported by Frodo, even though Sam and many others do the actual work of rebuilding, requiring simple manual labor. And finally, it is not Frodo but Sam, the gardener and forester, who emerges as the real "hero" of the reconstruction—and the only Hobbit ever elected mayor for four terms in the Shire—while Frodo, for various reasons, is unable to cope.

Tom Bombadil (and the River's Daughter)

One of the most curious characters in Tolkien's work is Tom Bombadil. Tolkien admitted that during the writing of *The Lord of the Rings* he himself seemed unsure of who Tom Bombadil was or what he might represent in the overall fabric of the trilogy. Bombadil exists, in a sense, apart from or alongside the mainstream of the narrative and the underlying mythology. He appeared earlier in *The Adventures of Tom Bombadil*, a collection of poems published in 1934, and Tolkien commented in a 1954 letter that Bombadil had been grafted into *The Lord of the Rings* early on while he was still struggling with the story line: "I put him in because I had already 'invented' him independently . . . and wanted an 'adventure' on the way. But I kept him in" (*Letters*, 192). This may contribute to the difficulty of knowing precisely what to make of Tom. As Tolkien acknowledged in another letter, "Even in a mythical Age there must be some enigmas, as there always are. Tom Bombadil is one (intentionally)" (*Letters*, 174).

Not surprisingly, then, as endearing as he is, Tom Bombadil does not quite fit into Middle-earth. For example, there is an inconsistency in the fact that both Bombadil and Treebeard are referred to as the oldest beings in Middle-earth. "Eldest, that's what I am," Tom says of himself. "Mark my words, my friends: Tom was here before the river and the trees; Tom remembers the first raindrop and the first acorn. . . . He knew the dark under the stars when it was fearless—before the Dark Lord came from Outside" (I/vii). Glorfindel also refers to him as "First" (II/ii). Gandalf later contradicts this, it seems, when he says of Treebeard: "Treebeard is Fangorn, the guardian of the forest; he is the oldest of the Ents, the oldest living thing that still walks beneath the Sun upon this Middle-earth" (III/v). Is Bombadil wrong about himself? Is Gandalf wrong about Treebeard? Or did Tolkien himself make a mistake? Peter Jackson, pressed to keep his film adaptation of *The Fellowship of the Ring* under four hours, chose to omit Tom altogether. But there is much in Tom Bombadil's character that has a bearing on the world of nature. The fact that he does not quite fit into Middle-earth is ironic in this respect: he may be the most explicit, concrete embodiment of the natural world—an incarnation, we might say, of environment itself. Tom may not *fit into* Middle-earth because he *stands for* it.

The most satisfying interpretation of Tom Bombadil, then, is that he is the representation or personification of nature: an earth spirit. This is suggested in several ways by Bombadil's description and behavior and can be felt in his unpretentious naturalness, even his earthiness. His voice is deep and glad, careless and happy. When he first appears in the story, he comes "charging through the grass and rushes like a cow going down to drink" (I/vi). He is most like the Hobbits in his love of the earth and the timeless pleasures of a simple rustic lifestyle. Perhaps this is why

Tom Bombadil likes to visit Farmer Maggot: the two are kindred spirits. In a letter written in 1937, before Bombadil had been more fully developed as a character who later finds his way into Middle-earth, Tolkien described him as "the spirit of the (vanishing) Oxford and Berkshire countryside" (*Letters*, 26).

This role expands when he enters *The Lord of the Rings*. We can see it in the appropriateness of his marriage to Goldberry; Bombadil is the earth spirit, while she is the river's daughter—a naiad, or water spirit. Jamie Williamson notes that the description of Goldberry "moves quickly from very brief, conventional observations of her individual physical appearance to a dense fabric of natural images." Her "physical being, her body, is seen as indivisible from forget-me-nots, water-lilies, and reeds, from beads of dew, living pools and waterfalls, and it is these which form our image of her." Williamson concludes, "This welter of imagery . . . serves to situate her, not in a timeless world, but in the cyclic time of the world of nature, where rippling streams and living pools beget and nourish reeds and lilies according to the rhythm of the seasons. Her body is emblematic of the natural world independent of 'those that go on two legs.'"[25]

In another letter, Tolkien wrote, "Goldberry represents the actual seasonal changes in such lands" (*Letters*, 272), thus strengthening the idea that Tom and Goldberry are physical embodiments of the spirit of nature. If these suggestions are not persuasive enough, Galdor's comment at the Council of Elrond also supports the idea: "Power to defy our Enemy is not in [Bombadil]," he says, "unless such power *is in the earth itself*" (II/ii, emphasis added). Bombadil's power is equated precisely with the natural potency of the earth—the brute fact of its existence and its resistance against forces of destruction. He is almost the opposite of Gandalf, who describes Bombadil as "a moss-gatherer," whereas Gandalf sees himself as "a stone doomed to rolling" (VI/vii). Gandalf is an embodied spirit, one of the Ainur who, in Tolkien's mythology, takes incarnate form as a member of the ancient order of Istari sent by the Valar to aid Middle-earth. It could be said, then, that whereas Gandalf is the physical incarnation of something spiritual, Bombadil is the spiritual personification of something physical.

Just as we get comfortable with this understanding of Bombadil, however, we stumble over comments Tolkien made in later letters that seem either to contradict his earlier statements or to revise them as

Bombadil's character developed further. In a letter from April 1954 he states, "Tom Bombadil . . . represents something that I feel important, though I would not be prepared to analyze the feeling precisely." He goes on to explain that Bombadil represents the inclination to take "delight in things for themselves without reference to yourself, watching, observing, and to some extent knowing." To Bombadil, "the question of the rights and wrongs of power and control" are "utterly meaningless," and "the means of power quite valueless" (*Letters*, 178–79). To some degree, then, according to this letter, Tom Bombadil represents the pursuit and love of selfless knowledge of the created world and its history, independent of any power or advantage that such knowledge might bring to the knower. We see this manifest in several ways in *The Lord of the Rings*. He is both a gatherer of knowledge, plying the four hobbits with questions when they arrive at his home, and a treasure-house of freely shared knowledge that comes pouring forth in stories. "He told them tales of bees and flowers, the ways of trees and the strange creatures of the Forest, about the evil things and good things, things friendly and things unfriendly, cruel and kind things, and secrets hidden under brambles." After a time with Bombadil, the hobbits "began to understand the lives of the Forest, apart from themselves" (I/vii). This is crucial.

In a letter of September 1954, Tolkien explains more of this aspect of Bombadil's character: "He is then an 'allegory,' or an exemplar, a particular embodying of pure (real) natural science: the spirit that desires knowledge of other things, their history and nature, *because they are 'other'* and wholly independent of the enquiring mind, a spirit coeval with the rational mind, and entirely unconcerned with 'doing' anything with the knowledge" (*Letters*, 192). Bombadil gathers knowledge because he wants to know and to learn. He is a pure scientist, with no interest in technology; he has the desire to know and to understand, but without the desire to manipulate. "He merely knows and understands about such things as concern him in his natural little realm" (*Letters*, 192).

Thus, besides representing nature in a concrete sense, Tom Bombadil can also be said to represent knowledge, but without the quest for power that often accompanies it both in Middle-earth and in our world. Put another way, Bombadil personifies science as a fundamentally distinct thing from technology or even from applied science. He is science in the sense of knowledge for its own sake, without regard to its utility in any particular application, rather than science as an exercise of technical capability for the purpose of manipulating the world.

A third way we can understand Tom Bombadil may seem, at first, to stand in direct contrast with the second. That is, he can be seen as pure power—but if so, it is power without the will to dominate. "Tom Bombadil is the Master," Goldberry tells the hobbits, but he is not the lord of anything (I/vii). As Tolkien wrote in 1954, "He is master in a peculiar way: he has no fear, and no desire of possession or domination at all" (*Letters*, 192). There is nothing in him that craves the oppression of other wills. Thus, even though he is immensely powerful, he embodies Foster's ninth principle of simplicity: "Reject anything that will breed oppression in others."[26] Even the Ring "has no power over him," Gandalf tells the Council. "He is his own master" (II/ii). When Bombadil speaks—which is usually in song—his words can have a powerful effect on reality. He commands the tree to release Merry and Pippin, and it does. He commands the wight to exit its barrow, and it departs. If this is magic, it is different from the sort we might encounter elsewhere—in the Harry Potter books, for example. Bombadil utters no magic spell or incantation. There is no battle, nor is there any resistance to his commands. His word alone is enough.

The closest we come to anything like this is Gandalf, whose words also hold power; he simply commands a door to stay shut, a fire to light, or a bridge to break asunder. Thus, despite their differences in other ways, just as Farmer Maggot and Bombadil are kindred spirits in their earthiness, Gandalf is like Bombadil in relation to power. Perhaps this is why Gandalf goes to visit Tom at the end of the trilogy: they appreciate each other's differences but have enough in common to appreciate their fundamental similarity. With Gandalf, however, there is some strain involved in the use of such power. After uttering a shutting spell on the door in Moria, the Balrog breaks it and Gandalf is exhausted. "I have met my match," he says, "and have nearly been destroyed . . . I am rather shaken"; shortly thereafter he says he is "weary" (I/v). In opposing spiritual evil, Gandalf's use of power drains him, but with Bombadil, it is effortless, done with a smile and a song.[27]

In summary, then, Bombadil can be said to represent nature, knowledge for its own sake, or pure power. The first associates him with something physical, the earth; the second and third associate him with nonphysical concepts. At first glance, these three understandings seem not only different but perhaps even contradictory. However, the apparent contradictions can be resolved; all three of these explanations form a complete ontological picture in which *being, knowledge,* and *power* are essentially united. If Bombadil is the personification of nature in Middle-earth, then he also represents natural science in its purest form as knowledge of that world's being and history. Such knowledge is potentially powerful, but Bombadil chooses not to use it to aggrandize his own position. He has no need to do so, because the use of power would not provide him with any greater knowledge, nor would it enhance his essential being.

Behind all this, Tolkien may be suggesting that the self-abnegating act of giving up the will to dominate is itself very powerful and the soul of simplicity. "Simplicity brings freedom," Foster explains, resulting in balance and joy, for under these conditions, "the lust for status and position is gone because we no longer need status and position."[28] Paradoxically, giving up power is an alternative and more profound form of empowerment. The intimate knowing that Bombadil exhibits is even more potent than the superficial pursuit of power; in its self-denying negation of the power syndrome, the kind of being and knowing exemplified by Bombadil is a form of love. It is the knowing and sharing implied in the seventeenth-century sense of the word when a man and a woman "know" each other in intimacy. In his simplicity, in his freedom from domination and from the will to dominate, as an incarnation of the world and of joyful knowledge of the world, Bombadil can be said to represent selfless love of the created order—in our view, the foundation for the most authentic form of environmentalism.

The Glory of Its Beginning: Ilúvatar and Creation

Wendell Berry begins his essay "Conservation and Local Economy" by noting, "In our relation to the land, we are ruled by a number of terms and limits set not by anyone's preference but by nature and by human nature."[29] So far in this chapter we have observed several aspects of a value system that provides what might be called "terms and limits" in Middle-earth: a value system that the previously discussed characters submit to. We have seen in the work of Yavanna that the created world, the life of Arda—especially the life of plants and animals represented by the Two Trees—is important, valuable, and good apart from any practical usefulness to its inhabitants. We have seen in the Hobbit race an appreciation and enjoyment of the world for what it is, not merely for what can be done with it. We have seen in Tom Bombadil the value of knowing and loving the world for what it is. And we have seen in him and in the Hobbits the value of simplicity exemplified by well-tilled earth and the work of one's hands.

All these values are important aspects of the environmental ethic that can be found in Tolkien's work. However, we have not yet seen the basis for any of them. That is, although we have seen that some in Middle-earth hold these values, we have not seen the origins of or reasons for these particular values as opposed to other ones. Why, in Tolkien's mythology, is self-denial better than exploitation and tyranny? Why is it better to love the earth and seek to preserve it rather than to ignore or despise it and use it destructively? Are the answers to these questions tied to a view of reality in which some things are right in an objective or absolute sense while others are not, or are these merely matters of preference? It is thus reasonable to ask whether Tolkien provides any basis for his ecological perspective beyond his own personal preference.

The answer is that Tolkien's environmental ethic is presented as a transcendent one. It is based on principles about creation that are implied throughout Tolkien's writings about Middle-earth:

1. The universe is the work of a divine creator.
2. The created world is good; it has inherent worth and beauty.
3. Creation has a purpose: to bring pleasure to its creator and to those who dwell in it.
4. The created order and its inhabitants are vulnerable to evil embodied in a cosmic enemy.
5. The mission of people dwelling in the world is to acknowledge the goodness of the earth, fulfill its purpose, and assist in its restoration from evil.

All five of these principles can be derived from a careful analysis of the mythology summarized in *The Silmarillion* and alluded to or built on in the other writings, and each has analogues in our world. What will be obvious to attentive readers is that Tolkien's environmental vision is a profoundly meaningful outgrowth of his Catholicism and is therefore, at bottom, Christian. In a letter from 1953, Tolkien himself wrote, "*The*

Lord of the Rings is of course a fundamentally religious and Catholic work: unconsciously so at first, but consciously in the revision" (*Letters,* 172). Many others have commented on the degree to which elements of Catholic belief can be discerned in Tolkien's works, and we can add little to these observations.[30] What we expand on here, though, are Tolkien's interjected "of course" in the statement above and his reference to both conscious and unconscious aspects of the work's Christian foundations.

When Tolkien writes that the work's foundations are "of course" Christian, he implies that the underlying myth's debt to the Christian story is, or ought to be, self-evident to the reader. When he notes that this indebtedness was unconscious at first, he suggests it is inevitable that he—a man who in another letter said, "I am a Christian . . . and in fact a Roman Catholic"—would base his imagined world on the worldview comprehended in his religious belief (*Letters,* 288).[31] Interestingly, Tolkien goes on to explain why he avoided putting in overt references to "anything like 'religion'" and why he often deliberately *removed* them: elements of religiosity or cultic practice, he states, are best "absorbed into the story and the symbolism." Elsewhere he declares that the explicit references to Christian religion in the Arthurian legend are "fatal" to its effectiveness as a fairy story: "Myth and fairy-story must, as all art, reflect and contain in solution elements of moral and religious truth (or error), but not explicit, not in the known form of the primary 'real' world" (*Letters,* 144). Thus, although there are obvious parallels between the Christian story and the mythic substratum of his legendarium, the refusal to draw overt connections is intended to increase the effectiveness with which Tolkien's deeply held beliefs, including those with environmental implications, are communicated to readers.

The five principles listed above, then, are transcendent in the sense that they are based on something beyond the personal preference of the author or of any one character or group of characters inside or outside the story in any particular time or culture. They are based on Middle-earth's creation mythology as recorded by the Elves, and if it is a true mythology, then the principles apply objectively to all inhabitants of Middle-earth whether they acknowledge them or not. In the world of Middle-earth they provide a sufficient explanation for the environmental positions adopted by the inhabitants of that world, and in our world they provide plausible reasons for the healthy, respectful treatment of the earth—objective reasons, if the underlying principles are true of our world as well. In any case, these principles transcend particular personal or cultural value systems, at least in the sense that they are shared by many of the great philosophical and religious traditions of human history. Echoing Berry's observation, we too would say that we are ruled by certain principles of nature and of human nature that set the limits on and prescribe the consequences of our behavior. Just as in Tolkien's myth, these principles are not established by the idiosyncratic preferences of anyone in particular—Tolkien said, "I do not think 'opinions,' no matter whose, are of much use without some explanation of how they are arrived at" (*Letters,* 399). In our view, the best foundation for an environmental consciousness is a Christian one identical with, or at least comparable to, Tolkien's.

These five principles are operative throughout *The Hobbit* and *The Lord of the Rings,* even though these books make only veiled references to the divine or angelic powers described in the creation myth at the start of *The Silmarillion.* To understand the roots of these principles in Tolkien's mythology, it is useful to examine Tolkien's creation myth and its roots in the biblical tradition.

We begin with the opening words of the *Ainulindalë,* the first text in *The Silmarillion,* which describe the creation of Middle-earth: "There was Eru, the One, who in Arda is called Ilúvatar." Though it actually says nothing at all about it, this is a simple yet profound introduction to Tolkien's view of nature. What it tells us is that Middle-earth does not begin with Men or Elves or Dwarves or Hobbits, or even with the Ainur. It begins with Eru Ilúvatar, whose names mean "the One" and "the Father of All." There is great mythical significance in Tolkien's giving Middle-earth this beginning. Eru is self-existent. He simply is (and was), like the great "I am" of scripture. As the name Ilúvatar suggests, everything else is either created by him as "the offspring of his thought" or brought into being in a derivative sense by created beings using materials at their disposal from Ilúvatar's original act of creation. Tolkien's term for this process is *subcreation.* As the *author* of creation, Eru alone can make the ultimate claim to *authority* within the world he has created. As the mythology goes on to explain, the power to "bring into Being" things of one's own—the "Imperishable Flame" or the "Secret Fire," as it is called—lies only with Ilúvatar. Not even the mightiest of the Ainur, who, though powerful, are themselves only created beings, can do so. When Melkor, the enemy, goes alone "into the void places seeking the Imperishable Flame," he cannot find it (*Silm*, 16); when Aulë tries to create living and breathing creatures of his own, he finds that the Dwarves, as products of his own fashioning, are only puppets. "Why dost thou attempt a thing which thou knowest is beyond thy power and thy authority?" Ilúvatar asks him (*Silm*, 43). The Ainur, Valar, Maiar, Istari, and Children of Ilúvatar all have subordinate roles in the ongoing process of creation set in motion at the beginning, and each has varying degrees of authority derived from that of the maker, but there are limits, even for the most powerful. Ilúvatar's question to Aulë gets at the very heart of Tolkien's ecology for Middle-earth, for we can imagine Ilúvatar asking any of the inhabitants: "Is what you are doing with creation in keeping with the authority given you by your creator and the creator of the world?" The parallel application in our world is obvious.

The second principle, that creation is good, follows from the first, for Tolkien goes on to root the goodness of creation mythically in the implied goodness of its creator. The act of creation takes the form of song:

> The glory of its beginning and the splendour of its end amazed the Ainur, so that they bowed before Ilúvatar and were silent. . . .
> Then the voices of the Ainur, like unto harps and lutes, and pipes and trumpets, and viols and organs, and like unto countless choirs singing with words, began to fashion the theme of Ilúvatar to a great music; and a sound arose of endless interchanging melodies woven in harmony that passed beyond hearing into the depths and into the heights, and the places of the dwelling of Ilúvatar were filled to overflowing, and the music and the echo of the music went out into the Void, and it was not void. Never since have the Ainur made any music like to this music. (*Silm*, 15)

The imagery is glorious and leaves no doubt that this music is a good thing. But the physical creation is somehow an incarnation of that song, a bringing into physical being of that which at first is only a vision. Or, one might say that although the music existed first and would have been beautiful even if it had never taken physical form, it is only a prophetic vision of the physical creation wherein it would be fulfilled. What we see, then, is that Arda, or, more broadly, Eä, is not good merely because someone happens to like it; it is inherently good as the product of the inherently good creator Ilúvatar. Turning this around, Ilúvatar likes—or, rather, loves—Arda because it is his good work; it is good because it is both the object and the product of his love. Its value is inherent in its origin. Steven Bouma-Prediger summarizes this as a Christian principle, derivable from the biblical creation story and reinforced in such various passages as Psalm 104. "Most importantly," he points out, "rocks and trees, birds and animals are valuable simply because God made them. Their value resides in their being creations of a valuing God, not in their being a means to some human end."[32]

This leads to the third principle. In his creation myth, Tolkien speaks not only of creation's goodness but also of its *purpose*. To use a different word, Ilúvatar the creator has a *will* for creation—that is, a desire or plan. The *Ainulindalë*, Tolkien's story of the creation of Middle-earth, is full of language describing the will and purpose of the creator, and this language has mythic significance. The first spoken words in Tolkien's mythological corpus are those of Eru expressing his purpose: "Of the theme that I have declared to you, I *will* now that ye make in harmony together a Great Music" (*Silm*, 15, emphasis added). A little later, it is said of Manwë and Ulmo that they "have from the beginning been allied, and in all things have served most faithfully the purpose of Ilúvatar" (*Silm*, 19). At one level, in terms of respecting the created world, the sentient creatures who share it do not necessarily need to know what the overall purpose for creation is; the fact that Ilúvatar has a purpose for his creation implies that the beings who inhabit it ought not to usurp it for their own desires. By analogy, a child entering a parent's kitchen ought not to eat a plate of cookies if the child is told that the parent has a purpose for those cookies, even if the child does not know what that purpose is.

Furthermore, there is one sense in which the purpose of Arda and Eä should *not* be stated—at least not in the ordinary sense of purpose. Middle-earth is not the creation of a utilitarian deity. For Eru Ilúvatar, the world exists to be enjoyed by him and by those he creates to enjoy it. It is good because it exists; its purpose is to *be* and to be a pleasure for those who witness, participate in, and share in its creation. Of course, this in itself is a purpose, though not strictly practical, and it is expressed throughout the *Ainulindalë* and elsewhere. It is deeply embedded in the creation account. Immediately after expressing his will to the Ainur, for example, Ilúvatar goes on to say to them, "ye shall show forth your powers in adorning this theme" (*Silm*, 15). That is, the Ainur are to enrich creation, making it more beautiful. And they are to do so in keeping with Ilúvatar's theme. Many of the Ainur (those known as the Valar and the Maiar) even go so far as to enter, or "descend," into creation to work from within, where they are thereafter "bounded in the World, to be within it forever" (*Silm*, 20).

As for delight, the story goes on to speak of the "desire" and "love" of the Ainur for the created world. Simply in looking upon the world, "their hearts rejoiced in light, and their eyes beholding many colours were filled with gladness." Thus as they work to adorn creation, they also delight in its splendor and beauty. The earth becomes "as a garden for their delight." It is even suggested that it is their love of the world, as much as any external law, that binds the Valar to it, "so that they are its life and it is theirs." All this is part of Ilúvatar's purpose. Ilúvatar speaks to Ulmo in particular of the "beauty" of the created world evident in the "cunning work of frost . . . the height and glory of the clouds, and the everchanging mists . . . and the fall of rain upon the Earth." It is a beauty that persists despite the war Melkor has made upon it. Ulmo understands that the beauty of creation is a good thing that is worth delighting in. Immediately after he speaks of joining with Manwë in the task of making melodies forever for the delight of Ilúvatar, it is said that "Manwë and Ulmo . . . in all things have served most faithfully the purpose of Ilúvatar." This clearly speaks to Tolkien's mythic concept of Ilúvatar's purpose. Likewise, when Aulë, who serves the creator and is one of the chief contributors to the shaping of the world, is contrasted with Melkor, the main difference is that whereas both have the creative spirit of a craftsman, Aulë takes delight in things for their own sake, not for the power or wealth they might bring him. He delights "in the deed of making, and in the thing made, and neither in possession or in his own mastery; wherefore he gives and hoards not" (*Silm*, 18–21). And the suggestion in the preceding passages is that created beings (like children in their parents' kitchen) can choose voluntarily to serve Eru's purpose or not, as is the case with Melkor.[33] In either case, Eru has a purpose for all of creation: it is for delight and for beauty, to be enjoyed for its own sake, not for hoarding or destruction or for the mastery that can be accomplished through its possession, use, or domination.

The importance of this can be seen in the differences between the mythology of Middle-earth and the contrasting mythologies of our world. An alternative mythology, for example, might be one in which the universe and the life within it are seen not as the results of a divine creative purpose but rather as the products of chance. In such a mythology, there could be no ultimate purpose; purpose instead would have to be constructed by individual creatures or cultures, and no single provisional definition would establish or prove its priority over others. This would naturally be reflected in how creatures within such an imagined world treated the rest of the universe. As an example, let us take two rival purpose-claims modeled on the basic structures of such a universe: One individual might prefer modern technological conveniences—an air-conditioned house, a big-screen television, an SUV, and a computer with a high-speed network connection. To such a person, these things would be more important than clean air, clean water, good soil, and species diversity. In a world with no inherent purpose, it would be difficult for such a person to find common ground with someone who preferred a simpler lifestyle that placed fewer demands on the world's limited resources. Dialogue between two such imaginary persons would become either an abstract debate—an argument over which value system is better—or a power struggle. The abstract argument would depend on the definition of "better," which in this hypothetical world could only be defined in utilitarian terms and in terms of individual preference. No appeal to more fundamental purposes could be made, and ultimately, the debate could be resolved only through the exercise of power whereby one preference would win out by subduing or destroying the other. The sort of harmony willed by Ilúvatar would not be possible.

Tolkien's Middle-earth, by contrast, has an inherent purpose; it is the deliberate creation of Ilúvatar, and no decision of Elf, Dwarf, Man, or Hobbit can diminish its inherent goodness or change the purpose for which it was made: to cause its inhabitants to rejoice in its glory both by participation and by attribution and to make Ilúvatar glad. When Ilúvatar reveals to Ulmo, the lord of waters, that he has redeemed Melkor's effort to destroy his works by creating frost, snow, clouds, mists, and rain, Ulmo's response indicates his understanding of the purpose of the Valar and the physical world. He says, "I will seek Manwë, that he and I may make melodies for ever to thy delight!" (*Silm,* 19). In one letter, Tolkien explains a similar principle about our primary world, writing that the purpose of life in the human world culminates in "moments of exaltation" when we call on all creation to join in the chorus echoed in Psalm 148 and Daniel 2, "Praise the Lord . . . all mountains and hills, all orchards and forests, all things that creep and birds on the wing" (*Letters*, 400).

This idea is echoed in Wendell Berry's explanation of the fundamental purpose of creation and its basis for a credible environmental ethic of stewardship. The beginning of the biblical creation account in Genesis 1:28, Berry reminds us, includes the charge to the first two humans, "Be fruitful and multiply and replenish the earth and subdue it." Far from providing a warrant for misuse of the environment, Berry says:

> The ecological teaching of the Bible is simply inescapable: God made the world because He wanted it made. He thinks the world is good, and He loves it. It is His world; He has never relinquished title to it. And He has never revoked the conditions, bearing on His gift to us of the use of it, that oblige us to take excellent care of it.

And he finds the culmination of this purpose at the other end of scripture:

> Many passages take us beyond a merely economic stewardship, but the one that has come to seem most valuable to me is Revelation 4:11, because I think it proposes an indispensable standard for the stewardship both of things in use and of useless things and things set aside from use: "Thou art worthy, O Lord, to receive glory and honour and power: for thou hast created all things, and for thy pleasure they are and were created."[34]

The highest purpose of the creation is the glory of its creator, a glory it shares as an embodiment of the loving care with which it is created and tended. We might point out, too, that in the threefold division of "things in use . . . useless things and things set aside from use," there are analogues for the three environmental domains in the scheme of this book: *agriculture*, which uses the environment for food; *horticulture*, in which the pragmatically "useless" aesthetic quality of the world is cultivated for the purpose of beauty; and *feraculture*, which sets portions of the environment apart from use to preserve its wild character.

The coinage *feraculture* is almost, but not quite, an oxymoron, and our triad of terms requires explanation. *Culture*, from the Latin *cultus*, originally had two meanings—one connected with tillage of the soil, and the other with ritual or religious reverence. Modern English reflects both senses: we speak of soil *cultivation*, but also of *cultivation* in the abstract sense of refinement—we *cultivate* a taste for fine wine; a *cultured* individual enjoys fine art, music, and literature. *Culture* in the broadest sense refers to the physical objects, places, and activities and the aesthetic, intellectual, moral, and religious concepts that a society or civilization holds in highest regard or reverence, while *cult* refers pejoratively to fanatical, obsessive reverence for a person or object of ritual veneration. In the first sense, then, *agriculture* denotes physical cultivation of the soil (Greek *agros*), and *horticulture* refers to the cultivation of plants (Latin *hortus*). The second sense of *cultus* is latent in these familiar terms, however, and ought to be emphasized more: the best agriculture should both cultivate the soil physically and respect it spiritually; horticulture should cultivate plants for both their practical uses and their aesthetic qualities. Our invented term *feraculture* is meant to highlight the second sense of *cultus*, suggesting a reverence for the wilderness that includes refraining from using it for pragmatic or commercial purposes—tillage, mining, drilling, and the like, or *cultivation* in the first sense. We are inspired in the use of this term by Berry, who writes in "God and Country" that we ought to have (1) "the ability to use well" the things of this world, (2) "the goodness or the character required to limit use" of these things, and (3) the character to recognize when we ought "to forbear to use" them.[35]

The application of these ideas in our world is obvious. Among those for whom Tolkien's myth is plausible, extending its underlying principles to our behavior might go a long way toward resolving conflicts between rival views—or at least provide common ground for discussion about how the environment ought to be treated.

This leads us to the fourth principle that can be seen in Tolkien's creation myth. Although there are beings who appear to serve the purpose of Ilúvatar—sometimes consciously, sometimes not—there are also those who stand in opposition to that purpose, who in their rebellion wage war on creation. Chief among these is the Ainu named Melkor, later called Morgoth by the Elves. His violent opposition to the essential values inherent in Ilúvatar's creation can be seen in the profound mythical language of the music: "Then the discord of Melkor spread ever wider, and the melodies which had been heard before foundered in a sea of turbulent sound. But Ilúvatar sat and hearkened until it seemed that about his throne there was a raging storm, as of dark waters that made war one upon another in an endless wrath that would not be assuaged" (*Silm*, 16). The imagery here is all violent. It is later said that Melkor's theme "essayed to drown the other music by the violence of its voice." What we notice is that much of that violence is directed toward the physical earth and the things that grow there. Ilúvatar says to Ulmo: "Seest thou not how here in this little realm in the Deeps of Time Melkor hath made war upon thy province? He hath bethought him of bitter cold immoderate . . . [and] devised heats and fire without restraint." Melkor's goal is to destroy the beauty of Ulmo's fountains and clear pools and to quell the music of the sea (*Silm*, 19). A little later, in the *Quenta Silmarillion*, we read that Melkor "looked down upon [Arda], and the beauty of the Earth in its Spring filled him the more with hate." Thus he attacks the world and sets up his abode there in order to do it harm. The result? "Green things fell sick and rotted, and rivers were choked with weeds and slime, and fens were made, rank and poisonous." He casts down the lamps of the Valar and spills destroying flame over the earth (*Silm*, 36–37). There are considerable implications to this. Even without being told Ilúvatar's purpose for creation, we might guess what it is by seeing Melkor's opposition and rebellion against it. In waging war against Ilúvatar, the mythical enemy attacks not the creator himself but the beauty of his creation. His hatred for Ilúvatar equates to a hatred for his creation, and vice versa.

We now turn to the fifth mythic principle identified at the start of this section—essentially, Man's response to the first four principles. Before doing so, however, let us return briefly to the notion raised earlier of an objective or transcendent basis for an environmental ethic. This is clearly suggested by the words of Aragorn when he first meets Éomer on the Plains of Rohan. "Good and ill have not changed since yesteryear," Aragorn tells the horse lord, "nor are they one thing among Elves and Dwarves and another among Men. It is a man's part to discern them, as much in the Golden Wood as in his own house" (III/ii). Aragorn, one of the chief voices of wisdom in Tolkien's works, asserts that morality is not temporally, spatially, or culturally subjective. Aragorn's words have important environmental implications, even to the people of Rohan.

Shortly after this remark, we learn that in order to build a fire to burn the bodies of their dead enemies, Éomer's people have cut down living trees from Fangorn Forest. Earlier, the cutting of Fangorn's trees is seen as unequivocally evil, an act associated with the Orcs of Isengard. Yet here, the people of Rohan—a basically good people, the reader is led to believe—do the same thing. Aragorn explains: "They were many, and they do not heed the wrath of Fangorn, for they come here seldom, and they do not go under the trees" (III/ii). The implication is that the Rohirrim have tried to justify their actions not on moral grounds but on pragmatic ones: they believe that they can escape the consequences. In Aragorn's wisdom, however (and in Tolkien's), such a justification is unacceptable—cutting living trees from Fangorn is morally wrong, whether it is done wantonly by Orcs or for some ostensibly practical reason by Men.

Faramir, another of the great and wise heroes of the Third Age of Middle-earth, makes several comments similar to those of Aragorn, also communicating something about the transcendent nature of morality in Tolkien's myth. At one point he says to Frodo, "I would not snare even an orc with falsehood" (IV/v). As important as winning battles is to the survival of his people, the moral goodness of speaking the truth is more important than a military victory. At another point, when his father Denethor criticizes him for his gentleness, saying, "Gentleness may be repaid with death," Faramir replies, "So be it" (V/iv). His response is simplicity itself. Faramir indicates that the virtue of gentleness stands higher than the military virtues prized by his father. Faramir's willingness to die strongly suggests a basis in objective morality and not in mere personal preference. In Tolkien's system of thought, there is an implied relationship between this subtle virtue and an environmental ethic of care for the created world: much of the violence in Middle-earth is done either directly or indirectly to the earth itself, and it reflects an attitude of hostility toward Ilúvatar, the created beings he calls his Children, and the world he has created for them to dwell in—both of which he loves for their own sake.

Many other examples can be cited, but it would be tedious to elucidate more of them here. On the one hand, many of us might feel the temptation to reject a moral system such as this, with its seemingly uncompromising absolutism. On the other hand, it can be seen as a necessary—and desirable—feature of his environmental ethic that

Tolkien imagines it as deriving its moral weight from the objective authority of divine law. Tolkien's environmentalism is firmly rooted in the Christian understanding of creativity, love, humility, and responsibility, and we believe this perspective provides the foundation—if not the only one, then at least one of the best—for a viable environmental ethic. Christian convictions are by no means necessary for an appreciation of this perspective, but acceptance of Tolkien's views on these matters requires an understanding of the basis for his perspective.

Let us turn now to the fifth principle in Tolkien's ethic. Both the Ainur and the Children of Ilúvatar (Men, Elves, Dwarves) are called to value the earth's goodness, to acknowledge its purpose, and to bring restoration from the harm caused by the rebellion of Melkor and his followers. Throughout the early parts of *The Silmarillion,* we certainly see this purpose at work among the Valar who serve Eru. Their efforts are poured into the labors of making the earth beautiful, fulfilling the purposes of Eru revealed in the music—for example, in Yavanna's creation of the Two Trees and Varda's making of stars—and healing the wounds caused by Melkor.

Perhaps the most important statement of purpose for the Elves, also called the Quendi, is expressed by Ulmo. In addition to serving "most faithfully the purpose of Ilúvatar," Ulmo is presented in *The Silmarillion* as one of the wisest of the Valar, one of the most deeply instructed in music, and one with a particularly intense love for Men and Elves. When the Valar decide to call the Elves to the undying land of Valinor, Ulmo is initially opposed to the summons. This may seem odd, but the explanation that follows makes perfect sense. We are told that some of the Valar, of whom "Ulmo was the chief," feel "the Quendi should be left free to walk as they would in Middle-earth, and with their gifts of skill to order all the lands and heal their hurts." We already know that from the beginning the Elves have a great love for the beauty of the earth. But what Ulmo adds to this understanding is a clear statement of what the Elves are *meant* to do with that love: they are intended to use all their gifts and skill to redress the hurts of Melkor. Their mission is to heal the hurts of the land. Ulmo, however, does not win the debate. The Elves are summoned west to Valinor out of Middle-earth, and those who follow abandon their original purpose. We are told that "from this summons came many woes that afterwards befell" (*Silm*, 52).

Man's purpose in Middle-earth is not explained in such straightforward terms in *The Silmarillion*. The narrative does say that Men "would stray often," not using their gifts in harmony with the design of Ilúvatar's music, implying that Men in Middle-earth are intended, like Elves, to use their gifts in harmony with his design (*Silm*, 42). In his essay "On Fairy-stories," however, Tolkien writes more explicitly about the human race in our world, and what he says about our purpose relates closely to what we learned about the purpose of Elves in the mythology of Middle-earth. A few words from the end of that essay suffice to end this chapter: "Redeemed Man . . . has still to work, with mind as well as body, to suffer, hope, and die; but he may now perceive that all his bents and faculties have a purpose, which can be redeemed. . . . In Fantasy he may actually assist in the effoliation and multiple enrichment of creation" (*TL*, 66). Thus, Man is to assist creation; to help it flourish, bear leaf, and be enriched. Although these comments were made in a specific argument promoting the value of fairy stories and fantasy literature, they speak more generally to the ultimate purpose for which, in Tolkien's view, humankind exists. The statement also applies to Tolkien's own work: his own imaginative fictions provide a fitting response to the need for works of literature that create a plausible image of a complex ecology and environmental ethic.

Chapter 2

Gandalf, Stewardship, and Tomorrow's Weather

❀

In *The Lord of the Rings,* when Gandalf first appears in Rohan at Meduseld, the golden hall of King Théoden, the notorious Gríma (son of Gálmód) gives him an icy reception. Gríma first calls Gandalf "Master Stormcrow"—repeating Théoden's earlier use of the pejorative nickname—and then adds the title "Láthspell," which means "ill news."[1] Gandalf responds by calling Gríma by his better-known nickname, "Wormtongue," a title that is equally pejorative and far more accurate.[2] Gandalf's purpose in this encounter is to restore Théoden to health so that he can take action against the evil that threatens not only the land of Rohan but also all of Middle-earth. Wormtongue opposes that purpose. It is not long, however, before the wizard lifts his staff, thunder rolls, lightning flashes, and Wormtongue is seen sprawled on his face, silenced and defeated (III/vi). Wherever Gandalf goes, there are electrifying confrontations, and these confrontations always involve competing visions for the community and the world.

Among the most intense confrontations in *The Return of the King* are those between Gandalf and Denethor. As steward of Gondor, Denethor is the acting ruler of the last kingdom of Númenóreans, which—aside from Rohan—is the only kingdom of Men between Mordor and the Misty Mountains.[3] As such, it is the major obstacle that stands between Sauron and domination of all Middle-earth. At issue in these confrontations are Gandalf's and Denethor's opposing ideas of what a steward should be and do. When the wizard comes to Gondor, offering both aid and counsel in the war against Sauron, Denethor essentially refuses that counsel, saying of himself, "The Lord of Gondor is not to be made the tool of other men's purposes, however worthy." He goes on to add, "And the rule of Gondor, my lord, is mine and no other man's, unless the king should come again" (V/i). For Denethor, stewardship is all about rule and authority. He divides the world into tools and the users of tools; rulers (including stewards), he explains, are those who use others as tools but are not themselves used. Denethor later goes so far as to compare his stewardship of Gondor with Sauron's rule over Mordor. Sauron "uses others as his weapons," he says to Pippin. "So do all great lords, if they are wise, Master Halfling. Or why do I sit here in my tower and think, and watch, and wait, spending even my sons?" (V/iv). Amazingly, Denethor actually suggests here that Sauron is a great and wise lord—a model for other kings—because he has learned how to make use of tools. Denethor even imitates the Dark Lord in his unwillingness to serve another's purpose, even if that purpose is worthy; thus he resists Gandalf's good counsel, seeing both Gandalf and Aragorn only as rivals to his power. In Denethor's political economy, wisdom is in knowing how to rule others: how to use them and spend them like money, even if those "others" are his own sons.

By contrast, Gandalf gives a very different picture of stewardship, saying to Denethor:

> Well my lord Steward, it is your task to keep some kingdom still against that event [the return of the king], which few now look to see. In that task you shall have all the aid that you are pleased to ask for. But I will say this: the rule of no realm is mine, neither of Gondor nor any other, great or small. But all worthy things that are in peril as the world now stands, those are my care. And for my part, I shall not wholly fail of my task, though Gondor should perish, if anything passes through this night that can still grow fair or bear fruit and flower again in days to come. For I also am a steward. Did you not know? (V/i)

This is one of the clearest indications of Gandalf's role in Middle-earth. He is a steward. In claiming this role, Gandalf makes no connection between stewardship and rule; he neither claims nor wants the rule of any realm, great or small. In reminding Denethor that he is a steward and that his task as steward is "keep[ing] some kingdom still" for the returning king, Gandalf makes it clear that a steward exists to serve others, and not vice versa. Of course, Gandalf also makes this clear through his actions when, despite their differences of opinion, he offers aid to Denethor. There is a stark contrast between Gandalf's actions as a steward and Denethor's. In many ways, the future of Middle-earth depends on which view of stewardship will win. The same might be said of our world today.

Use and Misuse of the Term *Steward*

Wendell Berry writes that he has "too little faith in the long-term efficacy of public stewardship" but much more faith in "the long-term efficacy of private stewardship," meaning in part that individuals and communities, and not just vague corporate or political entities, must be involved in stewardship. He sees as a major component of our modern ecological problems "the lack of a general culture of land stewardship."[4] The survival of our world, our country, or our society rests on our understanding of our roles as stewards—or, one might say, on competing visions of what a steward should be and should do.

One of the most significant aspects of Tolkien's environmental vision, and one informing all areas of his ecology, is his clarification of the real role of a steward. In the specific context of environmental stewardship, and especially the stewardship of wilderness and trees, he provides the model of the Ents, already mentioned briefly and explored more thoroughly in chapter 5. More generally, he gives us Gandalf—both the wizard's *words* about stewardship and his explicit *model* of stewardship. This is especially important in today's culture. In contemporary environmental discourse, the words *steward* and *stewardship* have acquired negative connotations; for some, it is as if their main understanding of stewardship has come from Denethor rather than from Gandalf.

Although the problem is not universal, and there are hopeful signs for a positive revaluation of the term,[5] even within the context of Christianity the terms have been misused. Jim Ball outlines four widely divergent ways in which the term *stewardship* has been used in the evangelical Protestant communities.[6] At one extreme, the rhetoric of so-called wise-use stewardship has been used to justify the exploitation of nature with an attitude of what Ball calls "extreme arrogance." This is akin to the approach of Denethor, who seldom even uses the word *steward* to describe himself, preferring the title *Lord*. Denethor does not hesitate to use exploitative methods to achieve his goals. Gandalf would not describe such an attitude as stewardship, and he certainly would not call it wise. Nonetheless, there are some who approach the world in this way, using the word *stewardship* arrogantly to describe what they are or are not doing and seeking to justify their behavior in Christian terms—a false justification, in Tolkien's understanding of Christianity.

It is understandable, therefore, that proponents of environmental responsibility sometimes react negatively to ideas of stewardship that seem to be borrowed from Christian doctrines or to the word *stewardship* itself. Because of such misuse, it is tempting to simply look for a different term altogether to describe what Gandalf is modeling. In a book whose subject is Tolkien's environmental ethic, however, *stewardship* is the appropriate term: it is the term Tolkien used in his writing, and it is a term he used with full awareness of its implications for Christian belief.[7] We must therefore make the effort to understand what that term means. Tolkien does this through the contrast between Gandalf and Denethor; he makes it clear that the true model of stewardship is that which is sometimes called *Christian stewardship*, which we define simply as stewardship of the kind modeled by Gandalf.

What is this Christian, or Gandalfian, concept of stewardship? One approach to understanding the word, appropriate to the study of Tolkien the philologist, is the historical and etymological approach. The word *steward* comes from two Old English words, *stig* and *weard*. A *stig* is a hall; in the Germanic tradition, it is a medieval mead hall, the place where a ruling chieftain gathered his followers for feasting and reward after success in battle. Later, the meaning of *stig* broadened to include inns and other forms of lodging.[8] A *weard* is a "lord," "keeper," or "guardian," and it has a modern derivative in *warden*. Today, when a child becomes someone's *ward*, that person is responsible for protecting and nurturing the child until he or she comes of age or until the child's parents become capable of caring for the child. Thus, a *stigweard*, or *steward*, is the keeper or warden of the mead hall. The word implies a set of responsibilities, and medieval law and social custom specified a number of things that a good steward could and could not do. The Anglo-Saxon *stigweard* was a host in charge of taking care of the guests of the hall; he was not, however, the king of the hall. Rather, the steward was responsible to a higher authority, namely, the king or chieftain. Later medieval codes required a steward to oversee the agriculture and husbandry of a feudal estate in his lord's absence—a frequent situation, owing to the widely disparate locations of the manors under a feudal lord's demesne. Thus the steward's responsibility included an explicit environmental component. In the realm of Gondor in the Third Age of Middle-earth—a realm modeled closely on feudal European civilization[9]— a steward was the one left in charge of a kingdom when a king went off to war. The steward had authority in the king's name until the king returned, but ultimately he was accountable to the rightful king for all his actions.

The gospels record several parables concerning stewards, including a "faithful and wise steward" who is ready and waiting for his lord's return from a journey afar (Luke 12:42–44), a bad steward who oppresses those under his care (Luke 12:45–46), and an "unjust steward" accused of wasting his lord's goods (Luke 16:1–2). Though the bad steward is a stock figure in medieval narrative, medieval literature provides at least one impressive example of a good steward, and it is one that we know Tolkien was intimately acquainted with. The Middle English romance titled "Sir Orfeo" tells the story of Sir Orfeo, the king of Tracience, whose wife Eurydice is spirited away by the king of the underworld. Leaving his kingdom in the hands of a steward, Orfeo goes on a ten-year search for his wife. Arriving at last in the underworld, he pleases its king by his harp-playing and thereby recovers his wife. Returning to Tracience in disguise, Orfeo discovers that the steward is still loyal to the absent king; overjoyed to find Sir Orfeo still alive, he gladly surrenders the throne to its rightful ruler with magnificent ceremony. When Orfeo and Eurydice die after a long and happy reign, the throne reverts to the steward—now designated its rightful successor.

The supernatural elements of the "Sir Orfeo" story may derive from undocumented Celtic sources, but most scholars recognize biblical symbolism in the idea of an absent but returning king and a faithful steward. The story survives in a number of versions in Old and Middle English, but what is interesting about this particular rendition is its happy ending, which is unique among the English versions and represents a significant departure from the classical legend of Orpheus on which it is based. Further, it is of interest to us here because Tolkien prepared a modern English translation of the story that—along with his translations of *Sir Gawain and the Green Knight* and *Pearl*—was edited by his son Christopher and published in 1975. Though no other writing by Tolkien survives on the subject, we can be certain that Tolkien regarded it as an example of a story marked by "eucatastrophe"—a "sudden joyous turn," a "miraculous grace" at the climax of a good fairy story—in which he perceives "a far-off gleam or echo of evangelium [good news] in the real world" (*TL*, 62–64). Clearly, Tolkien had examples of both good and bad stewards to work from in composing his own works.

In the political sense, there are three important aspects of stewardship: (1) responsibility for taking good care of the kingdom in the king's absence, (2) ultimate accountability to the king for carrying out that responsibility, and (3) surrender to the king's authority upon his return. The second and third aspects require explicit acknowledgment of the king's authority over the steward, and the third is central to the title of the final book in *The Lord of the Rings*.

Returning to Ball's discussion of the four uses of the term *stewardship* in the Christian community, we have the second use, or what he calls "anthropocentric stewardship." This acknowledges the lordship of God but still views nature as merely a resource; it does not acknowledge the world's intrinsic worth as the good handiwork of a good creator. Although this is perhaps not as blatant a misuse of the term as the first case, in that it at least acknowledges some responsibility, it is still a long way from how Tolkien used the word himself and understood its meaning in the Christian sense.

A third use of the word *steward* gets at the notion of "caring management," which sees humans in the roles of both lord and servant, as gardeners and managers, with the rest of creation having intrinsic value apart from that bestowed on it by those who tend and nurture it. In *The Silmarillion*, the Elves seem to be called to this model of stewardship. When Ulmo argues against summoning the Elves to Valinor, he speaks of using "their gifts of skill to order all the lands and heal their hurts." This implies a perspective in which the Elves are seen as servants; however, the idea of "ordering" the land also suggests the exercise of authority over it or the imposition of some structure that might not otherwise naturally exist. As we explore in chapter 4, in their relationship to the natural world, the Elves are perhaps best described not as agriculturalists or conservationists but as horticulturalists. Even when it is undertaken rightly and lovingly, horticulture implies some rule over the land and its products—some aspect of a ruler choosing what the land will produce and how it will be arranged.

If we judge by the fruits of their labors, Tom Bombadil and Beorn both seem to fit this model as well. Both are gardeners of some note, both act as managers of their respective domains, and both show great loving care for the realms under their dominion. Tom is said to be a "master," and though he never tries to change the character of Old Man Willow or destroy him, he does take steps to keep him under control. He has also carved out a small area of the Old Forest for his cottage and garden, and this involves the imposition of order and structure on part of the woods. The edge of the Old Forest bordering on his cottage is said to be "clipped and trim as a hedge," and he has various trails through the woods (I/vi). Likewise, Beorn, a wonderful caregiver for the creatures in his household, is clearly the ruler of his realm—and a powerful one at that. The animals follow his commands, but woe to anyone who attempts to tamper with the animals he tends.

Ball's fourth use of the term *steward* is what he calls "servanthood stewardship." This idea not only sees the intrinsic value of creation but also conceives of humans as servants within it. Any notion of human rule or authority is gone altogether. When Gandalf says, "For I also am a steward," his vision comes closer to this model of stewardship than to the third. He is there to offer aid; he will give any aid that Denethor asks for. He is not there to exercise authority and claims the rule of no realm, great or small. Nor is this empty rhetoric: Gandalf's actions lend credence to his words. Putting these two together, we might say that he exists for others, but others do not exist for him.

For what *others* does Gandalf exist? Asked another way, what is Gandalf's purpose? He answers the question himself when he says, "All worthy things that are in peril as the world now stands, those are my care." In this way, Gandalf identifies himself with Ilúvatar's mission for his Children, implying too the essential goodness of creation. In the first chapter, we discuss the fundamental concept that Ilúvatar creates a world with inherent value and goodness—that is, of inherent worth, or full of "worthy things." Gandalf sees this as clearly as anyone in Middle-earth and understands the value—even the necessity—of working to protect it. We might consider, for example, Gandalf's treatment of Shadowfax and the other horses. He addresses them not as beasts of burden but as friends and fellow laborers—partners in the war against Sauron—even asking permission to ride. "Time presses, so *with your leave*, my friends, we will ride. *We beg you* to use all the speed that you can. . . . I will set Gimli before me, and *by his leave* Shadowfax shall bear us both" (III/v, emphasis added). When he rides, Gandalf uses no saddle. He does not "ride" Shadowfax in the ordinary sense: the horse consents to bear him. "He has come for me: the horse and the White Rider. We are going to battle together" (III/v).

Gandalf as steward models what Steven Bouma-Prediger describes as the ecological virtue of respect for creation, which relates to the value of creation—the second principle listed in the previous chapter. "*Respect* names an understanding of and proper regard for the integrity and well-being of other creatures. A respectful person shows both esteem and deference to the other, because of the unique nature of that other. That which has intrinsic value calls forth a looking back—a respecting—which acknowledges and regards that God-given value."[10] Gandalf's definition of success in this role is equally telling. Even if Gondor should perish in the war, he will not have wholly failed if anything survives that can "still grow fair or bear fruit and flower again in days to come." This is a powerful statement, and the nature imagery is neither incidental nor gratuitous. Gandalf explicitly includes all life—everything that can grow fair and bear fruit or flower—as being under his care; everything alive is considered a valuable component of the whole created order that must be defended from harm. And if any part of Ilúvatar's created world of Middle-earth is imperiled, that part falls especially within Gandalf's domain. Although most of Gandalf's efforts are aimed at marshaling the Elf, Dwarf, Human, and Hobbit opponents of Sauron,[11] the ultimate purpose of his work is the protection and preservation of all life in Middle-earth. He knows that if his efforts are unsuccessful, those who care for the land as good stewards will be replaced by those who despoil it (the harmful work of such malevolent agencies is explored in chapter 8), and this will have environmental consequences for all of creation, not merely for the Children of Ilúvatar.

It is implied that if Gondor or any good thing within it should perish, then Gandalf's mission will have failed—at least in part. His desire is for the survival and the flourishing of all such things, and the loss of any of them would be costly. When Théoden asks Gandalf whether it is inevitable that "much that was fair and wonderful shall pass for ever out of Middle-earth," Gandalf replies somberly, "The evil of Sauron cannot be wholly cured, nor made as if it had not been. But to such days we are doomed" (III/viii). Any loss of life is to be grieved; all things that grow fair are to be protected.

Stewardship and Nature

We have seen so far that Tolkien's definition of good stewardship falls somewhere between what Ball describes as caring management and servanthood stewardship, perhaps combining some elements from both models, but one far from the negative extreme of careless domination and exploitation. But this is only the beginning of Tolkien's model of environmental stewardship. Just as his legendarium provides a complex ecology involving feraculture, horticulture, and agriculture, so his model of stewardship is deep, complex, and profoundly illuminated in his writings. Tolkien's model of stewardship is so important for an understanding of his mythology that we must explore it further.

One of the most important expressions of this stewardship model comes in Gandalf's words to his young disciple Frodo. Frodo bemoans the fact that the One Ring has come to him and that he is now responsible for dealing with it. "I wish it need not have happened in my time," says Frodo. Gandalf's reply approaches the heart of stewardship. "So do I, and so do all who live to see such times. But that is not for them to decide. All we have to decide is what to do with the time that is given us" (I/ii). The first thing to note in Gandalf's words is that something is *given* to Frodo—namely, time. The lesson is so simple as to be easily overlooked, but the principle Gandalf assumes here is that time is not earned, nor can it be won. Despite all metaphors to the contrary, time is a gift that cannot be saved any more than it can be bought or sold: it can only be spent or invested. Frodo's stewardship must begin with the acknowledgment that what he has was given to him. The next thing we must note is that Frodo is responsible for his *use* of that gift; he must decide what to do with it. No one else—not even Gandalf—can make the decision for Frodo. Frodo must avoid the paralysis that can set in when responsibilities require hard choices.

A modern syndrome that can be just as paralyzing as the need to choose between difficult alternatives has been described as the "victim mentality." Frodo laments his bad luck in being born into such a time; he feels that he is somehow the victim of circumstances and would like to be exonerated of the need to choose a right course of action. Frodo would like to believe that because his bad luck is undeserved, he should not be held responsible for dealing with it. Gandalf can sympathize with Frodo, but this does not change the fact that Frodo is ultimately responsible for what he does or does not do. This discussion can be generalized in several ways. First, although Gandalf specifically mentions time, the conversation is not principally about the time in history in which Frodo finds himself; it is about the Ring. Frodo is already a steward, whether he likes it or not. For the moment, he is the custodian of the Ring. Of course, the Ring is not a good thing, and its possessor is exposed to the potential, or even the likelihood, of both doing and suffering great harm because of it. But the opportunity to help destroy the Ring—an opportunity that Gandalf implies is Frodo's duty—might well prove to be a very good thing, even if at great personal cost to Frodo and those loyal to him. More specifically, then, we could say that Frodo is a steward not so much of the Ring as of the *responsibility* that his possession of the Ring places on him. In this way, Frodo can be seen as a steward both in the traditional sense—as the recipient of the material resources Bilbo has left to him as heir (his home, estate, gardens, and so forth)—and in the sense of his being responsible for the right use of all his skills, abilities, and capacities to do good.

The most important generalization, however, is from Frodo to the reader. Taken at face value, Gandalf does not speak merely of *Frodo's* time and responsibilities; he speaks of *all* people's. Of course, according to the internal logic of the novel, this means Frodo, Gandalf, and all the other characters alive in Middle-earth at the end of the Third Age. But, in one of the many instances when the implications of the narrative slide imperceptibly from the inner world of fantasy to the outer world of reality, Tolkien advances a point that is applicable to both. He articulates a moral imperative that he implies is a universal principle applicable to all people, including *us*. "This is what it means to be a steward," he says to us. The concept is so important to Tolkien that he reiterates it several times throughout the trilogy and elsewhere in his writings. It can be seen, for example, in Aragorn's challenge to Éomer to act: it is his responsibility to choose, and he must be either with Sauron or against him.

The broader implications of stewardship can also be seen in the confrontation in Meduseld with which we began this chapter. Gandalf reminds Théoden both of his gifts—his strength, his rule, his time, his hope—and of his responsibility to use those gifts:

"It is not so dark here," said Théoden.

"No," said Gandalf. "Nor does age lie so heavily on your

shoulders as some would have you think. Cast aside your prop! . . . You live. Gondor and Rohan do not stand alone. The enemy is strong beyond our reckoning, yet we have hope at which he has not guessed. . . . Cast aside regret and fear. . . . Do the deed at hand." (III/vi)

Here, Théoden's fulfillment of his stewardship duties as king—his doing of the "deed at hand"—has an impact not only on the people of Rohan but also on the land itself. It is clear that the Rohirrim are wonderful caretakers of their horses and grasslands. However, they have not always acknowledged the value of the adjacent forests. At the start of the story, Théoden in particular has lost sight of the far-reaching impact of his decisions and of the fact that he has allies. He seems to have forgotten that he is part of a community—not just the local or regional one in his kingdom of Rohan, but also what might be called the "international" community of Middle-earth, or even the "global" one of Arda. Wormtongue would blind him to this; Gandalf must remind him of it. The effects of Théoden's stewardship ripple outward and affect Rohan, Fangorn, Isengard, and Gondor.

Toward the end of Book V of the trilogy, Gandalf presents an even more telling explanation of stewardship. Though it is a time of war, with the most important battle yet to come, he speaks of stewardship specifically using the imagery of what must be called, in modern environmental terms, a "land ethic." Speaking to the gathered captains at the Last Debate, he says: "Other evils there are that may come; for Sauron is himself but a servant or emissary. Yet it is not our part to master all the tides of the world, but to do what is in us for the succour of those years wherein we are set, uprooting the evil in the fields that we know, so that those who live after may have clean earth to till. What weather they shall have is not ours to rule" (V/ix). Gandalf reiterates some of the same principles he has outlined earlier for Frodo. Nobody is responsible for the time, talents, or decisions of others. We need not "master *all* the tides of the world," he says, using a maritime image. Each is responsible for the stewardship of his own time, talents, and possessions in "those years wherein we are set." Here, however, Gandalf takes a further step in his choice of imagery. The explanation of the captains' duties uses natural metaphors with profound significance for environmental stewardship. He speaks of "uprooting" evil as one would uproot weeds. He speaks of weather. Most important, he speaks of leaving "clean earth to till." The implications of these potent remarks are twofold: (1) we exercise our stewardship in relation to the earth, and (2) we fulfill those duties not through exploitation but through caring management that leaves the earth good, clean, and wholesome for future generations. It should be remembered here that Gandalf's point is not primarily an environmental one, but his terminology implies his counsel for the generalized health and well-being of all Middle-earth, including its environment.

Taken in the context of similar imagery throughout Tolkien's works, these natural metaphors cannot be accidental or incidental. When Gandalf challenges the captains to be good stewards of their time and abilities by going to war against Sauron, Tolkien is, in effect, challenging his readers to be good stewards of the earth. Figuratively speaking, we do battle against evil in our own world—akin to Sauron's evil in Middle-earth—by uprooting whatever is bad and unhealthy in the fields familiar to us and by acting in such a way as to leave the earth fruitful, habitable, and, as far as possible, beautiful. We may not be responsible for weather patterns in our own time, but we may bear a heavy burden of responsibility for the climate of the future and for the quality of the environment that we will bequeath to our descendants.[12] We must ask ourselves: what kind of earth are we leaving for the generations that will follow us? In the Prologue to *The Lord of the Rings*, Tolkien makes very clear that the reason the Shire is so prosperous and its agrarian culture so successful is that the people of the kingdom of Arnor who lived in Eriador generations earlier were good stewards who left clean earth and healthy soil for the Hobbits' later use. Our wisest course would be to follow their example. We explore this more fully in the next chapter.

But Gandalf goes still further in his charge to the Captains of the West. He connects stewardship with the battle against evil. In fighting against Sauron, the captains are "uprooting" evil itself. Sauron is not merely an inconvenience; he is more than just somebody who interferes with the personal preferences of others in Middle-earth. When Sauron blights the land of Mordor, burns forests to the ground, befouls the air with the smoke of his furnaces, and wages war on the free peoples of Middle-earth, he is doing "evil," Gandalf says. Tolkien does not beat around the bush; here he has Gandalf use the absolutist language of objective morality. The comment that Sauron is merely a "servant or emissary" suggests that a deeper form of evil lies behind Sauron's. Tolkien's mythology—formalized in *The Silmarillion* but subtly pervasive throughout the legendarium—includes both good and evil as objective realities that transcend individual disposition or behavior. As we suggested earlier, in using such language, Tolkien implies that our stewardship responsibilities have inevitable consequences in terms of an objective environmental ethic in which some practices can be seen as objectively good or evil. Our use of our time and our treatment of the earth are not merely matters of personal preference: there are right and wrong ways to fulfill our duties as stewards of the earth. Tolkien would have us do right.

Man's Mission Revisited

We can now return to Tolkien's mythology and to what it might suggest for the mission of the human race on our planet. To understand this, we must look collectively at several races in Middle-earth. In Tolkien's mythology, Men and Elves together are called the Children of Ilúvatar, implying a special relationship with their creator. Elves, who are called the Quendi in their own tongue, are known as the Firstborn, while Men, also called the Atani, are the Followers. This special relationship between creature and creator also applies to Hobbits, because in the Prologue to *The Lord of the Rings,* Tolkien explicitly says that they are a branch of the human race. And it also applies to Dwarves, although their situation is different. Dwarves are created separately from Men and Elves; although their physical form is made by the Vala Aulë, they are given the breath of life by Eru himself and are considered his "children by adoption" (*Silm,* 44). Thus, Elves, Men, Hobbits, and Dwarves are all the Children of Ilúvatar.

To some degree, then, what can be said about the Elves' role in creation with respect to their special relationship to the creator applies in general to all the Children of Ilúvatar. In terms of the mythology itself, however, it applies most directly and completely to Elves. Tolkien wrote in his famous 1955 letter to Milton Waldman that the mythology is not anthropocentric but focuses instead primarily on the Elves; as a result, his mythology develops the environmental mission of the Elves to a much greater degree than it does that of Men. Indeed, although the Prologue cites a positive example of Men's treatment of the soil in the Northern Kingdom of Arnor, in the history of Middle-earth, the effect of Men's presence is generally destructive, a result of that race's characteristic mode of activity: war. However, in the mythology of *The Silmarillion,* Men clearly share the status of Children of Ilúvatar along with the Elves.

In our world, however—the world that is Tolkien's reference point as well as ours—Tolkien's readers constitute only one race. In creating the various races that inhabit his imaginary world, Tolkien borrowed different aspects of the one sentient race that he knew intimately by observation and participation: humankind. In what we might call Tolkien's "anthropology," different aspects of the human race are distributed—and not always evenly—among the various sentient creatures of Middle-earth; Elves, Dwarves, Hobbits, and Men variously exhibit characteristics that, in our world, are embodied as a whole in human beings.[13] In this respect, then, although the stewardship mission assigned to them by Ilúvatar may apply in different ways to the races and peoples of Middle-earth, when transferred into terms compatible with our world, the divergent environmental implications of that mission all apply with equal validity to humankind. The basic point for all these races is that, although they are a *part* of nature, they also somehow *transcend* nature, and in Tolkien's environmental vision, this fact has direct implications for us as human beings.

Put another way, although everything created in Eä and Arda is of value to Eru Ilúvatar, only Elves, Men, Dwarves, and Hobbits are called his Children. The nature of this relationship is important and, perhaps to some degree, controversial. It is said in the *Ainulindalë* that the world of Eä is created as a "habitation" or "dwelling" for Eru's Children, who, at the time, have not yet been created, and that the subcreative work of the Ainur is for the purpose of preparing Arda as their home. "And so it was that as this vision of the World was played before them, the Ainur saw with amazement the coming of the Children of Ilúvatar, and the habitation that was prepared for them; and they perceived that they themselves in the labour of their music had been busy with the preparation of this dwelling, and yet knew not that it had any purpose beyond its own beauty" (*Silm*, 18). Thus, in Tolkien's ecology, part of the purpose of creation is simply "its own beauty." But another part of its purpose—one that exceeds or goes beyond that beauty—is as a dwelling. By no means does this statement place nature ontologically in an inferior or subservient role to Men or Elves; nature is Eru's creation, just as his Children are. But it does mean that, from the beginning, nature's purpose is intimately bound to their coming into the world. Although other living beings—the *olvar* and *kelvar,* as Yavanna refers to them—are valuable in and of themselves, and although their status as beloved creatures of Ilúvatar is unquestionable, they are important in a different way from the sentient beings who populate Middle-earth. As for various aspects of the physical world—the winds of Manwë, the waters of Ulmo, the stars of Varda, and the ore and material substances of the ground to which Aulë is devoted—these, too, are part of the habitation prepared for Elves and Men, in relation to whom their significance is largely derived.

Readers who consider human beings in the same category as other forms of life in the biosphere and not, ontologically, of a different order from the rest of nature might be dissatisfied or even uncomfortable with Tolkien's assigning to humans a higher status in the biological hierarchy. The point that we can draw from Tolkien is this: if a plausible case can be made for the idea that human beings have no special privilege in the natural order, then, by implication, the purpose of Arda and Eä—insofar as such can be conceived—cannot be seen as deriving from or directed toward Man in particular, any more than it would be for any other animal, plant, or inanimate feature of the natural world. But in Tolkien's vision, Arda is brought into being for the Children of Ilúvatar—for Elves and Men.

At this point, a reference to the Judeo-Christian creation account is in order, especially as it pertains to the biblical portrayal of the special relationship of humans to God and the implications of that relationship for our environmental mission. One of the most important biblical passages outlining the role of humankind in relation to the environment occurs early in the book of Genesis. After the creation of the heavens and the earth and after the generation of all plant and animal life, Adam and Eve, the first human beings, are created. In creating them, God says, "Let us make man to our image and likeness: and let him have dominion over the fishes of the sea, and the fowls of the air, and the beasts, and the whole earth, and every creeping creature that moveth upon the earth." The passage goes on to say, "And God created man to his own image: to the image of God he created him: male and female he created them" (Genesis 1:26–27).[14] Repeated four times here is the word *image* or *likeness,* describing the special place humans have in creation. Although it is said many times of both humans and animals—and also of the earth itself—that God created them, no other creature is said to bear God's image; in this respect, humans are unique. We might note the close similarity with Tolkien's portrayal of Elves and Men as the unique Children of Ilúvatar. One of the main characteristics of a child is its "likeness" to its parent or parents—a bearing of the parent's image. This is a point that Tolkien explicitly makes in numerous places in his writings, including early in his creation myth, when Aulë explains to Ilúvatar (in defense of his own actions) that a child behaves the way he does in part because "he is the son of his father" (*Silm,* 43).

In the biblical creation story, it is stated immediately after the creation of man and woman that "God blessed them, saying: Increase and multiply, and fill the earth, and subdue it, and rule over the fishes of the sea, and the fowls of the air, and all living creatures that move upon the earth" (Genesis 1:28). Taken together, this passage and the previous one have aroused a great deal of controversy concerning the prescriptions for and the limits on human involvement in environmental processes. The term *dominion* in particular—perhaps justifiably—has aroused much suspicion, with its suggestion of domination or domineering overlordship. Taken in the best sense, these remarks define a human role that emphasizes responsibility, prudence, and care for the world. At worst, they might be understood as providing a warrant for imprudent, irresponsible exploitation of the environment in an attitude of contempt.

Although Tolkien drew on many mythical sources for his legendarium, most notably Old Norse, when it came to the most important aspects of his creation myth, he drew heavily from the biblical account. The problems some readers may have with the implications of Tolkien's mythology are the same ones many have had with the biblical creation myth. But Tolkien's mythology is consistent with the best interpretation of the biblical passages, and the biblical commands are best understood as emphasizing responsibility, humility, and loving care in environmental stewardship. Because all the races and peoples of Middle-earth represent facets of humanity, we can simplify the application of Tolkien's mythology to our world by saying that just as Middle-earth exists for the Children of Ilúvatar, so, according to the biblical understanding, our world exists for the children of God—humans. Once this idea is asserted, it raises the possibility—or, indeed, the historical reality—of human exploitation of nature. If the earth exists for the use of humankind, what are the ethical constraints on humanity's efforts to obtain and use natural resources in whatever way furthers human purposes? Why should we *not* do whatever we want with oil, water, soil, iron, air, uranium, or any other resource?

One of the most frequently cited essays published early in the modern history of environmentalism is Lynn White's "The Historical Roots of Our Ecological Crisis" (1967). It has been reprinted and anthologized a number of times in the literature of ecology and environmental studies, and White's ideas have played an important role in shaping the modern environmental consciousness. In the essay, White expresses something of the hypothetical response we just outlined concerning the idea that human beings enjoy a special privilege in the natural order owing to their status as God's Children. White says, for example, "Man shares in great measure, God's transcendence of nature. Christianity . . . insisted that it is God's will that man exploit nature for his proper ends. . . . By destroying pagan animism, Christianity made it possible to exploit nature in a mood of indifference to the feelings of natural objects."[15] Without even delving into Tolkien's likely response to this statement, there are a number of flaws in White's reasoning. One is that the exploitation of nature is never *merely* exploitative of the earth; it is always exploitative of other humans too. William Deutsch and Bryan Duncan capture this notion in the title of their paper "Everyone Lives Downstream."[16] They suggest that even if we *were* free to use the earth in whatever manner we wished, we would not be free to use it in a way that would be harmful to other people. Tolkien's ecology would not support such an idea (we return to this notion momentarily). But by polluting the earth, air, and water in order to extract what we want, we almost always enrich the already wealthy and privileged while causing sometimes immeasurable suffering to both the environment and other people, generally the poor and underprivileged. In Middle-earth, this principle is illustrated in the detrimental effects of Saruman's exploitative practices on the inhabitants of the Shire, which we explore in chapter 8. In Tolkien's terms, even the underprivileged are Children of Ilúvatar, and their suffering as a result of the exploitation of nature is no more warranted in his imaginary world than it is in our own. In his book exploring the classic spiritual disciplines of Christianity, Richard

Foster addresses the issue of environmental responsibility with respect to the excessive amount of resources used by wealthy Americans and the effects of this consumption on the rest of the world. He asks the pointed question: "Do we sip our coffee and eat our bananas at the expense of exploiting Latin American peasants? In a world of limited resources, does our lust for wealth mean the poverty of others?"[17] Foster believes that anyone who shares his Christian faith must ask these questions.

There is a second serious flaw in White's rather broad-brushed denunciation of the Christian tradition. Again, to use Tolkien's mythic vision, the idea that Arda exists as a *habitation* for the Children of Ilúvatar is not the same as saying that it exists for whatever purposes they want to pursue. Let us use a real-world example: When a landlord rents a home to tenants, he expects it to be used as a domicile. He does not intend for them to use its timbers for firewood, to extract the copper wiring in the walls and sell it to recyclers, or to gut the structure and use it to store grain. Tolkien specifies that Arda is created as a habitation, not as raw material for other purposes. Tenancy implies a certain low-level form of stewardship, and as Gandalf tells the gathered Captains of the West, they are responsible for leaving the world habitable for succeeding generations. Thus, when White remarks that we now think "we are superior to nature, contemptuous of it, willing to use it for our slightest whim,"[18] he describes a perspective that is not—as he suggests—the natural outgrowth of Christian attitudes but one that is radically at odds with Christian faith. It is also at odds with Tolkien's vision of environmental stewardship, rooted as it is in the Catholic tradition.

So what should we make of White's charge that this faith tradition makes possible—even demands—the exploitation of nature? In exploring the foundations of the ecology of Middle-earth, readers who are appreciative of Tolkien's writing and steeped in White's rhetoric might find it appealing to try to explain away some of Tolkien's anthropocentrism. It would be tempting, for example, to say that Tolkien drew more from pagan myths or that he blended Christianity and pantheism, drawing his environmentalism from the latter. Of course, Tolkien did draw imaginatively from many pagan myths, but his representation of the special relationship of Men and Elves to their creator—though not necessarily at odds with some elements of paganism—seems especially compatible with the Christian view. Much of the depth of his environmental vision comes not despite the fact that, as White says, "man shares, in great measure, God's transcendence of nature," but precisely *because* of the transcendent nature of creatures made in the image of their creator.

Dominion, Denethor, Authority, and the Fall

Returning to the creation accounts, the most troublesome word is *dominion*. It is used both in the biblical passage from Genesis and in Aulë's statement to Yavanna. Given the importance of the Genesis passage, Tolkien's use of the same word seems more than coincidental. In Genesis, God grants dominion to the human race. In *The Silmarillion*, Aulë says that Eru will give the Dwarves dominion to "use all that they find in Arda" for their own purposes. Does this imply ecological exploitation? Tolkien himself acknowledges the possibility of such an interpretation. In *The Silmarillion*, when Ilúvatar breathes life into the Dwarves, Yavanna the tree-grower hears about it from Aulë the smith, and she chastises him: "Because thou hiddest this thought from me until its achievement, thy children will have little love for the things of my love. They will love first the things made by their own hands, as doth their father. They will delve in the earth, and the things that grow and live upon the earth they will not heed. Many a tree shall feel the bite of their iron without pity" (*Silm*, 45). To some degree, then, it is prophesied that the Dwarves will see the earth itself and the living things growing on it as existing primarily for their own personal use. For this reason, Yavanna predicts that they will not love the earth for its own sake but rather will appreciate it only in utilitarian terms. They will love it for the things that they can do *with* it "by their own hands," she says. But Yavanna's final statement in this passage is perhaps the most telling. Because the Dwarves are created apart from Ilúvatar's plan and thereby do not have a proper love of Arda *as Arda*—a love of the things of Yavanna's making as well their own—nature as a whole will suffer. It should be noted, however, that in Tolkien's mythology such an attitude is portrayed as not in keeping with Eru's will and as harmful. The Dwarves' exploitative attitude is a result of Aulë's moral fault, his impatient fall into "folly," as he describes it. The religious word *sin* might even come into play here.

Even Aulë—who, in a dim recollection of the vision of the Children of Ilúvatar, gives the Dwarves both their form and their love of the earth—acknowledges that such an attitude is wrong in any of the races inhabiting Arda. We see this clearly in his dialogue with Yavanna:

> "And though the things of thy realm have worth in themselves, and would have worth if no Children were to come, yet Eru will give them dominion, and they shall use all that they find in Arda: though not, by the purpose of Eru, without respect or without gratitude."
>
> "Not unless Melkor darken their hearts," Yavanna said. And she was not appeased, but grieved in heart. (*Silm*, 45)

We see again that the misuse of and disrespect for the created world results either from Melkor's darkening the hearts of Eru's Children with evil or from some kind of falling away from the will and purposes of Eru. Also expressed, once again, is that the things of Arda—that is, the rest of creation apart from the Children—have worth "in themselves," independent of the world's inhabitants. The earth would have worth even "if no Children were to come." As Manwë explains to Yavanna, Eru gives consideration to "even the least sound of the least voice" (*Silm*, 46).

Whatever one makes of the biblical use of the term *dominion*, it would be convenient to say that in *The Silmarillion*, Aulë is simply mistaken when he uses it. After all, he has recently fallen into folly, even if he is forgiven and restored by Ilúvatar. Aulë here echoes a form of usage seen elsewhere in Tolkien's writing. Ilúvatar's use of the term *dominion* can be seen as merely a statement of fact about the ontological dynamics of Tolkien's imaginary world. In our world, if in a crude exercise of authority we want to destroy the earth, we are capable of doing so. The same can be said of Denethor, who has authority in Gondor. His authority does not provide him with a warrant to do whatever he wants, but in Middle-earth, as in our world, any authority can be abused. One can be a good steward or a bad one. In theory, and very nearly in fact, Denethor's position as steward permits him to undertake actions that would destroy his kingdom. And he almost does.

Biblically, we can say something even stronger, and since Tolkien viewed his works as fundamentally, if subtly, Christian, it is worth taking a moment to do so. One of the more important New Testament passages for a Christian understanding of environmental stewardship is found in Romans 8:19–22: "For the expectation of the creature waiteth for the revelation of the sons of God. For the creature was made subject to vanity: not willingly, but by reason of him that made it subject, in hope. Because the creature also itself shall be delivered from the servitude of corruption, into the liberty of the glory of the children of God. For we know that every creature groaneth and travaileth in pain, even till now." This passage speaks of the suffering of *all* creation, and in context it clearly refers to nonhuman aspects of creation. The author, Paul the apostle, associates that suffering with human failure and corruption. Because humans, the children of God (or "sons of God," in this passage), have been given dominion over nature, all of nature "groaneth and travaileth in pain" because of human corruption. But the first critical point here is that the suffering of creation is a result of humans acting in ways contrary to God's purposes.

The second critical point is that the ultimate goal is for the creation to be "delivered" from corruption and misuse. Humans are meant to share with the rest of creation "the liberty of the glory" of God. In the biblical view, corruption of nature results from misuse of human dominion; the appropriate use of human dominion is the freedom of creation. It follows that people ought to work toward freeing creation from corruption. This is what Ulmo argues the Elves ought to be doing in Middle-earth and why they should remain there rather than come to Valinor. The Children of Ilúvatar are physical creatures who are a part of nature and share much in common bodily with nature. But as transcendent beings they are also moral creatures who can be assigned the moral calling of caring for nature.

This brings us back to the question of what Ilúvatar *means* for his Children to do with the dominion he has granted them. And here Tolkien was certainly exploring another aspect of the biblical creation myth from which many of his ideas came. In Genesis, God commands man to "subdue" the earth and to "rule over" its creatures. As with the word *dominion,* much has been made of the words *subdue* and *rule,* which are unquestionably troublesome. In their full, original context, however, these words make much better sense. First, it should be remembered that God is said to have blessed all living things *prior to* the creation of humankind, saying, "Increase and multiply, and fill the waters of the sea: and let the birds be multiplied upon the earth" (Genesis 1:22); some translations read "be fruitful and multiply." Here, God's plan is for the fruitfulness of his creation, and when he gives human beings authority over it, it is in the context of their fulfillment of that plan. In an article explaining the theology of "creation-care," Calvin DeWitt calls one of his three principles of stewardship the "fruitfulness principle":

> The fish of the sea and the birds of the air, as well as people, are given God's blessing of fruitfulness.... God's Creation reflects God's fruitful work of giving to land and life what satisfies.... As God's work brings fruit to Creation, so too should ours. As God provides for the creatures, so should we who were created to reflect the God whose image we bear. Imaging God, we should provide for the creatures.[19]

Second, and more generally, throughout the first chapter of Genesis, which recounts the six stages in the process of creation, the statement "God saw that it was good" is repeated. This phrase, which functions as something of a litany in this highly patterned, formulaic account, refers to the creator's pleasure in all the details of the created realm prior to and culminating in the creation of humankind. As we have seen, Tolkien makes the same point numerous times in his creation myth, just as he includes statements paralleling the remark in Genesis that God saw the creation of humans as "very good."

Although Genesis 1:28 has aroused a great deal of controversy in environmental circles, less has been made of the clarification of this command in Genesis 2:15, which states, "And the Lord God took man, and put him into the paradise of pleasure, to dress it, and to keep it." The New International Version translates this slightly differently: "The Lord God took the man and put him in the garden of Eden to work it and take care of it." Other translations substitute "cultivate" and "keep" for "work" and "take care of." This statement does not suggest that Adam and Eve are free to do whatever they wish; the very next sentence contains a prohibition imposing limits on their actions. Regardless of the translation, the statement prescribes to humankind a transcendent moral obligation, and the concept employed here implies nurture, encouragement, and protection of life. Humans are defined in biblical terms not as exploiters of the environment but as its caregivers.

Most important, perhaps, is what comes prior to the command in Genesis 1:28. As we note, the book of Genesis gives fourfold emphasis to the idea that humans are created in God's likeness and are his image-bearers. It is in *this* context that the authority of dominion is given, along with all subsequent commands. A right understanding of dominion thus involves its exercise as God's image-bearers. Humans are to imitate God as his stewards in the cultivation and keeping of the earth he created. DeWitt goes on to explain the importance of this explanatory command in another of his three principles of environmental stewardship:

> Genesis 2:15 expects human people and their descendants to *serve* and *keep* the garden. The word "keep" is the Hebrew word *"shamar,"* which means a loving, caring, sustaining kind of keeping. This word is used in the Aaronic blessing, "The Lord bless you and *keep* you" (Num. 6:24). When we invoke God to keep *us*, it is not that God would keep us in a kind of preserved, inactive state. Instead it is that God would keep us in all of our vitality, energy and beauty. . . . It is the kind of rich and full keeping that we should bring to God's garden, his creatures and to all of Creation. As God keeps his people, so should people keep Creation.

As DeWitt explains, loving, caring, and sustaining are the predominant ideas. We need to keep creation by blessing it in the same way that we ourselves wish to be blessed, exercising our authority over creation in the same way that we want God to exercise his authority over us. Similarly, W. Dayton Roberts explains the Genesis passages as follows:

> The verbs used in Genesis to describe Adam's responsibilities—*serving, watchful care, ordering* and *controlling*—make us think of a benevolent overseer, one who reflects the Creator's own concern for the well-being of creature and Creation. In the words of theologian William Dyrness, Adam's ministry is "a reflection of the loving, ordered relationships of God himself."[20]

This servanthood, watchful care, and ordering constitute precisely the sort of stewardly care demonstrated and encouraged by Gandalf. In other words, the vision described by DeWitt and Roberts is very much in keeping with Tolkien's idea of environmental care portrayed decades earlier in his mythology.

All the above suggests something of what Tolkien understood as the concepts of authority and dominion outlined in the book of Genesis. The next thing we need to observe in Tolkien's myth is that even if nature is under the authority of the Children of Ilúvatar, they themselves are under the authority of the Valar, who are called the Lords of the West. To Elves and Men, they are like gods. Manwë, their king, "is dearest to Ilúvatar and understands most clearly his purposes. He was appointed to be, in the fullness of time, the first of all Kings: lord of the realm of Arda and ruler of all that dwell therein" (*Silm*, 26). Incidentally, we might note that even when Fëanor rebels against Manwë's kingship, he still calls Manwë by his title: "Manwë Súlimo, High King of Arda" (*Silm*, 85).

Even the Valar, including Manwë, do not have absolute authority to do whatever they will; they are under the authority of Eru Ilúvatar and are responsible to their creator. We see this, for example, when the Vala Aulë creates the Dwarves. Almost immediately, Ilúvatar challenges him, asking, "Why dost thou attempt a thing which thou knowest is beyond thy power and thy authority" (*Silm*, 43). Aulë can do a lot, but the limits of his authority are prescribed by Ilúvatar. Much later in mythic history, when the Men of Númenor raise a great fleet to wage war in Valinor against the Valar, Manwë temporarily relinquishes his authority. This is described in the *Akallabêth*, which says, "Then Manwë upon the Mountain called upon Ilúvatar, and for that time the Valar laid down their government of Arda. But Ilúvatar showed forth his power, and he changed the fashion of the world" (*Silm*, 278). Manwë and the rest of the Valar cannot be acting out of fear: they have the power to destroy the host of Númenor at any moment. But rather than fight against any of Ilúvatar's Children, they act as servants and relinquish their authority to the higher prerogatives of their creator.

Any lordship or authority possessed by the Children of Ilúvatar is subordinate to the authority of another in the cosmic hierarchy. Theirs is granted to them as a gift by a higher authority, and Elves and Men are always responsible to it, even when they fail to acknowledge it. In Tolkien's universe—and Tolkien's concept of stewardship—authority under Ilúvatar does not mean autonomy without limitations and without responsibility.

The last thing we notice about authority in Tolkien's myth is what happens when characters try to act as though there is no limit on their freedom and as though their autonomy does not imply great responsibility—that is, when they do not acknowledge the higher authority of Ilúvatar. The great drama at the center of the *Quenta Silmarillion* is the fall of the Elves in Valinor. This cataclysm, which results in great destruction of the environment, is caused by the Noldorin Elf Fëanor, who comes to see the Silmarils, the three fabulous jewels he has created, not as works of craftsmanship to be shared and enjoyed by others but as his sole possession. Shortly after the creation of the Silmarils, we read, "The heart of Fëanor was fast bound to these things that he himself had made" (*Silm*, 67). Not long after, the language grows stronger: "For Fëanor began to love the Silmarils with a greedy love, and grudged the sight of them to all save to his father and his seven sons; he seldom remembered now that the light within them was not his own" (*Silm*, 69). This is particularly significant when we remember the Silmarils' mythic function as repositories of the paradisal light of the Two Trees—mythic symbols in their own right, representing all life in Arda. Because they are fashioned from the substance of the earth, the Silmarils also stand in some sense for the physical realm of Arda. Fëanor's hoarding of them, then, symbolically suggests a desire to control Arda and all the life it holds.

Fëanor is so caught up with his own authority as craftsman, artist, and jewel-smith that he fails to acknowledge that the light of Telperion and Laurelin and the substance of Arda captured in the Silmarils are not his to possess. Tolkien explains this in a letter, written in 1950: "But the chief artificer of the Elves (Fëanor) had imprisoned the Light of Valinor in the three supreme jewels, the Silmarilli, before the Trees were sullied or slain. This Light thus lived thereafter only in these gems. The fall of the Elves comes about through the possessive attitude of Fëanor and his seven sons to these gems." Tolkien goes on to explain the result of this possessiveness—namely, what the Elves' fall looks like: "They pervert the greater part of their kindred, who rebel against the gods, and depart from paradise, and go to make hopeless war upon the Enemy" (*Letters*, 148). The Elves' cataclysmic fall, then, can be traced in Tolkien's myth to a wrong attitude toward the created order, one of greed and covetousness that makes personal claims on other elements of creation without acknowledging the creator's prior, and higher, claim.

Similar comments can be made about Númenor and the great fall of Man. In many ways, this fall echoes that of the Elves; it is a fall that stems from a loss of respect for Númenor, the island realm granted them by the Valar, and it results in the gross mistreatment of not only that land but also other areas of Middle-earth colonized by Men. One of the other names for Númenor is Andor, which means "Land of Gift," and initially the Men of Númenor acknowledge with gratitude the gift of this realm from the Valar and Ilúvatar above them. They are not covetous of what they do not have, and they are thankful to and dependent on Ilúvatar; they offer the first fruits of the harvest to him in a hallowed temple on Mount Meneltarma. During this time, they grow "wise" and "glorious"; they live under the protection of the Valar and in friendship with the Elves, increasing "in stature both of mind and body." Most tellingly, they are known as "Men of peace." When they visit the shores of Middle-earth and meet with lesser representatives of their race still dwelling in darkness, they teach them many things, including the healthy agricultural practices of their island home: "Corn and wine they brought, and they instructed Men in the sowing of seed and the grinding of grain" (*Silm,* 260–63).

When the shadow of evil falls on them, however, they become "proud" and "eager for wealth," and they begin to exert dominion over lesser Men, "taking now rather than giving" (*Silm,* 265). Although they become wealthier and more powerful as a result, they do not become any happier. Eventually, they cease to see Númenor as a gift and begin to think of it as their right. They become exploiters. In much of Tolkien's writing, some of the most telling symbolism of moral and ethical failure involves images of death and destruction in the natural world. In the *Akallabêth,* one such image is Nimloth, the White Tree of Númenor. A descendant of Telperion, one of the Two Trees made by Yavanna, Nimloth is thus also mythically symbolic of the whole realm of nature and the life within it. The text of the *Akallabêth* links the fate of Nimloth with the fate of Númenor. Among other things, the "fortunes of [the kings'] house were bound up with the Tree" (*Silm,* 272), and when men ceased to care for it, it was believed that Númenor itself would fall and its line of kings would come to an end (*Silm,* 269).

This is indeed what happens. First manifest as pride and greed, the evil growing among the Númenóreans becomes evident in their poor care of the earth, represented by their declining interest in tending to Nimloth. In the days of Ar-Gimilzôr, one of the most evil kings of Númenor, the White Tree "was untended and began to decline" (*Silm,* 268). Not long after, Ar-Pharazôn, the "mightiest tyrant that had yet been in the world since the reign of Morgoth" (*Silm*, 274), fells the tree altogether and burns its wood in a blasphemous, idolatrous offering to Morgoth. From then on, fire and smoke rise to form a continuous reeking cloud over the land—much as in Saruman's realm of Isengard or Sauron's land of Mordor (*Silm*, 273). One can only assume that because some sort of fuel is required for fire, many more fair trees of Númenor are burned besides Nimloth. This brazen affront to the Valar and Ilúvatar culminates in the Númenóreans' raising a great armada to assault the realm of Valinor. In their great pride, they not only disobey Manwë and forsake their role as stewards, but they even begin to imagine themselves as more powerful than the Valar. In response to this aggression, Ilúvatar overthrows their fleet as well as their land—though in mercy he spares a remnant of their people.

In tying the fall of Númenor to the death of this symbolic tree, Tolkien also provides a strong counterexample to Lynn White's comment that "to a Christian a tree can be no more than a physical fact." White suggests that the destruction of a tree or an entire forest—even ancient redwoods—is of no particular interest or importance to a person of Christian belief.[21] If Christianity were nothing more than a scientific or technological system of thought built on naturalism, one might agree that, within that system, a tree could be nothing more than a vegetable organism useful for building or burning. Similarly, to an animal—a squirrel, for example—a tree is nothing more than a source of nuts, a place to escape from predators, and a nesting site. But if humans are more than mere animals, if their being transcends mere physical existence in some way, they can see a tree as something more.

In Tolkien's mythology, a tree certainly can be—and almost always *is*—far more than a simple physical fact. Tolkien believed that the Christian myth offers not a lower but a higher view of all the created order, including trees. In a seminal conversation between Tolkien and C. S. Lewis described by Humphrey Carpenter, Lewis, shortly before his conversion to Christianity, expressed his firm belief in the worthlessness of myths as statements of truth: "Myths are 'lies and therefore worthless, even though breathed through silver.'" Tolkien responded as follows:

> "No," said Tolkien. "They are not lies. . . . You look at trees," he said, "and call them 'trees,' and probably you do not think

twice about the word.... To you, a tree is simply a vegetable organism, and a star simply a ball of inanimate matter moving along a mathematical course. But the first men to talk of 'trees' and 'stars' saw things very differently. To them, the world was alive with mythological beings.... Christianity is exactly the same thing—with the enormous difference that the poet who invented it was God Himself, and the images He used were real men and actual history."[22]

A tree is never *just* a tree, according to this fundamentally Christian view of the world to which Tolkien gives imaginative support over and over again.

Right Stewardship and the Mission of Man

All this brings us to a final restatement of what environmental stewardship really means in Tolkienesque terms. Stewardship is simply the proper exercise of authority granted by a higher authority, bound by limits and circumscribed by consequences. When Tolkien gives the Men and Elves of Middle-earth a special relationship with their creator, making them the Children of Ilúvatar, their environmental responsibilities are not diminished but dramatically increased. Tolkien's myth illustrates the potential for disastrous misuse of this stewardship responsibility when its source is abandoned or forgotten, and similar potential for exploitation is evident in other myths. For example, in the modern materialist myth that sees humankind as simply a part of the physical world, equal in value to plants, animals, and other elements of nature, by definition, everything the human race does is a part of the natural order; everything is "natural" in the everyday sense of the word. Fouling rivers with toxic waste and filling the atmosphere with poison are as *natural* as woodland creatures expelling *their* wastes into the humus.

Describing an interview with Aldous Huxley a year or so before his death, Lynn White wrote that one of Huxley's favorite topics of discourse was "Man's unnatural treatment of nature and its sad results."[23] But taken at face value, White's remarks suggest that human beings are merely equal with the other animals—that they are a part of nature and not, as Tolkien's myth would have it, the Children of Ilúvatar. If so, Huxley's comment makes no sense. Tolkien, however, might agree with Huxley on the deeper issue: humankind *has* treated nature unnaturally, and the results have been sad, even tragic. But in saying that human beings have acted unnaturally, Huxley—accidentally and perhaps unwittingly—acknowledges that humankind is not merely part of the natural order. Although White takes issue with some of Huxley's comments, he fails, seemingly, to miss the deeper point.

At the same time, Tolkien clearly presents the Children of Ilúvatar as physical creatures—specifically, as beings of both spirit and body. Much has been said about the goodness of Arda, the material creation of Ilúvatar, and we need not belabor the point here; however, we need to be clear that these statements apply to the physical bodies of the Children as well. This might be inferred from many different passages in the legendarium, but it is explicitly stated in the commentary "Athrabeth Finrod Ah Andreth," a passage from *Morgoth's Ring: The Later Silmarillion:* "There are on Earth 'incarnate' creatures, Elves and Men: these are made of a union of *hröa* and *fëa* (roughly but not exactly equivalent to 'body' and 'soul')."[24] Furthermore, the transcendent nature of the Children, their higher status and association with Ilúvatar, does not mean that their bodies are not important. The commentary goes on to explain that *hröa* and *fëa* "were designed each for the other, to abide in perpetual harmony," and that "the separation of *hröa* and *fëa* is 'unnatural,' and proceeds not from the original design, but from the 'Marring of Arda,' which is due to the operations of Melkor"(*MR,* 330–31). Tolkien did not accept certain aspects of Platonic thought, neither that associated with first-century Gnostics nor that associated with modern neo-Platonists, for whom the abstract realm of thought and idea, the spiritual world, is infinitely superior in being and goodness to the physical world and physical bodies. Thus, Elves who die do not remain disembodied but are reunited with their physical forms.[25]

There is, here, strong resonance with the biblical passage cited earlier that speaks of the groaning of creation. The next verse goes on to say, "even we ourselves groan within ourselves, waiting for the adoption of the sons of God, the redemption of our body" (Romans 8:23). The redemption Paul writes about here—described in the same breath as the awaited freedom for the created world—is a bodily resurrection. Fred Van Dyke, in "Ecology and the Christian Mind," summarizes the consequences of this understanding for our world:

God gave form from void, a unique form out of a myriad of possibilities, to a heaven and an earth which had neither. . . . It is not an illusion. Its material substance is neither an imperfection, as Aristotle thought, a necessary evil, as Plato thought, nor an illusion, as Buddha thought. Rather, as soon as nature is understood to be a *creation,* we understand that its material substance is not some imperfection in form but the essence of it. That is why we can now begin to deal honestly with the things in creation as *creatures,* not as imperfect, evil, or unreal. And we can begin to see ourselves, not as souls trapped in physical bodies (which even some Christians mistakenly believe), but as creatures with a composite nature: body, soul, and spirit.[26]

In making the Children of Ilúvatar bodily creatures who exist both as part of the natural world and as stewards over Arda's goodness—in having Men and Elves (and Hobbits and Dwarves) share, as White puts it, "in great measure, God's transcendence"—Tolkien's myth provides an imaginative foundation for a transcendent environmental ethic rooted in a form of Christian stewardship that recognizes, even celebrates, the goodness of the physical world.

Van Dyke makes another point that could be a summary of either the biblical understanding of humanity's purpose or Tolkien's purpose for the Children of Ilúvatar:

Stewardship of creation is demanded by something greater than the survivalist mentality inherent in many modern environmental appeals. It is demanded by humanity's unique position in creation as the image of God. So we are exalted by this demand, to act, in a limited but very real sense, as God's servant and representative to other creatures in this present age. But we are also, in the same acts of stewardship, humbled, for we also are creatures, and we stand accountable before God for the outcomes of any actions we take.[27]

In Tolkien's myth, nature exists and is good prior to and apart from the presence of the Children, yet it is intended to be their habitation. As stewards and tenants, the Children are given authority over the world, but not to do with it what they will. Rather, theirs is an authority accompanied by the responsibility to care for and nourish Ilúvatar's good creation. Indeed, although Arda is meant as their habitation, its value should not be reduced to this purpose in a simplistic or utilitarian way, and there is certainly no sense in which their authority is conducive to its misuse and destruction. It would be more correct—more true to Tolkien's total vision—to say that the purpose of both Arda and the Children of Ilúvatar is to serve together the purposes of their creator. In fulfilling this purpose—an opportunity and an obligation we are inclined to describe as a "mission"—they are responsible to care for the creation on behalf of its creator.

Part II

"The Succour of Those Years Wherein We Are Set"

A Complex Ecology of Agriculture, Horticulture, and Feraculture

Chapter 3

Hobbits and the Agrarian Society of the Shire

One of J. R. R. Tolkien's closest friends for many years was fellow writer C. S. Lewis. Lewis is the one other author whose influence on the modern genre of fantasy comes close to that of Tolkien; the two names are often mentioned together. Lewis's *Chronicles of Narnia* introduces readers to the fantasy world of Narnia, and as the landscape and history of this world unfold over seven books, we see a growing portrait of what appears to be a preindustrial agrarian society. Most of the natural descriptions of the realm are either pastoral or wild, and until the final book of the series, there are no signs of anything that might be called industrialization. When we finally do see preliminary signs of a dependence on what today might be called *agribusiness*—that is, Calormen's commercial growing of food for export to Narnia—this marks the end and destruction of Narnia.

In Lewis's books, bread and beer, butter and milk, onions and potatoes, fruits and nuts, and wines and fruit drinks appear on the tables of Narnia's residents, but there are almost no visible signs of any actual agricultural work. In our travels through Narnia, we meet no farmers and see no farms: no dairy farms to produce the butter and milk, no vineyards to make the wine, no farm fields planted with potatoes and onions. Although there is mention of orchards being planted at the end of *The Lion, the Witch, and the Wardrobe*, and they reappear at the start of *Prince Caspian*, readers encounter neither pastureland nor cropland.[1] Agriculture must exist *somewhere* in Narnia, but Lewis never shows it to us. Besides a few references to hunting, we do not know where food comes from. It appears as if by magic. In fact, two of the most memorable meals in the series—the feast provided by Father Christmas in *The*

Lion, the Witch, and the Wardrobe and the grapes of Silenus in *Prince Caspian*—*do* appear by magic.

Tolkien, by contrast, gives us many visible signs of agrarian society, especially in a place called the Shire in a region of Middle-earth known as Eriador. Though he refrains from detailing all the particulars of Shire economy and technology, even in the midst of an epic adventure of heroic fantasy he somehow manages to give us significant glimpses of the Hobbits' ways of living and working on the land. In the Prologue to the Second Edition of *The Lord of the Rings,* and in the portions of the narrative set in the Shire, Tolkien shows us working farmland and many signs and implements of agriculture and a small-farm economy. Among other things, he presents visible mills, such as Ted Sandyman's in Hobbiton; farms such as the one at Bamfurlong worked by Mr. Maggot and his family in the Marish; and vegetable gardens such as those tended by Sam Gamgee and his father, the Gaffer. Also specifically mentioned in the first several chapters are turnip fields, cornfields, mushroom farms, plows, harvests, and markets.[2] We even see evidence of the agricultural way of life when a battle is fought in the Shire at the end of the trilogy: the Hobbits build their barricades from old farm carts and wagons; though a few of them have hunting bows and knives, most of their weapons are such simple farm tools as axes, heavy hammers, and staves (VI/viii). Nibs Cotton defends his farm with a hayfork. In the Prologue, readers learn that Hobbit technology is simple, involving nothing more complex than forge bellows, water mills, and hand looms.

The point here is not to criticize Lewis or his writing. Lewis no doubt had a positive environmental perspective that is well worth exploring; Lewis and Tolkien shared a basic Christian understanding on which such ideas would have been based. But Lewis expressed his environmental vision differently. In other words, *The Chronicles of Narnia* is not deficient because it fails to show visible signs of agrarianism; rather, Tolkien's writing is distinctive because it does show such signs.

In addition to images of agrarian society, Tolkien provides positive portrayals of the farmers who make that agrarian society possible. For example, when in Minas Tirith the young boy Bergil, son of Beregond, boasts to the Hobbit Pippin that his father is a Guard—one of the most honored positions in Gondor—Pippin replies simply, but with no lack of pride, that his own father "farms the lands round Whitewell . . . in the Shire" (V/i). Besides the four travelers—Frodo, Merry, Pippin, and Sam—two of the most heroic Hobbits in the Shire are Farmer Maggot and Farmer Cotton.

One possible criticism of Tolkien is that these images are purely romantic, giving an idealized and unrealistic vision of a pastoral landscape. Many noted writers in agrarian and environmental studies have noted the danger of such romanticism. Norman Wirzba has written: "It is dangerous to romanticize local community life, especially when we remember that local communities have often been susceptible to various forms of provincialism. Farming communities, for instance, have not always been respectful of the contributions of women, nor have they been very welcoming of foreigners or people with new ideas. The result has often been a form of communal claustrophobia."[3] Brian Donahue warns of a different problem associated with the romanticizing of agrarianism: "Most suburbanites are not agrarians, of course—their romanticized vision of rural life has been called pastoral, or arcadian. They want to live within a quaintly farmed landscape, but few want to be farmers."[4] We could add that few suburbanites know anything at all about farming, and many would not enjoy the smell of manure wafting from freshly fertilized fields.

It is certainly the case that Tolkien wrote in a period when images of agrarian life were romanticized, and both he and Lewis were influenced by these pastoral visions, indicating a reaction against industrialization and a desire to return to the perceived ideals of the previous century. Humphrey Carpenter points out that Tolkien's association with the rural countryside was further romanticized by the death of his mother:

> His mother's death had severed him from the open air, from Lickey Hill where he had gathered bilberries, and from the Rednal Cottage where they had been so happy. And because it was the loss of his mother that had taken him away from all these things, he came to associate them with her. His feelings towards the rural landscape . . . now became emotionally charged with personal bereavement. This love for the memory of the countryside of his youth was later to become a central part of his writing, and it was intimately bound up with his love for the memory of his mother.[5]

There are elements of not only rural romanticism but also a personally charged emotional romanticism in Tolkien's writing.

This romanticism is not necessarily bad, however. Discussing the nostalgia often associated with the American Amish communities, David W. Orr also mentions eighteenth-century agrarian England:

> For many this is not nostalgia, but an awareness that in some places and at some times people did get the relation between culture and land right, and that remembrance haunts the modern mind. Jacquetta Hawkes, for example, once described rural England of the eighteenth century as characterized by a "creative, patient, and increasingly skilled love-making that persuaded the land to flourish." Such times and places were not perfect by any means, but they did represent an exceptional quality of life.[6]

We would argue that the same holds true of Tolkien's views. A certain amount of idealism in an agrarian vision may be a good thing. Some of the passages we cite earlier in this book suggest that if it inspires us to strive for it, such an imaginative portrayal of an ideal is exactly what we need. Part of the argument of this book is that Tolkien provides just this kind of imaginative inspiration.

But one of the most important points of this chapter is that Tolkien goes far beyond the merely romantic. We might consider, for example, Wirzba's criticism that nostalgic idealism ignores the fact that farming communities have not always "been very welcoming of foreigners or people with new ideas." Often throughout the narrative, Tolkien makes this criticism of the residents of the Shire. Within the first few paragraphs of meeting him, Farmer Maggot refers to Bilbo's travels as "strange doings" in "foreign parts" and speaks in a derogatory manner of "outlandish folk." When he gets ready to give Frodo, Sam, and Pippin a ride in his wagon, his wife warns him against arguing with "foreigners." Rather humorously, Tolkien shows just how extreme this agrarian provincialism can be: farmers on one side of the Shire are even distrustful of Hobbits from the other side of the Shire. Maggot, a resident of Buckland, comments to Frodo, "You should never have gone mixing yourself up with Hobbiton folk," adding, "Folk are queer up there" (I/iv). Of course, Hobbiton folk say the same thing about those from Buckland: "They're queer folk in Buckland," Gaffer Gamgee the gardener says (I/iii). This attitude, endemic to the Shire's farms, can be read as an implied critique of rural provincialism in our world.

J. R. R. Tolkien probably had no desire to be a farmer himself. However, his brother Hilary spent much of his adult life associated with agricultural pursuits. Carpenter tells us that Hilary worked for a time on a Sussex farm for the Brookes-Smith family. In 1911 the Tolkien brothers spent a memorable summer holiday on a walking trip of Switzerland with the Brookes-Smiths. Later, after his war service, Hilary had an orchard and garden near Evesham, and he sold his produce in a local market. When Tolkien and his wife and children went to visit Hilary, they were "pressed into service to help on the land."[7] We can assume, then, that Tolkien had a realistic understanding of at least some aspects of the agrarian life.

Returning to the two most important farmers in *The Lord of the Rings*, it is not surprising that neither is portrayed in a naïvely romantic way. They are not stereotypical bumpkins, to be sure, but they are not perfect either. Farmer Maggot shows both courage and common sense when he helps the companions across the bridge to flee the Black Riders near the start of the tale (I/iv). Farmer Cotton is a key figure in rousing the Shire at the end of the tale (VI/viii). Both figures are first and foremost farmers, with agriculture in their veins, wisdom in their thoughts, and dirt under their fingernails. But they also succumb to a certain amount of provincialism. Maurice Telleen makes a telling comment:

> A funny thing about cultures is that they produce people who understand more than they know. Sort of like osmosis. So the old agrarians, to get back to our subject, knew a lot about local soil, local weather, local crops, animal behavior, and each other. They depended on each other. It almost defines that much abused word, provincial. It was very provincial and no doubt carried a load of both inertia and foolishness, along with wisdom.[8]

Telleen might well have been describing the farmers of the Shire.

Through the Shire and its farmers and gardeners, Tolkien offers us a vision of the complex interdependencies of people, community, and land comparable to modern environmentalists' recognition that healthy human culture requires responsible agricultural use of the land.

A central issue in this vision of responsible agriculture is that when we use the soil to produce food and other commodities necessary for life, we ought not take more from it than we put back into it. Short-term agricultural policies must not jeopardize the soil's long-term fertility. The idea informing both modern thinking on the subject and Tolkien's perspective, exemplified in the Shire, is that of *sustainable agriculture*, which Tolkien portrays as an implicit concern in the societal mores of the people who live there.

In this chapter, we look more closely at the images and portrayals of agrarian society in the Shire. We explore the Shire as it reflects the Worcestershire of Tolkien's youth and contributes to his imagined history of Middle-earth. We then observe his portrayal of the individual agrarian—the farmer. Finally, to understand the importance to our culture of imaginative portrayals of such societies, we return to the exploration of stewardship begun in the last chapter, especially the virtue of self-sacrifice, examining how it is worked out in the particular virtues illustrated by the tenants of the Shire.

Hobbit Agriculture and the Worcestershire of Our World

Although there are numerous examples of good environmental stewardship in Tolkien's work, including glimpses of other healthy agrarian communities such as the settlement of Beorn and the West Marches of Rohan elsewhere in Middle-earth, the image is portrayed most persuasively in the culture of the Hobbits of the Shire. Although *The Hobbit* does not use the name "the Shire," it does contain the first published account of the Hobbits' land: it is "a wide respectable country inhabited by decent folk, with good roads, an inn or two, and now and then a dwarf or a farmer ambling by on business" (*H*, 65). By the time *The Lord of the Rings* was published, the conception of this country as a rural idyll had grown in Tolkien's mind, and *The Fellowship of the Ring* included a Prologue giving a historical and geographical account of the Hobbits, their society, and their culture. Hobbits, we learn, "love peace and quiet and good tilled earth," their "favorite haunt" being the "well-ordered and well-farmed countryside." At the time of the events described in the novels, "growing food and eating it occupied most of their time," and the Hobbits have "hardly any 'government.'" All the duties of officialdom are discharged by a mayor, under whom a postmaster and a sheriff exercise the delegated responsibilities of a messenger service and a watch, the latter being a kind of rudimentary police force. Although this last group becomes more sinister during Saruman's despoliation of the Shire toward the end of the story, their traditional duties make them "in practice rather haywards than policemen, more concerned with the strayings of beasts than of people." In other words, even the "governmental" officials of the Shire are as interested in the management and protection of livestock, fields, pastures, and farmsteads as they are in control of the people under their jurisdiction.

In short, these people are depicted as living a rural life and enjoying the pleasures of an agrarian society. As mentioned, Tolkien refrains from detailing all the particulars of their economy and technology, but the glimpses he provides are sufficient to form an impression of how a successful agrarian society might look—an impression that is both believable and compelling. As already suggested, at first glance this impression is so compelling—so idealized—that some object to it as unrealistic: a lovely picture, but one unrelated to reality. The objection is legitimate: no actual agrarian society in our world, no matter how successful and prosperous, can match the picture presented in *The Lord of the Rings*.[9] Yet, even though the image Tolkien portrays is not identical with any historical reality, we would be reluctant to agree that it is therefore unrelated to reality.

It is well known that Tolkien drew images of the Shire partly from his own childhood memories of Worcestershire and the West Midlands. In the summer of 1896, when he was five years old, his widowed mother moved herself and her two children to a cottage in the hamlet of Sarehole, in Yardley Parish, just outside Birmingham. Though now a part of the village of Hall Green in the city of Birmingham in Warwickshire, in Tolkien's youth, Sarehole was a quiet setting. According to biographer Carpenter, traffic on the road outside the Tolkiens' gate consisted of little more than "the occasional farm cart or tradesman's wagon." Indeed, the setting Carpenter describes is one of almost idyllic beauty:

> Over the road a meadow led to the River Cole, little more than a broad stream, and upon this stood Sarehole Mill, an old brick building with a tall chimney. . . . [T]he water still tumbled over the sluice and rushed beneath the great wheel. . . . Hilary Tolkien was only two and a half, but soon he was accompanying

his elder brother on expeditions across the meadow to the mill, where they would stare through the fence at the water-wheel turning in its dark cavern.[10]

We should not be surprised to learn, as Carpenter points out, that "the effect of this move on Ronald [J. R. R.] was deep and permanent. Just at the age when his imagination was opening out, he found himself in the English countryside."[11] In an interview, Tolkien commented on how his childhood in rural Worcestershire engendered in him "a particular love of what you might call central Midland English countryside, based on good water, stones and elm trees and small, quiet rivers and so on and of course rustic people."[12]

The four years the family spent in Sarehole appear to have furnished Tolkien with a rich store of remembered images and experiences, leading to the creation of the Shire as a quiet country of exclusively agrarian concerns. Tolkien later remarked that the period from 1896 to 1900 was "the longest-seeming and most formative part of my life." As he said, "it bites into your memory and imagination even if you don't think it has."[13] Those familiar with Peter Jackson's film adaptations of Tolkien's work could easily read Carpenter's description of Sarehole as a description of the second scene in the first film, which shows Gandalf's wagon as the only vehicle on the road. Ted Sandyman's mill on the Water in Hobbiton is clearly associated with the mill on the River Cole, and a number of other locations near Tolkien's childhood home also find analogues in his fictional world.

Even the name "the Shire" suggests associations with real-world agrarian society. Here, a word of explanation is in order for non-British readers. There are certain native associations of the word *shire* that Tolkien would have assumed on the part of his initial English audience. Seldom used in American English, the word has nuances of meaning that refer to the less densely settled counties in central and southwestern England, generally those that have *-shire* as part of their names, and particularly those described as the traditional "ceremonial" counties, in contrast to the modern administrative and metropolitan counties. Even today, one of Worcestershire's tourist boards describes the county as follows:

> Worcestershire presents a pleasant undulating surface of hill and dale, watered by the Avon, Leam, and Tame. The climate

is mild and healthy, and the soil, except some cold stiff clays on the higher grounds, is fertile. It consists chiefly of a strong red loam adapted for wheat and beans, or a sandy loam for barley and turnips. Much land is kept in permanent pasture for grazing. Formerly the county was thickly wooded (that part N. of the Avon being called the Forest of Arden), and fine timber is still abundant.

Again, the connections are clear. Except for beans, which are not mentioned among the agricultural products of the Shire,[14] all the other features of the Worcestershire landscape and vegetation mentioned here have counterparts in the Hobbits' world. Tolkien once described the Shire as "more or less a Worcestershire village of about the period of the Diamond Jubilee"—that is, 1897, during Tolkien's residence there.

By the time Tolkien began *The Lord of the Rings* in 1938, however, the scenes of his childhood idyll were gone. Already threatened at the close of the nineteenth century by the steady advance of industrial and suburban sprawl, the village of Sarehole was incorporated into the city of Birmingham not long after the Tolkiens moved away.[15] By then a burgeoning manufacturing metropolis, Birmingham almost tripled in size in 1911 when the parishes of Northfield, King's Norton, and Yardley—where Sarehole was situated—were absorbed into the city through the Greater Birmingham Act. The countryside at that time was undergoing significant change, a fact that can be inferred from the increase in Yardley's population in the decades up to and including the Tolkiens' brief sojourn there. In the seventy-year period from 1831 to 1901—scarcely more than a single lifetime—Yardley's population soared from 2,488 to 33,946, an increase explainable in large part by Birmingham's spread.[16]

Thus, the Shire of Tolkien's adult imagination must have been conceived partly in compensation for the destruction of the English countryside that occurred during his own lifetime. This would certainly account for some romantic elements; like many creations based on beloved memory, it is a re-creation of a best-loved boyhood home that no longer exists. Indeed, as an imaginative invention, it is a re-creation of an original that in some sense *never* really existed—certainly not in the form presented by the fiction. Nonetheless, although it is an imaginary country in a work of literary fantasy, the Shire has sources in the historical past of the real world in which Tolkien lived, and to some extent it can be identified with any rural, fertile landscape that sustains crop farms and pastures, dairy cattle and other livestock in the present day.[17]

Tolkien's Imagination and the History (and Future) of the Shire

If the Shire has roots in the real world of Tolkien's childhood, it also has roots in his fertile imagination. The "internal" history of the Hobbits' land is probably even more important than its "external" history, for in creating the Shire, Tolkien explored how a cultivated, civilized agrarian society might originate and how it might be managed in such a way as to exist for an extremely long time without jeopardizing the health and productivity of its most important resource: the soil.

In the Prologue before the story of *The Lord of the Rings* actually begins, Tolkien adopts the pose of an unbiased, scholarly, perhaps slightly pedantic editor. He offers "a few notes" describing some of the more important aspects of "this remarkable people" purportedly "collected from Hobbit-lore." The opening paragraph gives us some of these details, but it also achieves several subtle but important objectives in the framing of the tale. It begins, "Hobbits are an unobtrusive but very ancient people, more numerous formerly than they are today; for they love peace and quiet and good tilled earth: a well-ordered and well-farmed countryside was their favourite haunt." The quiet and peace-loving Hobbits are presented in ideal terms as farming people whose "well-ordered" country bespeaks personal virtues of prudence and industry, while their "well-farmed countryside" suggests a successful tradition of agricultural skill and care. What the reader is likely to miss, however, is Tolkien's use of present-tense verbs in this and other paragraphs. The implications of this grammatical choice are clear: Hobbits have existed from ancient times, they still exist, and in some undefined way their world is *our* world.

In a later paragraph, Tolkien makes this more explicit: "Those days, the Third Age of Middle-earth, are now long past, and the shape of all lands has been changed; but the regions in which Hobbits then lived were doubtless the same as those in which they still linger: the North-West of the Old World, east of the Sea." Tolkien not only suggests that their history is a part of our own ancient—if forgotten—history, but he also indicates that in a very real sense, their story is our story, for "in spite of later estrangement Hobbits are relatives of ours." Though the exact nature of the relationship between Hobbits and ourselves "can no longer be discovered," they are said to have spoken "the languages of Men" and to have "liked and disliked much the same things as Men did." As to why they now "avoid us with dismay and are becoming hard to find," the reader is left to infer that changes in the society and culture of "the bigger and clumsier races"—among whom Tolkien includes us, the "Big Folk"—are responsible (Pro).

Elsewhere in the opening paragraphs we are told that the Hobbits have "a close friendship with the earth" and "do not and did not understand or like machines more complicated than a forge-bellows, a water-mill, or a hand-loom." Hobbits disdain the sort of "progress" characterized in our own world by assembly-line manufacturing, industrial farming, advanced agricultural technology, agribusiness, or the needless use of complex machinery when simpler tools will do (Pro). Hobbits are willing to use simple devices to further their farming techniques, but they do not employ technological interventions that might endanger the quality of the soil, water, and air—the environmental sources on which their culture is directly dependent. In fact, they are willing to sacrifice short-term personal convenience for greater long-term good. As to the mythic estrangement between Hobbits and Men, the implications are clear: having abandoned "friendship with the earth," and having become enamored with mechanical technology, modern humanity has all but severed its harmonious relationship with the natural world, becoming more like Saruman, who—as Treebeard says—has "a mind of metal and wheels" (III/iv).

In the next part of this account we learn more about the historical background of the agrarian world of the Shire and its Hobbits. In a sketch of their history, we learn that in the year 1601 of the Third Age, 1,400 years before Bilbo's farewell birthday party, the pioneers Marcho and Blanco Fallohide obtained permission from Argeleb II, tenth king of Arthedain, for Hobbits to cross the Bridge of Stonebows and take the land beyond to dwell in.

> At once the western Hobbits fell in love with their new land, and they remained there, and soon passed once more out of the

history of Men and of Elves.... There for a thousand years they were little troubled by wars, and they prospered and multiplied.... The land was rich and kindly, and though it had long been deserted when they entered it, it had before been well tilled, and there the king had once had many farms, cornlands, vineyards, and woods.... The Hobbits named it the Shire, as the region of the authority of their Thain, and a district of well-ordered business; and there in that pleasant corner of the world they plied their well-ordered business of living, and they heeded less and less the world outside where dark things moved, until they came to think that peace and plenty were the rule in Middle-earth and the right of all sensible folk.... They were, in fact, sheltered, but they had ceased to remember it. (Pro)

In the Third Age of Middle-earth, at the time of the Shire's founding and settlement, Arthedain—one of the three realms of the Northern Kingdom of Arnor—is already in a long period of decline; within 300 years it ceases to exist as a political entity. According to Tolkien, the Hobbits' earliest tales indicate that they went through a period of wandering before their entrance into Eriador and had already diverged into three main groups, based on their settlement patterns: highlands and hillsides (Harfoots), flatlands and riversides (Stoors), and woodlands (Fallohides). We note that the Hobbits have not built cities or fortifications, and although each settlement group is described as having its own distinct cultural traditions, it is implied that they all underwent a transition from a primitive, migratory form of subsistence living to the establishment of a culture closely defined by the soil and landscape. Such a culture can only be based on such agricultural practices as seasonal tillage and harvest, storage of harvested grain, soil fertilization, and the preservation of seed for future planting—all of which require long-term familiarity with regional, local, and microenvironments and, of course, permanent settlements. Also implied is a recognition of the importance of careful land use to prevent erosion and exhaustion of the soil and to preserve its life-supporting fertility. Tolkien is careful to characterize the attitude conducive to the founding and survival of such a culture as one of "love."

Although the landscape that becomes the Hobbits' Shire had "long been deserted when they entered it," they do not find it to be virgin wilderness; although it is uninhabited, it is not a wasteland. This may seem a minor point of history, but it should not be overlooked that the Hobbits owe the foundation of their culture to a prior stewardship ethos: the first Hobbits move into a land that had been settled almost 2 millennia before.[18] Under its earlier inhabitants, Men of the Northern Kingdom of Arnor, the land had been "well tilled, and there the king had once had many farms, cornlands, vineyards, and woods" (Pro). The agricultural practices in this part of Arnor created the conditions under which the Hobbits are able to begin farming this land again and sustain this activity over an exceedingly long period. Frodo's comment that when things are in danger, "some one has to give them up, lose them, so that others may keep them" (VI/ix), and Gildor's reminder that "others dwelt here before hobbits were; and others will dwell here again when hobbits are no more" (I/iii), are programmatic of the Shire's maintenance, both in its history and in its prehistory.

After the Hobbits establish their home in the Shire, and after "a thousand years . . . little troubled by wars," they have "prospered and multiplied . . . and become accustomed to plenty," living in a "district of well-ordered business," plying "their well-ordered business of living" (Pro). We will return to the personal virtues that these descriptions imply, but embedded in these words is a light touch of something like irony: if Hobbits are susceptible to any general moral failing, it is the temptation to regard comfort as a given. Tolkien remarks, "they came to think that peace and plenty were the rule in Middle-earth and the right of all sensible folk" (Pro). If the Hobbits of the Shire represent an idealized agrarian society, it is not the picture of paradise. Tolkien includes the subtle implication that even Hobbit culture is vulnerable to the personal vices of self-aggrandizing self-centeredness in which "business" overtakes "living." One of the recurring themes in *The Hobbit*, prominent especially in the opening chapter, is the smugness of Bilbo's comfortable middle-class life, and one aspect of Bilbo's personality that the narrator repeatedly satirizes is his excessive concern for matters of business. In this passage from the Prologue, which is written at least partly from the Hobbits' perspective, we are led to understand that the phrase "all sensible folk" is meant to apply primarily, and maybe exclusively, to Hobbits themselves. A hint of xenophobia may be detected.

Nonetheless, as we have seen, Hobbits as a race are portrayed as being more in touch with nature than are Men in Middle-earth or human beings in our world. Nature is of fundamental value in and of itself, in contrast to the merely instrumental value of complex technology. Hobbits disdain the sort of industrial and technological "progress" characteristic of our modern world. And although the Hobbits love comfort, they are not willing to use artificial interventions to secure comfort if doing so will endanger the environment in the long term. Apart from the immediate pleasures afforded by work itself, their entertainments are the simple ones of food and drink, song and dance, long walks and hot baths, gossip and storytelling. Their agriculture—and thus their culture—is sustainable, presumably indefinitely.

Maggot and Cotton: Hobbit Farms and Farmers

Important to Tolkien's portrayal of agrarian society are his portrayals of the individuals who make it possible, especially the farmers. Wendell Berry has written that despite the many environmental difficulties of modern life, he has seen "enough good farmers and good farms, and a sufficient variety of both," to convince him that "an ecologically and culturally responsible agriculture"—that is, of the kind depicted in Tolkien's Shire—"is possible." Two obstacles stand in the way, however, of the fulfillment of this possibility: (1) as an occupation, farming "has low public standing"; and (2) "good farmers are rare."[19] John Gardner once wrote that it is almost axiomatic that in modern America no novel concerning farmers can succeed in gaining a wide readership. Farmers are popularly perceived as "hicks," says Berry, and many of the pejorative terms for members of the rural, agricultural populace substantiate his claim that the popular perception of farmers in our modern, urban culture accords no great esteem to people who work the soil to produce food.[20] Tolkien shows his own awareness of this in many ways. Even within the Shire, where farmers are more honored than elsewhere in Middle-earth (or in our world), there is a hint of class snobbishness by the wealthy Frodo and his friends toward Maggot, the farmer. Frodo's inclination is to regard Maggot as unimportant, and if not for his recent experiences, no doubt he would be surprised to learn that of all the folk of the Shire, Tom Bombadil would be spending time with Maggot (I/vii).

Although Tolkien's portrayal of the agrarian society of the Hobbits is relatively generalized, he includes an appreciative and somewhat detailed description of two Hobbit farmers: Farmer Maggot and Farmer Cotton. These two farmers form bookends of the story, appearing in Books I and VI, respectively. Farmer Maggot first appears when Frodo, Sam, and Pippin are departing from Hobbiton and try to take a shortcut across his farm. Although his name, Maggot, may seem pejorative—in fact, it means "grub worm" or "earthworm," not housefly larva—the epithet "Farmer" is an honorific one. Pippin describes him with admiration as "really a stout fellow." Merry describes him as "a shrewd fellow," commenting, "A lot goes on behind his round face that does not come out in his talk. . . . [H]e has the reputation of knowing a good many strange things." Tom Bombadil, whose character is particularly significant to the portrayal of harmony between people and the land, regards Farmer Maggot as "a person of more importance than they imagined." Tom says, "There's earth under his old feet, and clay on his fingers, wisdom in his bones, and both his eyes are open," indicating the esteem in which Tom holds him.

Here again, Tolkien gives us enough practical details about the farmer, his farm, and his farm family so that the picture is not simply a romanticized dream. Farmer Maggot's tame, well-ordered farmstead at Bamfurlong includes a turnip field and "a large house and farm-building" made of brick; like Maggot himself, it is "stoutly built." The farm family includes Maggot and his wife, three daughters, an unspecified number of sons, and several other hobbits "belonging to the farm-household." Frodo describes Mrs. Maggot as "a queen among farmers' wives" in gratitude for her generosity in packing a basket of mushrooms for him to take on his trek toward Crickhollow. Earlier, upon their arrival at Bamfurlong, we are told that Mrs. Maggot "brought out beer in a huge jug, and filled four large mugs" (I/iv). Tolkien here draws on medieval history in delegating to the lady of the house the role of ceremonial welcomer and dispenser of alcoholic beverages,[21] making a *queen* out of the farmer's wife. Frodo's words, though figurative, are not an exaggeration.

The scene in which the hobbits join the members of the farmstead at their evening meal is described in terms that evoke the hobbits' love of simple pleasures and, at the same time, presents a positive portrayal of farm life:

Two of Maggot's sons and his three daughters came in, and a generous supper was laid on the large table. The kitchen was

> lit with candles and the fire was mended. Mrs. Maggot bustled in and out. One or two other hobbits belonging to the farm-household came in. In a short while fourteen sat down to eat. There was beer in plenty, and a mighty dish of mushrooms and bacon, besides much other solid farmhouse fare. The dogs lay by the fire and gnawed rinds and cracked bones. (I/iv)

Despite the gruffness of his initial appearance, Maggot is an excellent host, and his household is a welcoming one. It abounds in the type of food and drink—solid farmhouse fare—most favored by Hobbits. And if there is a mythic quality to this scene, it is of the homey, humble sort, mundane in its evocation of rustic domestic peace and plenty. Even the dogs are provided for.

At the other end of the story, Farmer Cotton is an important character. Although we see much less of Cotton's farm than we do of Maggot's, we see enough of the farmer himself to make him worthy of notice. For example, we actually learn the names of Cotton's children: Jolly, Nibs, Nick, Tom, and Rosie. Although the Cottons seems a little less knowledgeable about the outside world than does Maggot (and a little less interested in knowing about it), Farmer Cotton is very knowledgeable about his own land. When the four travelers return to the Shire at the end of their adventures, the Cottons "asked a few polite questions about their travels, but hardly listened to the answers: they were far more concerned with events in the Shire." Among other things, Farmer Cotton understands the importance of good agrarian economics; he perceives, for example, that one of the causes of the Shire's troubles is that Pimple owns "a sight more than was good for him." In fact, Pimple has become a figure analogous to an agribusinessman in our world. He does not merely own farms; he owns "plantations." Furthermore, he exports the crops he grows (VI/viii). In this way, Pimple introduces into the Shire two problems discussed elsewhere in this book: when those who work the land do not have a personal stake in its well-being, and when the food grown is not eaten by those growing it, attention to the practical virtues of agrarian life and work wanes. When it comes to caring for the land, Farmer Cotton is a wise man and Pimple a fool.

Cotton is also courageous, which is most clearly shown when it comes to defending his land. The importance of defending the farm is a subject we explore in chapter 7 in the context of another of Tolkien's characters, Farmer Giles. At the end of *The Lord of the Rings*, it is Farmer Cotton who stands alone in the ring facing the first group of ruffians. Later, Cotton is one of the most important figures in helping to rouse the Shire. In addition to his courage, his knowledge is important; throughout the Shire's hostile occupation by Saruman and his henchmen, he makes careful note of how many ruffians there are, how they are armed, and where they are stationed. The four returning travelers rely largely on his knowledge as they undertake the defense and reclamation of the Shire. Farmer Cotton is one of Tolkien's important heroes, heroic not only for his courage but also for his knowledge of the land and his wisdom in understanding how best to care for it.

Attachment and Sacrifice

Given the genre in which he was writing, we can safely observe that the breadth of Tolkien's vision of agrarian life is astounding. The next question is what he did with it—or perhaps what the Hobbits would do without it. Early in *The Lord of the Rings*, there is a point when Frodo learns the true nature of the magic ring he has received from his uncle Bilbo. After Gandalf sketches for Frodo the history of this ring and the perils it poses, the two sit at Bag End discussing what action Frodo ought to take. Frodo's realization comes almost casually, but it is a critical and dramatic moment:

> "I cannot keep the Ring and stay here. I ought to leave Bag End, leave the Shire, leave everything and go away." He sighed.
> "I should like to save the Shire, if I could. . . . I feel that as long as the Shire lies behind, safe and comfortable, I shall find wandering more bearable: I shall know that somewhere there is a firm foothold, even if my feet cannot stand there again."
> (I/ii)

Ultimately, as all readers of the tale know, Frodo resolves to take the One Ring out of the Shire and make for Rivendell, where the quest for Mordor really begins. For the moment, however, he equivocates, expressing the strength of his personal, emotional attachment to the Shire and its gardens, pastures, fields, and woods, its farmlands and quiet villages.

He loves them and wishes he could stay and enjoy them indefinitely. Yet he also recognizes that the preservation of his homeland may require him to relinquish any personal claim on it. In his willingness to forgo his "firm foothold" in a "safe and comfortable" land, Frodo's sacrificial nature—which plays a key role in the success of his quest—begins to emerge into the foreground. His words evoke a strength of character that he already possesses at the beginning of the story and that develops and grows during the course of his quest for Mount Doom. But they also indicate—and are predicated upon—a close attachment to the land, the local culture, and the landscapes of home, which is characteristic of the Hobbits as a race.

At the end of the story, just before leaving the Shire for the last time, Frodo returns to this theme. In one of his last conversations with Sam, he tells his gardener and fellow Ring-bearer that he is leaving for the Grey Havens and departing Middle-earth. In tears, Sam replies, "But . . . I thought you were going to enjoy the Shire, too, for years and years, after all you have done." Frodo's reply is telling: "So I thought too, once. . . . I tried to save the Shire, and it has been saved, but not for me. It must often be so, Sam, when things are in danger: some one has to give them up, lose them, so that others may keep them" (VI/ix). His words here echo his comments much earlier in the story, though by the end, there is almost certainly a deeper understanding of their meaning and a greater conviction of their validity. This attitude of sacrificial humility is expressed throughout *The Lord of the Rings*. It is expressed broadly in terms of the preservation of people's lives and freedoms and more narrowly, but perhaps even more fundamentally, in terms of the protection of the natural environment in the landscapes of Eriador, Gondor, Rohan, and all of Middle-earth. Environmental stewardship of the sort discussed in the previous chapter sometimes requires people to relinquish certain claims—or to restrain themselves from certain kinds of behavior deriving from such claims—to ensure the transmission of the natural environment in a fertile and habitable condition to those who will come after.

This attitude is probably best explained on the basis of the biblical model of stewardship exemplified in the life of Jesus in the Gospels and developed in the Pauline epistles.[22] It is a model characterized by servanthood in which Jesus is shown humbly relinquishing his divine rights and claims to save the world he loves. Assuredly, self-sacrifice is not a uniquely Christian virtue—many who are not of the Christian faith exhibit sacrificial qualities and perform sacrificial acts of heroic proportions—but heroic self-sacrifice is essential to the meaning and purpose of the Incarnation and to the biblical pattern of stewardship that Christians are enjoined to imitate. This pattern is central to Tolkien's theory of literature and to his application of that theory in creating his characters. He concludes the epilogue of "On Fairy-stories" by calling the Incarnation—the story of Christ's humiliation and sacrifice—the central "eucatastrophe of Man's history" and the Resurrection the eucatastrophe of that story (*TL*, 72).[23] It should come as no surprise, then, that the virtues of humility and sacrifice are also central to Tolkien's environmental vision and crucial to the construction of the most important characters illustrating it: Faramir in Ithilien, Éomer in Rohan, the sons of Elrond in Rivendell, Frodo in the Shire, and Gandalf in all of Middle-earth.

Tolkien's concept of stewardship is defined not only by what one does but also by what one does not do and by what one gives up. Thus Gandalf, the model steward in Tolkien's writing, also gives up his life for his companions at Khazad-dûm. Of course, self-sacrifice for the land and for one's friends is not the only response that Frodo and others are called on to make: there are also active ways of reacting to the various forms of evil and its various effects in Middle-earth. Gandalf, Aragorn, Frodo, and many others are engaged at one level in a strategy of abnegation and self-denial for the sake of others, and at another level in an active campaign of resistance against Sauron, Saruman, the Orcs, and their agents in the War of the Ring. Among other things, it is a fight, and the environment provides the most basic background sphere of action against which the moral battle for the freedom of Middle-earth takes place. Frodo's relinquishment of the "firm foothold" he has helped preserve must be placed alongside many things that he and others do to resist tyrannical evil in Middle-earth.[24] The tension between his desire to remain at home in the land he loves and his recognition that he must leave it in order to save it reflects two aspects of stewardship. Both are necessary for the kind of stewardship Tolkien shows us in his writings: heartfelt devotion to a particular place and the people who live there; sacrificial willingness to do what is necessary to protect and preserve it. These are necessary agrarian attitudes, and they are Christian virtues.

Leaving Home: Mutual Dependence and the Others Who Will Follow

Frodo's attachment to the Shire and the significance of his sacrifice become more poignant once he makes the decision to undertake the quest to destroy the One Ring, both during his final months at Bag End and especially on his journey away. As Frodo contemplates his imminent departure, interpreting it as a form of "exile," he comments that he feels both very small and "very uprooted" (I/ii). We have already pointed out that Hobbits are a race defined by their identification with the soil: their style of architecture and their very name derive from their homes built in holes in the ground; going barefoot, they are in constant contact with the soil; their culture is based on sustainable agriculture in a small-farm economy. Thus, it is probably more than coincidental that Frodo uses the terminology of growing things rooted in the soil to characterize his sense of belonging in the Shire and his sense of alienation upon having to leave it.

As plans move forward for his journey eastward, Frodo grows more and more reluctant to leave. When he finally sets out, he has good reason to regret the decision he has made: the villages, inns, farmlands, and pastures of his country have never seemed so beautiful to him. Tolkien uses the poignant imagery of autumnal harvest to indicate Frodo's deep-seated sense of affection for the land that he must now leave behind: "The Shire had seldom seen so fair a summer, or so rich an autumn: the trees were laden with apples, honey was dripping in the combs, and the corn was tall and full." On the night of his departure, looking back at "the light of the last farm" twinkling among the trees, Frodo waves farewell, wondering if he will ever "look down into that valley again" (I/iii). The deep tension between Frodo's love of the Shire and his sacrificial relinquishment of it reflects the mutual interdependency between people and their homeland that is a key feature of the agrarian ideal underlying *The Lord of the Rings*. The landscapes through which Frodo and his companions move once they depart are described similarly as an ideal rural countryside. With the announcement, "now we're off at last," Frodo, Sam, and Pippin leap over "the low place in the hedge" at the bottom of the garden path and take "to the fields, passing into the darkness like a rustle in the grasses," going down a narrow lane and then through more fields, "along hedgerows and the borders of coppices" (I/iii).

Another important aspect of the Hobbits' sense of stewardship enters the narrative at this point. On the second night after their departure from Hobbiton, after narrowly escaping a Black Rider, Frodo, Sam, and Pippin encounter in the woods a company of the Noldor—the High Elves. Gildor, the leader of this company, warns the hobbits that their enemy is pursuing them. Frodo replies that he had not expected to meet danger "in our own Shire." Gildor's answer is telling: "But it is not your own Shire. Others dwelt here before hobbits were; and others will dwell here again when hobbits are no more. The wide world is all about you: you can fence yourselves in, but you cannot for ever fence it out" (I/iii). From the longer-range perspective afforded by the longevity of his race, Gildor asserts that people dwell on the land for only a brief time; others come after. This highlights the fact that however much they feel at home there, the Shire does not "belong" in an absolute sense to any of them. This brings us back to the idea that a steward is not an owner but a caretaker of something that belongs to another. Frodo's understanding of this concept is important for his ability to comprehend and put into action the heroic self-sacrifice discussed earlier. It is important for the hobbits to hear this from Gildor, and Tolkien saw it as an important principle for his readers to ponder as well.

The impossibility of complete isolation is brought home poignantly at the end of the trilogy when, finding the Shire under the heel of Saruman and his henchmen, the four hobbits discover widespread, wanton destruction of their once-beautiful land. We return to this destruction toward the end of the book when we explore the devastating environmental impact of policies other than those adopted by the Hobbits and examine the Hobbits' progress in restoring their land to its former fertility and beauty. But Gildor's words here emphasize an awareness of the transience of life on earth as a precondition to the attitude of sacrificial stewardship that Frodo exhibits.

The Impact of Hobbits and the Shire

In some ways, we have only begun to explore the Shire and the ecology Tolkien models there, and the Shire is only one such model in Tolkien's legendarium, not to mention in his other writings that do not concern Middle-earth. Further exploration, however, would no doubt discover the same ideas at work in other ways. We therefore summarize

Tolkien's portrayal as follows. At once respectful of the inherent dignity of the natural environment and respectful of the dignity of those who work the soil, in the Hobbits of the Shire, Tolkien depicts a people in harmony with the creation of which they are a noble part. Their local and regional economy is based on an agrarian system dependent on sustainable agriculture; they extract from the soil only such bounty as the harvests can provide, affording them not only subsistence but also the comforts resulting from abundance. The Shire represents an idyllic agrarian, preindustrial society where people can live comfortably at home in the natural world. It has romantic elements, but it is also much more. It is an agrarian ideal in the good sense: a picture that can inspire readers to take appropriate steps that in some small way can introduce the best elements of the Shire into the real world while avoiding some of the myopic pitfalls of Hobbit provincialism.

Although many readers of *The Lord of the Rings* respond enthusiastically to various components of Tolkien's imagined world, in recent decades the Shire and the Hobbits in particular seem to have attracted the greatest share of admiration. The Shire's portrait of preindustrial English village life has led many readers to try to emulate certain superficial, stereotyped features of the Hobbits' world: tea drinking, pipe smoking, cheese making, beer brewing, and the growing and eating of such simple foods as potatoes, turnips, and mushrooms. The popular-cultural longevity of the Shire's attractive power is evident in the borrowing of names from *The Lord of the Rings* for such things as pets, boats, recipes, health-food restaurants, natural food cooperatives, arts and crafts shops, country inns, personal nicknames, computer user names, titles of popular songs, and so on. Names related to Hobbits and the Shire seem particularly dominant. All this suggests that there is something about the imaginary land of the Shire that people want to imitate in the real world and incorporate into their own lives. To some degree, it might even be said that a certain strain of serious modern environmentalism owes its lineage to the "back to the earth" alternative lifestyles of the 1960s, which resonated with Tolkien's writing and to which Tolkien contributed through his fictional portrayal of the Shire. As Carpenter writes, the books' "implied emphasis on the protection of natural scenery against the ravages of an industrial society harmonised with the growing ecological movement, and it was easy to see *The Lord of the Rings* as a tract for the times."[25]

It remains to be seen whether and to what extent such a harmonious dwelling of people on the land can be attained in the real world—that is, attained by many people in a very general way. Nevertheless, environmental writers like Wes Jackson, Wendell Berry, Gene Logsdon, and others have not been deterred from trying to foster an alternative perspective on farming, food production and consumption, agriculture, and the economic and cultural issues surrounding them as part of the broader environmental movement.[26] We suggest that the name J. R. R. Tolkien belongs on this list. His perspective on Christian stewardship—heartfelt devotion to a particular place, knowledge that the place ultimately does not belong solely to us, and willingness to give it up to preserve it for others—is his plan for how such an idyllic vision can have a positive influence on this world.

Chapter 4
Horticulture and the Aesthetic of the Elves

The Enjoyment of Food and Gardens

The first appearance of Elves in the story line of *The Lord of the Rings* occurs on the second night of Frodo's journey through the Shire on his way to Rivendell. Preparing to sleep alfresco in Woody End, beside the road to Woodhall in the Eastfarthing, Frodo, Sam, and Pippin hear a group of travelers singing an Elvish song of Elbereth. As the hobbits wait in the shadows, a company of elves led by Gildor Inglorion passes by, starlight glimmering in their eyes and hair. Frodo points out that these are High Elves, few of whom "now remain in Middle-earth, east of the Great Sea"; they are the "fairest folk" among the three kindreds of Elves, who now seldom visit the Shire (I/iii). These elves are passing through Eriador, leaving Middle-earth on their way to Valinor across the sea in the farthest west. The mythic and environmental implications of their permanent abandonment of Middle-earth are profound and worth exploration, but at this point in the plot, their appearance on the outskirts of the Shire once again raises an interesting practical problem that is unresolved by Tolkien here or elsewhere in *The Lord of the Rings*: where does their food come from?

The episode has several overt narrative functions. First, and most

Tolkien's imaginative creation and portrayal of a culture devoted to the cultivation and conservation of the soil—that of the Hobbits—is one important facet of a comprehensive environmental ethic. To illustrate a contrasting dimension of Tolkien's environmentalism, we now turn to another race of people in Middle-earth: the Elves.

important, Frodo and Gildor's conversation concerning Frodo's quest for Rivendell adds to the urgency of his journey, which is soon to change from simple departure to desperate flight; the ominous references to the Black Riders, along with Gildor's advice to "make haste, and neither stay nor turn back" (I/iii), heighten the narrative tension and deepen the reader's sense of foreboding. Second, the hobbits' encounter with the elves satisfies a desire expressed by Sam in the first chapter, a desire that serves as something of a leitmotif throughout the novel. But third, and most relevant for our purposes, the episode gives the fullest narrative description anywhere in the trilogy of the preparation and eating of food by Elves.

The meal comes after a march of some miles to the forested hills above Woodhall, when Frodo and his companions halt with their elven guides in a kind of open-air camp, a wide space of grass surrounded by trees. "There is a fire in the hall, and food for hungry guests," says an elf standing beside Pippin. Then the scene of the meal is described.

> At the south end of the greensward there was an opening. There the green floor ran on into the wood, and formed a wide space like a hall, roofed by the boughs of trees. Their great trunks ran like pillars down each side. In the middle there was a wood-fire blazing, and upon the tree-pillars torches with lights of gold and silver were burning steadily. The Elves sat round the fire upon the grass or upon the sawn rings of old trunks. Some went to and fro bearing cups and pouring drink; others brought food on heaped plates and dishes. (I/iii)

The "hall," as it turns out, is not like the splendid Meduseld of Théoden or even the simpler hall of Beorn, where Bilbo and the dwarves are nourished on their journey in *The Hobbit*. It is a natural hall whose roof is made of tree boughs. The floor is the grass; the chairs are old tree trunks. The scene is illuminated by gold and silver light.

The scene has an earlier counterpart in chapter 8 of *The Hobbit*, when Bilbo and the dwarves stumble upon Green-elves feasting in Mirkwood. There, the aroma of roasting meat tantalizes the starving travelers, and we are reminded that Thranduil's people are hunters. Here, although Gildor's folk demur and call the meal "poor fare," the woodland feast includes bread "surpassing the savour of a fair white loaf to one who is starving," fruit as "sweet as wildberries and richer than the tended fruits of gardens," a fragrant beverage "cool as a clear fountain, golden as a summer afternoon," and apples of such high quality that Sam is provoked to remark later, "If I could grow apples like that, I would call myself a gardener" (I/iii). This short list is not exhaustive, and Sam and Pippin are said to remember little of that night's food and drink. However, attentive readers are left to ponder the complexities involved in the transport of not only the kinds and quantities of foods indicated but also the cups, plates, serving dishes, and other equipment needed by the Elves and those to whom they might offer hospitality during their westward trek.

Although the hobbits' recollection of the scene is noticeably vague, the details that *are* mentioned emphasize the aesthetic qualities of the setting as opposed to any particulars concerning the food and its preparation. In the phrase "richer than the tended fruits of gardens," there is a faint suggestion that the Elves do not engage in any sort of organized farming or even gardening but simply partake of the earth's bounty as it occurs naturally. In contrast, the loaves of bread—and later, the *lembas,* or way-bread of Lothlórien—hint at an entire invisible industry in which grain is cultivated and harvested, ground, refined, and baked. Also, the cool, clear, golden beverage served suggests viniculture of a far greater sophistication than fits these people's characteristics. Food seems simply to materialize as needed for this feast, with no indication of how or where it comes from. From a narrative perspective, this is altogether appropriate. The scene is described from a Hobbit's point of view. And while Hobbits visiting other Hobbits might notice such details as what vegetables are planted in their gardens or what kind of mill wheel they use or where the dishes come from, a Hobbit among High Elves—especially for the first time—would be too awed to take note of such mundane details.

In any case, although Tolkien was fully capable of depicting realistically many aspects of agrarian life, his description of Elves emphasizes other characteristics of this race. Whereas the agrarian society of the Shire shows how a group of people can draw on the life-giving fecundity of the soil for an extremely long time—perhaps indefinitely—without permanently depleting or exhausting it, the Elves illustrate a different outlook. Although they are as dependent on the earth for food as are the Hobbits or any other race in Middle-earth, the Elves are concerned primarily with the aesthetic qualities—the physical beauty—of the created world.

This is not to say that the Hobbits' view of nature has no aesthetic dimension. Although the focus of the previous chapter is on the Shire's agrarianism, the Hobbits also keep flower gardens and have great appreciation for trees. With respect to the raising of crops, the delight that Tolkien ascribes to the Hobbit lifestyle makes it clear that their pleasure in the fruitfulness of the earth involves more than simple sustenance or survival. It also goes beyond the salutary moral effects of hard work on personal and communal character, for the focus of the Hobbits' agrarian culture is directed toward the final stage of the process: the consumption and enjoyment of food and the social customs connected with eating. The fulfillment and joy that Hobbits derive from the results of their labor are both biological and social, and culinary aesthetics play a significant part in the sociability of their communal culture. Nonetheless, their agriculture has a pragmatic side; in the Shire, as in all the civilizations in Middle-earth, eating is a physical necessity, and Hobbits work toward that end.

The glimpses we are afforded of the Elves involve an altogether different focus. It is not merely that the reader is not shown the pragmatic side to their agrarian pursuits; it is that no agrarian pursuits are shown whatsoever. Though we sometimes see Elves engaged in the act of eating, *The Lord of the Rings* gives us little detail concerning the enterprises necessary to obtain food. Neither does *The Silmarillion*, befitting its high mythic tone; nor does *The Hobbit*, where such a description might fit very well with the narrative voice. With the exception of Thranduil's folk in Mirkwood, we are not told whether the Elves of Middle-earth engage in small-scale gardening, organized farming, or some sort of economic trade for the food they need for survival. In all the known civilizations in our world, it is a general principle that the long-term sustainability of a culture depends on the degree to which activities connected with biological survival can be invested with social and communal meaning through customs and rituals persisting over a long period. When it comes to the Elves, however, we have no indication of how and where—or even whether—they store agricultural commodities for long-term use, how and where they prepare food, or what social traditions sustain such activities.

What is relevant to the narrative—and what is an important aspect of the overall ecology of Middle-earth—are the aesthetic pursuits of the Elves. Despite the lack of details regarding the practices they use to acquire their food, the Elves are at least as environmentally aware as the Hobbits are, and in many ways, their environmentalism is more sophisticated. Even more than Hobbits, Elves identify themselves, and are identified by others, with the life of Middle-earth and see themselves as stewards and guardians of its beauty.[1] As many passages throughout the novels indicate, from their earliest mythic origins to the attributes they display in the stories of Bilbo's and Frodo's quests, the Elves' main concern is for the beauty of Arda (the earth) and indeed of all Eä (creation). If the Hobbits represent sustainable agriculture at its imaginative best, Elves can be seen as expressing Tolkien's view of *sustainable horticulture*.[2]

Some discussion of what we mean by "sustainability" with reference to horticulture may be necessary. The phrase on which this neologism is modeled speaks of sustainability in practical terms having to do with farming methods that do not threaten the soil's long-term ability to produce healthful crops. Agricultural techniques that rely on the application of herbicides and pesticides to improve crop yields but permanently poison the soil and water supply, practices such as the overuse of or reliance on biotic monocultures that deplete the nutritive qualities of the soil, or activities that cause the permanent loss of topsoil are considered "unsustainable." The long-term result in such cases would be the ultimate collapse of the agricultural system as a whole. Horticulture—by which we mean the cultivation of plant life and the landscapes that support it for purely aesthetic purposes—is of a different character altogether. Although, as with agriculture, one could speak about the sustainability of horticulture's results, with regard to the Elves, sustainability has more to do with threats *to* horticulture from other sources.[3] In our world, the question to be asked is: can aesthetic valuation of the environment be sustained in the face of threats posed by industrial, technological, and even agricultural imperatives considered essential by our modern economy?

This question lies at the heart of some conflicts between conservationists and preservationists whereby the aesthetic value of wilderness landscapes is weighed against the purported economic benefits of mining, timber cutting, or even farming those areas. It is one thing to frame an argument for preserving landscapes of natural beauty for the sake of maintaining biological diversity, ecological balance among species, or purity of subterranean aquifers. It is another to argue for their preservation purely on aesthetic grounds. And yet, such an argument is sometimes made, often under heavy opposition.

The state of Vermont, for example, has a rich and varied landscape that is considered beautiful by residents and visitors alike. But preservation of its aesthetic qualities—considered by some to be the state's most important natural resource—is achieved only with great effort to resist the economic appeal of mining operations, corporate agribusiness, and other activities that might bring financial benefits but at tremendous aesthetic cost. Even within environmental constituencies, aesthetics play a role in decision making and policy formation. For example, some groups recognize the need to decrease our reliance on the combustion of fossil fuels and quite reasonably point to wind power as an alternative source of energy production. But as soon as the massive wind-powered turbines needed to implement this shift are proposed for a site that has particular aesthetic qualities treasured by others, a struggle ensues over which is more important: energy independence or aesthetic value. In eastern Kentucky, part of the argument against the strip-mining of coal has to do with soil and water quality, part of it has to do with the cultural impact of the region's economic collapse after the coal is depleted and mining operations cease, and part of the argument is framed in aesthetic terms: strip-mining leaves a poisoned, uninhabitable, and ugly landscape in its wake.

Struggles like this occur regularly throughout the country and around the world as more and more societies confront the hard decisions necessitated by the dwindling of more costly natural resources. Again, the question might be: under what conditions does a wilderness landscape's undisturbed beauty override its economic usefulness? Or, under what circumstances is the relatively higher aesthetic value of small farms, pastureland, vineyards, and orchards expendable for the sake of highway construction, industrialization, or urbanization? How sustainable is the aesthetic view in the light of such pressures?

Tolkien has made the dilemma somewhat simpler in his legendarium, where the Elves' aesthetic preservationism is joined to the moral defense against the evils of Morgoth and Sauron. For the Elves, maintenance of the beauty of Middle-earth—in *The Lord of the Rings,* of Lothlórien in particular—is inseparable from freedom from the enslaving and environmentally destructive objectives of the Dark Lord. It is also counterposed against the more benign but, for them, utilitarian interest of the Dwarves, whose mining operations are sometimes but not always undertaken with attention to subterranean natural beauty. Indeed, in terms of aesthetics, the Elves are most sharply contrasted with the Dwarves, who value the environment primarily as a source of fuel, building materials, and precious gems and metals.[4] There is a telling moment when the dwarf Gimli and the elf Legolas first enter Minas Tirith together. Gimli immediately comments about the stonework: "There is some good stone-work here, but also some that is less good, and the streets could be better contrived." Certainly some of Gimli's evaluation is based on the pure aesthetic beauty of the work. But some of the dwarf's concern is utilitarian, particularly with respect to the streets and the gates to the city. "When Aragorn comes into his own, I shall offer him the service of stonewrights of the Mountain, and we will make this a town to be proud of." Even to the degree that his concern is aesthetic, Gimli makes no mention of living things. Legolas's response makes for a clear contrast. "They need more gardens," said Legolas. "The houses are dead, and there is too little here that grows and is glad. If Aragorn comes into his own, the people of the Wood shall bring him birds that sing and trees that do not die" (V/ix). Gardens that grow and are "glad" make glad the hearts of those who perceive their beauty, and gladness of heart is part of the overall freedom from oppression that the surviving Elves of Middle-earth—at Lothlórien and Rivendell—strive to protect.

Elvish Kingdoms of Wood and Stone

In the total oeuvre of Tolkien's Middle-earth canon, a number of Elvish communities are described. Some are pictured in detail, and some—such as those in Hithlum and Dorthonion in the First Age of Middle-earth—are only briefly sketched. Besides the numerous different and diverse communities of Quendi (Elves), there are numerous significant divisions within the race; these divisions might be called kindreds or subraces of Elves. The first division is between the Eldar, those who respond to the summons of the Valar and begin the journey toward Valinor and Aman and the True West in the earliest days of their prehistory, and the Avari, "the unwilling," who never begin the journey and play no significant role in Tolkien's legendarium. Furthermore, among those who begin the journey, some never reach Aman, choosing instead to stop along the way and remain in some part of Middle-earth. This results in the Calaquendi (the Elves of the Light, or High Elves, who reach Aman in the days of the Two Trees) and the Moriquendi (the Elves of the Darkness, who never see the light of the Two Trees either because they never begin the journey or because they do not complete it). Unlike the Avari, many of the Moriquendi do play a significant role in the history of Middle-earth shared by Tolkien. Galadriel of Lothlórien is one of the Calaquendi; Thranduil of Mirkwood is one of the Moriquendi. This division is significant enough that the two groups speak different languages: Quenya and Sindarin.[5]

The Eldar themselves can be subdivided into three peoples: the Vanyar, the Teleri, and the Noldor, each of which has its own kings and lords. All the Vanyar reach Aman, as do many of the Teleri, and they never return to Middle-earth. Many of the Noldor, however, do return to Middle-earth, in exile from Aman, and become known as High Elves. The Teleri, the largest of these three groups of Eldar, can be further subdivided, for most of those who forsake the journey and remain in Middle-earth are the Teleri. These become the Sindar (Grey-elves) and the Nandor (Green-elves). Though there is rarely open war among the Elves, the various Elvish kingdoms are not always friendly with one another. And some—usually the Noldor—are more friendly to Men and Dwarves than the other Elves are. The Elves of Doriath are resentful of the return of the Noldor and mistrust them because of the doom of their exile. King Thingol bans the tongue of the Noldor from his realm.

The point of this survey is not, however, to emphasize the differences but to suggest that the many dissimilarities among the various Elvish kingdoms are outweighed by their similarities. The most disparate Elvish communities are still more like one another, especially in their relationship with the earth, than any Elvish kingdom is to any kingdom of Man, Dwarf, or Hobbit. As Tolkien points out in *The Hobbit,* in his description of the Sindarin Elves of Mirkwood:

> They differed from the High Elves of the West, and were more dangerous and less wise. For most of them (together with their scattered relations in the hills and mountains) were descended

from the ancient tribes that never went to Faerie in the west. There the Light-elves [Vanyar] and the Deep-elves [Noldor] and the Sea-elves [Teleri] went and lived for ages, and grew fairer and wiser and more learned . . . before coming back into the Wide World. . . . Still elves they were and remain, and that is Good People. (*H*, 218–19)

Tolkien thus suggests a strong link among the various kindreds of Elves based on their common traits. In particular, whether Noldorin or Sindarin, Calaquendi or Moriquendi, and whether described in detail or only sketched, none of the descriptions of any Elvish community emphasizes agrarian concerns. Most contain no mention of such matters at all, a sharp contrast to Tolkien's descriptions of the Shire. Several, however, emphasize the Elves' interest in environmental beauty. At one point in Rivendell, Bilbo comments that even the Hobbits' robust appetite for "music and poetry and tales" is nothing compared with that of the Elves, who "seem to like [these things] as much as food, or more" (II/i). Though spoken in and of Rivendell, this comment is true of Elves as a race and is illustrated in every Elvish community the reader glimpses.

It is well worth looking at the descriptions of various important Elvish kingdoms that appear throughout the history of Middle-earth: Nargothrond, Gondolin, and Doriath (three kingdoms in the First Age of Middle-earth described in *The Silmarillion*), as well as Thranduil's realm in Mirkwood (visited by Bilbo and company in *The Hobbit* and mentioned in *The Lord of the Rings*), Elrond's community at Rivendell, and Lothlórien, the Elvish realm portrayed most clearly in *The Lord of the Rings*. Although readers of *The Hobbit* and *The Lord of the Rings* may think of Elves primarily in association with forests—most notably Lothlórien and Mirkwood—it is interesting to note that all three of the First Age kingdoms mentioned are associated with rocks, caves, and underground fortresses. This may stem in part from the necessity of defense; the First Age is one of war against Morgoth, and all three of these kingdoms in the region called Beleriand are hidden. Nargothrond[6] is hidden underground, Gondolin is geographically hidden within the Encircling Mountains, and Doriath is hidden and protected, through enchantment, by the Girdle of Melian.

Nonetheless, descriptions of these kingdoms emphasize natural beauty. The Hidden Realm of Doriath is the only one of the three associated primarily with trees and woods. It comprises the great Forest of Region and the smaller adjoining forests of Neldoreth and Brethil. These forests are replete with beautiful glades, golden trees, green hills, and unfading grass. Numerous rivers—the Esgalduin, Aros, Mindeb, and the mighty Sirion—all flow through the boundaries of Doriath. It is also the home of Lúthien, one of the most important figures in all the histories of Middle-earth and "the most beautiful of all the Children of Ilúvatar." Flowers spring from the earth of Doriath, and birds sing, when Lúthien passes (*Silm*, 165).

At the heart of Doriath, on the River Esgalduin, Thingol and Melian construct Menegroth, a subterranean hall "hewn in the living stone." It is interesting that even the caves of Menegroth are described in terms filled with natural beauty, and it is no accident that Tolkien describes the rock as "living stone." It is also no coincidence that the original home of Melian[7] is the gardens of Lórien, in the land of Aman, and that she—the most beautiful of Irmo's people—sings daily at the time of "the mingling of the lights" of the Two Trees; Melian "was akin before the World was made to Yavanna herself" (*Silm*, 55). Thus the beauty of Doriath and Menegroth is a particular beauty that recalls that of Valinor. Under Melian's tutelage, the Sindarin Elves create in their sylvan stronghold in Beleriand artistic images recalling "the wonder and beauty of Valinor beyond the Sea." The aesthetic motifs are natural:

> The pillars of Menegroth were hewn in the likeness of the beeches of Oromë, stock, bough, and leaf, and they were lit with lanterns of gold. The nightingales sang there as in the gardens of Lórien; and there were fountains of silver, and basins of marble, and floors of many-coloured stones. Carven figures of beasts and birds there ran upon the walls, or climbed upon the pillars, or peered among the branches entwined with many flowers. (*Silm*, 93)

Later, Melian has the halls decorated with artistic tapestries illustrating the deeds of the Valar, and it is called "the fairest dwelling of any king that has ever been east of the Sea" (*Silm*, 93).

Nargothrond, founded by Finrod Felagund, is not described in as much detail, although it is "the greatest by far" of the realms of Beleriand in the First Age. It is a land of mountains, rivers, and coastland, a sparsely populated "region of meads filled with many flowers" and a coastal marsh "empty of all living things save birds of the sea" (*Silm*, 120–21). Its name is derived from the river Narog that flows through and protects the heart of the realm. We learn that Finrod's realm is inspired by Thingol's and modeled after it, and thus indirectly reflects the beauty of Valinor. Likewise, even Turgon's stone city of Gondolin intentionally emulates the beauty of Valinor and remembers the light of the Two Trees. It is described as a fortress of great beauty founded as "a memorial of Tirion upon Túna," the Valinorean city of Turgon's birth. In it, "shining fountains played," and there stand two trees—the golden Glingal and the flower-adorned silver Belthil—"images of the Trees of old." It is said that "Gondolin upon Amon Gwareth became fair indeed and fit to compare even with Elven Tirion beyond the sea" (*Silm*, 125–26).

Moving forward in time to the Third Age of Middle-earth and to Tolkien's better-known works, there are three more kingdoms to note. In *The Hobbit*, at the eastern edge of Mirkwood, we see a society of sylvan Elves under the kingship of Thranduil, the father of Legolas. As in the three great kingdoms mentioned previously, Thranduil's people have an underground fortress in stone. "The king's cave was his palace, and the strong place of his treasure, and the fortress of his people against their enemies" (*H*, 219). When Thorin and company are taken prisoner, they and the burglar Bilbo spend considerable time in these caves. Nonetheless, the Elves of Mirkwood are associated more with the forest than with caves; they are known as Wood-elves, not Cave-elves. "In fact the subjects of the king mostly lived and hunted in the open woods, and had houses or huts on the ground and in the branches" (*H*, 219). When we first meet them, they are feasting in a wooden glade. "Their gleaming hair was twined with flowers; green and white gems glinted on their collars and their belts; and their faces and their songs were filled with mirth" (*H*, 206). We later learn that their king adorns himself likewise with images of nature. "On his head was a crown of berries and red leaves, for the autumn was come again. In the spring he wore a crown of woodland flowers. In his hand he held a carven staff of oak" (*H*, 223).

Through the eyes of Bilbo, the reader gets only a few more hints of the life of the Elves of Mirkwood. Again, although the folk of this community enjoy feasting, none of the descriptions suggests any agrarian concerns. In fact, we are told explicitly that although the Elves "were very fond of wine," they did not grow any grapes themselves. They provide for themselves partly by hunting and partly through trade with "their kinsfolk in the South" and "Men in distant lands" (*H*, 228). What is emphasized is the Elves' interest in environmental beauty: an appreciation of the value and artistry of the natural world.

Of the two Elvish kingdoms appearing in *The Lord of the Rings*, the physical attributes of Rivendell, also called Imladris, are described much more sparsely than those of Lothlórien. Bilbo describes it as "a perfect house, whether you like food or sleep or story-telling or singing, or just sitting and thinking best, or a pleasant mixture of them all." His statement that "time doesn't seem to pass here: it just is," evokes an atmosphere of otherworldly, almost Valinorean perfection. There is a "high garden above the steep bank of the river." It is not a vegetable garden but a place of natural beauty "filled with a faint scent of trees and flowers, as if summer still lingered in Elrond's gardens." Later, the beauty of Rivendell's natural surroundings is amplified as Frodo walks "along the terraces above the loud-flowing Bruinen," watching "the pale, cool sun rise above the far mountains, and shine down, slanting through the thin silver mist." Providing an important instance of the green-silver-gold motif and an echo of the beauty of Westernesse, which is sacred to the Elves, the passage goes on to note the glimmering of "the dew upon the yellow leaves" and "the woven nets of gossamer twinkl[ing] on every bush" (II/i). Despite the prevalence of feasting, however—and in marked contrast to the feasting of the Hobbits in the Shire—there is never any indication of where the food at Rivendell comes from.

Of the three Elvish realms described in *The Hobbit* and *The Lord of the Rings*, Lothlórien is painted in the most vivid detail. In *The Fellowship of the Ring*, as the Company (now bereft of its leader Gandalf) escapes Moria through the Dimrill Gate and makes for Lothlórien, descriptions immediately focus on the beauty and mystery of this enchanted forest. Aragorn indicates the direction in which he plans to lead them, and "they looked as he pointed, and before them they could see the stream leaping down to the trough of the valley, and then running on and away into the lower lands, until it was lost in a golden haze." Legolas then exclaims, "There lie the woods of Lothlórien," which he calls "the fairest of all the dwellings of my people" (II/vi). Many passages emphasize visual images that evoke the characteristics of the Two Trees treasured by the Elves: "There are no trees like the trees of that land. For in the autumn their leaves fall not, but turn to gold. Not till the Spring comes and the new green opens do they fall, and then the floor of the wood is golden, and golden is the roof, and its pillars are of silver, for the bark of the trees is smooth and grey" (II/vi). Here Legolas is describing mallorns—trees that he has never seen but are so important in Elvish lore that he knows them through legend. Similarly, the valley of the Silverlode is seen by Frodo as "a sea of fallow gold tossing gently in the breeze"; the mallorns crowning the hill of Cerin Amroth are "like living towers" in which "countless lights were gleaming, green and gold and silver" (II/vi).

We also learn much of what the Elves think about their realms from their various names. The Elves who dwell in Lothlórien are called the Galadhrim, which means "tree people," based on the Sindarin *galadh* ("tree"); the center of their sylvan society is Caras Galadhon, the "city of the trees." Thus their own name emphasizes their particular horticultural devotion. Although these people's interest in the natural world focuses, to a great extent, on arboreal life, the full range of their horticulture is much richer. For example, there are numerous descriptions of flowers and grass. The very name *Lothlórien* points to the Elves' interest in natural beauty and its preservation: *Loth* derives from a Sindarin word meaning "flower," making Lothlórien "Lórien of the flower." The realm of Galadriel and Celeborn is a place adorned with floral beauty, where the golden and white elanor and niphredil blossom. The name *Lórien* also recalls something important. Lórien is a name often used by the Elves to refer to Irmo, a Vala and one of the Fëanturi, or "masters of spirits." More accurately, however, Lórien is the name of Irmo's dwelling in Aman, a place known for its gardens—"the fairest of all places in the world"—where the Valar "find repose and easing of the burden of Arda." *The Silmarillion* tells of "the trees that flower in the gardens of Irmo" (28); these trees are tended by Melian, in whose realm Galadriel and Celeborn, the rulers of Lothlórien, dwell for many years. Curiously, Treebeard, perhaps the only character in Middle-earth who loves words and language as much as Tolkien himself, translates *Lothlórien* not as "Lórien of the flower" but simply as "Dreamflower" (II/iv). Treebeard is likely recalling that Irmo is also a "master of visions and dreams" (*Silm*, 28). But he may also be saying something about the nature and power of Lothlórien to capture and preserve through its horticulture the dreamlike, otherworldly beauty of Valinor. He also points out to Merry and Pippin that the original name of Lothlórien was Laurelindórenan, "Land of the Valley of Singing Gold" (II/iv).

It is also relevant to recall here that among his other talents, the young Tolkien seriously pursued artistic endeavors as a painter, sketch artist, and illustrator.[8] The illustrations gathered in *J. R. R. Tolkien: Artist and Illustrator* give ample proof of his skills in this area; among the most satisfying pieces of work is a watercolor of a tree—not just any tree, but a golden-leaved mallorn. The narrative passages in *The Lord of the Rings* that describe the beauties of Lothlórien reveal the artistic eye with which Tolkien viewed these imaginary scenes. One of the most detailed is this:

> They were standing in an open space. To the left stood a great mound, covered with a sward of grass as green as Springtime in the Elder Days. Upon it, as a double crown, grew two circles of trees: the outer had bark of snowy white, and were leafless but beautiful in their shapely nakedness; the inner were mallorn-trees of great height, still arrayed in pale gold. High amid the branches of a towering tree that stood in the centre of all there gleamed a white flet. At the feet of the trees, and all about the green hillsides the grass was studded with small golden flowers shaped like stars. Among them, nodding on slender stalks, were other flowers, white and palest green: they glimmered as a mist amid the rich hue of the grass. Over all the sky was blue, and the sun of afternoon glowed upon the hill and cast long green shadows beneath the trees. (III/vi)

The linguistic imagery is rich and focuses entirely on the natural beauty of the place. In short, it is a complete picture of horticultural activities, capturing both the tree itself and the flowers at its feet. Nature writer and poet Robert Siegel comments on the importance of Tolkien's level of descriptive detail with regard to the natural world, especially in Lothlórien:

> Tolkien finds that looking closely at nature can help one climb outside of himself and gain a sharp, contemplative awareness of the world. An example of this is when Frodo "discovers" the

bark on a tree in Lothlorien: "As Frodo prepared to follow him, he laid his hand upon the tree beside the ladder: never before had he been so suddenly and keenly aware of the feel and texture of a tree's skin and of the life within it. He felt a delight in wood and the touch of it, neither as forester nor as carpenter; it was the delight of the living tree itself."

For Tolkien, nature (when uncorrupted) is alive and manifests the goodness of Eru, or the One. It has deep, spiritual significance, reflective of Tolkien's own deeply spiritual nature. Legolas, the elves, and Lothlórien all seem to live in a constant contemplative awareness of nature, all time, and space. As the company travels, they are refreshed by the landscapes they travel through (except where nature has been corrupted, as in the Old Forest). Like the waybread, *Lembas,* bits of nature renew their strength.[9]

Beauty, Nature, and Reflections of Heaven

We can now begin to put this all together. As suggested earlier, the Elves' preoccupation is with the cultivation, refinement, and preservation of the aesthetic qualities of the created world. Rivendell and Lothlórien, two remaining realms of a once much greater Elvish presence in Middle-earth, are described as surviving outposts where a remnant dwell before their total and final withdrawal. In the scene described earlier, when Gildor and company make their first appearance near Woodhall in the Shire, they tell Frodo, "We are Exiles, and most of our kindred have long ago departed and we too are now only tarrying here a while, ere we return over the Great Sea. But some of our kinsfolk dwell still in peace in Rivendell" (I/iii). At the time this was first published, in 1953, readers could only infer the whole mythic panorama of Elvish history from disparate remarks scattered throughout the novel and its appendixes. That history includes their awakening at Cuiviénen in the farthest east of Middle-earth, their summons to the farthest west by the Valar, the sundering of their three kindreds, Fëanor's creation of the Silmarils and the epic feud over them, the Elves' war against Morgoth, the flight of the Noldor to Beleriand and Eriador after his defeat, and their gradual migrations westward again toward Valinor. Once *The Silmarillion* was published in 1977, a fuller understanding of this lengthy history became possible for readers, and we are now in a better position to comprehend the latent significance of passages in *The Fellowship of the Ring* in which Elves play an important role.

The narrator describes the scene at Woodhall, telling us of the Elves' torches that burn steadily "with lights of gold and silver." Though it is only a minor element of physical description and scene setting, this reference to "gold and silver" light is far from gratuitous or haphazard; it draws on an aesthetic system running through the whole of the Middle-earth canon, one that connects trees, green leaves, and the beauty of the environment with Elves and golden and silver light.[10] In chapter 1 we explored the mythic centrality of Yavanna in *The Silmarillion* as a quasi-divine being whose role is that of "lover of all things that grow in the earth." All living things "have their worth," she says, but among the *olvar* (plants), "I hold trees dear," and it is on their behalf that she sues for the creation of the Ents before the throne of Manwë. Yavanna herself is seen at times "standing like a tree under heaven, crowned with the Sun," from whose branches "spilled a golden dew upon the barren earth." Thus, as we noted, of all the Valar, Yavanna embodies Tolkien's fullest expression of ecological stewardship in his overall environmental vision. Yavanna's creation of Laurelin and Telperion, the Two Trees of Valinor, is said to be her greatest work, and their creation is described as fundamental in its mythic importance: "about their fate all the tales of the Elder Days are woven" (*Silm*, 38). The aesthetic qualities of the Two Trees contribute to the particular horticultural interest of the Elves.

First of all, the Two Trees replicate the lights of Illuin and Ormal, the Two Lamps made by Yavanna and her spouse Aulë in the Spring of Arda. We get a first glimpse of Yavanna's connection to the fertility of the ground here, for in the light of the lamps, "the seeds . . . that Yavanna had sown began swiftly to sprout and to burgeon," arising in "a multitude of growing things great and small, mosses and grasses and great ferns, and trees whose tops were crowned with cloud . . . but whose feet were wrapped in a green twilight" (*Silm*, 35). Melkor's destruction of these lamps brings an end to the Spring of Arda, and immediately after this, through singing, Yavanna brings Laurelin and Telperion into being. As we saw in the first chapter, this mythic narrative lays heavy emphasis on the specifics of their physical beauty. What we note now is that the golden and silver light in the Elves' camp near Woodhall points directly back to the Two Trees and Yavanna's role in beautifying the world with trees and flowers.

Why are the Elves particularly associated with Laurelin and Telperion? In the *Valaquenta*, we learn that their light is confined primarily to Valinor, the Blessed Realm in the west beyond the mountains of the Pelóri, while to the east Middle-earth lies "in a twilight beneath the stars," a darkness haunted by Melkor and the evil creatures wrought by him. It is in this environment that the Quendi and Atani—Elves and Men, the Children of Ilúvatar—are brought into being. Ilúvatar, it is said, sat "for an age . . . alone in thought." Then, he spoke: "Behold I love the Earth, which shall be a mansion for the Quendi and the Atani! But the Quendi shall be the fairest of all earthly creatures, and they shall have and shall conceive and bring forth more beauty than all my Children; and they shall have the greater bliss in this world" (*Silm*, 41).

The Quendi are especially beautiful in appearance and particularly skilled at conceiving and creating beauty. They are also especially dear to the Valar, who, when they first encounter them, are "filled . . . with the love of the beauty of the Elves." Desiring their fellowship, the Valar "summoned the Elves to Valinor, there to be gathered at the knees of the Powers in the light of the Trees for ever." Three kings of the Elves are brought to Valinor, where they are "filled with awe" for the Valar and the "light and splendour of the Trees"; returning east to their people at Cuiviénen, they persuade some of their race to undertake the journey westward (*Silm*, 49–52). The first among the three kindreds who respond to this summons are given "a land and a dwelling-place among the radiant flowers of the Tree-lit gardens of Valinor," where they "raised a high green hill" called Túna, on which falls the light of the Two Trees. The Elves establish Tirion, a city "with white walls and terraces" bathed in the trees' light. Shining on the Bay of Elvenhome beyond, the radiance of the Blessed Realm streams forth, "kindling the dark waves to silver and gold" and causing the first flowers to bloom east of the mountains of Aman (*Silm*, 59). Thus, by implication, when "lights of gold and silver" are said to burn steadily from the elves' torches in the Shire, the whole history of the Elves is subtly invoked: their own beauty, their love for the beauty of nature, their skill in creating things of beauty, and their love for the light of the Two Trees in the beautiful realm of Valinor to which they are summoned.

Several passages of the hobbits' description of Lothlórien make it clear that Tolkien intends the reader to understand this place as something of an earthly paradise—a version or an echo in Middle-earth of the Undying Lands of Valinor in Westernesse, to which all the Elves are drawn and some remember with deep longing. When Frodo steps onto the far bank of the Silverlode, "it seemed to him that he had stepped over a bridge of time into a corner of the Elder Days, and was now walking in a world that was no more. In Rivendell there was memory of ancient things; in Lórien the ancient things still lived on in the waking world. Evil had been seen and heard there, sorrow had been known; the Elves feared and distrusted the world outside: wolves were howling on the wood's borders: but on the land of Lórien no shadow lay" (II/vii). Later on, when Frodo's eyes are opened after his blindfolded march deeper into this land, the verdant beauty of the landscape is likened to that of "Springtime in the Elder Days." Frodo feels like he is "in a timeless land that did not fade or change or fall into forgetfulness." Sam says, "I feel as if I was *inside* a song, if you take my meaning." Later he comments, "If there's any magic about, it's right down deep, where I can't lay my hands on it," and he says, "It's like being at home and on a holiday at the same time" (II/viii). One of the effects of this land—the deep "magic" Sam refers to—is an apparent sharpening of the senses. Frodo, blindfolded, "found his hearing and other senses sharpened. He could smell the trees and the trodden grass. He could hear many different notes in the rustle of the leaves overhead, the river murmuring away on his right, and the thin voices of birds in the sky." And when he places his hand on the trunk of a mallorn, "never before had he been so suddenly and so keenly aware of the feel and texture of a tree's skin and of the life within it. He felt a delight in wood and the touch of it, neither as forester nor as carpenter; it was the delight of the living tree itself."

In this enchanted place whose floral and arboreal beauty is preserved, cultivated, and enhanced by the Elves' care over it, those who enter Lothlórien are vouchsafed a taste of both the ideal perfection of the natural order and the sensory capacity to appreciate its qualities. As we shall see, this is no hopeless or tragic nostalgia for lost and unrecoverable perfection, but rather a foretaste of expected and longed-for final fulfillment in a restored world. The Elves, fairest of the Children of Ilúvatar, are drawn to the gardens of Lórien and the light of the Two Trees in never-fading Valinor; in their own realms in Beleriand and elsewhere in Middle-earth, they both cultivate and preserve the memory of the beauty of the undying lands, re-creating it in artistic motifs recalling the flowers of Valinor; the green, gold, and silver lights of the Two Trees; and the living pillars of Oromë, "the Lord of Forests" (*Silm*, 29). In exile in the east, their strongholds at Rivendell and Lothlórien exist in order to restrain—and ultimately defeat—Sauron's evil, fulfilling the Elves' purpose in the moral dimension. But in light of the fact that the dominion of evil under Sauron and, by extension, Saruman marks the ruination of much that is beautiful in the environment, the Elves' mission is also discharged through their creation and preservation of natural beauty.

Aman and the Final Implications of Tolkien's Cosmology

As we know, Frodo's quest is completed and the Ring is destroyed; the Elves' long campaign of resistance against Sauron succeeds. With their purpose in Middle-earth—the preservation of freedom and beauty—accomplished, what is to become of Galadriel, the Galadhrim, Lothlórien, and indeed all the Elves in Middle-earth after the defeat of Sauron? Speculating on the present danger and its aftermath, Haldir, the sentry who leads the Company into Lothlórien, says:

> "The world is indeed full of peril, and in it there are many dark places; but still there is much that is fair, and though in all lands love is now mingled with grief, it grows perhaps the greater.
>
> "Some there are among us who sing that the Shadow will draw back, and peace shall come again. Yet I do not believe that the world about us will ever again be as it was of old, or the light of the Sun as it was aforetime. For the Elves, I fear, it will prove at best a truce, in which they may pass to the Sea unhindered and leave the Middle-earth for ever. Alas for Lothlórien that I love! It would be a poor life in a land where no mallorn grew."
> (II/vi)

Galadriel, too, seems to foresee Frodo's mission as part of the final chapter in the history of the Elves in Middle-earth before Lothlórien fades and they must depart. Having refused Frodo's offer of the Ring, she says with a note of sadness, "I will diminish, and go into the West." This tone is echoed in her farewell speech to Sam: "Our spring and our summer are gone by," she says, "and they will never be seen on earth again save in memory" (II/viii). As she and the other Elves fear, Lothlórien is doomed to fade. We are told that neither Frodo nor Aragorn will ever return to that place of beauty, and the sentences describing their last glimpse of Lothlórien might equally describe its final diminishment and disappearance: "Lórien was slipping backward, like a bright ship masted with enchanted trees, sailing on to forgotten shores, while they sat helpless upon the margin of the grey and leafless world" (II/ix).

The outcome of the Elves' mission, it seems, is actually a mixture of success and failure. Haldir speculates that it will be not a victory but "at best a truce." The One Ring is destroyed, Sauron is defeated, the free people of Middle-earth are delivered from the prospect of enslavement under a Dark Lord, and the physical world itself is spared from environmental devastation of the kind seen in Mordor and at Orthanc. Yet the power of the three elven rings is also depleted; the Elves must leave Middle-earth behind and, along with it, the reflection of Valinor's beauty preserved in Lothlórien. At the end of *The Lord of the Rings,* Frodo departs Middle-earth after the War of the Ring, and with him go Elrond and Galadriel, the greatest among the Noldor in the Third Age of Middle-earth. The world must now pass under the dominion of Men, much of its former beauty surviving only as a distant memory.

We must caution, however, that the sense of failure that accompanies the Elves' passing should not be attributed to flaws inherent in their environmental aesthetic. Indeed, if there is failure at all, it is because of flaws in the Elvish character and, to the extent that all the races of Middle-earth represent aspects of the human race in our world, flaws that are present in humanity. Like the other races in Middle-earth, Elves are presented as fallible. They are fallen creatures whose moral faults ultimately doom their efforts. To a great extent, their failure resides in the effort to resist all change, stemming from their prideful, selfish desire to have things as they once were. Yet their efforts to preserve the beauty of nature keep the memory of Valinor alive not only for themselves but for all races. We can read Haldir's remarks pessimistically, but we can also interpret them otherwise: there may be many dark places in the world, and it may be full of peril, but "still there is much that is fair"; though love may now be "mingled with grief, it grows perhaps the greater" as a result of their efforts. In the moral sense, the Elves' mission has been a success, made more poignant, perhaps, precisely because—

like Frodo's success—it is achieved at their own expense, costing them much that they hold dearest and love the most.

In *The Lord of the Rings*, we are told, the Elves—along with Frodo, Bilbo, and Gandalf—depart Middle-earth from the Grey Havens: "And the ship went out into the High Sea and passed on into the West, until at last on a night of rain Frodo smelled a sweet fragrance on the air and heard the sound of singing that came over the water. And then it seemed to him that as in his dream in the house of Bombadil, the grey rain-curtain turned all to silver glass and was rolled back, and he beheld white shores and beyond them a far green country under a swift sunrise" (VI/ix). Frodo, it seems, has gone to Aman, to the land of Valinor where the Elves were summoned eons earlier. But in the final sentence of the concluding section of *The Silmarillion*, published more than two decades later, the narrator indicates more clearly in metaphysical terms what Frodo's sea voyage on the white ship from the Grey Havens really means: "In the twilight of autumn [the ship] sailed out of Mithlond, until the seas of the Bent World fell away beneath it, and the winds of the round sky troubled it no more, and borne upon the high airs above the mists of the world it passed into the Ancient West, and an end was come for the Eldar of story and of song" (*Silm*, 304).

We must recall that after the end of the Second Age, the beautiful land of the Valar in the west no longer exists within the confines of the world, for as we learn in the *Akallabêth*, after the cataclysmic downfall of Númenor, "the land of Aman and Eressëa of the Eldar were taken away and removed beyond the reach of Men for ever . . . and the world was diminished, for Valinor and Eressëa were taken from it into the realm of hidden things" (*Silm*, 279). The realm of Arda, now a globed world, retains the memory of a beautiful land of perfection that, though physically inaccessible, still exists as something of a transcendent reality. The narrator of the *Akallabêth* states that the Eldar are "permitted still to depart and to come to the Ancient West and to Avallónë." Here, we come to one of the most important aspects of Tolkien's environmentalism because it touches on his theory of literature. The passage that follows says:

> Therefore the loremasters of Men said that a Straight Road must still be, for those that were permitted to find it. And they taught that, while the new world fell away, the old road and the path of

the memory of the West still went on, as it were a mighty bridge invisible that passed through the air of breath and of flight (which were bent now as the world was bent), and traversed Ilmen which flesh unaided cannot endure, until it came to Tol Eressëa, the Lonely Isle, and maybe even beyond, to Valinor, where the Valar still dwell and watch the unfolding of the story of the world. (*Silm*, 281–82)

We can explain the narrator's statements at the end of *The Lord of the Rings* and the specific choice of words in the final paragraph of *The Silmarillion*: the ship on which Frodo, Bilbo, and Gandalf sail takes them beyond the "Bent World" and above the "round sky" to the Blessed Realm.

In Tolkien's invented cosmology, Valinor has become an otherworldly realm—in Christian terms, a version of heaven. All the longings the Elves feel for Valinor may be reinterpreted as a recollection of and a desire for transcendent beauty that can no longer be fulfilled in this world. This explains the particularly sharp poignancy of their desire and the source of their sadness. Even among the exiled Dúnedain, lore masters are said to declare, "Avalónnë is vanished from the Earth and the Land of Aman is taken away, and in the world of this present darkness they cannot be found. Yet once they were, and therefore they still are, in true being and in the whole shape of the world as at first it was devised" (*Silm*, 281).[11]

This has direct implications for any who share Tolkien's Christian faith. The remembrance of the lost paradise of Eden, the longing for the future paradise of heaven, and visions of what these paradises were or will be like are never excuses for ignoring responsibility in the present world; they govern how that responsibility is to be fulfilled. Belief in heaven does not invalidate work on earth but rather should motivate it. At the end of the chapter "The Field of Cormallen," the elf Legolas speaks (in verse) of his longing for that heavenly realm:

Long are the waves on the Last Shore falling,
Sweet are the voices in the Lost Isle calling,
In Eressëa, in Elvenhome that no man can discover,
Where the leaves fall not: land of my people for ever! (VI/iv)

Almost in the same breath, he offers his practical help to Aragorn for healing the wounds of the earth. "In days to come, if my Elven-lord allows, some of our folk shall remove hither; and when we come it shall be blessed for a while. For a while: a month, a life, a hundred years of Men" (VI/iv). Both in their love of the beauty of Valinor and in their reverence for its memory expressed in the realms founded during their long exile, the Elves of Middle-earth represent the highest form of aesthetic valuation of the natural order. This is at the heart of Tolkien's environmental vision, and it is one of the chief points of this book.

Chapter 5

Woods, Wildness, and the Feraculture of the Ents

"I don't know about sides. I go my own way.... I am not altogether on anybody's side, because nobody is altogether on my side, if you understand me: nobody cares for the woods as I care for them, not even Elves nowadays" (III/iv). These remarks, vocalized by Treebeard the Ent in conversation with Merry and Pippin, capture in a few words another crucial part of the environmental ethic espoused by Tolkien in *The Lord of the Rings* and elsewhere in his writing. Wilderness in general, and forests in particular, must be cared for and preserved, and the necessity of doing so transcends all political boundaries, alliances, or "sides." Thus, Treebeard expresses both his sorrow over the lack of care for the natural order—even among the Elves, who, apart from the Ents, are the most ardent devotees of nature—and his single-minded independence and devotion to the preservation of woods and wilderness. Treebeard's words here and elsewhere attest to a love for the unpopulated landscapes of Middle-earth. He is the story's best spokesman for the forests of Middle-earth, and his perspective specifically illustrates the value and importance of wilderness.

In this chapter, we focus primarily on Fangorn Forest and on Treebeard, exploring the ecology of wilderness made evident through them. However, the Ents (also called the Onodrim) and their realm in Fangorn represent only one part of Tolkien's expansive vision of wilderness preservation, even as feraculture is only one part of the complex picture of his complete ecology.

Ents as Spokesmen and Shepherds

To understand the role of the Ents in Middle-earth, it is helpful to return to the story of their beginning in prehistory, before the coming of Elves,

Men, Dwarves, or Hobbits to Arda. As mentioned in previous chapters, in the beginning Ilúvatar creates the semidivine, angelic beings called the Ainur, who assist in composing a series of musical themes through which the created universe is brought into being—literally sung into existence. Some of the Ainur, we are told, then descend into the realm of Arda to assist further in its creation and care. Some of these are known as the Maiar, but the greatest and most powerful are the Valar, the "Powers of Arda," which, according to the narrator, Men often regard as gods.

Each of the Valar has a kind of lordship or dominion over an aspect of the world in which his or her creativity plays a decisive role. Elements of the natural world such as the wind, stars, clouds, water, stone, and earth are included among these. In and of itself, this bespeaks of the value of nature—the wild, untamed earth—independent of the Children of Ilúvatar. The Vala Yavanna is the "Giver of Fruits"; like the fertility goddesses of many mythologies—for example, the Old Norse goddess Freya, the Roman goddess Venus, the sacred Algonquian earth mother Nokomis, the Pawnee Atira, and the Japanese Inari—Yavanna is "the lover of all things that grow in the earth, and all their countless forms she holds in her mind, from the trees like towers in forests long ago to the moss upon stones or the small and secret things in the mould." Mostly, however, she is associated with trees:

> In the form of a woman she is tall, and robed in green; but at times she takes other shapes. Some there are who have seen her standing like a tree under heaven, crowned with the Sun; and from all its branches there spilled a golden dew upon the barren earth, and it grew green with corn; but the roots of the tree were in the waters of Ulmo, and the winds of Manwë spoke in its leaves. Kementári, Queen of the Earth, she is surnamed in the Eldarin tongue. (*Silm*, 27–28)

In the earliest days, when the world is newly formed, Yavanna sows into the ground of Arda seeds that germinate, sprout, and flourish into "a multitude of growing things great and small, mosses and grasses and great ferns, and trees whose tops were crowned with cloud as they were living mountains" (*Silm*, 35). As explained in the first chapter, the act for which Yavanna is best known is the creation of the Two Trees of

Valinor. Yet we must remember that it is through Yavanna that *all* plant and animal life comes into existence.

Because of her association with floral—especially arboreal—life, Yavanna occupies a special position in the mythology and cosmology of Middle-earth. It is Yavanna who is especially grieved by the abuse of the living creatures in the world, plants as well as animals. And among the Valar it is Yavanna who is most clearly positioned against the negative environmental implications of mechanical technology, even in its nascent stage under the creative impulse of the blacksmith Aulë—ironically, her spouse. Her acute concern for the natural world leads her to an explicit expression of her function as guardian of the trees, and the scene in which this idea is developed is worth exploration.

Early in the history of Arda, Melkor wreaks widespread destruction on all the works of the created world. Lamenting in particular how living things have been blighted under his poisonous influence, Yavanna says to Manwë, lord of the winds and heavens and king of the Valar, "All my works are dear to me. Is it not enough that Melkor should have marred so many? Shall nothing that I have devised be free from the dominion of others?" Manwë asks what she holds dearest in all her realm, and Yavanna answers:

> "All have their worth . . . and each contributes to the worth of the others. But the kelvar [animals] can flee or defend themselves, whereas the olvar [plants] that grow cannot. And among these I hold trees dear. Long in the growing, swift shall they be in the felling, and unless they pay toll with fruit upon bough little mourned in their passing. So I see in my thought. Would that the trees might speak on behalf of all things that have roots, and punish those that wrong them!" (*Silm*, 45)

Yavanna speaks here not only of the value of nature but also of its fragility and the great loss when parts of it are destroyed. Then come two ideas that even Manwë finds strange at first: plants and animals have moral significance and can be wronged, and those who do harm to nature ought to be punished.

Manwë demurs at first, but Yavanna reminds him that while he was busy with the winds and rains of heaven, she "lifted up the branches of great trees to receive them," and they "sang to Ilúvatar amid the wind and the rain." Here Tolkien echoes an idea found in many places, particularly in his own religious tradition: all aspects of creation—animals, plants, mountains, water, stars, and winds, as well as men and angels—participate in praise to the creator. Perhaps the most notable biblical expression of this is found in Psalm 148, one that Tolkien expressed a particular appreciation for. It begins, simply, "Praise the Lord!" and then calls on all creation to join in: sun and moon, stars, sea monsters, fire, hail, snow, clouds, beasts, cattle, young men, and virgins. Verse 9 is especially notable with regard to the words of Yavanna: "Praise the Lord ... Mountains and all hills; *fruit trees and cedars.*" With the rest of creation, trees have transcendent, spiritual value. This has been explored by Steven Bouma-Prediger, who comments on Psalm 148 and on related ideas found in Psalm 104, noting the important biblical ideas that "the human creature is but one creature among God's many creatures" and that any cultivation of the earth must be done "in harmony with the needs of other creatures and in such a way that all creation is enabled to sing praises to God the Creator, since the chief purpose of all creatures is to glorify God."[1]

Although, unfortunately, this important biblical principle has been ignored at times in Christendom, it continues to find expression in the Christian tradition (as it should), including in numerous Protestant hymns.[2] For example, "All Creatures of Our God and King," written by St. Francis of Assisi (1182–1226)—Lynn White's candidate for patron saint of ecologists—begins, "All creatures of our God and King / Lift up your voice and with us sing." It then calls on inanimate aspects of creation, including the "burning sun," the "silver moon," the "rushing wind," the "clouds that sail," and the "flowing water," to "make music for thy Lord to hear."[3] Not surprisingly, Tolkien includes in his legendarium not only ideas resonating with this great Catholic saint and hymn writer but also a character who seems almost Franciscan in conception. As Bradley Birzer points out, the wizard Radagast "embodies elements of St. Francis of Assisi and the Czech mythological figure Radegast, often imagined as a bird tamer. Like St. Francis, Radagast is described in *The Silmarillion* as 'the friend of all beasts and birds' and in *Unfinished Tales* as dressed in 'earth brown' like a Franciscan."[4]

As for Manwë, it seems that he understands this principle. After some inner deliberation and consultation in spirit with the creator Ilúvatar, he returns to Yavanna and answers, "When the Children awake, then the thought of Yavanna will awake also, and it will summon spirits from afar, and they will go among the kelvar and the olvar, and some will dwell therein, and be held in reverence, and their just anger shall be feared." He adds that the eagles, the Lords of the West, will also "go forth with wings like the wind," and Yavanna rejoices, saying, "high shall climb the trees of Kementári" for the eagles to nest in. But Manwë corrects her. "Nay," he says, "only the trees of Aulë [i.e., mountains] will be tall enough. In the mountains the Eagles shall house, and hear the voices of those who call upon us. But in the forests shall walk the Shepherds of the Trees" (*Silm*, 46). Here, Manwë, the wisest and most powerful being in Arda, speaks of the importance of the two great icons of wilderness: mountains and forests. Each will have its defenders in the service of the Valar: the eagles of Manwë in the mountains, and the Ents in the forests. In other words, Yavanna's wish for a spokesman on the trees' behalf has been answered; Manwë's statement amounts to nothing less than a prophetic foretelling of the eventual creation of Treebeard and the other Ents, the Shepherds of the Trees.

As treelike beings endowed with the ability to speak on behalf of the trees, the Ents are also shepherds who not only lead their flocks, figuratively, but also defend them against harm. As we see in *The Two Towers*, the Ents are prepared to punish those who wrong the trees. The value of the forests that the Ents represent, embody, and defend is made evident by Tolkien's inclusion of such figures in the narrative and the founding mythology of Middle-earth.

This valuation goes beyond trees and forests to include the whole concept of wilderness. Ents provide the reader with a perspective that highlights the value of unordered nature—Middle-earth in its original form. The places they favor are the free domains of birds, beasts, and other creatures that are either sparsely populated or wholly unpeopled by Elves, Men, Dwarves, or Hobbits. And typically, these areas are (or were originally) covered in dense forest. As the quotation at the beginning of this chapter indicates, Ents care for these places, expressing their respect for them by letting plants, flowers, and trees grow according to the principles inherent in their nature, countenancing neither the conversion of these lands to civilized use nor the organized cultivation of growing things.[5]

Indeed, Ents are strongly positioned against technologies in which the natural environment is used wastefully for ostensibly civilized purposes

—technologies that require the felling of trees for warmth and cooking, for example, or for the fueling of forges, smithies, and the like. Treebeard reserves his greatest hostility for the wizard Saruman, who, with "a mind of metal and wheels . . . does not care for growing things except as far as they serve him for the moment" (III/iv). Treebeard characterizes Saruman as "a black traitor" and a "tree-slayer" and particularly deplores Saruman's Orcs' wanton destruction of trees for malicious pleasure. Thus, in Treebeard we encounter an environmental perspective that is suspicious of any use of the natural landscape for destructive, selfish reasons, even when the perpetrators claim some practical justification for their purposes. For the Ents, even justifiable usage—in modern environmental politics, "wise use"—has to be situated on an ethical continuum whose furthest extreme is simple environmental waste and destruction.

By a specific set of ecological definitions, in modern environmental terms Ents might be called preservationists, Elves (and Entwives) conservationists, and Hobbits agriculturalists. In these terms, conservation might be called the management of the earth in an effort to preserve a balance among species and to control its use for the extraction of benefits without destroying it. Preservationism, in contrast, tends to be more species specific in its objectives and to regard the environment more atomistically rather than wholistically or organically. The ethics touching on these domains in Middle-earth is informed by a view compatible with that of John Elder, who writes:

> Within the wilderness ethic . . . there is an impulse to get back, to recover an understanding that the natural world has integrity and value beyond our human enterprises. . . . In this regard, wilderness possesses great spiritual value. It offers a realm for human activity that does not seek to take possession and that leaves no traces; it provides a baseline for strenuous experience of our own creaturehood.[6]

In many places throughout Tolkien's oeuvre, woods and forests—often wild, untamed, and trackless—serve as a potent image for the primordial value of the natural order, irrespective of and sometimes inimical to the self-centered concerns of Elves, Men, and other beings.

It should be said from the outset, however, that Tolkien portrays the position of neither the Ents nor the Elves nor the Hobbits as being fundamentally right or wrong in opposition to the others". Our emphasis throughout this book is on the comprehensive complexity of Tolkien's environmentalism. Although in some ways it is both exemplary and inspiring, the picture of Middle-earth afforded in the novels is by no means that of an Edenic paradise. The "Eden" phase in the history of Middle-earth (and of Aman, which we only glimpse in *The Lord of the Rings*)—has passed away eons earlier, shortly after the dawn of the First Age. None of the three ecological spheres we examine in this book enjoys an entirely untroubled relationship with the races that inhabit or visit it. Yet all contribute positively, and all three together are necessary for a complete ecology.

Ents and the Essence of Being

We can further understand the importance of Ents, and thereby the importance of Tolkien's ecology as portrayed through Treebeard and his kind, by studying the etymology of the word *Ent*. It has been observed that Tolkien used Old English to represent the "translated" language of the people of Rohan and applied the historical relationships between Old English and other Germanic dialects as an "overlay" for the relationship between Rohirric and the other branches of the languages of the Edain, the humans in Middle-earth (App F). Given these facts, there is authorial warrant for analyzing *Ent* not as a Quenya or Sindarin Elvish word but as an English one. Tolkien says in the appendixes that "Ent was the form of their name in the language of Rohan," and the language of Rohan, in its historicized translation, is "Old English." Even within the framework of *The Two Towers*, Tolkien indicates that the name is not haphazardly chosen.

What are Ents? This is also Théoden's question. After his recovery from the moral poison of Wormtongue, as he and Gandalf ride toward the Battle of Helm's Deep, Théoden, King of Rohan, catches his first glimpse of the Ents of Fangorn Forest. "What are they, Gandalf?" he asks. In terms that echo *The Silmarillion*—and that clarify what Manwë refers to in his prophecy—Gandalf explains to Théoden:

> They are the shepherds of the trees. . . . There are children in your land who, out of the twisted threads of story, could pick the

answer to your question. You have seen Ents, O King. Ents out of Fangorn Forest, which in your tongue you call the Entwood. Did you think that the name was given only in idle fancy? Nay, Théoden, it is otherwise: to them you are but the passing tale; all the years from Eorl the Young to Théoden the Old are of little count to them; and all the deeds of your house but a small matter. (III/viii)

Clearly, Gandalf associates Ents with storytelling and sees something fitting in the relationship between the word *Ent* and the creatures it describes. But why is the name no "idle fancy"?

First, although the word is obsolete in Modern English, in Old English it means "giant," a variant spelling of the more often encountered *eoten*. More precisely, the word *Ent* is a modernization of two apparent Old English synonyms found in *Beowulf*: *ent* and *eoten*, the latter cognate with the Old Norse *jötunn*, meaning "giant." Tolkien, however, glossed the word as *troll*, which can be seen in *The Lord of the Rings* when he uses the names *Ettenmoors* and *Ettendales*, translated by Aragorn as the "troll-fells" and "troll-country," respectively (I/xii). Based on this gloss, in preliminary drafts of the novel, Tolkien even had an early scene in which Gandalf's imprisonment is due to a hostile Giant Treebeard (*Shadow*, 363).[7] This concept obviously changed, however, and Treebeard became the benevolent Ent we know today. The association of giants with trees is unique to Tolkien, but the analogy is natural: most species of trees are taller than humans. But what led to the change from Ent as troll to Ent as Shepherd of the Trees?

In Tolkien's world, Ents are still giants and are, in a way, still related to trolls, which are said to have been bred by Morgoth in mockery of them. But they are also somehow connected to the *essence* of Middle-earth. Something of Treebeard's deeper role—his connection to the essential matters of his world—is suggested in Pippin's attempt to describe his eyes:

"One felt as if there was an enormous well behind them, filled up with ages of memory and long, slow, steady thinking; but their surface was sparkling with the present: like sun shimmering on the outer leaves of a vast tree, or on the ripples of a very deep lake. I don't know, but it felt as if something that grew in the ground—asleep, you might say, or just feeling itself as something between root-tip and leaf-tip, between earth and sky—had suddenly waked up, and was considering you with the same slow care that it had given to its own inside affairs for endless years." (III/iv)

The image here is one of deep and profound understanding. We see in Treebeard both wisdom and knowledge, both earth and sky, and both past and present. An analogue of this can be found in the mythology of ancient Scandinavia, where Yggdrásil, the "World Ash," is the pillar of the world, its branches holding up the roof of the sky, its trunk anchoring the center of the earth, its roots reaching down into the Well of Being where the three Norns—Urð, Verðandi, and Skuld (that which was, that which is, and that which is to come)—weave the fates of human beings.

Certainly the role, or task, of the Ents—their work as preservationists, shepherds, defenders of woods and wilderness—is also central to the essential connection between Treebeard and the whole realm of Middle-earth. As mentioned earlier, Ents are created (presumably by Ilúvatar) specifically in answer to Yavanna's wish for someone or something to speak on behalf of all living things. Tolkien associates this defense of the woods and wilderness of Middle-earth with the wise preservationism ascribed to Treebeard and imaginatively invites readers to make the same connection.

This raises another interesting etymological point. In his letters, Tolkien dismisses any association of the word *Ent* with the philosophical language of being or ontology (*Letters*, 211–12; see also 334–35). But the *Oxford English Dictionary* (*OED*) relates the word both to the botanical world and to abstract philosophical terms associated with "essential being." It cites *Ent* as an obsolete word with two senses. The first sense is that of "scion" or "graft," with a citation from *Hexham's Dutch Dictionary* of 1648: "Eester, an Ent, a Scion, a Sprig, or a Graft." Already the discussion is in the realm of botany and forestry. This is certainly one plausible explanation for how Tolkien's concept of *Ent* could have changed from giant troll to the Onodrim. The second sense of the word, though, derives from the late Latin *ens, entis*, and the *OED* cites an article from the ninth edition of the *Encyclopaedia Britannica*: "Starting from the formula 'the Ent (or existent),' the Nonent is existent unity . . . which reason discovers beneath the variety and mutability of things." The second sense of the word *Ent* is philosophical, and it describes a concept very close to that of "essence of being." The *OED* refers us to another entry, *Ens*, where we learn that the word means "something which has existence; a being, entity, as opposed to an attribute, quality, etc." or "an entity regarded apart from any predicate but that of mere existence." Finally, the editors of the dictionary tell us, *ens, entia* (and *ent*, we can surmise—a hypothetical abbreviation) means "essence." Putting all this together, then, an Ent can be said to be a giant as well as a scion, a sprig, or a graft and thus a tree, connected to (dare we say, "rooted in") the essence of being.

Tolkien disavowed this final meaning, and we must take his remarks seriously. Nonetheless, it is one of the hallmarks of Tolkien's philological perspective that words conceal levels and layers of meaning that are often unrecognized or unacknowledged by those who use them. Certainly Tolkien was a writer who had keen insights into the sources and meanings of words and their implications. Despite his disclaimer against any *intention* to invest *Ent* with philosophical implications, those implications are nonetheless present in the linguistic resources Tolkien drew on to create the Onodrim. Even if the connection between the word *Ent* and the essence of being is purely coincidental or unconscious, it is a coincidence that fits the character of Treebeard, as does the connection between giant and sprig. The philologist doth protest too much, we might opine.

Another related point about Treebeard is that he represents language itself, specifically the history of language. Among his other traits, Treebeard has a particular interest in and knowledge of linguistic matters. He thus fulfills the concept of the "fitness" between words and the things they name, suggested in the passage by Gandalf quoted earlier. This extends to Treebeard's knowledge of his own name: "I am an Ent, or that's what they call me. Yes, Ent is the word. *The* Ent, I am, you might say, in your manner of speaking. Fangorn is my name according to some, Treebeard others make it. Treebeard will do" (III/iv). What the reader soon learns about Treebeard is that he is something of a philologist and a linguist; he is also a philosopher of language. Taking up a position that, in our world, was debated by the Platonic philosophers and arises from time to time in subsequent history, Treebeard says that there is a connection not only between names and things but also between names and stories:

"I am not going to tell you my name, not yet at any rate.... For one thing it would take a long while: my name is growing all the time, and I've lived a very long, long time, so my name is like a story. Real names tell you the story of the things they belong to in my language, in the Old Entish as you might say. It is a lovely language, but it takes a very long time to say anything in it." (III/iv)

In linguistic-historical terms, Entish—Treebeard's language—echoes features of a well-recognized primitive stage in the development of the Indo-European languages.[8] Further evidence of this appears in Appendix F of *The Lord of the Rings,* where Tolkien notes that the Ents' language "was unlike all other: slow, sonorous, agglomerated, repetitive, indeed long-winded." The Ents themselves are natural linguists, "skilled in tongues, learning them swiftly and never forgetting them."

Philology was Tolkien's great love. As he repeatedly wrote in his letters, and as T. A. Shippey has illustrated even more fully, *The Lord of the Rings* is a philological novel inspired by philological principles.[9] In the character of Treebeard, Tolkien ties together his profound love of language and one of the novel's most important advocates for wilderness preservation. Treebeard speaks on behalf of the trees and forests of Middle-earth, indicating the value of wilderness. More particularly, the Ents serve both as an incarnation—or in*arbor*ation—of the vegetative life of that world and as sentient stewards of the untamed sylvan domain that is their province. The association between Treebeard's use of language and the essential life of the natural order may be one of Tolkien's most profound inventions.

The Forest for the Trees

Earlier we mentioned that one difference between conservation and preservation is the atomistic view of the latter: not only is wilderness as a whole important, but each individual species and indeed each individual member is important as well. As Robert Siegel comments, "For Tolkien the individual details of nature have spiritual significance that ascend a ladder from the physical world to the spiritual."[10] Love of the wild forest stems from a love of trees in general and of individual trees, and it can work in the other direction as well. Perhaps even more than a love of woods or forests, this love of individual trees is characteristic of Tolkien and is evident in his written works.

Further evidence of Tolkien's high regard for trees can be gathered from a variety of sources besides his fiction writing. Published photographs of the author in adulthood, for example, show him sitting or standing near some of his favorite trees. In his youth, before his particular gift for mythmaking and storytelling was fully developed, Tolkien discovered a talent for artistic illustration—in particular, for pencil sketches, pen-and-ink drawings, and watercolors. Trees were among his favorite subjects, and some of his most successful artistic endeavors were his depictions of trees. In his profoundly significant autobiographical allegory "Leaf by Niggle," the title character devotes his entire life to the painting of a single tree—with both a forest and a mountain range visible in the background, representatives of the wildness that is the central subject of this chapter.

Over the course of his life, in letters and in the prefaces to his books, Tolkien commented on his special love for trees. In 1955, for example, he wrote, "I am . . . much in love with plants and above all trees, and always have been; and I find human maltreatment of them as hard to bear as some find ill-treatment of animals" (*Letters*, 220). He echoes this theme much later in his printed response to a newspaper article on forestry: "In all my works I take the part of trees as against all their enemies," decrying the "stupidity" of "the destruction, torture and murder of trees perpetrated by private individuals and minor official bodies" (*Letters*, 419–20). In letters written during the Second World War, he details the beauty of England's trees for the benefit of his son Christopher, then serving in the Royal Air Force in South Africa.[11] In a letter written almost thirty years later—again to Christopher—he comments admiringly on the late-spring leafing out of oaks and ash trees, birches, beeches, and limes. However, lest indiscriminate use of tree imagery be ascribed to his works, in a 1972 letter Tolkien rejects a reader's hypothesis that the etymology of Aragorn's name includes an association with trees.[12] Still, in 1963, four days after the death of his lifelong friend C. S. Lewis, Tolkien describes his bereavement in these terms: "I have felt the normal feelings of a man of my age—like an old tree that is losing all its leaves one by one: this feels like an axe-blow near the roots" (*Letters*, 323, 341).

Indeed, it is remarkable to see how much and how often Tolkien wrote and thought about trees. Although in the introduction we denied that he was a "nature writer" in the usual sense of that term, some of his writing about trees might well be associated with that category. Tolkien preceded the modern environmental movement, but he was certainly aware of at least one of the great poets in the nature writing tradition: Gerard Manley Hopkins. Although we do not know what Tolkien thought of Hopkins's poetry, there is good evidence that he considered Hopkins a worthwhile model as both an author and a Christian thinker and that he had some level of interest in the life and work of the nineteenth-century poet. Tolkien even read from Hopkins's personal correspondence and quoted from it in a letter to C. S. Lewis (*Letters*, 127–28).

In that light, Hopkins's poem "Binsey Poplars Felled" (1879), mourning the loss of a stand of aspen trees, may be considered at least as corroborating Tolkien's view:

> My aspens dear, whose airy cages quelled,
> Quelled or quenched in leaves the leaping sun,
> All felled, felled, are all felled;
> Of a fresh and following folded rank
> Not spared, not one
> That dandled a sandaled
> Shadow that swam or sank
> On meadow and river and wind-wandering weed-winding bank.

One could easily imagine this poem as a direct inspiration for Tolkien's poem in *The Lord of the Rings* in which Bregalad the Ent laments the loss of his beloved poplars at the hands of the Orcs:

> O rowan mine, I saw you shine upon a summer's day,
> Your rind so bright, your leaves so light, your voice so cool and soft:
> Upon your head how golden-red the crown you bore aloft!
> O rowan dead, upon your head your hair is dry and grey;
> Your crown is spilled, your voice is stilled for ever and a day. (III/iv)

There is a striking similarity between the two poems in imagery, meter, length, and emotion. Both poems begin with a similar phrase: "My aspens dear" and "O rowan mine." Hopkins has the alliterative "quelled" and "quenched," while Tolkien uses "spilled" and "stilled," rhymes that echo the repeated "felled" in Hopkins's poem. Even the types of trees are similar—both are small, silvery hardwoods usually associated with mountain landscapes. But the deepest similarity is the tone of emotional attachment to the trees and his corresponding bereavement at their loss: "All felled, felled, are all felled . . . Not spared, not one," Hopkins writes, expressing grief at the completeness of the annihilation. Before Bregalad even begins his verse, he says, "The Orcs came with axes and cut down my trees. I came and called them by their long names, but they did not quiver, they did not hear or answer: they lay dead." Both poems work to the same effect. Readers may argue whether Tolkien succeeded as a poet, but his efforts in poems like this are akin to those of Hopkins, who, not unreasonably, can be considered among modern nature writers.

Tolkien's love of trees represents something of an incipient or implicit environmentalism and evokes a certain form of nature writing, yet it goes deeper to concepts foundational to the legendarium as a whole. Another positive example of the mythic significance of trees—not only en masse, in woods and forests, but also as individuals—appears in *The Return of the King* (VI/v), where a tangible sign of Aragorn's right to rule as Gondor's returning king is the discovery of a tree, a silver sapling on the side of Mount Mindolluin. This sapling, as Gandalf explains, is a descendent in the line of the White Tree, Nimloth the fair, from a seedling of Galathilion. Galathilion, in turn, is the offspring of the fruit of Telperion, the Eldest of Trees whose creation early in the First Age of Middle-earth, in the Spring of Arda, is described in *The Silmarillion*. This White Tree is the heraldic symbol of the survival and longevity of the City and the Realm of Gondor and a living counterpart of the withered tree in Gondor's Court of the Fountain. Aragorn's transplanting it there after his coronation heralds the closing of the tumultuous Third Age and the dawning of the Fourth Age in which the Elves will fade and—with environmental results that can be surmised—dominion of the earth will pass to the Second Children of Ilúvatar: Men. In the mythology of Valinor and of Middle-earth, as in many mythologies in our own world, trees play a crucial, even a central role.

Primordial Forest and Deforestation

So far, we have dealt only with Ents. However, a comprehensive view of forests-as-wilderness in Tolkien's entire mythic oeuvre would have to take into account not only Fangorn Forest and Treebeard the Ent but also the forests of Lothlórien, the Old Forest, and Mirkwood—three wooded wilderness areas of western Middle-earth during the Third Age. And it would also have to consider the vast forests of Beleriand that provide the setting for much of the action of the First and Second Ages of Middle-earth in *The Silmarillion*. These include Taur-im-Duinath, described as the "Forest between the Rivers" south of the river Andram, "a wild land of tangled forest in which no folk went, save here and there a few Dark Elves wandering"; Taur-en-Faroth, the "Forest of the Hunters," a "great wooded highlands" rising from the river Narog north of Nargothrond; Taur-na-Neldor, or Neldoreth, the "Forest of Beeches" forming the northern and smaller part of the land of Doriath; and Region, the "denser and greater woods" forming the southern portion of Doriath between the rivers Aros and Esgalduin (*Silm*, 123, 153; 55, 91–96; 114, 122, 168; 55, 93, 96–97, 233–34). The fact that the background landscape of Tolkien's imagined world includes so many forests is itself worthy of note.

Many passages in the Middle-earth canon comment on specific characteristics of trees and forests, contributing narrative details for the sake of verisimilitude—which Tolkien elsewhere calls "the inner consistency of reality." But they also hint at deeper moral and ethical implications. The world in which *The Lord of the Rings* is set, for example, includes both the woods of Lothlórien and the Old Forest. Lothlórien exhibits the positive results of careful preservation and stewardship by the Elves under Celeborn and Galadriel. The Old Forest, however, once part of the vast forest of Eregion, displays a certain malevolent ill will toward destructive intruders. By the time Frodo and his companions enter it at the end of the Third Age, this forest has become suspicious of all outsiders—a trait also evident in Treebeard—and is hostile even to wandering Hobbits, who pose no genuine threat. Yet the Old Forest is still worthy of preservation; though he is Master, Tom Bombadil makes no attempt to cultivate the forest or turn it from wild to tame. He even permits Old Man Willow—an undeniably dark-hearted being—to continue living.

One measure of the slow degradation of the natural environment in Middle-earth is the reduction of forestlands over many millennia of history. During the Council in Rivendell, Elrond—a character portrayed by Tolkien as one of the wisest in Middle-earth—remarks, "Of the Old

Forest many tales have been told: all that now remains is but an outlier of its northern march. Time was when a squirrel could go from tree to tree from what is now the Shire to Dunland west of Isengard. In those lands I journeyed once, and many things wild and strange I knew" (II/ii). Here Elrond makes an explicit connection between forests and wildness. There is also a suggestion that these things "wild and strange" are worth knowing and that tales about them are worth telling—in short, that wilderness is valuable. The implication is that the loss of wilderness and of the great forests—the deforestation of the "one wood"—is sad and regrettable.

Hugh Keenan, writing about the importance of trees in Middle-earth, notes: "The life history of these living trees demonstrates the literal and symbolic import of their preservation. For as the forests have disappeared by being pushed back, burned, or cut down, the land and its people have suffered. The return of the forests to Isengard and to the Shire signals the return of life to the dead and dying lands."[13] According to Keenan, Tolkien's writing associates deforestation with "dead and dying lands." Of course, the Ents provide an ideal voice for expressing this. Later on, Treebeard makes a comment similar to Elrond's, describing a "once upon a time" when "there was all one wood . . . from here to the Mountains of Lune." He makes use of the same "time was" phrase as Elrond: "Those were the broad days! Time was when I could walk and sing all day and hear no more than the echo of my own voice in the hollow hills" (III/iv). Another of Middle-earth's wisest figures, Treebeard is giving the hobbits more than a geography or history lesson; it is an environmental one as well. The Ent is in full agreement with Elrond: the loss of Middle-earth's great forests is tragic. And when the Ents later recover a portion of it in Isengard, or when the Hobbits do so in the Shire, even this limited extent of reforestation is worthwhile, symbolic of nothing less than "the return of life."

Although the attacks on Fangorn by Saruman and his Orcs are described briefly in *The Lord of the Rings,* the long-term process of widespread deforestation is not detailed or even hinted at there. But in a philological essay on the names of rivers in Middle-earth published posthumously in *Unfinished Tales,* Tolkien ascribes the catastrophic reduction of this extended forest to two negative forces: the Númenórean shipwrights' greedy desire for timber, and Sauron's stratagems in his war against the Elves in the middle of the Second Age:

> In the earlier days, at the time of the first explorations of the Númenóreans, . . . Minhiriath and Enedwaith were occupied by vast and almost continuous forests, except in the central region of the Great Fens. The changes that followed were largely due to the operations of Tar-Aldarion, the Mariner-king, who formed a friendship and alliance with Gil-galad. Aldarion had a great hunger for timber, desiring to make Númenór into a great naval power; his felling of trees in Númenór had caused great dissensions. In voyages down the coasts he saw with wonder the great forests, and he chose the estuary of the Gwathló for the site of a new haven entirely under Númenórean control. (*UT*, 262)

This haven, named Lond Daer, becomes the center for the extensive logging operations that follow. At first, the native inhabitants of these lands do nothing to halt the harvesting of timber. Later, however, when more extensive felling of trees starts to destroy their forests, they respond with violence. This, in turn, provokes the Númenóreans to even more rapacious activity:

> The native people were fairly numerous and war-like, but they were forest-dwellers, scattered communities without central leadership. They were in awe of the Númenóreans, but they did not become hostile until the tree-felling became devastating. Then they attacked and ambushed the Númenóreans when they could, and the Númenóreans treated them as enemies, and became ruthless in their fellings, giving no thought to husbandry or replanting. (*UT*, 262)

At first, we learn, logging is confined to the banks of the Gwathló, the river dividing the lands of Minhiriath and Enedwaith in the southern part of Eregion, and the cut timber is floated down this river to the haven at Lond Daer. Eventually, however, the Númenóreans drive "great tracks and roads into the forests" north and south from the banks of the Gwathló. As a result, "The devastation wrought by the Númenóreans was incalculable. For long years these lands were their chief source of timber, not only for their ship-yards at Lond Daer and elsewhere, but also for Númenór itself. Shiploads innumerable passed west over the sea" (*UT*, 262). Shortly thereafter, during the war in Eriador between Sauron and the Elves, "the denuding of the lands was increased." Although the exiled natives at first welcome Sauron in the hope of claiming a victory against the Númenóreans, within short order Sauron's raiders "made much havoc on the fringe of the forests, setting fire in the woods and burning many of the great wood-stores of the Númenóreans." By the time Sauron has been defeated and driven out of Eriador eastward into Greenwood the Great—renamed "Mirkwood," reflecting his evil influence—"most of the old forests had been destroyed." The river Gwathló now flows through a land that, once surrounded by thick forest, has become "a land . . . far and wide on either bank a desert, treeless but untilled" (*UT*, 263).

What are we to make of this history? The later deforestation is due to Sauron and is readily associated with evil in its most personal form. The earlier destruction of the forests, however, is due to the Númenóreans, who at that time are at war with Sauron. Is it, then, justified? There are several hints that the answer is no. The first is the association between deforestation and "a great hunger," which is to say, "lust"—Númenor's desire to make itself into a great naval power. Tolkien's sympathies are never with those who are hungry for power. The mariners' environmental waste causes dissension first in Númenor and later in Middle-earth, and the narrative goes so far as to describe it as "incalculable" devastation. All this takes place as part of the downfall of the Númenórean civilization. Long before the modern environmental concern over destruction of the tree cover in U.S. cities or of South American rain forests, Tolkien had already associated the downfall of a great civilization with its lust for lumber. And he expressed this in chilling descriptions that could apply equally well to modern clear-cutting practices.

It is in this context that we see the hostility of the Old Forest. This hostility appears to the Hobbits only in "old bogey-stories Fatty's nurses used to tell him" (I/vi), but in reality it is characteristic of a much longer history of hostile relations between various races and Middle-earth's forests. By the time of the late Third Age, this hostility has hardened into something like a general environmental principle according to which Men and other races are alienated from the wild regions of the landscape. This situation is reflected in Tolkien's narrative descriptions of various forests, which often evoke an atmosphere of suspicion, hostility, and enmity, as illustrated by the scene of Bilbo and the dwarves' entrance into Mirkwood in *The Hobbit*. Along with the adjectives "gloomy," "strangled," and "blackened," the trees are said to be listening to the companions, who "thump along" out of the light and into the darkness. It is oppressive. "There was no movement of air down under the forest-roof, and it was everlastingly still and dark and stuffy." The description of the gloom as "a sort of darkened green glimmer" enhances the sense of eerie oppression, as do glimpses of things "scuttling behind tree trunks" and sounds of "grunts, scufflings, and hurryings in the undergrowth" (*H*, 124). This is an environment that is clearly not friendly to visitors.

Many years later, Frodo and his companions have a similarly disquieting experience in the Old Forest. Merry gives a preliminary account of the strange atmosphere there:

> "The Forest is queer. Everything in it is very much more alive, more aware of what is going on, so to speak, than things are in the Shire. And the trees do not like strangers. They watch you. They are usually content merely to watch you, as long as daylight lasts, and don't do much. Occasionally the most unfriendly ones may drop a branch, or stick a root out, or grasp at you with a long trailer. But at night things can be most alarming, or so I am told. I have only once or twice been in here after dark, and then only near the hedge. I thought all the trees were whispering to each other, passing news and plots along in an unintelligible language; and the branches swayed and groped without any wind." (I/vi)

This clearly suggests not merely a passive and indifferent danger but an active hostility directed toward the hobbits—or toward any who venture into the Old Forest. Soon the hobbits are forced to pick their way among "many writhing and interlacing roots," and the "uncomfortable feeling that they were being watched with disapproval" deepens to a sense of "dislike and even enmity." In response to a cry of anguish by Pippin, "the wood seemed to become more crowded and more watchful than before." Eventually they feel pressing in on them "the ill will of the wood." For Frodo, the wood has now become "abominable." In a desperate effort to encourage his companions, Frodo sings a song against despair, but the words include the ill-timed observations that "all woods ... must end at last" and "east or west all woods must fail." At that point, "a large branch fell from an old overhanging tree with a crash into the path," as the trees "seemed to close in before them" (I/vi).

At this juncture, the Old Forest has acquired an overwhelming sense of menace that, later in the afternoon, seems to guide the hobbits in a certain direction against their will, through "deep folds in the ground... discovered unexpectedly" or "wide moats and sunken roads ... choked with brambles." Of course, the end result of this misdirection is that the hobbits are guided irrevocably into the valley of the river Withywindle, where they are lulled into a stupefied state of drowsy enchantment. Just before dozing off, Frodo lifts his heavy eyelids and sees "leaning over him a huge willow-tree, old and hoary. Enormous it looked, its sprawling branches going up like reaching arms with many long-fingered hands, its knotted and twisted trunk gaping in wide fissures" (I/vi). Merry and Pippin are trapped in two of these fissures, and the hobbits' rescue is accomplished only by a natural force even more powerful than Old Man Willow: Tom Bombadil.

Again the reader learns that there is a troubled history between Hobbits and the Old Forest. The source of these difficult relations stems from the Hobbits' early occupation of the Shire in the Third Age of Middle-earth. Merry comments:

> "The trees do actually move, and can surround strangers and hem them in. In fact long ago they attacked the Hedge: they came and planted themselves right by it, and leaned over it. But the hobbits came and cut down hundreds of trees, and made a great bonfire in the Forest, and burned all the ground in a long strip east of the Hedge. After that the trees gave up the attack, but they became very unfriendly." (I/vi)

However, the root of the problematic relationship between the wild woodlands and the sentient beings[14] of Middle-earth is broader and older than any dispute between the Hobbits and the trees of Old Man Willow's forest. It goes back to the deforestation of the primeval forest discussed earlier.

Other trees and forests for which Treebeard and the Ents serve as shepherds and as spokesmen in Middle-earth often seem hostile to the plans and purposes of those who encroach on or travel through them. In *The Two Towers*, the Ents' suspicion of intruders is evident in the first moments of Treebeard's encounter with the hobbits. Pippin's remark concerning Fangorn Forest—"I almost felt I liked the place"—provokes Treebeard's reply: "Almost felt you liked the Forest! That's good! That's uncommonly kind of you. . . . Turn round and let me have a look at your faces. I almost feel that I dislike you both" (III/iv). Hostility is also apparent in the hobbits' first impressions of Fangorn: "It is all very dim, and stuffy, in here," said Pippin. He later adds, "Look at all those weeping, trailing, beards and whiskers of lichen! And most of the trees seem to be half covered with ragged dry leaves that have never fallen" (III/iv).[15] Merry, however, goes on to make a distinction between the atmosphere in Fangorn Forest and that in Mirkwood:

> "But the Sun at any rate must peep in sometimes," said Merry. "It does not look or feel at all like Bilbo's description of Mirkwood. That was all dark and black, and the home of dark black things. This is just dim, and frightfully tree-ish. You can't imagine animals living here at all, or staying for long."
> "No, or hobbits," said Pippin. (III/iv)

Though not hostile in the same way that Mirkwood is in *The Hobbit*, this forest still seems reluctant to admit them. Akin to this, of course—and on both sides of the line—is the Old Forest's hostility to these same hobbits in *The Fellowship of the Ring*, which culminates in Old Man Willow's trapping Merry up to his waist—and Pippin entirely—in a snapped-shut crevice in his hollow trunk.

Considering Tolkien's love of trees, we might ask why he would paint such a dark and even evil picture of Mirkwood and the Old Forest. In Fangorn, the reader's sympathies clearly lie with the Ents, but in Mirkwood and the Old Forest, it is with Bilbo and the dwarves and with the four hobbits. One answer is probably simply narrative in nature. We must remember that Tolkien above all wanted to tell a good story, and having these characters pass through a frightening and often hostile woods makes for a dramatic atmosphere. For the most part, however, even Tolkien's narrative choices are rooted consciously or unconsciously in deeper issues. A second answer, then, might be found in Sauron's evil effects on Mirkwood and perhaps the effects of other malevolent figures, such as the Barrow-wights and Old Man Willow, on the Old Forest. Certainly Morgoth and Sauron have the ability to corrupt things that are originally or essentially good. If Morgoth can twist and corrupt Elves to breed Orcs and can breed Trolls in mockery of Ents, then he can also corrupt nature.

But a third answer, and perhaps the one most relevant to our discussion, is that although the two places are certainly different in nature in terms of their hostile regard for destructive intrusion, ultimately there is no discrepancy between the Old Forest and Fangorn. The hostilities are ancient, and there is a long-standing desire to defend the forests and to punish those who do wrong. This can sometimes work through strange alliances. For example, the physical description of Old Man Willow in *The Fellowship of the Ring* is remarkably similar to that of Treebeard in *The Two Towers*. As the hobbits later learn from Treebeard, some trees "have bad hearts," and when Merry mentions the Old Forest as an example, Treebeard verifies the connection. Old Man Willow, we may presume, is one of these: an originally "good" tree that has gone "bad." Further information is provided later when, after the Ents' destruction of Isengard, Merry and Pippin mention a species called Huorns. These are either trees that have been "wakened" to sentient life or, more likely, Ents that have become more treelike; Merry says, "They stand here and there in the wood or under its eaves, silent, watching endlessly over the trees." The similarity with the Old Forest is also suggested when Merry says, "they can move very quickly, if they are angry," and you can suddenly find "you are in the middle of a wood with great groping trees all around you." They still have voices and can converse with Ents, but, says Merry, "they have become queer and wild. Dangerous" (I/vi). As noted earlier, the hostility of the Old Forest originates in its response to hostile penetration; "Greenwood the Great" is refashioned as "Mirkwood" only after Sauron enters it, and Treebeard's suspicion of outsiders is only the understandable result of Saruman's and the Orcs' malevolent treatment.

To summarize, between the Hobbits and the Old Forest, just beyond the borders of the Shire, there is a long and troubled history, and the episode in the first part of the trilogy illustrates a general principle in *The Lord of the Rings* and the mythology informing it: people are not always friendly toward the environment—toward wilderness in particular—and, in response, the environment is not always friendly toward people. In Middle-earth, as in our world, mistreatment of the natural world results in an environment that is less hospitable to its inhabitants: Man, Hobbit, Dwarf, or Elf. It should be noted that Tolkien portrays the natural world as originally neutral at worst—if not actually friendly—toward humans and other races, and the disharmony that grows between them is only the secondary response of an endangered environment.

Forests, Wilderness, and the Future

Before we conclude, it is worth mentioning that although forests provide primary and important images of wildness and wilderness in Tolkien's writing, they are not the only examples. Indeed, Tolkien's appreciation for other wilderness landscapes can be glimpsed in countless passages throughout the story. Among the many skillful narrative techniques he employs, alongside the detailed descriptions of localized settings, Tolkien often grants the reader panoramic glimpses of the vistas opening out before his characters. After the Council of Elrond, for example, as the Company of the Ring sets out on its journey, the travelers cross a bridge leading out of the deep valley onto "the high moor where the wind hissed through the heather." With one last glance back at Rivendell, "the Last Homely House," they enter one of the most deserted wilderness areas in Middle-earth. South of the Ford of Bruinen and west of the Misty Mountains, the landscape is "much rougher and more barren than in the green vale of the Great River in Wilderland on the other side of the range." As Frodo and his companions make their way south and east, we get a sense of the immensity of this landscape, and of its emptiness:

> Each day the land looked much the same as it had the day before. Yet steadily the mountains were drawing nearer. South of Rivendell they rose ever higher, and bent westwards; and about the feet of the main range there was tumbled an ever wider land of bleak hills, and deep valleys filled with turbulent waters. Paths were few and winding, and led them often only to the edge of some sheer fall, or down into treacherous swamps. (II/iii)

The travelers make their way "for many sunless days" against the icy wind blowing west from the mountains, sleeping by day in hollows or "hidden under the tangled thorn-bushes that grew in thickets in many places." A full fortnight passes in this way, and Gandalf remarks that they cover "five-and-forty leagues [150 miles] as the crow flies," indicating just how vast the distances are in this part of the continent.

About this time, the wind changes direction, "the swift-flowing clouds lifted and melted away, and the sun came out, pale and bright. . . . The travellers reached a low ridge crowned with ancient holly-trees whose grey-green trunks seemed to have been built out of the very stone of the hills. Their dark leaves shone and their berries glowed red in the light of the rising sun" (II/iii). Here, on the borders of the ancient Elvish country of Eregion, Frodo gets his first glimpse of Mount Caradhras, whose northern precipice, still largely in shadow, "stood up like a tooth tipped with snow" and, where the sunlight slants upon it, glowing red. Many other passages could be cited here, and readers no doubt have their favorites, but the point has been made: the wilderness of Middle-earth is vast, it is forbidding, and it is sometimes dangerous, but it is also beautiful. And in the ethos informing the creation of Middle-earth, it is of great intrinsic value.

Even more important, every great community or settled, cultivated area in Middle-earth is enhanced and made both more wonderful and more complete by its proximity to wilderness. The Shire is situated adjacent to the Old Forest; Rivendell, the Last Homely House, is at the edge of the Wild; Rohan is bordered by Fangorn as well as by mountains to the west and south; Minas Tirith sits at the foot of the White Mountains. Tolkien may be doing no more than following an imaginative tradition long used in fairy tale and romance of situating the hall, village, or castle at the edge of the dark and mysterious wood, but he uses this tradition well. Whether by accident or not, he paints a clear picture of the value and even necessity of juxtaposing civilization and wilderness.

So what can be said concerning the future of wilderness, forest, and untamed mountains? As readers of the books and viewers of the films know, the Ents join the war against the forces of enslavement and ecological waste, contributing to the overthrow of Saruman and thus, indirectly, to Sauron's destruction and the liberation of Middle-earth. For the moment, or perhaps for a long while, the overwhelming threat of disaster—including environmental disaster—is removed. The positive results of these developments for the natural world are suggested in a number of ways, including the flowering of the White Tree of Gondor, the Ents' reclamation of Orthanc, the preservation of the forests of

Fangorn and Lothlórien, and the restoration of fertility to the Shire in the record-breaking harvest of the year 1420 of the Third Age.

In the longer term, apart from a few scattered prophetic, eschatological passages concerning the eventual perfection of Arda at the end of time, Tolkien's writings contain only a few scattered details of future developments touching on Middle-earth, its inhabitants, or the environment. In the *Ainulindalë*, for example, we learn that beside the music of the Ainur, whereby the world is made, "a greater still shall be made before Ilúvatar . . . after the end of days," and in the *Quenta Silmarillion*, it is said that the constellation Menelmacar "forebodes the Last Battle that shall be at the end of days." Just before Aragorn's discovery of the sapling of Nimloth, Gandalf says, "The Third Age of the world is ended, and the new age is begun; and it is your task to order its beginning and to preserve what may be preserved. For though much has been saved, much must now pass away. . . . For the time comes of the Dominion of Men, and the Elder Kindred shall fade or depart" (VI/v). The implications for the environment are unclear, and readers are left to speculate what this might mean in terms of stewardship of the world under the dominant influence of Men—human beings. The brief, allusive remarks concerning relations between Men and the environment in the Prologue to *The Lord of the Rings* suggest a decline, with the "Big Folk" (human beings) living much less harmoniously with the natural world than the Hobbits do.

The melancholy, even elegiac tone of the final scene in which Treebeard appears suggests much the same thing. At the edge of Isengard, now "the Treegarth of Orthanc," Aragorn—the newly crowned King of Gondor—thanks the Ents for their role in their enemies' downfall and concludes with a blessing: "may your forest grow again in peace." But Treebeard's face "became sad," and his comments seem to foreshadow a loss:

> "Forests may grow," he said. "Woods may spread. But not Ents. There are no Entings."
>
> "Yet maybe there is now more hope in your search," said Aragorn. "Lands will lie open to you eastward that have long been closed."
>
> But Treebeard shook his head and said: "It is far to go. And there are too many Men there in these days." (VI/vi)

These remarks have to do with the ancient separation of the Ents from the Entwives, a rift that stems from the male and female Onodrims' unresolved argument concerning preservation of the wilderness versus its conservation for practical use. But Treebeard goes on to say farewell to Galadriel and Celeborn:

> "It is long, long since we met by stock or by stone. . . . It is sad that we should meet only thus at the ending. For the world is changing. I feel it in the water, I feel it in the earth, and I smell it in the air. I do not think we shall meet again."
>
> And Celeborn said: "I do not know, Eldest." But Galadriel said: "Not in Middle-earth, nor until the lands that lie under the wave are lifted up again. Then in the willow-meads of Tasarinan we may meet in the Spring. Farewell!" (VI/vi)

Frodo's song in the Old Forest says, "though dark they stand, / all woods there be must end at last," and "east or west all woods must fail." It appears that during the coming age, the wild forests of Middle-earth will diminish and, along with them, the Shepherds of the Trees will fade and vanish. Gandalf's comment here is even more pointed: "The New Age begins," he says to Treebeard, "and in this age it may well prove that the kingdoms of Men shall outlast you, Fangorn my friend" (VI/vi).

The wilderness areas of Middle-earth are greatly diminished when they are viewed as raw material for technological reshaping. In this process, the land loses its essential value—its goodness-as-created—in favor of a dubious instrumental value. Ultimately, this process threatens to deprive it of all value. In chapter 8 we discuss several local or regional landscapes where this in fact has happened. More generally, looking toward the future, Middle-earth is threatened with becoming a much diminished world when places like Fangorn and the Old Forest cease to exist, for once the environment is completely reshaped, the lifeforms that subsist within it lose the rooted sense of place on which they depend for meaning and for life itself.

Chapter 6

The Necessity of Margins in Middle-earth's Mingled Ecologies

The moral, ethical, philosophical, and theological issues contained in J. R. R. Tolkien's writings justify our claim that although his work is not generally acknowledged in contemporary "ecocriticism," his treatments of ecological responsibility and environmental stewardship are not merely gratuitous additions but reflections of the author's deeply held convictions. In the previous chapters, our exploration of Tolkien's threefold vision of environmental responsibility looked at the agrarianism of the Hobbits, the aestheticism of the Elves, and the preservationism of the Ents as valid responses of sentient creatures in the context of the created world they occupy. Although we examined the farmlands of the Shire, the cultivated trees and gardens of Rivendell and Lothlórien, and the wilderness areas of Fangorn and the Old Forest as separate, discrete domains, it is apparent that they are not really separable from one another. The forests, fields, and farms of Middle-earth are all part of a total environment, a larger whole. More important, they are dependent on and commingle with one another in the comprehensive ecology of Middle-earth.

With reference to the Bristol Cliffs near his home in Vermont, John Elder writes:

> Ecologists speak of the meeting between two ecosystems as an "ecotone," partaking of some of the physical attributes of each constituent environment and harboring some of the creatures from each as well. Within such a meeting ground, "edge-effect" prevails, in a diversity of species that exceeds those of the separate ecosystems as well as in the relative density of individual

organisms. An edge is a risky opportunity. It offers new sources of food for creatures venturing out from the fundamental safety of familiar ground, but also exposes them as potential sources of nourishment for fellow opportunists creeping in from the opposite side.[1]

Tolkien's environmental vision, we have asserted, is both complex and comprehensive, and this is partly because the imaginary world he created is largely based on the pattern of our own. One could almost read Elder's description as an account of what happens to the four hobbits—or what threatens to happen to them—as they move from the familiar, stable environment of the Shire through the various phases of their journey into the unstable wilderness of Eregion and then to Rohan, Gondor, Mordor, and back again to the Shire at the story's end. But Elder's salient point is that such places in the natural world are significant sources of rich interconnections across their boundaries. They can also be crucial to the overall health of the environments they delineate.

Similarly, in an essay titled simply "Margins," Wendell Berry cites the farming practices of the Peruvian Andes as a positive example of sustainable agriculture that "utilizes—indeed, depends upon—its margins." In these transitional environments, "wild and semi-domesticated species thrive"; agriculture of this kind "does not push its margins back to land unsuitable for farming . . . but incorporates them into the very structure of its farms." Berry describes this "accommodat[ion] of the margin within the form" as allowing "the wilderness or nature to thrive in domesticity, to accommodate diversity within unity." Further, the example of Peruvian agriculture leads him to see "how crude and dangerous are our absolute divisions between city and farmland, farmland and wilderness." He regards "integration of the human community with its natural margins" as a worthy goal.[2]

Berry concludes the essay by reasserting what he calls "the necessity of margins." We might draw a similar conclusion by observing that margins are necessary in Middle-earth. Over the course of the long narrative of *The Lord of the Rings*, Frodo and the other hobbits travel across a vast expanse of geography, into and out of various regions and locales that fit into the three major environmental domains we have outlined. In many places, the boundaries between these regions are sudden and distinct—for example, the gated wall separating Bree from the outside world, the Doors of Dúrin between the Elves' land of Hollin and the Dwarves' realm in Moria, the Pillars of Argonath at the northern boundary of the Kingdom of Gondor, or even the Black Gate or the fortified outpost at Minas Morgul behind which lies the ruined environment of Mordor. These sudden transitions often anticipate or coincide with important events in the plot or in the development of a character. But in other cases, there is significant overlap between environments, with much more gradual transitions from one to the next. It is these overlapping and commingling ecological zones—these margins—that this chapter addresses, for they have rather important theoretical and ecological implications.

Liminality, Ecotones, and Thick Margins

Before looking at several instances of ecotones in *The Lord of the Rings*, we must briefly mention some issues associated with borders and margins and connect the relevant ecological concepts with corresponding literary ones. Whether natural or artificial, the kinds of boundaries described here might be called liminal, from the Latin *līmen*, "threshold," and *līmes*, "boundary" or "limit." In the real world, and in the imaginary worlds envisioned in literature, such places can have enormous personal, social, and environmental significance.

Early in the twentieth century, anthropologist Arnold van Gennep used the term *liminal* to describe ceremonial rites of passage—occasions of social transition marking important milestones in the growth and maturation of an individual, a family, or a larger social group.[3] The significance of birth, death, marriage, graduation, promotion, retirement, and many other events is generally indicated by specialized forms of behavior designed to highlight their meaning and make them memorable. In the 1960s, Victor Turner refined this idea to define liminal events as "movements betwixt and between the *formerly* familiar and stable and the *not-yet* familiar and stable."[4] More recently, the concept of liminality has fueled a minor industry in literary criticism, as scholars have shown how marks of liminality—threshold moments—in literary texts are often assigned prominent symbolic and thematic meanings. Thomas Pison's "Liminality in *The Canterbury Tales*" is an important example of an early application of this theoretical concept to medieval literature, as is Sara Higley's 1986 discussion of *Beowulf*.[5] More recent attestations have literary scholars applying the idea to such diverse writers as Kingsley Amis, Ralph Waldo Emerson, Arthur Conan Doyle, and Maxine Hong Kingston, and even to animé films.[6] Perhaps more than anything else, the recent completion of two doctoral dissertations on liminality demonstrates an emerging preoccupation with this subject as a cutting-edge topic.[7]

Van Gennep, Turner, and most literary critics are interested primarily in cultural thresholds symbolized by feasts, parties, and social and religious rituals and in such man-made boundaries as doorways, mileposts, bridges, and walls. They are not interested in the edges or margins of whole environments. However, no one would dispute the fact that natural boundaries such as the edge of a forest, the entrance to a cave, or the shoreline of an ocean—edges defining the borders of wilderness, the subterranean world, or the sea—can have a powerful effect on people. Liminal sites like these often spell foreboding, sometimes engendering the contemplation of death and mortality, the brevity of life, or something metaphysical—good or evil—beyond the bounds of the visible world. In the chapter titled "Fog on the Barrow-downs," for example, at the moment the hobbits see the standing stones, they are on the threshold of the dangerous netherworld of the Ringwraiths, the ghostly undead Nazgûl, presaging the ultimate threat that the Ring poses to Frodo.

Analysis of liminal experiences has been fruitful in many disciplines besides anthropology and literature, including ecology and environmental studies. Naturalists working at about the same time as van Gennep in the early twentieth century began to use the term *ecotone* to describe transitions between one environmental domain and another. In an ecology textbook currently used in many university courses, *ecotones* are defined as "transitions from one type of ecosystem to another, for instance the transition from a woodland to a grassland."[8] This is an interesting example, for it is one of the important and prominent types of sharp, clearly demarcated transitions that Tolkien describes in *The Lord of the Rings*. We see it in *The Two Towers* at the edge of Fangorn Forest, where the forest meets the grassy plains of Rohan. Repeatedly, these passages mention the "eaves" of Fangorn Forest or its "edge."[9] Merry and Pippin encounter this distinct boundary when they escape from their Uruk-hai captors. Aragorn, Legolas, and Gimli encounter it as well, a short time later, while pursuing their friends. For both groups, this boundary gives them pause, and the crossing of it is a dramatic moment.

Here Tolkien gives us a narrative liminal space, but it is closely related to an important ecological one—an almost archetypal ecotone. More to the point of this book, environmental ecotones themselves are important in Tolkien's ecology. Middle-earth, it appears, cannot be divided rigidly into environmental domains without overlap or mutual involvement. Furthermore, in addition to sudden transitions—environmentally speaking, sharp demarcations between one ecosystem and another, such as the grassland-to-forest transition between Rohan and Fangorn—ecologists recognize that gradual transitions can be of great importance in the environment, and some of the most important ecotones we find in Middle-earth are of this gradual, or "thick," variety. Gildor's final comment to Frodo when they meet in the Shire may have other intentions or connotations, but it betrays a particular awareness of the boundary issues examined in this chapter: "The wide world is all about you: you can fence yourselves in, but you cannot for ever fence it out" (I/iv). There are echoes of the familiar in even the strangest surroundings.

It would not be possible to discuss all aspects of this important element in *The Lord of the Rings* here. As we state above, in the course of the story, the main characters traverse a great expanse of geographical territory, indicated by a multitude of narrative markers meant to clue the reader in to the importance of each boundary crossing. We confine ourselves in the remainder of this chapter to three main topics: (1) the ambiguous demarcations—that is, the thick margins and wide ecotones—dividing the agrarian world of the Shire from wilderness areas in the macroenvironment of Middle-earth; (2) the image of health, shown as a mingled ecology in the restoration of the Shire at the story's end; and (3) a liminal space of a different kind found in the house of Tom Bombadil and Goldberry, where many worlds come together in a profoundly rich ecotone.

Out of the Shire and into the Wild (But Not All at Once)

Early in *The Fellowship of the Ring,* an important scene takes place in a shadowy tunnel under a thick hedge near the eastern border of Buckland, an outlying region settled by Hobbits on the far side of the

Brandywine River. Frodo and company are discussing their departure from known regions of Buckland and the Shire into the dark, unknown, ominous Old Forest:

> Merry got down and unlocked the gate, and when they had passed through he pushed it to again. It shut with a clang, and the lock clicked. The sound was ominous.
> "There!" said Merry. "You have left the Shire and are now outside, and on the edge of the Old Forest." (I/vi)

In Peter Jackson's film interpretation of Tolkien's work, scenes of the Old Forest and Tom Bombadil have been excised entirely, and the hedge and locked iron gate that mark the clear transition into the Old Forest do not appear. However, Jackson seems to have realized that something important is happening here, so he included a variation of it. In the film version, it is a sunny afternoon, not a gloomy early morning, and the boundary is marked by a change in the color of the grass instead of a locked iron gate. Further, rather than Merry talking to Pippin, it is Sam talking to Frodo. When he steps across an imaginary line, Sam remarks:

> SAM: "This is it."
> FRODO: "This is what?"
> SAM: "If I take one more step, it'll be the farthest away from home I've ever been."

In the film, the liminal importance of this moment is reinforced visually by three large black birds perched ominously on a scarecrow in the background. These details highlight the significance of the event for Sam, a stereotype of Hobbit parochialism who also serves as an index character for the exploration of the natural world of Middle-earth. In the course of the story, it is Sam who develops most as a character, and crossing the border of the Shire into the wilder world outside is the first step in his initiation into maturity; for him, this is a significant threshold moment. But the liminality of this scene for all four travelers is no less marked in the book than it is in the movie. In fact, it is laced with unmistakable signs of foreboding. These include rather obvious narrational comments ("The sound was ominous") and formulaic auditory signals, including the clanging of a gate and the click of a lock. These details direct the reader to regard this unmistakably as the significant crossing of a boundary. Indeed, one of the most important environmental contrasts in Middle-earth is between farmland and wilderness—between the friendly, cultivated fields of the Shire and the wild, untamed realms summed up in the atmosphere of Fangorn and the Old Forest.

The reader is not disappointed. Soon hereafter, the travelers encounter changes in the environment that make unavoidable distinctions between the agrarian comforts of the Shire and the hostile forces outside it. In addition to the attacks of Old Man Willow and the Barrow-wights in the Old Forest and the Black Riders in Bree, on Weathertop, and at the Ford of Bruinen, the hobbits encounter significant opposition from the environment itself: malicious trees, briars, and underbrush in the Old Forest; fog on the Barrow-downs; parasitic insects in the Midgewater Marshes and the trackless marshes themselves; and rough terrain in what Aragorn specifically calls "wilderness" before their respite in Rivendell (I/xii).[10] The narrative tension of the first several hundred pages has as much to do with the natural hazards encountered after leaving their familiar homeland as it does with the specific threat of the Black Riders' pursuit. Nevertheless, however portentous the scene in which they cross the border of the Shire and enter the wilderness, the hobbits' escape from the agrarian world of the Shire is in other ways a gradual one. They first pass through marginal areas, liminal spaces of considerable breadth or thickness. These function as both narrative ecotones and ecological ones: overlapping settings that are not quite civilized but not quite wilderness either, having qualities of both.

In short, the agrarian world and the wilderness are demarcated by no visible dividing line—like that between Fangorn and the grasslands—with absolute farmland on one side and true wilderness on the other. So when do the hobbits actually find themselves in the wilderness? How wide is the liminal space? A definition of *wilderness* as "untrammeled," "undeveloped," "retaining its primeval character," and "without permanent improvements or . . . habitation"[11] would put this development much later in the story than their entrance to the Old Forest. After their departure from Bag End, the hobbits' journey takes them from the village of Hobbiton into the more sparsely settled areas eastward in the Shire, and then through the Green-Hill country and the tangled woods along the Stockbrook. Even within the Shire there are relatively less settled areas as well as areas of denser population. When the hobbits escape by ferry across the Brandywine River at night, they are outside the Shire, yet they enjoy another brief respite of civilization in Frodo's house at Crickhollow. On the following morning, they genuinely leave the Shire behind when they go under the High Hay into the Old Forest.

This marks a major shift: technically, they are now in the wilderness. As proof, their first serious setback occurs immediately thereafter in the nearly disastrous encounter with Old Man Willow, an embodiment of malevolent natural forces residing in the wilderness—the darker spirit of the primeval forest, as Treebeard later suggests. However, the threat is neutralized when they are rescued by Tom Bombadil, whose entrance into the story affords the hobbits yet another brief recovery. Tom's household is a peaceful outpost secure from the wilder forces of nature, with wholesome food, good drink, and the telling of tales—just the sort of thing Hobbits love when they are at home. After being rescued again by Bombadil on the Barrow-downs, they find their way to the village of Bree, which is described as "a small inhabited region, like an island in the empty lands round about" in the center of "a small country of fields and tamed woodland only a few miles broad" (I/ix). Bree even has a village inn on the model of Hobbiton's Ivy Bush and Bywater's Green Dragon.

As a result, although at many points early in the story the reader may be convinced that the hobbits have finally left the agrarian world and are out in the wilderness, it is almost 200 pages before the term *wilderness* in any way accurately describes their surroundings. The word first appears in the book after the departure from Bree, where we read, "On the third day out from Bree they came out of the Chetwood. The land had been falling steadily, ever since they turned aside from the Road, and they now entered a wide flat expanse of country, much more difficult to manage. They were far beyond the borders of the Bree-land, out in the pathless wilderness, and drawing near to the Midgewater Marshes" (I/ix). Even this assertion may not be fully persuasive, however. To the list of domestic outposts cited earlier, we must now add Rivendell, toward which Aragorn guides the hobbits after leaving Bree. Although it lies beyond the "Edge of the Wild" on a map of Wilderland published in *The Hobbit,* we may recall that the Elves call Rivendell "the

Last Homely House east of the Sea" (II/i), indicating that it is the last outpost of civilization *before* the wilderness begins. Also, there is a road that runs from Bree to Rivendell—albeit a dangerous one at times, and one that the company does not stick to—but its presence precludes the land's classification as wilderness by many definitions accepted in modern environmental discourse.

Therefore, it could be said that not until the Company of the Ring departs from Rivendell after the Council of Elrond do the main characters leave civilization and enter the wildest regions of Middle-earth.[12] Throughout the lengthy series of narrative developments all the way up to Bree and even, to a lesser degree, as far as Rivendell, at no point are the hobbits very far from reminders of the familiar comforts of home: Farmer Maggot's house, Crickhollow, the house of Tom Bombadil, the Prancing Pony Inn. Each place may be wilder than the one before, but the transition is gradual, and during the transition, elements of civilization, rural agrarianism, and true wilderness mix. Yet these spaces in the journey from cultivated agrarian life to real wilderness are all ecologically and narratively important and rich.

The ecological richness of these places is indicated by the variety of trees and vegetation either implied or explicitly mentioned in the hobbits' passage toward wilderness. After jumping the hedge at the edge of the garden at Bag End, the hobbits make their way westward down a narrow lane, heading south "along hedgerows and the borders of coppices" of unspecified type. They cross the Water, a stream "bordered with leaning alder-trees," then head eastward, climbing slopes grown with "thin-clad birches." They halt for the night in the "deep resin-scented darkness" of a fir wood, yet they are "still in the heart of the Shire" (I/ii). The second day's "zig-zagging" route takes them to a steep bank from which they look across "lower lands dotted with small clumps of trees," disappearing into the "brown woodland haze" of Woody End near the Brandywine River. In the afternoon, the terrain begins to change again. Now on level ground, the road ahead lies "through grass-lands sprinkled with tall trees, outliers of the approaching woods," apparently—based on subsequent references—oaks. After a close encounter with one of the Black Riders, they leave the road and strike a course parallel to it through "thick and tussocky grass" and uneven ground. The outlying trees of the approaching forest increase in density, as "the trees began to draw together into thickets." After sunset, the thickets have converged into a full-fledged cover of timber as they turn down a narrow lane winding "through a wood of ancient oak-trees" toward Woodhall. They pause shortly thereafter inside the "huge hulk" of a hollow tree—again, presumably, an oak. After another period of walking, upon hearing the approach of Gildor and the elves, they slip quietly off the path "into the deeper shade" under the oaks. They meet Gildor, who establishes their destination that night as "the woods on the hills above Woodhall" some miles away. Their final nighttime march on this second day's journey takes them through still denser woods, with trees that are "now younger and thicker," with "many deep brakes of hazel on the rising slopes." The late hours of the night are spent eating and talking with the elves in an outdoor hall pillared by living trees (I/iii).

On the third day's journey, further changes in vegetation make for difficult travel. Thickets grow "closer and more tangled," and the stream-bed they strike is "overhung with brambles." After going slowly and painfully through "bushes and brambles" alongside the stream, they wade across and come to "a wide open space, rush-grown and tree-less," then encounter "a belt of trees: tall oaks, for the most part, with here and there an elm tree or an ash." They journey through this belt as quickly as possible, "over patches of grass and through thick drifts of old leaves," halting at midday beneath an elm tree described as still in full leaf, though it is turning yellow with the waning of the year. The woods now "came to a sudden end," with wide grasslands stretching ahead; the lands become "steadily more tame and well-ordered," and they soon find themselves surrounded by "well-tended fields and meadows" in the approach to Farmer Maggot's land at Bamfurlong (I/iv). Though not necessarily liminal symbols in the fullest sense of the term, this catalog of tree species reveals how Tolkien uses natural images as indicators of subtle environmental change. These references serve not only to create a sense of forward motion but also to establish a picture of arboreal diversity even within the relatively small compass inside the borders of the Shire—a diversity associated here with the margin or the transition between agrarian and wild.

Another important boundary type appearing in Tolkien's narrative, and one worth examining, even though it seems somewhat humble, is the hedge. In Tolkien's writing, hedges play an important role, uniting his presentation of the agrarian idyll with evocations of liminality as the hobbits venture into the wider world. Hedges appear several times. After his birthday party, Bilbo's departure begins with his jumping over a low place in the hedge below Bag End (I/i). Seventeen years later—and narrated in almost the same words—Frodo walks "down the garden-path" and jumps over what we assume to be the same "low place in the hedge" before taking "to the fields, passing into the darkness like a rustle in the grasses" (I/iii). Hedges and gates appear again the next day as Frodo and his companions leave their difficult passage through Woody End and approach Maggot's farm at Bamfurlong. Maggot's house lies down a rutted lane running between "low well-laid hedges." At the ferry crossing at Bucklebury, there is a reference to wisps of mist "above the hedges," and the entrance to Frodo's house at Crickhollow is described as an opening through a "narrow gate in a thick hedge" (I/v). The crossing into the Old Forest, of course, is under a hedge, the High Hay, and the agrarian order of the landscape surrounding Bombadil's house includes a reference to the eaves of the forest as "clipped, and trim as a hedge" (I/vii). The list could go on, including hedges at Bree and at the gates of Moria.

The frequent reference to hedges is based on the traditional landscape of rural England. Whether created by leaving strips of natural vegetation to grow wild or by planting any number of species of bush, shrub, or tree, hedges have served historically as barriers for the containment of livestock, protection against intruders, and prevention of erosion; as a source of fruit and nuts, kindling, and timber; and as habitat for wildlife for hundreds of years in England. Traditionally, maintenance of hedges has been part of a program of wise agricultural management, and hedges' importance as a microenvironment has long been recognized. Their presence in the Shire befits the rural environment Tolkien has invented.[13]

The Restored Shire: A Mingled Ecology

The mingled ecologies and ecotones found not only in the gradual transition from the agrarian Shire to the wilderness but also within the Hobbits' land itself can be seen as contributing to the environmental health of the Shire. At the end of *The Lord of the Rings*, when the four hobbits return home, the important contributions of these ecotones are developed even more clearly. Our final image of the Shire following the War of the Ring is not one of tar-paper sheds, uprooted trees, or the smoking mill in Hobbiton—far from it. As an agrarian environment, the restored Shire exhibits all its earlier fecundity and more. Through the Lady Galadriel's gift, Sam enriches the soil of the Shire to such a degree that the harvest of 1420 becomes legendary for its bounty. But Sam's role, now far more important than that of Frodo's yardman or gardener, has grown to encompass elements of all three major ecosystems outlined in this book. He has learned much since first venturing beyond the Shire's borders.

Sam is introduced in *The Fellowship of the Ring* as his father's assistant in "the growing of vegetables—in the matter of 'roots,' especially potatoes." And his most significant role early in the story is clipping the grass at Bag End (I/i, ii, iii). After his adventure, however, his duties are much more extensive. Presumably, Sam's first encounter with Ents occurs only on the homeward journey after Aragorn's coronation, but he seems to have gained a perspective on the natural world that draws something from Treebeard's and now includes more than his employer's yard and kitchen garden. Although he is not mentioned specifically in the scene, Sam is surely present for Aragorn's parting blessing to Treebeard. "Now I thank you once more," says Aragorn, "and I bid you farewell. May your forest grow again in peace. When this valley is filled there is room and to spare west of the mountains, where once you walked long ago" (VI/vi).

The reforestation of Eriador, which, in Aragorn's mind at least, is a theoretical possibility, is overshadowed for Treebeard by the apparently inevitable extinction of his kind. He replies, "Forests may grow. . . . Woods may spread. But not Ents. There are no Entings" (VI/vi). There is indeed a change coming in the world: Treebeard feels it in the water, the earth, and the air.

Yet, even though "there are no Entings," there is Sam Gamgee. Grieving over the loss of the trees that "had been cut down recklessly far and wide over the Shire" (VI/ix), Sam attends to them as something of an expert in the management of forests and timberland. In addition to his other labors in the cleanup and restoration of Bag End, he is "often away in the Shire on his forestry work," planting saplings "in all the places where specially beautiful or beloved trees had been destroyed" (VI/ix). Though not exactly a counterpart to the Ents—he is not a Shepherd of Trees, like Treebeard—in his nurturing of them, Sam has become as much Treebeard's assistant as Gaffer Gamgee's. Aragorn's prophetic words concerning the reforestation of Middle-earth are fulfilled—at least in the Shire—by Sam. The Shire has its share of wooded terrain; there is the Woody End in the Green Hill Country, and the map of "A Part of the Shire" usually published with the book shows the southern tip of Bindbole Woods in the North Farthing. And even though elm trees traditionally do not grow there—a point of contention early in the novel at the Ivy Bush—there is the suggestion that that quarter of the Shire verges on woodlands. Under Sam's care, we may presume, the quality and extent of these forested areas remain secure, part of the mingled ecology in the complex environment of Middle-earth.

But what of the third environmental domain—the one we have described as horticultural—expressing the Elves' special interest in minimal cultivation of the natural world and the highlighting of its aesthetic qualities? Where in the Shire is there evidence of this response to the natural order? It has already been established that the Hobbits' love of flowers is evidenced in their nomenclature: "Half the maidchildren in the Shire" are called by floral names. In particular, Sam—who marries Rosie Cotton—has sisters named Daisy and Marigold; his own daughters are named Elanor, Daisy, Ruby, and Primrose. But Sam's principal horticultural achievement is the planting of the silver mallorn nut given to him by Galadriel. He uses it to replace the Party Tree felled during the Shire's occupation by the enemy:

> In the Party Field a beautiful young sapling leaped up: it had silver bark and long leaves and burst into golden flowers in April. It was indeed a *mallorn,* and it was the wonder of the neighbourhood. In later years, as it grew in grace and beauty, it was known far and wide and people would come long journeys to see it: the only *mallorn* west of the Mountains and east of the Sea, and one of the finest in the world. (VI/ix)

Though Sam initially believes that healing the Shire's environmental damage will take so long that "only his great-grand-children . . . would see the Shire as it ought to be," just a year after his return, the restoration of the Shire's farmlands, forests, and floral beauty is well under way. Tolkien's portrayal of a healthy Shire includes agriculture, horticulture, and feraculture all coming together, touching one another, overlapping, and commingling in places.

Bombadil's House: An Environmental, Social, and Mythical Ecotone

We now leave the Shire and turn our attention to a unique place in Middle-earth. It is found within the Old Forest on the edge of the Shire and bears a striking resemblance to certain cultural aspects of Hobbit life. In other ways, however, it is entirely different. We have already mentioned Tom Bombadil and Goldberry several times and discussed the environmental implications of their characters. We now look at them again in relation to ecotones and liminal spaces. Their house is a place with Shire-like amenities in the midst of the wild world beyond the Shire's borders. There, the hobbit travelers enjoy "food and cheer and song," which we regard as formulaic expressions of the simple pleasures especially favored by Hobbits. But the house of Tom Bombadil is more than an outpost of rustic comfort in the wilderness; in the terms we have used in this chapter, it is a liminal space—a "thick threshold"—where realms overlap. Some of this can be seen as a function of the complementary roles of Tom and Goldberry themselves. Several domains of the natural world coincide here, but something far deeper and far more significant for Tolkien's environmental myth also happens during the hobbits' sojourn. Tom and Goldberry create a space where the timeless mythic realm and the present natural world come together.

The first thing we note in this regard is that Tom and Goldberry are liminal characters. Goldberry is a mythic character that some regard as an embodiment of a river. That is, she is something of a nature goddess.[14] The colors green and gold are associated with her and are reminiscent of the mingled green and gold light of the mythic Two Trees, Telperion and Laurelin; by extension, in some sense, they make Goldberry akin to Yavanna. In Goldberry, the mythic and natural worlds commingle. Upon meeting her, Frodo immediately sings a song extempore in her praise, emphasizing her identification with natural beauty and the beauty of nature: she is "slender as a willow-wand" and "clearer than clear water," a "reed by the living pool" in spring and summer, a "river-daughter" fair as "wind on the waterfall" and "leaves' laughter" (I/vii).

Likewise, Tom belongs both to the real world of the present in which the hobbits live and breathe and to the mythic world in which temporal distinctions between the Elder Days and the present—between the First, Second, and Third Ages of Middle-earth—have little meaning. Tom knows the world and loves it, and because of this, he is able to teach the hobbits much about "bees and flowers, the ways of trees, and the strange creatures of the Forest" (I/vii). During their stay in his house, Tom teaches important environmental lessons to Frodo and his companions, who "began to understand the lives of the Forest, apart from themselves, indeed to feel themselves as the strangers where all other things were at home." This is a vision of pristine wilderness, suggesting a perspective on the created world in which the components of the natural environment—forests, mountains, rivers, and trees in their earliest natural state—belong "each to themselves." Tom belongs to the physical world of willow wands, flagstone floors, water lilies, and the like—the subjects of his songs praising the simple beauty of nature.

Yet, like Goldberry, Tom also belongs to the world of myth and legend, a concrete manifestation of things the hobbits have barely glimpsed, even in their stories and fairy tales. For example, just as in Lothlórien, where time seems either not to pass or to be irrelevant, during their stay in Bombadil's house, "Whether the morning and evening of one day or of many days had passed Frodo could not tell. He did not feel either hungry or tired, only filled with wonder" (I/vii). Tom is Eldest. Even to one as old and wise as Elrond—himself a mythic hero appearing in the old tales of Beren and Lúthien—Tom is part of a deeper and older myth, with names befitting his mythic stature. "Iarwain Ben-adar we called him, oldest and fatherless. But many another name he has since been given by other folk: Forn by the Dwarves, Orald by Northern Men, and other names besides" (II/ii). He is said to have been present in western Middle-earth when the Noldor first made their entrance from Valinor in the First Age. He has knowledge of the world "before the river and the trees" and can remember "the first raindrop and the first acorn," before the arrival of Elves, Men, and Hobbits. His knowledge goes back to the time "before the seas were bent," before the creation of the Sun and Moon, when "the dark under the stars . . . was fearless," and even earlier still, "before the Dark Lord came from Outside" (I/vii). Though he is apparently not a Vala, he seems to be knowledgeable of the mythic history of the land he inhabits because he has been a part of that history from the beginning.

Yet the fact that Tom is old does not produce in him a world-weary gravity of spirit—far from it. He hops around in yellow boots with a blue feather in his cap, and the nonsense or near nonsense of his rhymes bespeaks a playful levity unequaled anywhere else in Tolkien's works. The combination of trochees, spondees, and dactyls in his poems makes for a sprightly quickness, and readers with a finely tuned ear for poetry will note that even in prose, Tom's conversational discourse falls into these patterns. He thus belongs both to the world of myth and to the world of everyday, even childlike joy in the creation.

Most important, though, Tom belongs to the River's Daughter, his spouse Goldberry. When we first meet Tom, he is on an errand for her, and Goldberry contributes far more than incidental importance to Tom's mythic function as an embodiment of the life and spirit of unspoiled land. So few intact couples—spouses or lovers—appear in the novel that Tom and Goldberry's joyful coexistence merits careful consideration with the small handful of other couples: Galadriel and Celeborn in Lothlórien, Aragorn and Arwen, Faramir and Éowyn, and Sam Gamgee and Rosie Cotton. It need not be spelled out how important harmonious interactions between males and females are for the propagation of life, for the fertility and fecundity of the earth. And although each of these couples plays a crucial role in its own way, the union of Goldberry and Tom has special significance. In their relationship, we see a portrayal of ecologically diverse yet compatible forms of stewardship over the natural environment. In the background, of course, lies the myth of Yavanna and Aulë, whose division of labor is presented both as a harmonious complementarity and, at its worst, as a rivalry bordering on hostility. The Ents' legend of the Entwives is one of spousal disharmony, and their disagreement over the best way to tend to growing things—a preservationist versus a conservationist mentality—leads to the Entwives' departure. In the joyful spousal relationship between Tom and Goldberry, however, we see a rare picture of spousal harmony, a picture that is crucial to the environmental harmony it signifies.

This relationship makes passages set in their house something of a narrative ecotone, where their two different ecologies are depicted as coming together. We are not referring here to the organized house and garden surrounded by the wildness of the Old Forest. That ecology is certainly interesting, and it serves as an analogue to the ecotones in the Peruvian Andes mentioned by Berry, where wilderness "thrive[s] in domesticity to accommodate diversity within unity." What we mean here is Tom and Goldberry's ecology. Their house may be the most important narrative ecotone in the book, and their spousal harmony is the very thing that makes its ecotone possible in the stricter environmental sense.

The mythical qualities of the house are evident immediately. Upon entering it, Frodo falls under a spell of enchantment "deeper and nearer to mortal heart; marvelous and yet not strange." The supernatural aspect is also highlighted by the dreams the hobbits have there—except for Sam, who "slept through the night in deep content, if logs are contented." Merry, Pippin, and Frodo all have dreams that are presented in the text as portents, omens, prophetic glimpses of present and future events. These include Gandalf's captivity and escape from Orthanc, the flooding of the land around Isengard, and Frodo's final journey into the eternal world beyond death. Pippin's dreamed sensation that he "was not in an ordinary house at all" is accurate; the house is an otherworldly refuge where "nothing passes door and window . . . save moonlight and starlight and the wind off the hill-top" (I/vi).

Paradoxically, Tom's house is unexalted. It is an everyday house bordering "the eaves of the Forest," which are "clipped, and trim as a hedge," the path "well-tended and bordered with stone." It is a long, low house with low roof beams on "a hillside of turf." It has a kitchen garden in which pole beans grow, and it is furnished and decorated naturally in flagstone, earthenware, fresh green rushes, and water lilies (I/vi–vii). Yet, as soon as he crosses the threshold,[15] Frodo understands the joy "hidden in the songs we heard"—a joy that is a celebration of the miracles of the natural world, the ordinary created world that is extraordinary in its purpose and beauty. Again, this is a contrast of commingled worlds: the ordinary and the extraordinary, the mythic and the natural. Should we be surprised? As we noted earlier, Tolkien associated myth and fantasy with the power to show us the luminous, spiritual, sacred, and transcendent in nature and in the everyday environments of our quotidian world.

Although the four hobbits do not visit Tom and Goldberry when they return from their quest, the lessons they learn in the Old Forest and the harmonious relationship between Tom and Goldberry and between their domesticity and the surrounding wildness may be as much of an environmental model as the realms of Galadriel and Treebeard are. For the hobbits who must restore the ravaged Shire, that model is an inspiration contributing to the richness of the mingled ecology they bring to bear on the reconstruction of their own home.

Throughout the trilogy, Tolkien provides narrative clues to indicate the crossing of significant boundaries. In addition to architecture and other constructed markers, many are signaled by reference to changes in vegetation and alterations in the terrain, landforms, and such natural features as rivers, mountains, and grasslands. Broadening Wendell Berry's title "A Country of Edges" (describing Kentucky's Red River Gorge), we might see Middle-earth as a land of edges, the comprehension of which involves an awareness of its many environments.[16] At least in environmental terms, for one to understand Middle-earth, one must know its farmlands, gardens, forests, mountains, and grasslands; the boundaries that demarcate them; and the necessary margins uniting them into an environmental whole.

Chapter 7
The Ecology of Ham, Niggle's Parish, and Wootton Major

So far, we have focused on the mythology, characters, settings, and imagery related to the environment of Middle-earth as illustrated in Tolkien's legendarium. We now turn briefly to his best-known shorter works of fiction: "Farmer Giles of Ham," "Leaf by Niggle," and "Smith of Wootton Major," about which less has been written. As with the major texts, it would be inaccurate to describe any of these stories as works of environmental literature or as nature writing.

"Farmer Giles of Ham" is a comic piece whose rather unheroic protagonist is something of a rustic simpleton who is not taken very seriously either by the reader or by the other characters—at least not until the end of the story, and perhaps not even then. He defeats both a giant and a dragon largely by accident before he wins a second, only slightly more intentional victory over the same dragon and then a deliberate victory over a petty king. Although it can be argued that the story has a serious point, in *J. R. R. Tolkien: Author of the Century*, Tom Shippey suggests that Tolkien himself "felt no urge" to take the story's setting seriously. Shippey suggests that the story's humorous style belies its "more aggressive" underlying theme, but it is not by any means an environmental one.[1]

"Leaf by Niggle" is a story of autobiographical significance bordering on allegory. Its tone is much more serious than that of "Farmer Giles of Ham," and—not unlike Aulë's defense of his unauthorized creation of the Dwarves—the story seemingly serves as a defense of Tolkien's literary objectives and as a personal confession of his perceived failures as a writer. As Shippey explains, it is both a "personal apologia, and a self-critique."[2] The autobiographical reflections center on the value and purpose of art, the duties of an artist to society, and the writer's mortality. Environmental themes play a small but—we will argue—important background role.

Likewise, "Smith of Wootton Major," written toward the end of Tolkien's life, is a deep and profound work with personal reflections verging on allegory and autobiography. As with any of Tolkien's works of fiction, it should be read first and foremost for its narrative qualities as a story. But, like "Leaf by Niggle," it can also be understood otherwise: as an apologia for fantasy literature and fairy tale—or the literature of Faërie, as Tolkien might have said. As a story, it is a superb example of how and why the best works in that genre succeed in communicating profound narrative truth. Indeed, it is one of the best contributions to the genre the reader is likely to encounter. But like the other stories, it is not a statement of an ecological vision; its environmentalism is in the background.

Nonetheless, despite these caveats, significant glimpses of Tolkien's environmental perspective can be seen in these pieces and in the imagined geographies they describe: the town of Ham and the surrounding "Wild," Niggle's Parish and its adjacent forest and distant mountains, and the village of Wootton Major and bordering land of Faërie. Although they are not part of the Middle-earth canon, these three short stories support the general outline of Tolkien's environmental views examined in the earlier chapters of this book. They illustrate the same complex, unifying, overall ecology of agriculture, horticulture, and feraculture seen in *The Lord of the Rings*. They also suggest some of the same transcendent values connected with the fully Christian sense of stewardship discussed in chapter 2. Taken as a whole, one can draw from these short stories a significant environmental ethic.

Farmer Giles of Ham

"Farmer Giles of Ham" was the first of the three short stories to be written, and it is also the most lighthearted. It was first published in 1949, but Tolkien wrote it more than a decade earlier; it was conceived at roughly the same time he was working on *The Hobbit* and appears to have reached final form by 1938.[3] It is not surprising, therefore, that of the three works discussed in this chapter, Tolkien's environmental ideas are least fully developed in this piece. If "Farmer Giles" were all we had of Tolkien's work, it would be difficult (though not impossible) to find evidence of any significant ecological vision in his writing. Although we should avoid making too much of the story or reading too deeply into it, traces of Tolkien's developing vision can be seen in it.

A hint of an environmental orientation can be seen in the title of the story and the name of the main character. Giles is a farmer. He is not merely Giles; he is *Farmer* Giles, which is to say that his identity is wrapped up with his agrarian occupation. He does the work of farming without hurry or bustle, for "bustle has very little to do with business," he says, and he gives little thought to anything other than "his fields, his village, and the nearest market" (*WMFG*, 70). To raise an issue often cited by Wendell Berry, like all real farmers, Giles uses the term *business*, but he is not really interested in the business end of farming—certainly not in what the modern world calls agribusiness.[4] For example, we do not see him traveling to faraway markets to seek better prices for his goods. When fellow citizens of Ham suggest that he go to the court to be knighted, he replies, "I am a farmer and proud of it: A plain honest man" (95). Put another way, Giles is content with his role. He is, in the eyes of his king—and in his own terminology—a "rustic": a member of this romanticized and often insulted class (84). He belongs to the real world; he has no interest in being a knight or any other sort of hero—either of the countryside or of the Middle Kingdom. His primary interest is quite simple: he wishes to protect his homestead, his farm, from intruders. The point is made quite clearly by Tolkien's name choice for Giles's village: *Ham* is the Old English form of *home*.[5] Giles's farm is his home, and vice versa. The association of farm and home is clearly deliberate.[6]

We might broaden this into a more general principle: Farmer Giles is a defender of the agricultural way of life. This may seem out of place for so lighthearted a tale, and certainly the farmer himself would not presume to make so bold a claim. For Giles, it is merely a matter of protecting his property: "Property is property; and Farmer Giles had a short way with trespassers," we are told (77). Yet it should be remembered that *The Hobbit* ends up being a more significant and profound tale than it starts out to be. Perhaps "Farmer Giles of Ham" is also a little more weighty than Tolkien intended it to be. At the very least, we can see the same underlying set of presuppositions at work here, though probably unconsciously, that are at work in his more mythic and serious writing. In Giles, we see something of what Berry says makes a farmer a good one, distinguishing small farmers from agribusinessmen:

> In agriculture, the economy of scale or growth directly destroys land, people, neighborhoods, and communities. . . . And so good agriculture is virtually synonymous with small-scale agriculture—that is, with what is conventionally called "the small farm." . . .
>
> The practicality of the small farm may lie in the inherent human tendency to cherish what one has little of. I believe that land wasters always own or "control" more land than they can or will pay attention to. Some people, of course, will not cherish or pay attention to any land at all. But with land as with anything else, those who have a lot will tend to think that a little waste is affordable. When land is held in appropriately small parcels, on the other hand, a little waste tends to be noticed, regretted, and corrected, because it is felt that a little loss cannot be afforded. And that is the correct perception: it *cannot* be afforded.[7]

Berry could easily be describing Farmer Giles. Giles cherishes his land and his prized cow Galathea and cannot afford to lose them. He regrets any loss suffered by land or beast. Thus he is willing to do what it takes to preserve his land, even if it means facing a giant. As the narrator tells us, "he was more anxious about his property than his skin" (78).

Furthermore, as Berry goes on to say, protecting the individual small farm and protecting the way of life it represents are intimately linked, with the chain of support working in both directions:

> To these defenders [of the small farm] I want to suggest that it may be impossible to defend the small farm by itself or for its own sake. The small farm cannot be "developed" like a product or a program. Like a household, it is a human organism, and has its origin in both nature and culture. Its justification is not only agricultural, but is a part of an ancient pattern of values, ideas, aspirations, attitudes, faiths, knowledges, and skills that propose and support the sound establishment of a people on the land. To defend the small farm is to defend a large part, and the best part, of our cultural inheritance.[8]

In other words, defend the individual small farm, and you defend the whole "cultural inheritance"; defend the whole "ancient pattern of values," and the individual small farm reaps the general benefits. No doubt Berry did not have the blunderbuss in mind as a means of defense, but the two-way principle is the same, and though this no doubt stretches the story's application far beyond Tolkien's intention, we might well view Giles's giant as the mythical giant, something of an allegorical expression of the "giant" of commercial agribusiness.

Appealing once more to Tolkien's use of names, we can extend the connection between defending a farm and defending the whole agricultural way of life. The name Giles, or Aegidius, as he is known more learnedly, is the name of a Catholic saint. In both England and the rest of Europe, there are dozens of churches and chapels dedicated to St. Giles, including one in Oxford, where Tolkien spent most of his academic life. The name has rustic associations: as legend tells, a hind was sent by heaven to nourish Giles in his monastic hermitage, and the name Aegidius—from the word for "goat" or "goatskin"—was attached to him as a result. One of St. Aegidius's sacred functions is protection and defense of simple folks, farmers and rustics, and perhaps even their land. Although in Catholic tradition the main patron saint of farmers is St. Isidore the Farmer (1070–1130), one of St. Francis's earliest followers, St. Giles of Asissi (1190–1262), was a farmer in secular life and could legitimately be taken as a secondary patron of agrarians. And the connection goes even deeper. Giles's full surname is Agricola de Hammo, for which "Farmer from Ham" is merely a vulgar translation.[9] Giles can be said to represent the "agriculture of home"; by extension, he might represent every farmer and could be described as the Everyman of the rustic world, his village standing for the whole agrarian way of life.

This raises the question: who is Giles protecting his farm from? Or, returning to an earlier point, from what intruders? The first two intruders in the story are archetypal villains of Faërie, monsters akin to the ones Tolkien discusses at length in "*Beowulf:* The Monsters and the Critics": a giant and a dragon. In the short story, both represent the careless and wanton destruction of the farm. The giant is called the "desolation of gardens"; he "trampled on the crops, and flattened the mowing-grass"—not to mention trampling on several of Giles's sheep and his prize cow—in five minutes doing "more damage than the royal fox hunt could have done in five days" (71–72). The dragon is even deadlier, though perhaps not as bold. "He was cunning, inquisitive, greedy, well-armoured," and "especially large and ferocious." And "he did a great deal of damage in a short while, smashing and burning, and devouring sheep, cattle, and horses" (89, 92). Because the setting of this story is rural and agrarian, it stands to reason that the damage done by both monsters is mostly to agriculture: farms, fields, and livestock. But in traditional, even ancient, narrative terms, it is also significant that the monsters are precisely what they are: a giant and a dragon.

If we accept Tolkien's 1936 essay as reflecting his thoughts on the literature of Faërie in general—and not strictly on *Beowulf*—then the fact that Farmer Giles wards off monsters and not mere human foes lends greater mythic resonance to the defense of his farm—even in this mock-heroic form. Speaking of *Beowulf*, Tolkien writes, "I would suggest, then, that the monsters are not an inexplicable blunder of taste; they are essential" (*MC*, 19). Again, "Farmer Giles of Ham" has nothing remotely resembling the lofty seriousness that Tolkien recognizes in *Beowulf*. But the generic artifice of the mock-heroic style should not distract us from recognizing a similar mythic function for the monsters in Tolkien's short story. Tolkien goes on to say, "Most important is it to consider how and why the monsters become 'adversaries of God,' and so begin to symbolize (and ultimately to become identified with) the powers of evil, even while they remain, as they do still remain in *Beowulf*, mortal denizens of the material world, in it and of it" (*MC*, 20). These monsters are part of the common stock of both secular and sacred traditional narrative in medieval Europe, and just as Giles's protection of the land can be seen as "sacred" because it is undertaken in opposition to these particular monsters, mythically speaking the ravaging of the environment in this story is no mere incidental inconvenience. Giles's staunchest ally in Ham is the village parson, a representative of the church. Taken with their fullest mythic implications, in terms of traditional motifs, these monsters can be seen as symbols of the power of evil, adversaries of God, making Farmer Giles on some level a contender for divine agricultural or ecological justice.

Furthermore, Tolkien comments that in *Beowulf*, monsters are "of the material world, in it and of it," arguing that Beowulf's battle against evil does not take place in some vague spiritual realm but in a setting presented as geographically real. Applied more generally to the everyday life of the reader, the implication is that day-to-day battles in real life combine the physical and the spiritual realms in ways that may render them inseparable. Generalizing this idea further, it could be said that those who destroy the land are the enemies of God, and those who protect it, such as St. Giles and Farmer Giles, are performing a sacred, divine duty.

This brings us to the last of Farmer Giles's foes. Unlike the first two, the third intruder is not a monster but a human being—King Augustus Bonifacius—along with his royal retinue. To understand why a human foe is also important to the structure of this story, we must understand something of what the king represents, especially in relation to or in contrast with the title character. Augustus Bonifacius leads a life of luxury and excess; he is more interested in feasting and fashion than in the agricultural work that sustains his kingdom. The name *Augustus* suggests splendor and dignity, at least in the sense that these seem to be important to the king's sense of himself and his image. Having a good image and being well thought of are more important to the king than the substance of effective rule, and the abundance of titles and surnames he gives himself illustrates this: he calls himself Bonifacius, meaning "one who does good," and Ambrosius, connoting the famed food or fragrant nectar of the gods. But his later title, Tyrannus, is far more appropriate (*WMFG*, 84). Rather than one who does genuine good, he is more akin to a self-serving do-gooder, in the most pejorative sense of that expression. If offering a gift to a distant, rustic, local hero will help his image and cost him nothing but a worthless sword, the king is all too eager to oblige.

The contrast between the king's world and the rustic world of Ham is further emphasized when it is suggested that Giles leave Ham and go to the royal court. The farmer replies, "Honest men fare ill at court, they say" (95). Though Giles fires off this subtle but scathing indictment simply to save his own hide, the validity of the remark is demonstrated throughout the story. The court is rampant with conceit and deceit. King Augustus cares nothing for lambs, plowing, milk, or water (126). He seems to care little about any aspect of the agricultural life of his people, but only for the economic value he can extract from it. The comparison made between the damage done by the giant and that done by the fox hunt is telling; even the king's royal entertainment is more important to him than the land on which it takes place.

In short, then, the king represents human greed and selfishness. Just as Saruman brings the monstrous but distant evil of Sauron and the blasted landscape of Mordor closer to home and makes it more easily recognizable—first in Isengard and later in the Shire (see chapter 8)—so Augustus Bonifacius makes the monstrous environmental evil of the giant and the dragon more personal and recognizable. Despite the face—or faces—it wears, this kind of evil is no less damaging to the landscape. All this can be boiled down to one simple but important point: the heroes of this tale are those who care about and protect the agrarian environment; those who do not are the villains. Those who are involved in the day-to-day life of the soil, whether tilling the ground or lambing the ewes, are represented positively; their enemies—both monster and human—are those who care little for the land and run roughshod over it to entertain themselves, to feast themselves at the expense of the poor, or simply to fatten their treasuries.

Can we see the fullness of Tolkien's threefold vision—agriculture, horticulture, and feraculture—in this short, comic tale? No. But setting aside the rather marked generic differences, we do see strong hints of the agrarian component in it. We catch a glimpse of the incipient environmental perspective and suggestions of how Tolkien would develop these ideas years later in the narratives that would become part of the Middle-earth canon. There are seeds in "Farmer Giles of Ham" that germinate and bear fruit in "The Scouring of the Shire" in *The Return of the King*.

Niggle's Parish

"Leaf by Niggle," published in the *Dublin Review* in 1945, was conceived and written the previous year, after the Tolkiens' neighbor expressed nervousness about a large poplar looming over her house. The woman wanted to have the tree removed, but Tolkien considered this ridiculous and managed to prevent its being felled. But, "anxious about [his] own internal Tree," he began thinking. "One morning he woke up with a short story in his head, and scribbled it down," his biographer tells us.[10] As mentioned earlier, this story has been regarded as an autobiographical allegory.[11] However, at least one dimension of the story is so clearly suggestive of parallels with Tolkien's own self-conception and with religious perspectives on mortality that the distinction between application and allegory may be an excessively fine one.

The title character Niggle is initially introduced simply as a painter, much in the same way that Giles is presented simply as a farmer. Just as, on one level, "Farmer Giles" is only a story about a man's defense of his farm, on the surface, "Leaf by Niggle" is simply about a painter and his art. But the story is really about two things: the character flaws that prevent Niggle from being a more successful painter, and a deeply philosophical defense of art in relation to transcendent or eternal values. Part of this defense is the fact that Niggle's paintings, especially his leaves, are beautiful in and of themselves, at times even captivating. "A Leaf by Niggle has a charm of its own," says the mysterious Second Voice in the middle of the story. "He took a great deal of pains with leaves, just for their own sake" (*TL*, 85). But on a deeper level, the story's message is not "art for art's sake" but a defense of art for the sake of reality. The argument does not diminish the importance of art but elevates it to the status of transcendent value and, in addition, makes it part of a value system in which the beauty of nature is linked to things of eternal importance. Niggle's paintings, and in particular his tree, are, for many, the "best introduction to the Mountains" (95).

To understand the ecological implications of this story, we must begin with a detailed account of Niggle's great painting, described in one of the story's first visual images:

> It had begun with a leaf caught in the wind, and it became a tree; and the tree grew, sending out innumerable branches, and thrusting out the most fantastic roots. Strange birds came and settled on the twigs and had to be attended to. Then all round the Tree, and behind it, through the gaps in the leaves and boughs, a country began to open out; and there were glimpses of a forest marching over the land, and of mountains tipped with snow. (76)

Simple as it may seem, this picture provides a wonderful illustration of the complex environmental perspective discussed in earlier chapters. In the aesthetics of the tree itself, we have images associated with arboriculture as part of the more general horticultural devotion identified with the Elves of Valinor and Lothlórien. We learn later in the story that the tree actually comes to life in a landscape surrounded by hedges, where the two principal characters spend a great deal of time gardening and cultivating flowers, including new floral species imagined into life collaboratively. Again, this brings to mind Lothlórien and the Shire after its restoration. And the tree sustains other species of life: numerous strange and presumably wild birds. Then, behind the tree, there is a forest—it has a tamer part nearby and an untamed one farther away—while still more distant are the even wilder mountains. These images evoke the wilderness domain associated with the Ents in a picture that contains elements of both cultivated and wild beauty: conservation shading into preservation, horticulture shading into feraculture. It is a design replete with ecotones. These varied ecological components do not compete; rather, they complete one another, an effect captured in miniature in the "shining spray [of leaves] that framed the distant vision of the mountain" (80). Initially, we see the image of the mountain from a distance; it is only a vision, but visions can be powerful, especially when—as in this story—they come to fruition in reality.

This imagery is further developed toward the end of the story, after Niggle's painting has been given the gift of primary existence. Again, all these aspects are present in the real tree and in the surrounding region that comes to be known as Niggle's Parish:

> The birds were building in the Tree. Astonishing birds: how they sang! They were mating, hatching, growing wings, and flying away singing into the Forest, even while he looked at them. For now he saw that the Forest was there too, opening out on either side, and marching away into the distance. The Mountains were glimmering far away. (89)

They are now part of a cultivated region of a real world, and the tree and the surrounding garden provide sustenance and life for wild birds—this time, *real* birds.

The passage quoted above provides just a glimpse of the story's imagery. The plot of the story, though, is also significant to an understanding of Tolkien's ecology, even in places where it seems primarily personal or idiosyncratic. In the beginning of the story, Niggle has become so wrapped up in his private painting that he neglects his other duties: "nuisances" and "hindrances" he calls them. He neglects his neighbor, Parish. He neglects his garden, which is overrun with weeds. And he neglects to prepare for an inescapable, "wretched" and "troublesome" journey. The conflict between Niggle's painting and his other responsibilities is made explicit when his painting of the tree is moved to "a tall shed that had been built for it out in his garden (on a plot where once he had grown potatoes)" (75–77). The nature of the parenthetical comment emphasizes that Niggle's focus on his painting has been at the expense of his garden—not a flower garden, but one in which a nutritive staple once grew. A section of his land once used for humble agrarian purposes now has a storage shed erected on it.

Shippey has made a persuasive case for understanding this part of the story as an expression of Tolkien's anxiety over the pursuit of his imaginative writing (his "art") to the neglect of his own "garden," the academic world (his "field" of study). No doubt this is right. At the same time, a tension between art and the world in the wider sense also seems to be written into the story, and there are implications for the view of nature that we find to be part of Tolkien's environmentalism. Additionally, Niggle's neglect of his neighbor Parish is presented here as a lack of charity, a character defect that is healed when his art is transfigured into a real world of intense natural beauty. As a character, Niggle himself is transformed by the end of the story, and his transformation is part of the translation of a mere painting into the gift of nature.

In the story, Niggle's neighbor Parish is one of the many irritating interruptions preventing Niggle from making progress on his painting. Niggle does not like Parish very much, "partly because he was so often in trouble and in need of help." But also:

> He did not care about painting, but was very critical about gardening. When Parish looked at Niggle's garden (which was often) he saw mostly weeds; and when he looked at Niggle's pictures (which was seldom) he saw only green and grey patches and black lines, which seemed to him nonsensical. He did not mind mentioning the weeds (a neighbourly duty), but he refrained from giving any opinion of the pictures. (78)

Neither man understands the other. When Parish begs him for some canvas to repair a leaky roof, Niggle evades the request, and Parish's roof never gets fixed. In short order, Niggle is indicted by an Inspector of Houses for failing to attend to Parish's needs; the inspector, a tall man dressed in black, announces that he is "the Driver" and whisks Niggle away in a carriage, taking him to a rail station for his journey. "The train ran almost at once into a dark tunnel" (82).

Most readers recognize that Niggle's long-dreaded journey is that of death; the "Workhouse Infirmary" in the next section of the story represents purgatory, and the remainder of the story is an allegory of the afterlife.[12] Niggle undergoes extensive treatment through hard work, harsh medicines, and lengthy periods of inner reflection until, after an unspecified amount of time, he is finally declared "better," fit "to go on to the next stage."[13] By casting the story in this framework, Tolkien clearly suggests that issues of artistic integrity, kindness to one's neighbors, and the beauty and value of the natural world are not merely isolated, mundane concerns; they are interrelated, and they have transcendent spiritual significance.

The next section of the story takes Niggle by bicycle in spring sunshine into a land of "marvelous turf" where he finds his tree, the one he once labored over so long without finishing. Now it is finished, and it is real, "alive, its leaves opening, its branches growing and bending in the wind" (88). He lingers a while, simply admiring the tree, its individual "exquisite leaves," and the birds nesting in its branches. After some time, he turns toward the forest, glimpsed earlier through the branches in the background of his painting; it is now a part of the world of eternal reality into which he, and it, have been raised.

> The Forest, of course, was a distant Forest, yet he could approach it, even enter it, without its losing that particular charm. He had never before been able to walk into the distance without turning it into mere surroundings. It really added a considerable attraction to walking in the country, because as you walked, new distances opened out; so that you now had double, treble, and quadruple distances, doubly, trebly, and quadruply enchanting. . . . You could go on and on, but not perhaps for ever. There were the Mountains in the background. They did get nearer, very slowly. They did not seem to belong to the picture, or only as a link to something else, a glimpse through the trees of something different, a further stage: another picture. (89)

Just as the wildness of the mountains and the "distant Forest" complete the beauty of the tree and the cultivated regions, providing it with some of its "particular charm," the tree provides a point of entry into the wilderness seen "marching away into the distance." At the same time, the beauty and mystery of the nearby, the close at hand—in his old life, "mere surroundings"—are not diminished by proximity. It is the simultaneous presence of both perspectives—the familiarity of the close by, the wonder of the far away—that creates what Niggle calls the "considerable attraction" of the place.

He finds, though, that in this new land, "there were a number of inconclusive regions" still in need of work, still needing "continuing up to a definite point." Puzzled as to how to begin, and aware of the need for advice, he stumbles upon his old neighbor Parish "leaning on a spade," and together they begin to build a house and tend a garden. Niggle, who in his old country struggled unsuccessfully to make good use of time, now finds himself "the better of the two at . . . getting things done." Parish, once the consummate gardener for whom Niggle's painting was "That Daubing," now "often wandered about looking at trees, and especially at the Tree" (90).[14] They learn to work together and acknowledge their mutual need for each other: "Niggle would think of wonderful new flowers and plants, and Parish always knew exactly how to set them and where they would do best" (91). Niggle comes to value "Parish's Garden," and Parish admires "Niggle's Picture"; the eventual name for that place becomes the combined form "Niggle's Parish," suggesting a reconciliation between the practical and the artistic in a world of natural beauty combining both.[15] It is yet another sort of ecotone where two different "ecologies" come together and produce a vibrant life that can be found only where they mingle.

As their work on the house and garden nears completion, the two "allowed themselves more and more time for walking about, looking at the trees, and the flowers, and the lights and shapes, and the lie of the land. Sometimes they sang together; but Niggle found that he was now beginning to turn his eyes, more and more often, towards the Mountains" (91–92). In this and many passages from this section of the narrative, the unmistakable subtext is that the beauties of nature are valuable and to be enjoyed in and of themselves; at the same time, though, they point the way toward the deeper, richer beauty—again, the term *transcendent* beauty seems most apt—for which Niggle longs. Led by a shepherd up the grassy slopes, Niggle hikes into the "high pasturages" under the "wider sky" of the mountains. Here, the narrator breaks off, saying he "cannot guess what became of him" or what the mountains Niggle glimpsed are really like: "only those can say who have climbed them" (93).

The story ends with two conversations whose context is not clearly indicated. The first includes three characters named Tompkins, Atkins, and Perkins; most likely, the diminutive suffix *-kins* in all their names is meant to match their pettiness.[16] Theirs is a largely dismissive discussion of the value—practical or otherwise—of Niggle and his painting. Atkins, "nobody of importance, just a schoolmaster," who seems cautiously supportive of Niggle's art, keeps a fragment of the painting of the tree, a scrap of canvas with a single painted leaf, which he says he cannot get out of his mind. Councilor Tompkins does not understand this. His name—a diminutive of Thomas, the apostle forever associated with "doubt"—suggests the idea of a small-minded skeptic who does not understand the intrinsic beauty or value of art or nature. Tompkins cares only for "practical" use, by which he means "economic use." To him, flowers are merely "the digestive and genital organs of plants," and the idea that they are "pretty" is incomprehensible. Perkins—possibly a diminutive of "Peter"—disavows any knowledge of Niggle's art at all (93–95).

But there is an irony in all this. On the last page of the story, the First Voice and the Second Voice discuss the land, the tree, and its surrounding gardens as if they were a recreational resort or retreat. The Second Voice says the place does in fact have value, though not in the same utilitarian terms conceded by Tompkins.

> "It is proving very useful indeed," said the Second Voice. "As a holiday, and a refreshment. It is splendid for convalescence; and not only for that, for many it is the best introduction to the Mountains. It works wonders in some cases. I am sending more and more there. They seldom have to come back." (95)

Repeating the idea of forward progress, or of movement "further up and further in,"[17] this person or being—perhaps even a divine figure[18]—sees Niggle's painting and Parish's gardening as making a positive, practical contribution to the restoration and healing of others who are making the same journey. The land on which they have worked has value for its own sake and, in terms of community and communion, for the sake of others' well-being. Inasmuch as it is a heavenly realm, it also suggests that heaven is a place not of disembodied spirits floating on clouds but of fruitful agricultural and horticultural work.

Finally, the ultimate reconciliation of art and nature is symbolized in the name that the two voices agree this land ought to have:

> "The Porter settled that some time ago," said the Second Voice. "*Train for Niggle's Parish in the bay:* he has shouted that for a long while now. Niggle's Parish. I sent a message to both of them to tell them."
> "What did they say?"
> "They both laughed. Laughed—the Mountains rang with it!" (95)

As Shippey has pointed out, this is a comedy—not in the same way that "Farmer Giles of Ham" can be called a comic tale, but in the classical and Dantean sense of having a happy ending, a *eucatastrophic* one with a suggestion of final fulfillment in celestial harmony.[19] The environmental implications of its message have as much to do with Tolkien's belief in the value of the natural world as with the capacity of art to represent, fulfill, and complete it.

Wootton Major

"Smith of Wootton Major" was written much later than the two stories discussed above. It was begun in 1965 and first published in 1967, and not surprisingly, it reveals a more mature, sober, deeper level of thought. Like "Farmer Giles of Ham," it is about the importance of the natural world, and like "Leaf by Niggle," it is about the contribution that art (including literature) can make to it. But whereas the predominant culture in Ham is agrarian, with only occasional glimpses of distant mountain wilderness, in Wootton Major, agriculture is referred to only indirectly through the type of work done by the title character. Thematically, the predominant picture of Faërie in "Smith of Wootton Major" is that of feraculture—wilderness—and in that sense the story is much closer in tone to the final section of "Leaf by Niggle."

The story's most powerful images are those of the natural wilderness of Faërie, which is not subject to human domination or habitation.

Faërie is portrayed as a wild land that is both beautiful and dangerous, accessible to human appreciation but inimical to conquest, possession, or even the presence of human beings, except by permission of a transcendent authority. It is full of great mountains with impassable peaks, desolate shores with ever-present storms, and "Dark Marches of which men knew nothing" (*WMFG*, 26). There are places in Faërie where, even with the star given to him by the king of that land, Smith cannot go. This wilderness is protected from humans by its inhabitants. One thing that becomes clear to Smith over the course of his wanderings is that the star—which we can equate with Niggle's artistic gifts—is not a passport to go wherever he wishes. There are places that he is intentionally kept out of, even with his star.

Yet for all the danger and wildness, the land is also full of beauty—so much so that "some of [Smith's] briefer visits he spent looking only at one tree or one flower." Furthermore, there are hints that some of this beauty is not that of wildness but rather a beauty cultivated by the folk of Faërie. The Vale of Evermorn, the dwelling of the Queen of Faërie, is a place typified by images of ordered beauty. There are lawns there, for example, and some of the flowers grow in response to contact with the feet of the queen and her dancers. We might say that flowers spring forth where these supernatural figures "plant their feet." And yet here, we are told, the "green surpasses the green of the meads of Outer Faery as they surpass ours in our springtime." As we pointed out in an earlier chapter, the color green is a universal image of nature with special symbolic significance throughout Tolkien's works. The color green provides the reader of this story with a vision of nature richer than anything imaginable in the world—a potent image of supernatural horticulture (26–31).

Although this story does not directly depict agricultural scenes, its background is an agrarian world. For example, Smith is described as "the best smith between Far Easton and the Westwood, and he could make all kinds of things in his smithy. Most of them, of course, were plain and useful, meant for daily needs: farm tools, carpenters' tools, kitchen tools . . . and the like. They were strong and lasting, but they also had a grace about them" (23). The fact that "farm tools" are the first things mentioned suggests the agrarian nature of Wootton Major. The farm and kitchen implements described here are "plain and useful," intended to meet "daily needs"; they are not bejeweled finery indicative of the sort of greedy desire that so often leads to the extraction of wealth. Like the Shire, Wootton Major is technologically simple; Smith crafts hand tools, not complex machinery. And all these aspects of the agrarian life are connected with "grace," which suggests aesthetic qualities tinged with the spiritual and the sacred. What we have in Wootton Major—though the picture is only barely sketched—is a complete agrarian world situated on the borders of the beauty and wildness of Faërie.

The next thing to note about the setting for this tale is the abundance of nature imagery. As mentioned, "some of [Smith's] briefer visits he spent looking only at one tree or one flower," and the symbol of the King of Faërie is a great and beautiful tree: "Far off there was a great hill of shadow, and out of that shadow, which was its root, he saw the King's Tree springing up, tower upon tower, into the sky, and its light was like the sun at noon; and it bore at once leaves and flowers and fruits uncounted, and not one was the same as any other that grew on the Tree" (28). In mythic terms, this tree plays a startlingly similar role to the Two Trees made by Yavanna in *The Silmarillion*. Both images have spiritual qualities. Yavanna's trees are of sacred mythic significance, and in this story, the king's tree reaches into the sky, its glorious light suggesting the glory of the heavens. In both cases, the trees give off a light of their own.

Like "Leaf by Niggle," "Smith of Wootton Major" can be understood at least in part as autobiographical allegory.[20] Ideas found in "Smith of Wootton Major" share much in common with those expressed in "On Fairy-stories." In the latter, Faërie is described as "a perilous land" with "pitfalls for the unwary and dungeons for the overbold" (*TL*, 9), while in "Smith of Wootton Major," we read "that the marvels of Faery cannot be approached without danger, and that many of the Evils cannot be challenged without weapons of power too great for any mortal to wield" (*WMFG*, 24). The more important connection, though, is between the *author* of the essay and the *character* in the story. In the first paragraph of the essay, Tolkien describes himself as "a wandering explorer (or trespasser) in the land [of Faërie], full of wonder but not of information" (*TL*, 9). This could also be a fitting description of Smith, who, through the gift of the fairy star, becomes Starbrow, also a traveler in Faërie. The star is his passport into a world of deeper reality, just as Niggle's tree is part of a landscape through which he and Parish and many others after them gain entry to the deeper realities beyond. We also see that Smith, like the author of the essay, is full of wonder but not of information: "Some things he did not forget," we are told, "and they remained in his mind as wonders and mysteries." Later, when Smith becomes presumptuous about his freedom, he is viewed as a trespasser and told, "You don't belong here" (*WMFG*, 24, 26, 31).

Other than Smith himself, the most important characters in "Smith of Wootton Major" are the King and Queen of Faërie. There seem to be several levels of meaning in these characters. One aspect of the imagery—one we should expect, given the connection between the story and the essay—is that "Smith of Wootton Major" is also about the value and purpose of fantasy literature. It is fair to suggest here that Tolkien was writing a fairy story about writing fairy stories. The king and queen represent the real power of Faërie, as opposed to the dull and sugary imitations represented by the cakes of the onetime master cook Nokes. Yet even the sugary imitations, we are told, can help point people toward the deeper and truer things. "Better a little doll, maybe," the queen says to Smith the second time they meet, "than no memory of Faery at all. For some only a glimpse. For some the awakening" (37). Readers who detect an echo of the "introduction to the Mountains" in "Leaf by Niggle" are no doubt right.

With respect to Tolkien's environmental vision, however, perhaps the most important lesson of the story, and the backbone of Tolkien's environmental ethic appearing in all his works, is connected with stewardship: the idea that we are not owners of the land, nor even of our own time or abilities. These things are lent to us, and we are accountable for how we use them. Niggle's most precious gift is time, and he needs to learn to be a better steward of it. For Smith, the star is a tremendous gift to him as a smith and a craftsman, but it is also one that enables him to enter the land of Faërie. Such gifts, however, are not to be used merely for our own pleasure and purposes. This is later spelled out clearly in a conversation between Smith and the King of Faërie, who is still in the guise of Alf, the master cook:

> "Do you not think, Master Smith," said Alf, "that it is time for you to give this thing up?"
> "What is that to you, Master Cook?" he answered. "And why should I do so? Isn't it mine? It came to me, and may a man not keep things that come to him so, at least as a remembrance?"

> "Some things. Those that are free gifts and given for remembrance. But others are not so given. They cannot belong to a man for ever, nor be treasured as heirlooms. They are lent." (41)

Here the king corrects Smith, reminding him of what he may have known all along: the star was lent to him to be used only for a time, not to be held onto forever. This is a lesson in stewardship that Smith fundamentally understands, though it is difficult for him to put it into practice. He proves to be a good steward of his talents as a blacksmith—making many things that are useful, beautiful, and delightful but never making a single weapon—we are told, "he could have forged weapons that in his own world would have had power enough to become matter of great tales" (24), but he does not. He also proves to be a good steward of the star, freely returning it to the king when the time comes. Finally, the character of Alf (or Prentice), who is from the eternal realm of Faërie—indeed, the very king of a realm that could rightly be called heavenly—humbles himself to become incarnate in the world of men, coming first as a child and staying into adulthood. The transcendent significance and the biblical echo of this lesson in stewardship are unmistakable.

In these stories, it is in the context of stewardship that Tolkien presents natural images in which we can see hints or vestiges of an environmental vision. The land is not ours to be used, consumed, and disposed of as we wish. Tolkien teaches us that, like Smith and Farmer Giles, we are stewards of the environment, just as, like Niggle and Parish, we are stewards of our time and talents.

In *A Sand County Almanac*, Aldo Leopold says ethics involves the recognition that humans live in community with one another; a "land ethic," he writes, simply expands the idea of community to include other creatures and their habitats and, at its widest extent, the whole of the environment, the whole of creation.[21] In the context of the larger ethical system Tolkien understood as basic to reality, these stories suggest a transcendent perspective in which creation is seen similarly as intrinsically valuable and in which people are fulfilled ultimately as creatures in harmony with creation and the creator. In these three stories we see hints and reflections of this practical harmony in the same threefold vision of environmental stewardship that underlies *The Lord of the Rings*.

As in the lengthier novels, Tolkien explores developments of character in which right ethical relationships between people are implicated in a right understanding of their relationship with the natural environment. This, in turn, serves as an artistic foundation for Tolkien's exploration of the created physical world on a continuum with the transcendent world of eternal reality and of our stewardship responsibilities that touch on both.

Part III
"Uprooting the Evil in the Fields That We Know"

☙❦❧

Following the Vision, and the Consequences of Ignoring It

Chapter 8
Three Faces of Mordor

Just as Tolkien's environmental vision in his Middle-earth mythology is complex and comprehensive, including models of agriculture, horticulture, and feraculture and the principles of both conservation and preservation, so too the threats to that vision in *The Lord of the Rings* are distinguished by their breadth and complexity. The evils of Sauron and the dangers he poses to the ecology of Middle-earth are threefold: they appear in descriptions of the land of Mordor itself, in portrayals of Saruman's Isengard, and in the picture of a degraded Shire under Sharkey at the end of the story. Such a presentation not only enables readers to see the natural (or, rather, *anti*-natural) conclusion of Sauron's ecological nightmare but also provides—in images of the Shire under hostile occupation—a more realistic and accessible picture that comes much closer to home. Readers are shown what Mordor looks like when it is no longer far away but has come into their own backyards.

The Ephel Dúath, the Morgai, and the Plateau of Gorgoroth

Many readers of *The Lord of the Rings* have made the implicit connection between the devastated landscapes of Middle-earth and environmental destruction in our world. A memorable example of this is from the 1960s, when Tolkien was just beginning to reach a wider audience among American college students. It was reported in the late 1960s that Harvard University bulldozed a grove of beloved trees to make way for a new "culture center." In protest, on the half-finished building at the construction site, amidst torn-up ground, concrete blocks, and tangles of iron reinforcements, someone scrawled in black paint, "Another bit of Mordor."

Mordor indeed. The most dramatic aspect of Tolkien's vision of evil and its devastating effect on the natural environment is revealed in the extreme in Mordor. It is in this land, under the tyranny of the Dark Lord, that we see most clearly the sort of world that Middle-earth would become if left to the rule of Sauron and those like him. The picture is hideous, but it is one that must be confronted directly as we move toward a consideration of its applicability to our own environmental threats.

The reader first sees the tortured land of Mordor when, guided by Gollum, Sam and Frodo arrive at the Black Gate that guards Sauron's realm:

> Dreadful as the Dead Marshes had been, and the arid moors of the Noman-lands, more loathsome far was the country that the crawling day now slowly unveiled to his shrinking eyes. Even to the Mere of Dead Faces some haggard phantom of green spring would come; but here neither spring nor summer would ever come again. Here nothing lived, not even the leprous growths that feed on rottenness. The gasping pools were choked with ash and crawling muds, sickly white and grey, as if the mountains had vomited the filth of their entrails upon the lands about. High mounds of crushed and powdered rock, great cones of earth fire-blasted and poison-stained, stood like an obscene graveyard in endless rows, slowly revealed in the reluctant light.
>
> They had come to the desolation that lay before Mordor: the lasting monument to the dark labour of its slaves that should endure when all their purposes were made void; a land defiled, diseased beyond all healing—unless the Great Seas should enter in and wash it with oblivion. "I feel sick," said Sam. Frodo did not speak. (IV/ii)

"Dreadful," "loathsome," "gasping," "choked," "sickly," "fire-blasted," "poison-stained," "obscene," "desolation," "dark," "defiled," "diseased beyond all healing"—this must rank as one of the lengthiest and most gruesome passages describing environmental degradation in modern literature. It is worse than the Dead Marshes, Sam feels, for even in *that* dreadful land there are some rudimentary forms of life. In Mordor, the only hope for the restoration of life would be something on the order of a cataclysmic flood. A precedent for this speculation occurs at the end of the *Quenta Silmarillion,* when the Valar sweep across Middle-earth, destroy Morgoth, and split the northern world asunder, letting the sea roll in and change the shape of the western shores of Middle-earth forever. Another occurs at the end of the *Akallabêth,* when Ilúvatar drowns Númenor in recompense for its many offenses, not the least of which are offenses against the environment. Tolkien's acknowledged exemplar is the myth of Atlantis, but another undocumented influence is no doubt the biblical myth of the Great Flood. In that story, because of the continual evil and "wickedness of man" (Genesis 6:5), God uses a deluge to wipe humankind from the face of the earth, saving only Noah and the animals on his ark. However, events like this do not occur often in mythology, and the recurrence of such an event in Middle-earth is not presented as a likelihood until the end of time.

Upon looking at the desolation of Mordor, therefore, Sam understands how complete the disaster is: he concludes that "neither spring nor summer would ever come again" to that blasted land. Environmental devastation on this scale disrupts even the annual seasonal cycles. To describe this scene, Tolkien gives us one of the vilest literary images imaginable: the vomit of entrails. It is no wonder Sam feels sick. Tolkien draws from the imagery of war, industrialization, and urbanism, which in our world seem to run roughshod and rampant over the landscape as pasture, farmland, and undisturbed wilderness retreat as before an advancing enemy. The "high mounds of crushed and powdered rock" of Mordor remind us of the mountains of tailings and mining wastes that trouble our own environment. The ground in Mordor is not only "fire-blasted," as with bombs, but also "poison-stained," as when factories' toxic refuse contaminates the earth, the water, and the air. Although the modern notion of toxic waste dumps and Superfund cleanup sites had not yet been conceived, Tolkien certainly had plenty of opportunity to witness wanton abuse of a similar kind from the factories in the city of Birmingham. He also witnessed environmental devastation as a member of the Nineteenth Lancashire Fusiliers during World War I, where the horrors of trench warfare, poison gas, and the Battle of the Somme left a lasting impression on him (*Letters,* 303).[1] One of the saddest aspects of Tolkien's environmental commentary here is that the wastes figuratively described as filth and vomit are said to remain as a "lasting monument" of Sauron's work, to "endure when all [his] purposes were made void." We can only hope such a dismal sentence does not rest on all such places in our world.

Fortunately for their quest, Sam, Frodo, and Gollum turn aside from the gate and do not try to enter Mordor that way. Following a brief but important respite in Ithilien with Faramir, they finally enter Sauron's realm several days later, after their encounter with Shelob and Frodo's subsequent imprisonment in Cirith Ungol. Tolkien offers a visual description of Mordor as it would have been seen by the hobbits climbing down from the Ephel Dúath: "Slowly and painfully they clambered down, groping, stumbling, scrambling among rock and briar and dead wood in the blind shadows." Again, the imagery is just as vivid and painful from this microcosmic perspective as it is in the large-scale view from the Black Gate. We can feel the anguish of a lifeless landscape and the anguish imposed on those who pass through it: the shadows of blindness and death, the memory of trees reduced to "dead wood," and—shortly thereafter—the memory of water in beds of "now dry and withered stream[s]" as the hobbits stumble upon a tiny trickle of water:

> Out of a gully on the left, so sharp and narrow that it looked as if the black cliff had been cloven by some huge axe, water came dripping down: the last remains, maybe, of some sweet rain gathered from sunlit seas, but ill-fated to fall at last upon the walls of the Black Land and wander fruitless down into the dust. Here it came out of the rock in a little falling streamlet, and flowed across the path, and turning south ran away swiftly to be lost among the dead stones. (VI/ii)

Tolkien's imagery—that of an axe ripping apart the cliff—bespeaks violent destruction of the very shape of the landscape. And great violence *has* been done; even the less arresting images elsewhere contribute to the underlying sense of the environmental damage that has left nearly everything in Mordor either dead or dying: trees, rivers, stones, and even the air. When they look to the skies, they see that "Orodruin was still belching forth a great fume," an image made sharper by its jarring juxtaposition with the "sweet rain gathered from sunlit seas." If any of this water eventually falls on the land of Mordor in the form of rain, it is said to be "ill-fated." Water cannot last long in Mordor before it is polluted, sucked into the greedy earth, or evaporated and lost. It is not surprising, then, that Sam and Frodo sometimes simply speak generically of "the glooms of Mordor" (VI/ii).

The blight on the earth is most keenly felt by the hobbits when they first enter that land, when the contrasts between it and the living world are still sharp:

> Upon its outer marges under the westward mountains Mordor was a dying land, but it was not yet dead. And here things still grew, harsh, twisted, bitter, struggling for life. In the glens of the Morgai on the other side of the valley low scrubby trees lurked and clung, coarse grey grass-tussocks fought with the stones, and withered mosses crawled on them; and everywhere great writhing, tangled brambles sprawled. (VI/ii)

What little life remains is "harsh," "twisted," "bitter," and "struggling for life." Again the imagery is one of torture and violence: tussocks "fight" with stones; the withered mosses are "writhing," as if in the violent throes of death. When they fall from a ledge and land in a tangle of thorns, Sam says, "Bless me, Mr. Frodo, but I didn't know as anything grew in Mordor! But if I had a'known, this is just what I'd have looked for. These thorns must be a foot long by the feel of them" (VI/ii). The thorns have taken up—as if by the roots—the violent nature of the rocky soil they grow in. Yet they represent life, and even the twisted thorns are a blessing of sorts, for they cushion the hobbits' fall.

The hobbits find it surprising that there is any life at all, then. But there is some. Tolkien seems to suggest that even in the midst of such horror—even against the worst evils—nature exhibits a tenacious will to survive. Eventually, however, we see this struggle as doomed to failure if the evil is not stopped. When the hobbits come fully down off Ephel Dúath and onto the inner edge of the Morgai and the Plateau of Gorgoroth, we read, "the last living things gave up their struggle; the tops of the Morgai were grassless, bare, jagged, barren as slate" (VI/ii). The landscape of Mordor is both "bare"—devoid of vegetation—and "barren"—its fertility destroyed, no longer able to produce life. And the deeper they go beyond the marges, the worse it becomes:

> On the very edge of the last fence of Mordor ... the inner plain stretching away into a formless gloom ... only a grey light came to the dreary fields of Gorgoroth. There smokes trailed on the earth and lay in the hollows, and fumes leaked from fissures in the earth. ...
>
> Between them and the smoking Mountain, and about it north and south, all seemed ruinous and dead, a desert burned and choked. They wondered how the Lord of this realm maintained and fed his slaves and his armies. (VI/ii)

Again we see continuous gloom—a recurring image in descriptions of Mordor—gloom so deep that it no longer takes form. The environmental degradation is so bad that the earth itself has begun to emit noxious fumes. As in earlier passages, the imagery here is all of ruin and death: a desert made lifeless not through natural causes but through the actions of Sauron.

And still it gets worse, as the hobbits discover when they cross the plains toward Mount Doom. "Down on the stones behind the fences of the Black Land the air seemed almost dead, chill and yet stifling. ... For the hobbits each day, each mile, was more bitter than the one before, as their strength lessened and the land became more evil" (VI/iii). Shortly after escaping Cirith Ungol, while still on the Morgai, Frodo had told Sam, "I tried to remember the Brandywine, and Woody End, and The Water running through the mill at Hobbiton. But I can't see them now" (VI/ii). His remarks are already quite poignant, because these are the very reasons—the verdant woods and clean rivers of the Shire—that Frodo undertakes his quest. But after a few days in Mordor, Frodo has lost even more; his memory of *everything* he has ever enjoyed has been driven from him. "I know that such things happened, but I cannot see them," he tells Sam. "No taste of food, no feel of water, no sound of wind, no memory of tree or grass or flower, no image of moon or star are left to me" (VI/iii). These last few items are especially telling, for they are the things of nature and creation so loved by Hobbits. The environmental devastation wrought by Sauron not only kills life; in Frodo, it has killed even the memory of it.

At this point, we must ask what Sauron has done to destroy the environment of Mordor so effectively. And we should be alert to environmental implications for our own world. Although Tolkien suggests that

Mordor has been dead for a long time, there are hints—some suggestive imagery and some specific comments—about what has destroyed this land. The smoke pouring into the air from Mount Doom and from the ground itself suggests modern industry of the kind Tolkien must have observed as a child in or near Birmingham. But he also gives another specific explanation for the death of Mordor. When Sam wonders where Sauron's armies, massed on the Plain of Udûn, get food and water, the omniscient narrator provides insight that is unavailable to the hobbits themselves. "Neither [Sam] nor Frodo knew anything of the great slave-worked fields away south in this wide realm, beyond the fumes of the Mountain.... Here in the northward regions were the mines and forges, and the musterings of long-planned war" (VI/ii). This passage tells us several things. First, the form of agriculture practiced by the servants of Sauron is radically different from the small farms of Cotton, Maggot, and the Hobbits in the Shire. Instead, it more closely resembles mechanized, large-scale factory farming of the kind that has become prevalent in the modern world of agribusiness or the agricultural collectives of totalitarian regimes. It is agriculture of the most oppressive kind: that of slave labor. In terms decried by Wendell Berry and others, this alone is sufficient indictment of Sauron's environmental failures. Tolkien, however, gives us even more. We also see mines, slave-run forges, and militarism. And of course—like the greed that causes it—warfare in the real world damages the land like nothing else can.

Hidden in this indictment of industrial farming, mass-production manufacturing, and large-scale mining in service to the military machine is an even more subtle indictment. Berry, whose positions we have cited throughout this book, defends the idea of personal ownership of land, especially in the context of local community and the values of environmental stewardship, contrasting them with the negative effects of corporate and public ownership. Because the corporate absentee landowner does not dwell on the land whereby he makes money by producing food, digging mines, or building factories, he is not confronted with the environmental harm done by these activities. We see some of this reasoning in Berry's essay "Conservation and Local Economy," which outlines seven guiding principles for the use and care of land. We commend them all to interested readers, but among them, numbers II, IV, V, and VII are particularly relevant to Tolkien's presentation of the evil of Mordor:

II. Land cannot be properly cared for by people who do not know it intimately, who do not know how to care for it, who are not strongly motivated to care for it, and who cannot afford to care for it.

IV. People are motivated to care for land to the extent that their interest in it is direct, dependable, and permanent.

V. They will be motivated to care for the land if they can reasonably expect to live on it as long as they live. They will be more strongly motivated if they can reasonably expect that their children and grandchildren will live on it as long as they live. In other words, there must be a mutuality of belonging: they must feel that the land belongs to them, that they belong to it, and that this belonging is a settled and unthreatened fact.

VII. A nation will destroy its land and therefore itself if it does not foster in every possible way the sort of thrifty, prosperous, permanent rural households and communities that have the desire, the skills, and the means to care properly for the land they are using.[2]

Viewed from Berry's perspective, Sauron is a model of corporate landownership. Apparently the Dark Lord does not know it intimately, is not dependent on it, and thus is not motivated to care for it. It does not matter to him if he damages Mordor; there are other fields farther away where his slaves can produce the food they need to serve his war machine. In the north are his mines and his blasted earth, and if those fail—which they likely will—he will no doubt find or conquer others. But if Sauron's stewardship of the land is deficient, so is that of the Orcs and the Men who work it. As slaves, they have no compelling interest in its long-term health.

Saruman's Isengard

The image we have just painted of Mordor is stark and dramatic; no reader of Tolkien's work would want to live on the Plains of Udûn or anywhere near this place of such widespread environmental devastation. Now one could make the case that there are many places in our world where the environmental devastation is as extreme as that seen in the fictional land of Mordor. Abandoned strip mines and clear-cut timberlands provide two such examples. Yet another is the barren landscape that was once the bottom of the shrinking Aral Sea. As we mentioned earlier, the descriptions of Mordor were surely inspired at some level by the big-city industrialization of early-twentieth-century England. Blighted urban scenes were already well established in literature by Tolkien's time, as evidenced by some of William Blake's poetry and the novels of Charles Dickens. The latter's description of Coketown, in *Hard Times*, is particularly reminiscent of Tolkien's Mordor:

> It was a town of red brick or of brick that would have been red if the smoke and ashes had allowed it; but as matters stood it was a town of unnatural red and black like the painted face of a savage. It was a town of machinery and tall chimneys, out of which interminable serpents of smoke trailed themselves for ever and ever, and never got uncoiled. It had a black canal in it, and a river that ran purple with ill-smelling dye, and vast piles of building full of windows where there was a rattling and a trembling all day long, and where the piston of the steam-engine worked monotonously up and down, like the head of an elephant in a state of melancholy madness.[3]

Tolkien had plenty of descriptive and pictorial sources for devastated environments to draw on, not to mention his own imagination.

Nonetheless, such scenes may still feel remote to readers, and as a result, the fictional portrayals may not automatically invite a practical response. The problem with this image is that in some ways it is *too* horrific. Few people are likely ever to witness a landscape as blasted and lifeless as Mordor's; thus, as vivid as the picture is, it may seem like something of a remote abstraction. "Mordor is a long way away," Treebeard says to Merry and Pippin, as an explanation for why he has failed to take action in the past (III/iv). If Treebeard, the Shepherd of the Trees, feels the distance, how much more distant Mordor must seem to Tolkien's readers. Further, because Mordor is so dark and distorted, even a reader who is unsympathetic to environmental concerns can easily perceive the extremity of its description, identify it as undesirable, and agree that Sauron should be opposed—but without necessarily recognizing the need to address the *real* environmental evils that surround us in daily life.

Mordor, however, is only one part of a much fuller portrayal of the nature of environmental evil. The evils represented by Mordor and the effects of the tortured ecology of Sauron's realm are much more recognizable in Saruman's Isengard, where environmental destruction is defended by the very reasonable sounding arguments of the white wizard. A casual reader of the trilogy or a viewer of Peter Jackson's films might think that Saruman's only evil is his militarism and desire for power and that there are no environmental implications to his rule over Isengard or his plans for Middle-earth. But Tolkien gives a clear picture of the ecology of Isengard under the white wizard and what the land looks like under such rule.

The first glimpse of this picture comes at the Council of Elrond early in Book II, when Gandalf describes the transition the region has undergone under Saruman—from a land "green and fair" to one of "pits and forges" (II/ii). Pits and forges are, of course, our mines and industry: signs of "progress." It is a clear enough picture, and among its other features, good and bad, Jackson's film captures this scene quite well. One of the most compelling images in the movie *The Fellowship of the Ring* is of Saruman's transformation of Isengard from an ancient, positive symbol of the powerful and wise Númenóreans in a beautiful woodland bordering the forests of Fangorn into a seat of military power: part strip mine, part clear-cut, part factory, part military base. The most telling scene is when one of Saruman's Orc servants complains that the trees are strong, with deep roots, and thus hard to fell, and that more wood is needed for their furnaces. Saruman's reply is a command to take down *all* the trees—to lay bare (and barren) the land of Isengard.

The most complete description of Isengard is given in *The Two Towers* when Gandalf, Aragorn, Legolas, Gimli, Théoden, Éomer, and a company of Rohirrim approach it after the battle at Helm's Deep. We read, for example, that "most of the valley [around Isengard] had become a wilderness of weeds and thorns." This is not nearly as bad as the description of Mordor; there is still some life in Isengard, but probably only because Saruman has not had as much time as Sauron. The narration makes it clear that Isengard is moving very quickly in the direction of Mordor and Udûn as its ruler destroys more and more life, leaving only a fading memory. Trees, especially, are targeted. "No trees grew there," the reader is told, "but among the rank grasses could still be seen the burned and axe-hewn stumps of ancient groves." As for the road that had once been lined with trees, "instead of trees there marched long lines of pillars, some of marble, some of copper and iron, joined by heavy chains" (III/viii). Saruman apparently views smelted and manufactured products as superior to—more useful than—the living elements of the landscape.

Regarding the various forms of pollution, we also read, "Iron wheels revolved there endlessly, and hammers thudded. At night plumes of vapour steamed from the vents, lit from beneath with red light, or blue, or venomous green." We may recall Dickens's pistons working "up and down," rattling the windows in his fictional Coketown. Perhaps the most telling comments, however, are the simplest ones. "Once it had been fair and green. . . . It was not so now." This powerful emotional appeal to our memory of good things turned bad is repeated: "Once it had been green and filled with avenues, and groves of fruitful trees, watered by streams that flowed from the mountains to a lake. But no green thing grew there in the latter days of Saruman." It is an understatement when we read yet another profound and simple comment: "It was a sad country" (III/viii).

The other source of knowledge about Saruman and Isengard in detail is Treebeard. Earlier in *The Two Towers*, when the ent meets the two hobbits in Fangorn, Treebeard's words provide a great deal of insight because they include not only a description of what Saruman has done but also a moral judgment on those actions. When Merry and Pippin ask about Saruman, Treebeard has plenty to tell: "[Saruman] is plotting to become a Power. He has a mind of metal and wheels; and he does not care for growing things, except as far as they serve him for the moment" (III/iv). Contrary to the positive ecologies we discussed in chapters 3, 4, and 5, in Saruman's ecology growing things have no inherent value; to the white wizard, growing things are just that: things. Their only value is in how they can be used by Saruman to gain power. The connection to metal and wheels is also important, suggesting a replacement of nature—both agriculture and wildness—with machinery.

Implications of this value system can be seen in the destruction of the trees of Fangorn—a destruction carried out by the Orcs at the command of Saruman. As Treebeard describes it, "He and his foul folk are making havoc now. Down on the borders they are felling trees—good trees. Some of the trees they just cut down and leave to rot—orc-mischief that; but most are hewn up and carried off to feed the fires of Orthanc.

There is always a smoke rising from Isengard these days. . . . There are wastes of stump and bramble where once there were singing groves" (III/iv). It is evil enough, Treebeard suggests, to ravage entire forests even for such practical reasons as feeding forge fires. But it is even worse for the Orcs to destroy the trees for no purpose at all. "It is the orc-work, the wanton hewing . . . without even the bad excuse of feeding the fires, that has so angered us; and the treachery of a neighbour, who should have helped us. . . . There is no curse in Elvish, Entish, or the tongues of Men bad enough for such treachery. Down with Saruman" (III/iv). Saruman's actions constitute two kinds of evil: deforestation for utilitarian purposes and destruction of forests simply to let them rot. This is what we can expect from the likes of Saruman. A bad steward of his own land will probably be a bad steward of other people's, and the ill effects are bound to spill over into the surrounding landscape.

Tolkien also shows us Saruman's evil—in particular, the evil of his *anti*-ecology—in the manner in which he does battle. The Ents discover this in their attack on Isengard, as Pippin later explains to the others: "Suddenly up came fires and foul fumes: the vents and shafts all over the plain began to spout and belch. Several of the Ents got scorched and blistered. One of them, Beechbone I think he was called, a very tall handsome Ent, got caught in a spray of some liquid fire and burned like a torch: a horrible sight" (III/ix). Saruman, it seems, has used some sort of defoliating agent or other form of chemical warfare. Besides showing that he considers the trees and their guardians his enemies, this shows us that his war on Rohan is also a war against the land itself. Again, the mythic agent of destruction in the lands of Mordor and Isengard is shown in the image of industrial smokestacks: vents and shafts spouting and belching fire and foul fumes. Like Sauron and Morgoth before him, Saruman is destroying Arda, the creation of Eru.

Tolkien scholar and philologist Tom Shippey claims that, among other things, the character of Saruman provides a basis for the "strong applicability" of the mythology of Middle-earth. Though this comment was made in the context of Tolkien's philology and as a general statement about the mythic dimension of *The Lord of the Rings*, Shippey's ideas provide insight into ecological issues as well. As a philologist, he explains, Tolkien is exploring Saruman's nature as a consummate "technologist," even in the character's name. The word *saru*, a hypothetical (unrecorded) Mercian form of the West Saxon word *searu,* has puzzled Old English lexicographers for a long time. Shippey connects *saru-* and *searu-* with the *sare-* in the name Sarehole, whose mill became for Tolkien "an image of destructive technology." If *sare* means something similar to *saru,* then a *Sarehole* is a *searu-pit,* and Saruman is a *searu-man.* In this way, the wizard can be connected to the idea of destructive technology. Treebeard's comment about the wizard's mind accords precisely with Shippey's explanation of Saruman's name:

> The standard translation for *searo* here is something like "cunning," and this fits with other uses. . . . The word has ominous suggestions as well, in the adjective *searocræftig* or the noun *searoniþ,* "cunning-crafty," "cunning-spite." Finally it is connected also with treasure . . . [like the] treasure [that] *stayed with* its possessor, [and] gave him the "dragon-sickness" of which the Master of Laketown died.
>
> Saruman could then mean simply "cunning mind," itself an old designation for a wizard, and so suitable enough. But behind that, one may see that for Tolkien the Old English word expressed very accurately a complex concept for which we no longer have a term. What does Saruman stand for? One thing, certainly, is a kind of mechanical ingenuity, smithcraft developed into engineering skills. Treebeard says of Saruman that "He has a mind of metal and wheels"; his orcs used a kind of gunpowder at Helm's Deep, and later on he uses against the Ents a kind of napalm. . . . How suitable that "Sarehole" could be taken to mean "the *saru*-pit" or possibly "the sere pit, the withered pit."[4]

Saruman, as Shippey explains, is thus associated with metal and engineering, with the greedy desire to stockpile personal possessions that is itself associated with many environmental woes and, ultimately, with the withering of the land that results from both. He is in many ways the opposite of Samwise, son of Hamfast, the simpleminded rustic who is cunning in neither action nor speech. Cunning and craftiness may be positive traits when put to good use, but not when they are turned against the land or used only for the selfish accumulation of goods or power.

As for the "strong applicability" of the lessons we learn from Isengard, Shippey is surely right, particularly with regard to environmental concerns. He explains:

> The "applicability" of this is obvious, with Saruman becoming an image of one of the characteristic vices of modernity, though we still have no name for it—a kind of restless ingenuity, skill without purpose, bulldozing for the sake of change . . . the Sarumans of the real world rule by deluding their followers with images of a technological Paradise in the future, a modernist Utopia; but what one often gets . . . are the blasted landscapes of Eastern Europe, strip-mined, polluted, and even radioactive. One may disagree with Tolkien's diagnosis of the situation, and with his nostalgic or pastoral solution to it, but there can be no doubt that he has at least addressed a serious issue, and tried to give it both a historical and a psychological dimension nearly always missing elsewhere.[5]

One of the things that makes Tolkien's descriptions of Saruman and Isengard so valuable for us in the real world is that they show how someone like Saruman defends his actions with reasonable-sounding rhetoric, the benign surface of which conceals a more sinister purpose. These arguments are first voiced during the Council of Elrond; in his account of Saruman's betrayal of the order to which they both belong, Gandalf quotes Saruman's own words: "The time of the Elves is over, but our time is at hand: the world of Men, which We must rule. But we must have power, power to order all things as we will, for that good which only the Wise can see" (II/ii). Saruman's message is seductive. Sauron, by contrast, does not justify his tyranny by appealing to the idea of the "good"; indeed, Sauron's voice is never heard directly in *The Lord of the Rings*—nor do we see his face—which do doubt contributes to the potency of the abstract quality of evil he represents. Because he appears in embodied form similar to the other characters, however, Saruman seems much more real. And he not only speaks of doing good but also seems legitimately convinced of the goodness of his actions.

Norman Wirzba describes the type of rhetoric used by Saruman in this way:

The purveyors of the industrial, and now information and global, economies routinely claim the inevitability and necessity of their programs and plans, and then argue that agrarian ways are anachronistic, even dangerous, since they stand in the way of a bright future. History shows, however, that the prophets and salespeople of technological progress rarely reveal the whole story.[6]

Tolkien demonstrates in Saruman's rhetoric many of the things Wirzba writes about. Saruman speaks of the inevitability of what must come to pass and promises a bright future, with rewards for those who follow his agenda. Although his speech does not explicitly target agrarianism, we have already seen that his policies run roughshod over the land and thus prove inimical to its long-term health.

Part of what makes Saruman's language work so well, however, is that there is some truth in his words. When he says, "the time of the Elves is over," he is right. By the end of the trilogy, after the War of the Ring has ended, the two mightiest Elvish kingdoms—Rivendell and Lothlórien—are approaching or have already come to the end of their history. With Aragorn's reclaiming the throne of Gondor, the world of Men has dawned. Surely Gandalf knows these things: he is in close communion with the elves Elrond and Celeborn, and one of his principal goals throughout the final years of the Third Age is to help Aragorn gain his rightful throne. As to the need for power, once again we must concede that Saruman is right. Even Gandalf admits that strength is needed.

Saruman's speech continues, and for those who have seen the film version, the words are familiar:

> "A new Power is rising. Against it the old allies and policies will not avail us at all. There is no hope left in Elves or dying Númenor. This then is one choice before you, before us. We may join with that Power. It would be wise, Gandalf. There is hope that way. Its victory is at hand; and there will be rich reward for those that aided it. As the Power grows, its proved friends will also grow; and the Wise, such as you and I, may with patience come at last to direct its courses, to control it. We can bide our time, we can keep our thoughts in our hearts, deploring maybe evils done by the way, but approving the high and ultimate pur-

pose: Knowledge, Rule, Order; all the things that we have so far striven in vain to accomplish, hindered rather than helped by our weak or idle friends." (II/ii)

Again, Saruman uses language to suggest that his goals are good. He appeals to both wisdom and hope, and at least some of the values he espouses (in his words) are ones that Gandalf also affirms: knowledge and order. Saruman agrees that evil should be deplored and that patience is important. Gandalf might say similar things. For these reasons, among others, it is a seductive speech. Thus, at the end of Book III, when Saruman uses similar language with King Théoden and his men after the Battle of Helm's Deep, it is no wonder that many are taken in by what he says. The narrator records their reaction: "The Riders stirred at first, murmuring with approval of the words of Saruman; and then they too were silent, as men spell-bound. It seemed . . . Saruman stood beside a door of escape, holding it half open so that a ray of light came through" (III/x). It is powerful rhetoric!

Yet Tolkien clearly associates Saruman with great harm to the environment and, more specifically, with technological progress that comes at the expense of life, nature, and the earth. In an essay titled "The Uses of Prophecy," David W. Orr provides insight into the rhetoric of industrialization, which he says "rests on the simple and seductively powerful idea that we can exploit soils, forests, biological diversity, and minerals without adverse consequences, and that doing so is akin to our rightful destiny. That idea is widely known to be wrong, even perversely so, but it still exerts a powerful hold on the public mind and public policies."[7] Saruman exploits all the land around him for the purpose of increasing his power. He destroys the soil and forests of Isengard. He exploits the minerals. And he does so claiming that it is his rightful destiny—the rightful destiny of Man, whose time it is to rule the earth. That he is so successful in gaining power attests to the powerful hold such rhetoric has on the public mind. Tolkien brilliantly evokes the subtle manipulations of language, ideas, and people that can produce ecological disaster both in Middle-earth and in our world. Such is progress, and Tolkien has captured it in Saruman's all-too-familiar rhetoric.

Shippey's exploration of the character suggests that "Saruman, indeed, talks exactly like too many politicians. It is impossible to work out exactly what he means because of the abstract nature of his speech. . . . His message is in any case one of compromise and calculation." Shippey concludes that "Saruman is the most contemporary figure in Middle-earth, both politically and linguistically."[8] Saruman's is the rhetoric of many contemporary enemies of the environment. It is the rhetoric of agribusiness telling the family farmer that the ways of the small farm are over and that in order to survive he will have to adapt to new industrial techniques of food production—and then promising that if he follows this course, all will be better. In short, it is the rhetoric of *progress*.

Berry captures such a scenario in *The Gift of Good Land*:

> Take, say, fifteen eighty-acre Amish farms and join them together in the ownership of an "agribusinessman," who will get rid of the livestock, take out the fences, buy the large machinery necessary to farm on a big scale, and plant all twelve hundred acres in corn or corn and beans. Health will decline in everything from the soil to the community; soil loss may rise as high as six bushels per bushel of corn. This farmer-as-"agribusinessman" will be a life-long extravagant consumer of *everything* he needs, from fuel to fertilizer, from credit to extension courses in "stress management." He will be a good citizen of the economy. But whether he knows it or not, and sooner or later he will know it, this economy proposes to ruin him, as it has ruined millions of others, and sell him out to a larger "agribusinessman" who wants to "handle" 2400 acres and help the economy even more.[9]

This is what Saruman promises Gandalf: the opportunity to be a good citizen of the economy—*Saruman's* economy. But Gandalf is wise enough to see that such an economy would ruin anyone who participates in it. Along the lines Berry suggests, we can speculate further that Gandalf would ultimately be "sold out" to a larger enterprise: Sauron.

Saruman's words also contain a threat, of course, for he claims that such changes are inevitable, regardless of any attempt to stop them. A wise person would make sure that he is on the winning side, he suggests. "You can try to remain on a small farm," this logic says, "but I'll only find others to join my powerful monopoly and drive you out." Tolkien thus shows us this familiar voice—one that has taken many of us in—and reveals to us what the words really mean and how evil such a voice can be. Hidden in Saruman's speech is the desire for personal power, the power to order all things as he wills. It is a power that ruins its allies and any who try to buy into it.

At the beginning of this section, we claimed that Isengard is really just a reflection of the evil of Mordor and the effects of Sauron's tortured ecology. Eventually, we see the truth of this statement. Gandalf describes what he sees when he is kept as a prisoner atop Orthanc: "I looked on [the valley] and saw that, whereas it had once been green and fair, it was now filled with pits and forges. Wolves and orcs were housed in Isengard, for Saruman was mustering a great force on his own account, in rivalry of Sauron and not in his service yet. Over all his works a dark smoke hung and wrapped itself about the sides of Orthanc" (II/ii). There are two clear images of what Isengard represents. The first is militarism. Like Mordor, Isengard is something of a war camp where soldiers are being mustered for battle. We learn later that Isengard houses "warriors with great store of arms" and that "wolves were fed and stabled in deep dens beneath" (III/viii). The second image is one of industrialization: forges and the dark smoke they produce filling the air. That picture is expanded later when we read, "There Saruman had treasuries, storehouses, armouries, smithies, and great furnaces" (III/viii)—more factory imagery. As in Mordor, there are also suggestions of agribusiness. "Beneath the walls of Isengard there still were acres tilled by the slaves of Saruman. . . . Thousands could dwell there, workers, servants, slaves" (III/viii).

One of the most interesting descriptions reveals that the plain of Isengard "was bored and delved. Shafts were driven deep into the ground; their upper ends were covered by low mounds and domes of stone, so that in the moonlight the Ring of Isengard looked like a graveyard of unquiet dead" (III/viii). Isengard is not merely a ring but a "Ring . . . of unquiet dead." Michael Stanton has astutely pointed out that this description evokes the One Ring of Sauron.[10] The image is also suggestive of the Nine Rings animating the spirits of the dead mortal men who wear them. In neither case is the association accidental. As the narrator summarizes:

> Saruman had slowly shaped [Isengard] to his shifting purposes, and made it better, as he thought, being deceived—for all those

arts and subtle devices, for which he forsook his former wisdom, and which fondly he imagined were his own, came but from Mordor; so that what he made was naught, only a little copy, a child's model or a slave's flattery, of that vast fortress, armoury, prison, furnace of great power, Barad-dûr, the Dark Tower. (III/viii)

Ultimately, Isengard is both a reflection of Mordor and a foreshadowing of it. It shows the reader what Mordor will be like when Sam and Frodo arrive there, even as Mordor shows the reader what Isengard is destined to become—and what our world would become if we were to accept the rhetoric of progress along the lines of Saruman's. Tolkien scholar Kathryn W. Crabbe has summarized what we can learn from Isengard: "Parallel to the destruction or breaking of the creatures of Middle-earth, the destruction of the earth itself is a dramatic manifestation of evil. To follow Saruman is to follow death, to be sure, but Tolkien's images of death are most powerful when they depict the destruction of the land, the source of life itself."[11]

This is made all the more compelling by the contrast with Gandalf, imprisoned atop the tower of Orthanc amidst all the destruction. In the film version, as Gandalf sits in despair, a small moth flutters past him. Gandalf sees this as an opportunity: the moth might be used as a messenger. Yet despite his desperation and his awful predicament, he is unwilling to risk wounding the frail creature. Rather than grab it and possibly damage its wings, he gently folds his fingers around the moth, not even touching it. He then makes his request. This scene is not in the book, but it captures a respect for living creatures that is part of Tolkien's environmental vision.

The Shire under Sharkey

Peter Jackson's film adaptation can be commended for its portrayal of Tolkien's environmental perspective—at least in negative form—in its graphic depiction of the defoliation at Isengard. Unfortunately, the film does not explore these ideas, which appear in the chapter entitled "The Scouring of the Shire" toward the end of *The Return of the King*. When it comes to applying Tolkien's environmental ethic in our own lives, this is the single most important chapter in the entire trilogy. Not merely an epilogue or an afterword, it is the culmination toward which the previous sixty chapters point. The evils of Mordor appear a little closer to our frame of reference in the glimpses of Isengard, but they are brought *fully* home in the Shire. When the hobbits return to the Shire, they find that the long arm of Mordor has reached even there. In that chapter, Tolkien provides not only the clearest picture of what environmental evil looks like in our world but also his plan for how it must be countered—the subject of our final chapter.

Certain passages suggest that learning these important lessons and applying them to our lives is the chief significance of the "The Scouring of the Shire." Returning from their long journey, the hobbits find the Shire in ruins. The narrator tells us:

> There they had their first really painful shock. This was Frodo and Sam's own country, and they found out now that they cared about it more than any other place in the world. Many of the houses that they had known were missing. Some seemed to have been burned down. The pleasant row of old hobbit-holes in the bank on the north side of the Pool were deserted, and their little gardens that used to run down bright to the water's edge were rank with weeds. Worse, there was a whole line of ugly new houses all along Pool Side, where the Hobbiton Road ran close to the bank. An avenue of trees had stood there. They were all gone. And looking with dismay up the road towards Bag End they saw a tall chimney of brick in the distance. It was pouring out black smoke into the evening air. (VI/viii)

The key sentence is the second one: this is the hobbits' "own country." The damage here seems most evil because it is the land "they cared about more than any other place."

We must now pause to consider the places we ourselves care about the most. If we have been engaged in the deeper issues touched on by the story, it should not be difficult to see that it is the Hobbits that Tolkien leads us to identify with most. Other than their diminutive size, Hobbits are presented as normal people suddenly placed in situations that require them to be heroic. More than any other people in Middle-earth, they are like us. As Shippey explains, "That indeed is their main function . . . a figure essentially modern in attitudes and sentiment is imported into the historical world, to guide the reader's reactions, to help the reader feel 'what it would be like' to be there." With respect to *The Hobbit* in particular, he adds, "[Bilbo's] main failings are those which the child reader, and indeed the adult reader, would have if transported magically to Middle-earth."[12] Likewise, as we noted in chapter 3, the Shire is based on the farm country and rural villages of Tolkien's own England—the England of the early nineteenth century. And though it was fast disappearing even then, for all its nostalgic idealism, it is a familiar landscape—in the imagination, if not in reality—to English and American readers captured by the idyll.

We catch a glimpse of this form of evil penetrating the Shire and immediately think of our own homes. We see the destruction of old houses and the construction of new ones, not because there is anything wrong with the old ones but simply because, according to the standards of innovation and progress, the new are supposed to be better and therefore preferable. In our world, when the housing and construction industries consume resources, it is supposed to "stimulate the economy," or so we are told. What this really means is that the housing industry puts money into the hands of those who stockpile the raw materials needed for construction. In the Shire, the new buildings are closely associated with the felling of trees and the black smoke pouring from chimneys into the evening air above Hobbiton. In Mordor and Isengard, such smoke comes from vague and nameless sources—holes in the ground, giant belching mountains, and subterranean furnaces. In the Shire, however, the source of the smoke is specific and localizable: the tall brick chimney of the new mill.

The four travelers are able to recognize this as evil partly because they have seen it in a more overtly sinister form elsewhere in Middle-earth. Frodo and Sam have seen it in Mordor; Merry and Pippin have seen it in Isengard. When they first see Bilbo's old neighborhood after its devastation, comments by Sam and Frodo reinforce the idea of this chapter's applicability to our world:

"This is worse than Mordor!" said Sam. "Much worse in a way. It comes home to you, as they say; because it is home, and you remember it before it was all ruined."

"Yes, this is Mordor," said Frodo. "Just one of its works. Saruman was doing its work all the time, even when he thought he was working for himself. And the same with those Saruman tricked, like Lotho." (VI/viii)

Sam is simply saying aloud what Tolkien wants his readers to think. Readers of the trilogy have seen all these signs in the real world—the felling of trees, the destruction of lovely old houses to make way for rows of ugly new ones, the construction of factories with smoke-spewing chimneys—and perhaps have merely accepted them as the unavoidable side effects of "progress." Tolkien names them the works of Mordor, and those who plan or assist in these things serve Mordor, even if they do not know it. Surely this is what the anonymous graffiti artist at Harvard meant by the spray-painted scrawl: "Another Bit of Mordor."

"The Scouring of the Shire" is full of reflections of these bitter realities, a catalog of the manifestations of the evil of Mordor in "our own country." We see it from the moment the four hobbits return and begin asking the locals what has been happening:

> "Taking in folk off-hand like, and eating extra food, and all that [isn't allowed]," said Hob.
> "What's the matter with this place?" said Merry. "Has it been a bad year, or what? I thought it had been a fine summer and harvest."
> "Well no, the year's been good enough," said Hob. "We grows a lot of food, but we don't rightly know what becomes of it. It's all these 'gatherers' and 'sharers,' I reckon, going round counting and measuring and taking off to storage. They do more gathering than sharing, and we never see most of the stuff again." (VI/viii)

One of the first laws we hear about is a law against hospitality, one of the most important virtues strengthening a sense of community. A thread running through much of Wendell Berry's writing is the mutual interconnection between sound ecological practices and a strong sense of community. It is therefore no coincidence that the destruction of the community of the Shire—its old homes, its inns and other gathering places, and even the postal service that enables Hobbits to stay in touch—goes hand in hand with the destruction of the trees and gardens.

In Hob's description we see another detriment to good environmental stewardship: food production solely for export. A short time later, Hob returns to this issue: "All the stocks seem to have gone. We do hear that wagon-loads of it went away down the old road out of the Southfarthing, over Sarn Ford way. That would be the end o' last year, after you left. But it had been going away quietly before that, in a small way" (VI/viii). Tolkien suggests something that environmentalists have been saying for the past two decades with increasing frequency and urgency: healthy communities eat locally grown food, which feeds not only local people but also the local community and its economy. Among those with strong environmental commitments—both individual consumers and a growing number of dining establishments—there is now a healthy national trend toward purchasing locally grown produce. One potential consequence of a bad ecology is that people go hungry even when, as Hob says, they "grows a lot of food." But there is far more at stake. The consumption of farm products grown locally avoids the consumption of energy—fossil fuels—required to transport goods long distances from farm to market. Even more important, local consumption ties communities more directly to their own soil, which is more conducive to sound environmental stewardship and thus good soil health. The healthiest situation is when locally grown food is consumed by people who have a commitment to the long-term health of their own land, the soil on which the food is grown, and the rivers and ponds into which agricultural runoff flows.

People who have traveled to regions where much of the best produce is exported to foreign markets know that the results can be depressing. A tourist visiting Romania during the Ceaușescu regime in the 1970s or 1980s, for example, would have seen a rich and fertile land easily capable of feeding the people of that country. But at the time, most of the Romanian people—with the exception of Communist Party officials—were hungry, unable to enjoy the fruits of their own labor, which were destined for export. As if to rub their noses in this injustice, the government established "Dollar Shops" in popular tourist areas, especially near prominent hotels in big cities, which sold the best produce and the finest wines only to foreign visitors with foreign currency. Thus, the laborers who tended Romania's grape-rich area of Tulcea, famed for its vineyards, were denied access to the excellent fruit of Tulcea's vines. In the Shire it is beer, but the idea is the same: only the foreign "ruffians" are allowed to drink it.

It is not surprising, then, to find people in Romania or in the Shire sullen and depressed, reflecting the downturn of their situation and that of the land itself. When the hobbits return, "the land looked rather sad and forlorn; but it was after all the first of November and the fag-end of Autumn. Still there seemed an unusual amount of burning going on, and smoke rose from many points round about. A great cloud of it was going up far way in the direction of woody end" (VI/viii). In a classic instance of the "pathetic fallacy," Tolkien describes the land itself as "sad and forlorn," just as in pre-1989 Romania the disruption of people's access to the products of their labor affected the whole community in a palpable way.

It is important to note that trends like these do not unfold overnight. Like many bad environmental practices, they begin slowly and expand as people become accustomed to them. Tolkien points this out as well, showing how the woes in the Shire begin "in a small way," invisible at first, then continuing so inconsequentially that nobody complains, until the Shire's goods are being exported by "wagon-loads" and it is too late to stop it. Farmer Cotton later confirms what Hob has said earlier, explaining that Lotho ("Pimple") had already managed to acquire considerable land quietly before people knew what he was doing: "Of course he started with a lot of property in the Southfarthing which he had from his dad; and it seems he'd been selling a lot o' the best leaf, and sending it away quietly for a year or two. But at the end o' last year he began sending away loads of stuff, not only leaf. Things began to get short, and winter coming on, too" (VI/viii). Cotton raises two problematic issues, both of which begin quietly and grow slowly: the ownership of too much land by one person, and the move from using farmland to grow food for the local market toward using it for the larger-scale production of export (cash) crops. Had the four hobbits not returned when they did, the narrator tells us, the Shire might never have recovered. Until their return, most of the Hobbits of the Shire seem incapable of resisting their oppressors: Sharkey and his henchmen. Of course, is that the four travelers have been trained by Gandalf, Aragorn, and Treebeard to recognize evil and actively oppose it.

Another reason the Hobbits in the Shire do not resist until Frodo and his companions return is simply that they are slow to recognize the trend as a form of evil. It develops slowly and comes packaged in the progressivist rhetoric of Saruman. In the Shire, the terminology differs from that of Isengard, but the end result is the same. Pimple's and Sharkey's plans are disguised in the benign-sounding terminology of "gathering" and "sharing," terms that do not necessarily connote evil and in fact may be understood as forms of benevolence. Like much propaganda, the terms are simply ambiguous, and the lack of clarity serves to cover up the evil. Then there is the rhetoric of efficiency, which sounds good on the surface until the real meaning is clarified. Farmer Cotton explains: "Pimple's idea was to grind more and faster, or so he said. He's got other mills like it" (VI/viii). In his introduction to Aldo Leopold's collection *For the Health of the Land,* Scott Sanders writes that Leopold "disputed the views that bigger is better, that novelty is proof of vitality, that profit matters above all else. His skepticism about the dogma of endless growth is another quality that makes him seem like our contemporary."[13] Leopold and Tolkien both warn their readers to be wary of this form of rhetorical manipulation. Again, efficiency is not an evil per se; however, the means by which efficient methods are implemented and the goals toward which they are directed can cause problems for the community and the environment.

Perhaps the most important factor enabling this form of evil to creep into the Shire is that some Shire folk gain from the implementation of these policies at the expense of others. Pimple grows rich, presumably from exporting a considerable amount of the Shire's goods to feed Saruman and his armies in Isengard. Ted Sandyman—already presented as an arrogant character in the novel's opening chapters—now enjoys the prestige of owning large mills. Some of the shirriffs also seem to enjoy their newfound power. Farmer Cotton explains:

> "It all began with Pimple, as we call him," said Farmer Cotton. . . . "Seems he wanted to own everything himself, and then order other folk about. It soon came out that he already did own a sight more than was good for him; and he was always grabbing more, though where he got the money was a mystery: mills and malt-houses and inns, and farms, and leaf-plantations. He'd already bought Sandyman's mill before he came to Bag End, seemingly." (VI/viii)

Ultimately, it is this desire for money, property, and power, Tolkien suggests, that is at the root of the environmental evil foisted on the Shire.

This motive drives the accumulation of possessions and land, while the desire to rule others drives the separation of landowners from farmworkers. When people own more land than they can care for themselves, the principles of stewardship mentioned earlier in this book are nullified. As Frodo and Sam observe, this is nothing less than an extension of Mordor. Pimple's lust to "own everything himself" and "order other folk about" is exactly the motivation at work in the One Ring itself.

Writing further about the rhetoric of those arrayed against agrarian culture, Orr adds: "That they wish to bamboozle should astonish no one; that they get away with it, however, depends on a high level of public drowsiness and gullibility. But that is an altogether more complicated thing—a kind of co-conspiracy involving a combination of ignorance and apathy on one side and a desire to mislead on the other, all disguised by a language unhinged from reality."[14] Orr could easily be describing Lotho and the situation in the Shire. Of course, bamboozling is exactly what Lotho is doing. He gets away with it for a while because, as Tolkien clearly shows, many hobbits grow drowsy, gullible, and apathetic, while others, desirous of financial gain, become Lotho's co-conspirators. Although he has no Ring, Lotho and those driven by these motives can be seen as a little like Sauron.

In light of this, it is interesting to note that Farmer Cotton says Lotho "already did own a sight more than was good for him." If we take these words literally, the new ecology that Lotho helps Saruman usher in is not only bad for the Shire but also bad for Lotho himself. Likewise, for all his arrogance, Ted Sandyman goes from running his own small mill to being a cleaning boy in someone else's. The size of the new mill does little to ameliorate the degradation of his position, and even if he were the owner of the new one, it would not help him much. "You've got to have grist before you can grind," Farmer Cotton says, "and there was no more for the new mill to do than for the old" (VI/viii). Tolkien suggests that even those who knowingly go along with Saruman suffer in the long run. What we see, then, is that blame for the environmental woes of the Shire does not rest solely with Sharkey and his ruffians from the outside; the Hobbits themselves must bear some responsibility—both those who become his accomplices and those who passively stand by and allow the damage to be done.

Interspersed with these suggestions of how this kind of evil penetrates the Shire, Tolkien continues to show just how bad the results of Sharkey's distorted ecology are. Cotton describes the state of Hobbiton upon the travelers' return: "They're always a-hammering and a-letting out a smoke and a stench, and there isn't no peace even at night in Hobbiton. And they pour out filth a purpose; they've fouled all the lower Water, and it's getting down into Brandywine. If they want to make the Shire into a desert, they're going the right way about it" (VI/viii). As vivid as this description is, it falls short of expressing how bad things really are. Each new corner the four hobbits turn brings more signs of devastation, culminating at last when they reach Bag End:

> It was one of the saddest hours in their lives. The great chimney rose up before them; . . . they saw the new mill in all its frowning and dirty ugliness: a great brick building straddling the stream, which it fouled with a steaming and stinking outflow. All along the Bywater Road every tree had been felled. . . . Even Sam's vision in the Mirror had not prepared him for what they saw. The Old Grange on the west side had been knocked down, and its place taken by rows of tarred sheds. All the chestnuts were gone. The banks and hedgerows were broken. Great wagons were standing in disorder in a field beaten bare of grass. Bagshot Row was a yawning sand and gravel quarry. Bag End up beyond could not be seen for a clutter of large huts. (VI/viii)

Even after the battle is won, Saruman is defeated, and his ruffians are driven out, Tolkien continues to describe how much environmental damage has been done in so short a time: "The trees were the worst loss and damage, for at Sharkey's bidding they had been cut down recklessly far and wide over the Shire; and Sam grieved over this more than anything else. For one thing, this hurt would take long to heal, and only his great-grandchildren, he thought, would see the Shire as it ought to be" (VI/ix). Cotton says Sharkey's work is turning the Shire into "a desert." But Frodo and Sam, and Tolkien's readers, have a more specific name for it: Mordor.

In our world, such imagery is common in any region where industrialization has damaged or destroyed the environment; the result is barren landscapes, fouled water, polluted air. In Isengard and Mordor, environmental evil is associated with Saruman and his armies of Orcs or with the colossal but distant forces of Sauron. In the Shire, Tolkien shows us its more familiar face. The water is fouled by the "stinking outflow" of mills; the pollution continues all the way down into the Brandywine. The trees are felled by Men and Hobbits for new buildings, for fuel, and sometimes for no reason at all. Even the grass has been "beaten bare."

Our Great-grandchildren

The nature of Sam's grief leads to a final thought that provides an appropriate conclusion for this chapter. Sam foresees that the damage caused to the land under Sharkey will take a long time to heal. It will take at least two generations for the visible scars to disappear, we learn, and some of the damage may never be undone. In our own world, we all live with the effects of previous generations' environmental pollution. Traces of some of humankind's worst artificial toxins, for example, can still be found in people's bodies long after their use has been banned; the waste products of fossil fuels burned a hundred years ago can be found in the ice layers at both poles. We live with environmental problems unwittingly bequeathed to us by our predecessors. Once-beautiful landscapes are now wastelands, and many grasslands, woodlands, and wetlands are now severely reduced or have vanished forever.

In his introduction to Leopold's essays, Sanders addresses this issue, quoting from Leopold's "The Farmer as Conservationist":

> You cannot travel far in our prosperous country, nor read far in Leopold, without being reminded of loss. "Few acres in North America have escaped impoverishment through human use," he tells us soberly. "If someone were to map the continent for gains and losses in soil fertility, waterflow, flora, and fauna, it would be difficult to find spots where less than three of these four basic resources have retrograded."[15]

As we have seen in "The Scouring of the Shire," Tolkien shows us the retrograding of three of these basic resources. Soil fertility on Bagshot Row in the Shire has been obliterated, its once verdant hill now a gravel pit. The Water has been fouled all the way to the Brandywine. And in the trampled grass, decimated gardens, and hewn trees—symbolized by the cutting of the Party Tree—we see the "loss of flora" Leopold writes about. Given the destruction of their native habitats, we can safely assume that animals have also been displaced if not destroyed. And we must remember that this is only the Shire; the effects are much worse in places in or near Isengard and Mordor, which will never again support life. In his essay "Do We Want a Woodless Countryside?" Leopold comments, "In farming, as in war, it is often hard to retrieve mistakes."[16]

This leads back inevitably to Gandalf's comments about stewardship examined earlier in the book. Gandalf is concerned about the degree to which stewardship, good or bad, exhibits an attitude of consideration to future generations. Early in the story, the Hobbits of the Shire live in a healthy land well cared for by their predecessors, but in the three spoiled landscapes discussed in this chapter, we see the opposite: the soil and water of the Shire are now unable to support life because the stewardship principles needed for sound environmental policies have been suspended or abandoned altogether. These principles, noted by Sanders and Leopold and illustrated so clearly by Tolkien, are the explicit focus of Théoden and Gandalf, who foresee the effects after the Battle of Helm's Deep:

> "Yet also I should be sad," said Théoden. "For however the fortune of war shall go, may it not so end that much that was fair and wonderful shall pass for ever out of Middle-earth?"
>
> "It may," said Gandalf. "The evil of Sauron cannot be wholly cured, nor made as if it had not been. But to such days we are doomed. Let us now go on with the journey we have begun!" (III/viii)

Chapter 9

Rousing the Shire

The three-part picture of environmental woes painted in the previous chapter is bleak but far from hopeless. "The Scouring of the Shire" is only the penultimate chapter of *The Lord of the Rings*. In the final chapter, "The Grey Havens," Tolkien leaves his readers with an inspiring picture of hope for the restoration of the Shire—one that represents the culmination of his environmental vision in a kind of qualified optimism. In addition to the hope of healing and restoration at the end of the story, the reader also faces the sorrow of the Elves' departure from Middle-earth, and Sam's mallorn tree is small compensation. We are also reminded that many great heroes have fallen, and some wounds, like Frodo's, will not heal. Emotionally, the ending is complex.

Even with regard to the land itself, the Shire is not portrayed as perfect at the end of the story, just as the Shire before Saruman is not meant to be understood as perfect. Not only are there wounds to men and hobbits that will not heal, but there are also wounds to the earth. The picture Tolkien paints of the Shire fosters no illusion of complete freedom from corruption. Though it is now undergoing a process of restoration and environmental healing, it is a place that has been damaged and broken in many ways. Nonetheless, Tolkien provides hope for Isengard as well, and even—in a very limited way—for Mordor, wounded and blighted as they are.

Inasmuch as our world today suffers many of the same afflictions as Mordor, Isengard, and the Shire under Saruman's rule, it is appropriate to examine this hope. In this chapter we look briefly at the promise of healing in these three damaged landscapes. Then, turning to what must be done to bring this healing about, we continue the chapter with an exploration of the necessary attitudes, and chapter 10 extends the process from attitudes to action.

Hope and Healing

The easiest place to see the healing of the earth's wounds is in the Shire, where the process of restoration is so vivid that a quick summary will suffice as illustration, even for the most casual reader. The narrator tells of the Hobbits' homeland in the year following the War of the Ring:

> Altogether 1420 in the Shire was a marvellous year. Not only was there wonderful sunshine and delicious rain, in due times and perfect measure, but there seemed something more: an air of richness and growth, and a gleam of a beauty beyond that of mortal summers that flicker and pass upon this Middle-earth. . . . The fruit was so plentiful that young hobbits very nearly bathed in strawberries and cream; and later they sat on the lawns under the plum-trees and ate, until they had made piles of stones like small pyramids. . . . Vines were laden, and the yield of "leaf" was astonishing; and everywhere there was so much corn that at Harvest every barn was stuffed. (VI/ix)

"Richness and growth," "beauty," and "plentiful" fruit: these are fundamental goals of agrarian stewardship and, we might add, of horticultural and feracultural stewardship as well. They are signs of environmental health in an agrarian world. Tolkien paints an image of beauty and agricultural bounty: fruit, strawberries, cream, plums, grapevines, leaf, and corn. It is a picture meant to inspire hope. Certainly Middle-earth has been damaged. Yet the restoration of health appears as vibrant and beautiful in the Shire as ruination and lifelessness do in Mordor. Many a fortunate farmer in our world has known years of plenty like that of 1420 in the Shire, counterbalancing other years of failed harvests, want, and hardship.

Given the Shire's central, positive role throughout the trilogy in Tolkien's portrayal of the ecology of Middle-earth, it is also the focus of environmental healing in the concluding chapter. Yet Tolkien makes it clear that there is hope for the damaged environments elsewhere in Middle-earth as well. For example, although the land surrounding Isengard is even more scarred than the Hobbits' land, its restoration is glimpsed in several short passages, and these are worth examining.

This restoration begins with a mere promise. One of the more destructive acts that Saruman commits is damming the river Isen. When the Ents attack Saruman, they destroy the dam and free the river, flooding Isengard. "Water may come through," Treebeard warns Merry and Pippin as they prepare to break the dam, "and it will be foul water for a while, until all the filth of Saruman is washed away. Then Isen can run clean again" (III/ix). The progression from foul to clean water is of fundamental importance to the restoration of health in Middle-earth, and Treebeard's words constitute not only a warning but also a promise for the hobbits and for us in our world. For Isengard, the process is a washing away of filth and, in the removal of a constructed artifact—the dam—a return to a more natural state in which the wild river is allowed to flow unconstrained.

Of course, in the Shire, as in our world, healing is not instantaneous. The Isen will remain befouled "for a while," even as the Ents work toward its restoration. Some environmental damage heals only gradually, and in some cases, good things are lost forever. The more complete the devastation, the longer the time needed to undo it. Treebeard says elsewhere that trees that have stood since the dawn of time but stand no more cannot be replaced. Still, there is considerable promise, and later in the story Tolkien builds on this promise, showing the reader the beginning of its fulfillment under Treebeard's care and stewardship.

Months after the conclusion of the war with Sauron, as the members of the Company travel through Isengard on their way back to the Shire, they witness the early stages of environmental repair: "From Deeping Coomb they rode to Isengard, and saw how the Ents had busied themselves. All the stone-circle had been thrown down and removed, and the land within was made into a garden filled with orchards and trees, and a stream ran through it; but in the midst of all there was a lake of clear water" (VI/vi). The place is so transformed under the restorative care of the Ents that it calls for a new name, the Treegarth of Orthanc. Just as Sauron's One Ring is cast into the Crack of Doom on Orodruin, Saruman's *stone* ring—symbolic of his association with the Dark Lord—is thrown down and removed. The restoration has begun. Where Saruman felled trees and put up pillars of metal and stone, Treebeard has reversed the process. Though barely three months have passed since Saruman's fall, already there are orchards. The entrance to the Treegarth—the "tree enclosure"—is now between two tall trees that stand "like sentinels at the beginning of a green-bordered path" (VI/vi).

Treebeard's earlier vision is well on its way to fulfillment. Clean water now covers the former ruin, and the land is growing green again.

Of the three faces of environmental evil explored in this book—Mordor, Isengard, and the occupied Shire—only the first seems to be beyond physical help. Although the source of the damage to all three is ultimately Mordor, only the interior of that land—Gorgoroth and Udûn—is so scarred and lifeless that restoration seems unlikely. But elsewhere Tolkien gives us glimpses of hope even for Sauron's scarred land. When Aragorn becomes king, one of his first acts is to release Sauron's slaves and give them the lands about Lake Núrnen to work as their own (VI/v). In agrarian terms, this signals a return to the sound tradition of land owned, farmed, and cared for by those who live on it.

Although Tolkien never describes what Mordor might look like after its restoration, he does give other signs of hope through the commitment of two characters that readers have learned to love and trust. Éowyn of Rohan and Faramir of Gondor devote their lives to the health of Ithilien, a land bordering Mordor that has also been scarred by war. As if declaring herself a handmaiden of Yavanna—or perhaps even a mythic manifestation of Yavanna herself—Éowyn announces, "I will be a healer, and love all things that grow and are not barren" (VI/v). Her pledge gets at the heart of stewardship in an age of environmental devastation, and also at the importance of life in Tolkien's ecology—not only human life, though certainly this is included, but "all things that grow." As a shield-maiden of Rohan, Éowyn wins perhaps the single most important battle on the Pelennor Fields when she destroys the witch king, the chief of the nine Nazgûl. For such a tenacious, zealous, and skillful character to turn from the practice of warfare to the art of nurture, growth, and healing of the environment is a momentous development—a shift from *thanatos* ("death") to *bios* ("life"). Attentive readers may be encouraged.

Nor is Éowyn alone in her commitment. Faramir, to whom she is wed at the end of the tale, responds with a pledge of his own: "Let us dwell in fair Ithilien and there make a garden. All things will grow with joy there, if the White Lady comes" (VI/v). The reader is left with little doubt that these things can come to pass. Among other things, at a mythic level, this represents a reconciliation of gender differences that divide the Ents from the Entwives, fulfilling the tenuous prophecy in Treebeard's song that begins, "When Spring unfolds the beechen leaf"

(III/iv). It also echoes the marital, domestic, and environmental harmony illustrated by Tom Bombadil and Goldberry. Furthermore, hope is restored even for lands that have been part of Mordor. Aragorn gives Faramir the task of utterly destroying Minas Ithil in the Morgul Vale. Aragorn says that although the Morgul Vale has been so defiled that "no man may dwell there for many long years," nevertheless, "it may in time to come be made clean" (VI/v).

And so the vision of Middle-earth's restoration after Sauron's downfall looks promising. It is reasonable to ask, however, whether such a vision can possibly be fulfilled in our world. Is there any reality behind the fantasy, or is Tolkien's restorative vision no more than wishful thinking? Within certain limitations, we believe that Tolkien is thinking more than wishfully; properly applied, the resolutions imagined in the fantasy point toward potential environmental solutions in our world. Because we believe that Tolkien's environmental views are indeed applicable to our situation, we also believe that the best path toward fulfillment of his vision lies in implementing an ethic of environmental stewardship similar if not identical to the one developed in Tolkien's work.

Here again we raise a concern mentioned in our introduction. In everyday terms, Middle-earth clearly is not our world, and the distinction between fiction and reality is one that has to be maintained. By his own admission, Tolkien was not writing an allegory, so the applicability of environmentalism in *The Lord of the Rings* to the real world cannot be explained or pursued simplistically. But, we assert, there is much to be learned from Tolkien through the characters of Gandalf, Aragorn, Faramir, Galadriel, Théoden, Éowyn, the Hobbits, and even Gimli the dwarf.

As we noted earlier, Tolkien himself saw the connections between Middle-earth and our world as more than incidental. In a letter to W. H. Auden, who reviewed *The Fellowship of the Ring* in 1955, Tolkien remarked:

> What appreciative readers have got out of the work or seen in it has seemed fair enough, even when I do not agree with it. Always excepting, of course, any "interpretations" in the mode of simple allegory: that is, the particular and topical. In a larger sense, it is I suppose impossible to write any "story" that is not allegorical in proportion as it "comes to life"; since each of us is

an allegory, embodying in a particular tale and clothed in the garments of time and place, universal truth and everlasting life. (*Letters*, 212)

So, although we do not see *The Lord of the Rings* as a simple intentional allegory, we do find that the work "comes to life." Clothed in the garments of Middle-earth is a "universal truth" that is both written into the text Tolkien created and woven into the fabric of reality—the story we are in. Thus, in the second sense described above by Tolkien, we are providing what might be called an allegorical application of the legendarium's ideas to the particular topic of twenty-first-century environmentalism, suggesting that the principles embedded in his work *should* be brought to bear on environmental problems in the modern world. Frodo and Sam's combined remarks on continuities between the "old tales" and their story, and Tolkien's remarks on the subject of fantasy and reality in "On Fairy-stories," exemplify and strengthen the idea cryptically introduced in the 1955 letter.[1] If we are to learn anything from Frodo and company, then even as we respect the *boundary* between fiction and reality, we must also take some steps toward recognizing *connections* between the two and make the applicability explicit.

Being Roused (and Rousing Others)

When Merry and Pippin first arrive in Fangorn Forest early in *The Two Towers,* one of the first comments Treebeard makes about the coming war is a solemn foretelling: "It seems that the wind is setting East, and the withering of all woods may be drawing near" (III/iv). Here, Treebeard finally acknowledges the grave threat Sauron and Saruman pose to his realm. Specifically, he sees that the recent losses he has suffered—the Orcs' wanton burning and cutting of trees—will be just the beginning if he does not act soon. Situations like this occur several times in different places throughout the story. King Théoden of Rohan is in a similar strait when Gandalf, Aragorn, Legolas, and Gimli come to him. Despite the death of his son and the attacks on the Westfold villages, he has ignored the threats at the doorstep of his own realm. The first thing Gandalf must do is rouse him to a heightened awareness of the danger and the action he must take against it.[2] The hobbits must do the same when they return to the Shire. For Treebeard, the primary threat is against the environment; his trees are subjected to attack and destruction. For the others, the immediate danger is the threat of war, with environmental destruction as a secondary result. Even in the latter case, however, warfare serves as both a direct cause and a perfect metaphorical expression of the environmental threats in Middle-earth. Environmental conflict in our world, too, is in some ways a battle, and the change of attitude and behavior required to engage in it are similar to those required for waging war.

Applying this to the subject at hand, acknowledgment of environmental problems is important, but it is only a first step. As Norman Wirzba observes, "agrarianism is about learning to take up the responsibilities that protect, preserve, and celebrate life."[3] After recognizing the dangers, Treebeard and the Ents must still *act* against them. They must protect their arboreal flocks and preserve their forest. Treebeard says they must be "roused." But taking responsibility is never as easy as it appears. "We Ents do not like being roused," Treebeard says, "and we never are roused unless it is clear to us that our trees and our lives are in great danger" (III/iv). Inertia and complacency—especially reluctance to take any action that upsets a comfortable lifestyle—are the reason many of us are slow even to acknowledge the problems we face. Treebeard must overcome both the attitude that "Mordor is a long way away" and the resulting shirking of his duties.

The complacency in the Shire is similar. In the previous chapter, we saw that many hobbits initially are slow to address the evil surrounding them, and thus they are easily lulled into submitting to forces inimical to the agrarianism that defines their civilization. Eventually the evil takes so many forms that they are forced to recognize it for what it is. Yet even then they need to be roused to take responsibility and do something. "Shire-folk have been so comfortable so long they don't know what to do," Merry observes (VI/viii). It is much easier to sit and do nothing than to act. In the short term, it is also safer: ents and hobbits die in their respective battles against Saruman and his servants; many of King Théoden's knights die in battle, and Théoden himself falls at the Battle of the Pelennor Fields.

Fortunately, in their travels Merry and Pippin have already witnessed something of the "rousing" process: its necessity, the steps needed to bring it about, and especially its successful results. They know what to do. "'Raise the Shire!' said Merry, 'Now! Wake all our people!'" (VI/viii).

We can see the same principles at work in Meduseld as in Hobbiton and Fangorn. For too long Théoden has listened to Wormtongue's rejection of Gandalf as a "Stormcrow" or *Láthspell,* a bringer of bad news. Tolkien uses the imagery of awakening from sleep to describe his transformation: "It is not so dark here," says Théoden as he begins to return to consciousness. "Dark have been my dreams of late." He is described as breathing "free" air again, casting aside his crutch, and taking up his sword. Of course, the next question he asks is crucial: "What is to be done?" (II/vi).

What does King Théoden learn that makes him willing—even at the cost of his own life—not only to rise and oppose Saruman but also to go to the aid of Gondor against Sauron? What do Merry and Pippin learn from Treebeard that enables them to succeed in rousing the Shire?

We do not know exactly what Treebeard says to rouse the other Ents; the reader is not taken inside the Entmoot. Nevertheless, the narrative suggests at least three principal motivations—what we might call *prerequisite attitudes*—necessary to the successful rousing of these parts of Middle-earth:

1. The recognition that inaction results in further harm.
2. The abandonment of despair, and the trust that positive actions have positive consequences.
3. Sufficient care for the created world to do something about the danger.

Treebeard phrases the first of these principles in an interesting way: "'Of course, it is likely enough, my friends,' he said slowly, 'likely enough that we are going to *our* doom: the last march of the Ents. But if we stayed home and did nothing, doom would find us anyway, sooner or later. That thought has long been growing in our hearts; and that is why we are marching now'" (III/iv). Treebeard is saying that as costly as it may be to take action, it is far costlier to do nothing. This is a necessary aspect of overcoming the complacency of past comforts in order to take responsibility for the present and the future. For this reason, Treebeard is willing to risk his life. In the short term, it might seem safer for him and the Ents to hide in Fangorn, as they have been doing for eons. By following that easy path, however, doom—the withering of all forests— is certain to find them. Similarly, Merry and Pippin help the Hobbits of the Shire come to the same realization. Certainly there is risk involved in taking on the ruffians and reclaiming their farms, foodstuffs, inns, and the infrastructure of their society. But if they do nothing, Merry argues, the ruffians "will simply come down on us in force, corner us, and then drive us out or burn us in." Merry's conclusion is that they "have got to do something at once" (VI/viii). It is this diligence in making the threat of doom more widely known that rouses the Ents, the king of Rohan, and eventually the Hobbits.

Like the Ents, however, most people in the real world "do not like being roused." Along with their desire to see the Ents march to the aid of Rohan, readers of *The Lord of the Rings* may feel sympathy with their reluctance to embark on what may be their last march. Such efforts often involve risk and always require effort. For example, reducing our consumption of fossil fuels may require uncomfortable changes in our everyday habits. Reducing toxic emissions in automobile exhaust and in coal-burning power plants similarly would require real sacrifices for real people, including the loss of creature comforts that we may take for granted. Likewise, choosing to eat foods grown locally by sustainable methods that require good agricultural and environmental stewardship is not easy. Initially, it costs more; in the long run, however, the alternatives are even more costly—not merely economically but, more importantly, with respect to the environment. But in recognizing these things, we must understand that it is necessary to assume responsibility and take action, to change what we are doing and what we are failing to do.

The second principle goes hand in hand with the first. We must believe that action really can bring about change. Throughout Tolkien's works, the small and the mighty alike attempt great things, and many succeed. Saruman is one of the most powerful figures in Middle-earth, yet the Ents challenge him. Treebeard knows that when they are gathered together, the Ents are strong. "You do not know, perhaps, how strong we are," he tells the two hobbits (III/iv). By the time they return to the Shire, Merry and Pippin have already seen that even a powerful figure like Saruman can be overthrown when enough people are roused to get involved in the task. They are able to inspire other hobbits, so that even young Robin says to Sam, "If we all got angry together something might be done" (VI/viii). Robin is right; even though they are only a fraction of the size of the Ents, the Hobbits are strong in their own right. People often do not know how strong, both individually and collectively, they can be.

Put another way, this second principle really involves a choice of hope over despair—one of the central ideas in the application of Tolkien's trilogy to environmental concerns in our world. Tolkien's hope was informed by and founded on an understanding of the goodness of the world and the goodness and power of its creator, which was part of his Christian faith. Ultimately, Tolkien sees the outcome of any battle as being in the hands of the creator—in Middle-earth, Eru Ilúvatar; in our world, God. The reason for this transcendent hope is illustrated in *The Lord of the Rings* when the wise of Middle-earth recognize, or catch glimpses of, Ilúvatar's power at work. Gandalf tries to foster hope in Frodo at the start of the story by pointing to the assisting hand of a higher power. In answer to Frodo's questions concerning why the Ring has come to him, Gandalf says, "There was something else at work, beyond any design of the Ring-maker. I can put it no plainer than by saying that Bilbo was meant to find the Ring, and not by its maker. In which case you also were meant to have it. And that may be an encouraging thought" (I/ii). Gandalf leaves the completion of the logical inference unstated. Bilbo was "meant" to find the Ring not by *its* maker but by *his* (Bilbo's) maker, who also meant Frodo to have it. Gandalf is reminding Frodo that although Sauron the Ring-maker is powerful, there is another vastly more powerful force at work opposing the evil of Mordor.

Later in the tale, when Frodo and Sam are making the painful crossing of Mordor, we get a clearer glimpse of this power:

> There was battle far above in the high spaces of the air. The billowing clouds of Mordor were being driven back, their edges tattering as a wind out of the living world came up and swept the fumes and smokes towards the dark land of their home. Under the lifting skirts of the dreary canopy dim light leaked into Mordor like pale morning through the grimed window of a prison. (VI/ii)

The battle of the free peoples of Middle-earth against Mordor is fought not only on the ground but also in "the high spaces of the air"—by which Tolkien means the upper stratosphere, but which we may extend to the heavens. The fumes and smokes of Sauron's pollution are being driven away and replaced with clean air; freedom and release are coming to the dreary canopy of Mordor's prison. The passage invites two interpretations, one of them environmental and the other mythic or religious. On the one hand, the text imagines the very force of the winds above Middle-earth contending against Sauron's evil—figuratively represented as "air pollution"—and winning. In terms of the background mythology in *The Silmarillion,* this is a continuation of the cosmic battle of the Valar: the clean winds of Manwë are in active opposition against the foul reek of Sauron, Melkor's servant. On the other hand, the reader may perceive a faint echo of a biblical passage in which physical battle is seen as a manifestation of spiritual battle between the demonic forces of evil and the divine forces of good. In Ephesians, this battle is said to involve "the prince and power of the air" (2:2) and "spirits of wickedness" (6:12) and to take place *"in the high places"* (6:12)—or, as other translations say, "in heavenly places."[4] Based on an implicit trust in the creator, those who attempt to live out the principles of environmental stewardship as depicted by Tolkien may do so in the hope that some battles in this world can be won. They can say, along with Sam, "Look at it, Mr. Frodo! Look at it! The wind's changed. Something's happening. He's not having it all his own way. His darkness is breaking up out in the world there" (VI/ii).

Just as Gandalf's words of encouragement to Frodo constitute a challenge for the hobbit to have hope and to take action, religious faith in our world must not be offered as an excuse for doing nothing. As Tolkien says in the last sentence of "On Fairy-stories," "Redeemed Man has still to work ... but he may now perceive that all his bents and faculties have a purpose, which can be redeemed." Humankind has been assigned the task of completing and perfecting the divine works of creation, including reformation and restoration of the created order.

This second principle, the promise of hope, includes a warning. At one level, *The Lord of the Rings* illustrates the point that small people can sometimes accomplish great things. Frodo—a "Halfling"—achieves nothing less than the salvation of Middle-earth from a tyrannous conqueror. Yet Tolkien also shows us a balance between *pragmatism* and *faith.* We must take some action—we must *do* something—and there may be good reason to hope that our actions will succeed, but we must also be wise enough to choose our battles carefully. As a purely military example, during the Battle of Helm's Deep, Gimli the dwarf follows Aragorn and Éomer in a sally through a side door; he does not enter the fray at this juncture, however, because the enemies at this point are Men, who tower over him. Only at the last moment, when the smaller-statured Orcs make an ambush, does he enter the fight and save Éomer's life. His explanation? "I looked on the hillmen," he says, "and they seemed over large for me" (III/vii). Likewise, although the Ents undertake to oppose Saruman, they know that they cannot hope to mount an offensive against Sauron himself: "There is naught that an old Ent can do to hold back *that* storm," says Treebeard (III/iv, emphasis added). When Gandalf sends Bilbo and the dwarves on a seemingly impossible quest at the start of *The Hobbit*, he warns them not even to think about taking on Sauron (the Necromancer), which would be far beyond the combined might of all the Dwarf kingdoms together (H, 58). Such warnings do not suggest an approach born of timidity or passivity but rather one of common sense and prudence. Some battles are easily won; some are ambitious but not impossible; and some ought not be fought without considerable aid. Again, the explicit application of this point in Tolkien's narrative is to military battles, but, as with so many aspects of Tolkien's work—or the work of any great writer—ideas that are explicitly about one thing may touch on others. And in Tolkien's writing, military battles are tropes for so much more. With respect to the environment, then, we might begin by judiciously deciding which battles we are equipped to fight and which we are not.

Nevertheless, we must engage the battle at some level. The narrative of *The Lord of the Rings* often makes the point that neutrality is not an option. As Aragorn says to Éomer, "You may say this to Théoden son of Thengel: open war lies before him, *with* Sauron or *against* him" (III/ii). Again, although Aragorn's cause is not directly an environmental one, the principle holds. Maurice Telleen applies this idea specifically to environmental causes and ecological responsibility:

> Action or inaction has consequences: both benign and terrible, trivial and important, intended and unintended. We are born into a web of life that both precedes and follows us. Some of it is understood and much of it isn't. But we are each simultaneously part of the picture and one of the painters. Neutrality is not an option. Mindlessness is, but neutrality isn't. That sounds fairly eternal to me. I grant that it has little to do with harps or heaven, but a good bit to do with how and where we use our own time and place on earth.[5]

Telleen's remarks could easily function as a paraphrase of many speeches throughout the story by Gandalf, Aragorn, Elrond, and Galadriel. There is no neutrality. Inasmuch as inaction results in further harm, to do nothing is to support Sauron. It is also worth noting that in the use of the word *eternal,* Telleen might have in mind another attribute that is one of Tolkien's greatest strengths: the legendarium fundamentally takes spiritual conceptions out of the vague imagery of "harps and heavens" and demonstrates their significance in daily life in the real world—in "our own time and place on earth." Like many of the principles in this book, one can find not only spiritual roots but also practical applications in the material world.

The third attitude we see in Tolkien's portrayal of the response to evil in Middle-earth—the final prerequisite that ties the previous two together—is that in rousing oneself or others to action, one must care deeply about all forms of life. Certainly this includes, but should not be restricted to, human life. Many arguments in favor of environmental causes are based on economic and financial reasons anchored ultimately in individual, corporate, or governmental self-interest. For example, certain local financial benefits accompany the cleanup of polluted water sources; regional economies can be stimulated through ecotourism if certain wilderness areas are preserved from development; recycling and the use of alternative energy sources create new industries that in turn create jobs; and so forth. It is not that such actions are not valuable in themselves—they are. But often they are pursued not for their inherent value but for another, less honorable reason: they make somebody a lot of money. Too often, though, the argument goes the other way: much *more* money can be made even more quickly through rapacious logging, mining, or pumping operations or through the development of private or public lands that, in environmental terms, ought to remain undisturbed.

Aldo Leopold writes, "Many labored arguments are in print proving that conservation pays economic dividends." He is not interested in such economic motivations, however, and admits that he "can add nothing to these arguments."[6] In this regard, Tolkien and Leopold are in much the same camp. Characters in Middle-earth who are motivated primarily by economic self-interest—Bill Ferny, the Master of Laketown, and, to some degree, the race of Dwarves as a whole—are not Tolkien's heroes. When environmental stewardship is expressed in *The Lord of the Rings,* it is motivated not by economics but by other, higher reasons.

In Middle-earth, financial benefits are not only insufficient, but they are also largely irrelevant to the beautification and preservation of wilderness, the creation and nurture of gardens, and the restoration of fertility to pastures and farmlands.

For many, this could be seen as a weakness in Leopold's position and in Tolkien's environmental vision, or at least in their application to the situation we now find ourselves in. We live in a world that is driven by economic concerns at every level, including—increasingly—global ones. Economic incentives often seem to be a prerequisite to significant action. As Leopold asks:

> Can a farmer afford to devote land to woods, marsh, pond, windbreaks? These are semi-economic land-uses—that is, they have utility but they also yield non-economic benefits.
>
> Can a farmer afford to devote land to fencerows for the birds, to snag-trees for the coons and flying squirrels? Here the utility shrinks to what the chemist calls "a trace."
>
> Can a farmer afford to devote land to fencerows for a patch of ladyslippers, a remnant of prairie, or just scenery? Here the utility shrinks to zero.[7]

Some ecologically sound undertakings, in other words, can be justified on the basis of their economic value even when the real value lies elsewhere. But some efforts in the direction of environmental health may have only negligible economic worth, and the economic utility of others may add up to zero. If our environmental motivations are defined only on the basis of economic results, then our approach will differ fundamentally from Leopold's: we will not care about squirrels in the snag trees or ladyslippers in the fencerows. Leopold argues that even environmental programs that have no identifiable economic benefit are worthwhile.

Tolkien demonstrates this in his story. The environmental motivation that he authorizes best fits the category of transcendent values based on stewardship principles that are more universal than those of any particular culture, place, or time. If we comprehend Tolkien's claim that, as the handiwork of a good creator, the universe is inherently valuable, and if we understand this goodness to be independent of its practical usefulness or economic payoff, then the manner in which we treat it cannot help but be affected. If we understand the transcendent goodness and purpose of nature and humankind's transcendent mission as its stewards, we will take steps toward a willingness to endure the hardships and engage in the difficult labors required for its preservation and restoration—not because we stand to reap financial gains but because of the inherent goodness and implicit value of such efforts.

Wirzba's prescriptions involve taking responsibility for the protection and preservation of life in order to "celebrate" it. These three go hand in hand: protection, preservation, and celebration. We protect what we value in order to preserve it for continued celebration. Though it is a minor theme in *The Lord of the Rings,* references to celebration and merriment recur throughout the narrative. Faramir comments on the predicted happy outcome of Ithilien's restoration by saying that it is "with joy"—the essence of celebratory experience—that "all things will grow." The Hobbits celebrate beer, hot baths, and good fellowship with much joyful singing. The epic adventure as a whole begins with a birthday party whose Party Tree links the celebratory spirit with a potent symbol, in Tolkien's mythic oeuvre, of nature.

Sacredness and the Model of Love

But all the preceding may be too abstract in our search for an intellectual rationale. It might be simpler, and truer, to say that we do best when our motivation is a *selfless love of the world and all that it contains:* wind and sea; tree and grass; mountain, valley, plain, and all that they contain. So it is in Middle-earth, where the Glittering Caves of Aglarond move Gimli to make an impassioned speech infused by feelings one can equate only with this kind of love. One of the most startling examples of character development in Tolkien's novel is seen in Gimli after his encounter with Galadriel, whose love for Lothlórien is said to be "deeper than the deeps of the Sea" (II/vii). In coming first not to fear Galadriel, then to respect her, and finally to love her, Gimli learns to echo the love of natural beauty that characterizes the Elvish race as a whole. We see this most clearly when Gimli discovers the Glittering Caves of Aglarond during the Battle of Helm's Deep. He describes the caverns of Green-elves in Mirkwood as "hovels" compared with Aglarond, "immeasurable halls, filled with an everlasting music of water that tinkles into pools, as fair as Kheled-zâram in the starlight." He goes on:

> And, Legolas, when the torches are kindled and men walk on the sandy floors under the echoing domes, ah! Then, Legolas, gem and crystals and veins of precious ore glint in the polished wall; and the light glows through folded marbles, shell-like, translucent as the living hands of Queen Galadriel. There are columns of white and saffron and dawn-rose, Legolas, fluted and twisted into dreamlike forms; they spring up from many-coloured floors to meet the glistening pendants of the roof: wings, ropes, curtains fine as frozen clouds. (III/viii)

Gimli's ecstatic description of this subterranean environment continues at great length and with similar emotion, concluding with the statement, "It makes me weep to leave them." This is Gimli's longest speech in the whole trilogy; his repetition of Legolas's name—four times in all—bespeaks his heightened state of emotion.

Based on his limited—albeit growing—knowledge of Dwarves, however, Legolas comments with some cynicism that "one family of busy dwarves with hammer and chisel might mar more than they made" in those caves (III/viii). Gimli understands Legolas to mean that the economic value of the gems and treasures there might be the dwarfish motive for entering Aglarond. He is aghast at the suggestion:

> No dwarf could be unmoved by such loveliness. None of Durin's race would mine those caves for stones or ore, not if diamonds and gold could be got there. Do you cut down groves of blossoming trees in the springtime for firewood? We would tend these glades of flowering stone, not quarry them. With cautious skill, tap by tap—a small chip of rock and no more, perhaps, in a whole anxious day—so we could work. (III/viii)

Gimli immediately rejects the idea of exploiting these caves and, more importantly, rejects profit as a motive for other kinds of involvement with nature. Although Dwarves might be described as economically motivated,[8] Gimli's love for this place has nothing to do with economics. His expressions of love for it use imagery of the Elves' love for flowers and trees. This dwarf, whose zeal for the Mines of Moria is almost mythic, and whose earlier poem on Durin's realm focuses largely on hammers, anvils, chisels, mining, delving, and forging, now sets aside the stereotypical preoccupations of his race and compares rock formations to trees blossoming in springtime. Gimli's attitude originates partly from the depths of his character and the results of his personal choices, but part of it stems from Galadriel, who blesses him on his departure from Lothlórien in these terms: "Your hands shall flow with gold, and yet over you gold shall have no dominion" (II/viii). In other words, Gimli will not be economically motivated. Thus Legolas, finally sensing the real change, responds to Gimli's speech, "You move me, Gimli.... I have never heard you speak like this before" (III/viii).

Another character whose environmental position flows from, or is shaped by, a love of nature and growing things is Sam Gamgee. After the Shire is rid of its oppression under Saruman, his skills and hard labor are poured into correcting the environmental damage. In fulfillment of a prediction by Frodo, Sam becomes not only a great gardener but also a forester—which in the Shire involves the planting of trees, not the felling of them. Like Gimli, Sam's character develops. We first encounter him tending Bilbo's garden and clipping the grass at Bag End; his domain is limited to his father's area of expertise—"the growing of vegetables" and "the matter of 'roots,' especially potatoes" (I/i). Over the course of his adventures, his horizons widen and his horticultural skills broaden to include the nurture of trees. In the Mirror of Galadriel, his nightmare glimpse of the Shire's havoc climaxes in a vision of Ted Sandyman's felling of trees, and on his return home in the final chapters, it is the sight of the fallen Party Tree, "lying lopped and dead in the field," that finally reduces Sam to tears (VI/viii). In his expanded role, "in addition to all his other labours," he is "often away in the Shire on his forestry work." Aided by the soil from Galadriel's garden,

> Sam planted saplings in all the places where specially beautiful or beloved trees had been destroyed, and he put a grain of the precious dust in the soil at the root of each. He went up and down the Shire in this labour; but if he paid special attention to Hobbiton and Bywater no one blamed him.... The little silver nut he planted in the Party Field where the tree had once been; and he wondered what would come of it. (VI/ix)

As we learn, early the next year, a young sapling with silver bark and golden flowers springs up, "the only *mallorn* west of the Mountains and east of the Sea, and one of the finest in the world." Sam loves the Shire, and in particular he loves his own village; his nurture of growing things links him with Treebeard and Galadriel, the Ents and the Elves. In Sam, the three major ecologies of Middle-earth balance and are reconciled, and it is clear that this reconciliation is to a great extent the outgrowth of environmental love.

Myth and Wonder

Like Galadriel and Sam, many responsible readers will wish to nurture such love in themselves and in others, and as a work of literature, *The Lord of the Rings* provides an ideal example of how to do it. In the portions of the story concerning the rousing of Rohan, Tolkien shows how myth and fairy tale can help rekindle among the race of Men in Middle-earth a deeper appreciation for the spiritual significance and sacredness of nature. In turn, this rekindled appreciation can help engender a deeper love for the world and a corresponding desire for its protection and preservation. For Éomer, the process begins when he first meets Aragorn and sees him as a character come to life out of the ancient world of myth and legend. Aragorn reminds Éomer that the grass itself is the stuff of myth—"a mighty matter of legend though you tread it under the light of day!"—infusing it with the luminous quality of something beyond mere material substance.

This rekindling process is even clearer when Théoden first comes into contact with the Ents, a scene we described in chapter 5. In Rohan, the Ents are associated with fairy tale and legend, but through Gandalf, Théoden learns to see trees in a whole new light. He comes to understand that his is "but the passing tale" and that "all the deeds of [his] house but a small matter" (III/viii). Gandalf's discussion with Théoden captures a principle that, as Wirzba explains, is another fundamental prerequisite to taking responsibility—one that goes hand in hand with loving the earth: "The first requirement of such responsibility is that we give up the delusion that we live in a purely human world of our own making, give up the arrogant and naive belief that human ambition should be the sole measure of cultural success or failure."[9] Gandalf makes it clear to Théoden that the world is far larger than he has imagined, and its importance inheres in more than the existence of Men alone. Ents and their forests and wilderness are important, and Théoden's actions have far-reaching consequences that have an impact not only on Edoras but also on all of Rohan, on neighboring Fangorn Forest, and in fact on all of Middle-earth. And of course, Treebeard's actions affect Rohan as well. They are either allies or enemies.

In an article on interrelatedness appearing in a collection focusing on the Christian creation tradition, Paul Lutz makes this related observation, complementing the point made by Wirzba: "One of the most important concepts of ecology is that everything in the creation is related to everything else. *Interrelatedness* or interdependence is one of the most important ecological principles, but one that is extremely difficult to conceptualize."[10] Thus, the nonhuman world is important, as both Gandalf and Wirzba note, and it is a critical part of any "measure of cultural success or failure." But, as both Gandalf and Lutz note, the human world is intimately related to the rest of creation. These two facts lend far greater significance and urgency to the heroic actions Théoden contemplates and ultimately undertakes. And because the battle he fights is much more important than he realizes, Théoden has the support of unseen allies that he is unaware of. What Théoden does with this information, of course, is up to him. But by bringing Théoden—and readers—into contact with the mythical dimension of reality, and by showing the transcendent, even sacred, spiritual dimensions of nature in everyday life, Tolkien's story engenders a similar appreciation of the real world among his readers: it takes a principle that is "extremely difficult to conceptualize" and makes it clear and compelling.

Chapter 10

Environmentalism, Transcendence, and Action

※

In the previous chapter we examined how and why the various good stewards in Middle-earth are motivated to restore the regions of the environment for which they are responsible. We found that the formidable problems confronting them require a significant individual commitment to overcome complacency, take responsibility, embrace hope, and rouse others to meet the challenges they face. For all of them, environmental restoration in Middle-earth is motivated not by a desire for personal profit or economic gain but by a selfless and celebratory love of creation. But in practical terms, we still must ask how these principles and prerequisite attitudes apply; we must move from how these model stewards *think* to what they actually *do*.

In exploring this, we are also led to ask how these ideas might apply to us, members of the human race in the real world. If we share those attitudes, what are we to do? As we stated earlier, although *The Lord of the Rings* was not written as an allegory, the best interpretations of the novel meet Tolkien's criterion of *applicability*. In this way, at least in broad terms, our understanding of the work shares something with medieval allegorical exegesis—a point that Tolkien would no doubt agree with, despite his distaste for strict allegory. The environmental ethics discernible at the literal level of *The Lord of the Rings* suggest what we should understand, where this understanding leads us, and finally what we should do—exegetically, the *moralia*—in applying Tolkien's vision of environmental stewardship in our own lives. What is the *moral* of the story?

Just as Tolkien's story illustrates motivating principles, it also illustrates what the action guided by these principles should look like. By showing how the work in Gondor, Fangorn Forest, and the Shire is accomplished, the story answers the question concerning what one who shares these motivations should do. We conclude this book by examining this model of work and tying it to the principles presented in the previous nine chapters. Although our focus is on applications within Middle-earth, we hope that real-world applications will be self-evident for the reader. And we are convinced that Tolkien would strongly welcome such applications.

What Can I Do?

When the hobbit Robin Smallburrow first appears in the story in "The Scouring of the Shire," he is working as a shirriff and is therefore in some capacity a sympathizer with Sharkey and his occupying ruffians, though he claims not to like being in that position. Confronted by Sam Gamgee, Robin asks, "What can I do?" On the face of it, Robin Smallburrow's question is an excellent one; it is another way of asking how a society's environmental vision might be reflected in its mores— the customs essential to its well-being and survival. Of course, in the context of his discussion with Sam, Robin's question is really more rhetorical, and it is disingenuous. As demonstrated by his previous plea ("Don't be hard on me"), it is an evasive answer to Sam's charge that he "ought to be ashamed" of participating in the "nonsense" that Sharkey and his men have perpetrated on the Hobbits (VI/viii). Robin offers the reply as an excuse for passively consenting to the evils afoot in the Shire; his surname suggests the parochial nature of his imagination, his smallness of vision.

But Sam takes the question at face value. In answering Robin, he says in no uncertain terms that the young hobbit must take responsibility and join in the recovery and restoration of the Shire: if what Robin is doing is wrong—"if it has stopped being a respectable job"—then he must "give it up, stop Shirriffing," says Sam (VI/viii). Rephrased as an honest inquiry with practical application in our world, Robin's question might even be revised as a motto: What Would Frodo—or Sam, Pippin, or Merry—Do?[1] In any event, the question is addressed in earnest in several places and by several characters toward the end of *The Lord of the Rings*. It is addressed in the Shire, especially by Sam, and in Fangorn Forest and Isengard by Treebeard, who (as we discuss later) also formulates a workable response to the general question of what people should do in such circumstances. A particularly fitting example is Aragorn, who essentially asks this question when he returns to Gondor and takes up the throne in Minas Tirith. Unlike among the Hobbits, Ents, and Elves, there are few models of good environmental stewardship among Men in Middle-earth.[2] In Aragorn, however, as in Faramir, the depressing picture of Men is considerably ameliorated. Ilúvatar's prophetic suggestion that Men might ultimately "use their gifts in harmony" and contribute to "the glory of my work" is exemplified in Aragorn, fulfilling Tolkien's hopeful statement concerning Man's assistance in "the effoliation and multiple enrichment of creation."

As is the case with Gandalf, the importance of Aragorn's example appears most clearly when contrasted with that of Denethor. In "The Pyre of Denethor," just before Denethor immolates himself, Gandalf tells him there is much he can still do to right the wrongs of his poor stewardship. Denethor rejects this message, breaks his staff, and proceeds to lie down in a fiery death. His final act is perhaps the most vivid portrayal of a Man's abrogation of his responsibilities and refusal to do what good he can for the betterment of the world. By contrast, Aragorn fulfills the potential for one of the Dúnedain, a member of the "inscrutable," "self-cursed" race of Men—the Younger Children of Ilúvatar—to do much to heal the hurts of the world. Even before he is restored to the throne of Gondor, Aragorn is revealed on numerous occasions to be a healer. In "The Houses of Healing," Aragorn says of himself, "in the high tongue of old I am Elessar, the Elfstone, and the Renewer." The epithet "Renewer," or *Envinyatar* in the Elvish tongue, is as portentous for his role as a restorer of Middle-earth as is *Estel*, meaning "hope," the name given to him by his mother.

In four of the healing scenes in the novel—Frodo on Weathertop and Faramir, Éowyn, and Merry in Minas Tirith—the treatment Aragorn uses is *athelas*, a naturally occurring herbal remedy regarded by the herb-master of Gondor as useful only for headaches or "to sweeten a fouled air." But in Aragorn's hands, *athelas* is no mere air freshener or analgesic, and when he uses it to treat Faramir, its immediate effects are striking:

> Then taking two leaves . . . he crushed them, and straightway
> a living freshness filled the room, as if the air itself awoke and

tingled, sparkling with joy. And then he cast the leaves into the bowls of steaming water that were brought to him, and at once all hearts were lightened. For the fragrance that came to each was like a memory of dewy mornings of unshadowed sun in some land in which the fair world in Spring is itself but a fleeting memory. (V/viii)

The imagery is not incidental; *athelas* does much more than clear the air: it summons up—much like Tolkien's literature does—imagined sensations of a better, purer world. Wakened from unconsciousness, Faramir does not exhibit his father's paralyzing despair but immediately says to Aragorn, "What does the king command?" He is ready to serve, and when Aragorn tells him to rest, eat, and be ready when he returns, Faramir answers, "I will, lord. . . . For who would lie idle when the king has returned?" (V/viii).

Shortly thereafter, as the herb's sweet aroma wafts about the chamber of Éowyn, it seems as if "a keen wind blew through the window . . . an air wholly fresh and clean and young, as if it had not before been breathed by any living thing and came new-made from snowy mountains high beneath a dome of stars, or from shores of silver far away washed by seas of foam" (V/viii). Echoes of Valinor are unmistakable here; Éowyn too is revived, if not yet to hope, then at least to health and readiness, saying, "there are deeds to do." Finally, approaching Merry's bedside, Aragorn speaks hope into the moment: "These evils can be amended," he says, and the herb's fragrance steals through the room "like the scent of orchards, and of heather in the sunshine full of bees." Here are echoes of the agrarian Shire, and the restoration of Merry's health is indicated by his first words, so appropriate to a Hobbit: "I am hungry" (V/viii).

These scenes reveal in miniature the much broader healing mission that Aragorn fulfills as King Elessar, both within the realm under his command and beyond it. The first of these involves reconciliation between the stewards of Gondor and the kings in the line of Elendil. At Aragorn's coronation, as the last steward of Gondor, Faramir ceremonially "begs leave to surrender his office" and hands the white rod, a symbol of his stewardship, to his king. In a symbolic reversal of Denethor's breaking of the staff, Aragorn hands the white rod back to Faramir, declaring, "That office is not ended, and it shall be thine and thy heirs' as long as my line shall last" (VI/v). As we will see later, Faramir fulfills his role as steward in the restoration and enrichment of lands spoiled by occupation and war.

Crowned as King Elessar with the ancient crown of Gondor's last king, Eärnur, Aragorn undertakes widespread repairs in the city, making it "more fair than it had ever been, even in the days of its first glory." He adorns it with fountains and trees, and under his rule, "all was healed and made good," recovering and preserving for posterity the memory of its ancient glory long after the Third Age has ended. In acts of royal diplomacy afterward, Elessar dispenses peace, pardon, and freedom in the lands of Mirkwood, Dunland, Harad, and Mordor. He secures lasting bonds of brotherhood between Gondor and Rohan and between himself and Éomer, who departs for his own realm, "where there is much to heal and set in order" (VI/vi). Restoration under King Elessar also includes reunification of the ancient kingdoms of Gondor and Arnor.[3]

The environmental implications of the restored kingship of Gondor are symbolized further in imagery deeply resonant with Middle-earth's underlying mythology. In May of that year, Gandalf and Aragorn find a sapling growing on the stony slope beneath the snow of Mount Mindolluin. "Already it had put forth young leaves long and shapely, dark above and silver beneath, and upon its slender crown it bore one small cluster of flowers whose white petals shone like the sunlit snow." It is, exclaims Aragorn, "a scion of the Eldest of Trees," Telperion, the mythic tree of Yavanna, descended from Galathilion through Nimloth, and the heraldic insignia of the ruling house of Gondor. Aragorn receives this as a symbolic blessing on his reign, and Gandalf declares it a signal of the end of the Third Age, the fading of the Elves, and "the time ... of the Dominion of Men." In light of our earlier discussion of the term, at least insofar as King Elessar's reign is concerned, the idea of *dominion* should not be ascribed the pejorative connotations associated with it elsewhere in the legendarium and in what we have said is a distorted understanding of Genesis 1:26. The withered White Tree of Gondor is gently uprooted, the sapling is planted in the Court of the Fountain, and in June it is found "laden with blossom" (VI/v). On Midsummer's Day, King Elessar weds Arwen Undómiel, beginning a reign of 120 years that the appendix calls one of "great glory and bliss." It is described in the "Tale of Years" as a reign in which Aragorn's acts of grace, diplomacy, and benevolence reveal the best expression of power and dominion that characterizes the race of Men in Middle-earth.[4]

Leadership and Responsibility

In Théoden, Éowyn, Faramir, Éomer, and Aragorn, we see examples from the race of Men who effectively suppress the worst traits of their race and exercise their virtues to achieve the good purposes for which they are intended. It is evident that in Middle-earth, fulfilling one's personal responsibility and awakening or arousing it in others requires leadership. In Rohan, Théoden and, later, Éomer are kings, so technically, the people of the Riddermark must obey them, just as the Men of Gondor must obey Aragorn. Faramir's response to Aragorn, "What does the king command?" is paradigmatic. As such, readers might be unable to draw many direct applications: none of us are kings or queens; most of us are not subjects under monarchal rule but citizens of representative democracies. And though we are free to live out some of these principles ourselves, few of us have wide enough authority or leadership positions to enact ecological policies for the protection, preservation, or restoration of the environment. Most of what we can do we have to do ourselves.

The example of Treebeard, though, may inspire more than this small hope. As the leading Ent, it appears that Treebeard does have some degree of authority over the others. However, he does not merely order the other Ents about, and by permitting them their autonomy, his style of leadership and exercise of authority are more compatible with our expectations of how things ought to be than, say, Théoden's or even—as gracious as he is—Aragorn's use of regal power. At the same time, Treebeard does not wait for someone else—another Ent—to do something: he leads in his speech and in his action. He takes the initiative to call the Entmoot—"a gathering of Ents—which does not often happen nowadays," he says. It obviously takes some effort to do this, but he works hard. "I have managed to make a fair number promise to come," he tells the hobbits (III/iv).

Individuals who have worked in voluntary organizations will recognize how much background effort is implied by this innocuous statement. Further, one gets the sense that in both calling the Entmoot and addressing the participants, Treebeard must speak passionately about the need to protect and preserve Fangorn Forest. We are explicitly told that one of the important things he does is simply "going over all the facts," making clear to the others how much damage has already been done in their wilderness domain and how urgent the need for action is (III/iv). Treebeard then demonstrates a willingness to make sacrifices like the ones he asks the others to make. He acts, he sets an example, and others follow.

Still, even Treebeard has more authority than do most readers of Tolkien's works. Again, it is in the Hobbits and in the Shire where readers see models of leadership that are most applicable to our own situation. Just as in Fangorn, the rousing of the Shire requires leaders with a plan. Once the recovery of the Shire is well under way, Farmer Cotton says, "I said we could master them. But we needed a call. You came back in the nick o' time, Mr. Merry" (VI/viii). Like Treebeard, when Merry and Pippin lead, other hobbits follow and are able to bring about change.

The exercise of leadership involves taking responsibility for one's own actions. Like many of the ideas in Tolkien's works, this flies in the face of much modern thinking, which often resorts to blame-shifting and the adoption of a "victim mentality" precisely when it is most important that personal responsibility be acknowledged and acted on. When he confronts young Robin Smallburrow about his role as a shirriff under Saruman's control, Sam implies that Robin is abetting the harm being done to the Shire. Like many others under the ruffians' heel, the young hobbit shifts the blame to others for choices he has made, choices that contribute to the widespread ruin of the Shire. Sam replies that it is time to take responsibility for his own actions. Robin asks "what can I do?" because he would prefer to do nothing. As noted, Denethor also abrogates responsibility rather than choosing to do anything positive.

Treebeard's approach to the question of practical action comes much closer to the stewardship ideal that Tolkien exemplifies. His is a fulfillment of the understanding expressed by Gandalf, who says it may not be our responsibility to "master all the tides of the world," but we should do what we can with the time given to us. Global change may not lie within our purview, but personal and local change may well be possible. Treebeard articulates a plan of action consistent with this view; he is cognizant of the pervasive problems confronting him but adopts a qualified optimism nonetheless: "There are hollow dales in this land where the Darkness has never been lifted, and the trees are older than I am.

Still, we do what we can. We keep off strangers and the foolhardy; and we train and we teach, we walk and we weed" (III/iv). Treebeard is doing two things here. First, he acknowledges that evil is not merely a distant thing found only in Isengard and in the work of Saruman; it is present even in his own land. Second, he is taking responsibility at a simple and basic level: "we do what we can." This statement can be considered an honest and positive rejoinder to Robin's dishonest question, "What can I do?" For the Ents, doing what they can means not only fighting dramatic battles and training and teaching others what they should do but also demonstrating the application of these limited solutions in their own lives: "we walk and we weed." Here, Treebeard's choice of terms directly illustrates the adage about "walking the walk and talking the talk." Treebeard even goes so far as to accept some blame for the loss. "I have been idle," he confesses. "I have let things slip." In the immediate follow-up to his own confession, he does not sidestep his responsibility but steps right up to it: "It must stop! I will stop it!" (III/iv).

The same is true of Sam, who acknowledges that the death of Saruman does not mean that his work of rousing and restoring the Shire is finished. We can speculate that once the ruffians are expelled, it might be tempting for him and the other hobbits to pat themselves on the back for the good work they have done and then sit back—perhaps at the Green Dragon Inn in Bywater—have a pint or two, smoke their pipes, and, with much nodding and wagging of heads, lament in sonorous tones all the damage done by Saruman. No one would disagree that they would be justified in placing the ultimate blame squarely on the shoulders of the fallen wizard. Sam, however, takes another course: "I shan't call it the end, till we've cleared up the mess," he says gloomily, "and that'll take a lot of time and work" (VI/viii). Among the Men who are the best examples of leadership, it seems to be a part of their noble bearing that characters such as Aragorn, Faramir, Théoden, and Éomer do not need to ponder long or engage in endless self-examination before getting to work. Once they see what needs to be done, the aggressive nature of their race leads them simply to do it.

Community, Counsel, and Debate

It must be noted that building unity of the kind attempted by Treebeard and Sam is no easy task, as anyone who has tried to do so can attest. This often requires individuals to submit to the will of the group. Healthy submission, however, does not necessarily eliminate the need for or the value of debate. For some—particularly in parliamentary and academic traditions, in which resolutions are adopted through vigorous, formal debate—the term *debate* may have primarily negative connotations. A better word here might be *counsel,* meaning personal discussion and advisement, or *council,* referring to a constructive group discussion and debate. Within the strong communities in *The Lord of the Rings,* councils are occasions when important issues are raised, discussed, or even debated in the traditional sense, but all sides listen to one another; decisions are reached by consensus; and, in some cases, counsel is given to a leader.

Striking examples of this include, in the chapter "The Council of Elrond," the decision to undertake the quest for Mount Doom and, in the chapter "The Last Debate," the decision to march on the Black Gates. The first of these is the longest chapter of the trilogy. Tom Shippey points out that it is 15,000 words long and "consists entirely of people talking." Twelve different speakers from diverse backgrounds are present, seven of whom are introduced for the first time.[5] All those who speak are taken seriously and make important contributions. In yet another example, Treebeard's Entmoot in Fangorn Forest is a meeting at which many speak, and it takes three days for the Ents to weigh their options and make what appears to be a decision by consensus.

It is not that lengthy debate replaces action or that discussion is important in and of itself. What is important is the link between the two: action without discussion can be foolhardy; discussion without action can be pointless. Applying this to the modern world, it is important that environmental activism be undertaken in communal contexts, where plans are discussed, people listen to one another, and participants work together even when their opinions differ. Along these lines, it is crucial that in the councils described in *The Lord of the Rings,* the powerful do not simply force decisions on others. In Rivendell, neither Gandalf nor Elrond demands that his voice be heeded above the others. In fact, a careful reading of the chapter reveals the degree to which Gandalf and Elrond refrain from strongly steering the discussion or manipulating the group's deliberations to achieve a foregone conclusion—such devices are more typical of Saruman's rhetorical deceits. Along with the others, they weigh options and listen to divergent opinions.

Judith Kollmann notes that in *The Lord of the Rings, council* and *counsel* often go together; both, she says, "are chief means to wise decisions."[6] This is modeled, too, in the relationship between Gandalf and Aragorn as they lead the Company of the Ring south from Rivendell. They are said to "debate" which is the best path—Gandalf believes it is through Moria, but Aragorn prefers to cross the mountains at Caradhras. After a period of ongoing discussion, Gandalf finally says they must reach a decision before going farther. Aragorn replies, "Then let us weigh the matter in our minds, while others rest and sleep." Though he is older, wiser, and in many ways more powerful, Gandalf in the end yields to Aragorn. As he says earlier, "If you bring a Ranger with you, it is well to pay attention to him, especially if the Ranger is Aragorn" (III/iii). When the ascent of Caradhras fails, a decision must be reached once again concerning whether to attempt passage through Moria. This time, the two of them gather all nine members of the Fellowship and make a decision.

By contrast, Sauron and Saruman never seek the counsel of others. Their method involves deception, coercion, or both. As related by Gandalf in "The Shadow of the Past," Saruman invites Gandalf to what is supposed to be an opportunity for mutual discussion concerning the One Ring. Saruman has no intention of listening to Gandalf, however, and when Gandalf refuses to comply with his plan, Saruman simply takes him captive, locking him up to overpower him and circumvent Gandalf's wishes. As Kollmann points out, this is not genuine counsel but a mockery of it. Likewise, the Orc "councils" that appear in the narrative—among Grishnákh, Uglúk, and the three groups of Orcs involved in Merry and Pippin's capture (III/iii) or among Shagrat, Snaga, and Gorbag in Cirith Ungol (IV/x, VI/i)—represent distorted, unsuccessful negotiations. Both conclude with one leader's murder by his rival.

For these reasons, then, the characters Tolkien presents as "wise" frequently warn against disharmony and disunity among the opponents of Sauron. In Lothlórien, Galadriel warns the Fellowship, "Your Quest stands upon the edge of a knife. Stray but a little and it will fail, to the ruin of all. Yet hope remains while the Company is true" (II/vii). In Rohan, Gandalf tells King Théoden, "Behold! the storm comes, and now all friends should gather together, lest each singly be destroyed" (III/vi).

Throughout Tolkien's works there are many strong examples of the value and positive results of fellowship and community. The very title of the first volume of *The Lord of the Rings* is suggestive of the importance of *fellowship*, and it is worked out in many areas, including ecology. As we discussed in earlier chapters, in contrast with the Ents and the Entwives, Tom Bombadil and Goldberry provide a model of a successful ecological partnership early in the novel, while at the end of *The Lord of the Rings*, the Shire itself provides a model of a society in which agriculture complements horticultural concerns, both of which are complemented by the preservation of forests. The restoration of Isengard is not achieved by Treebeard alone; others of his kind march with him, and their restorative work is done cooperatively. Likewise, as we noted earlier in this chapter, Sam is not working alone to reclaim the Shire; "thousands of willing hands of all ages" are involved in the cooperative venture of cleaning up after Saruman.

The idea of nurturing a love of the earth in others assumes that there are others with whom we have a relationship. This other-directedness suggests that stewardship obligations are best lived out in the context of *community*, a word that is indicative of common causes pursued in a spirit of cooperation. As with many things, the need for unity is most apparent in situations characterized by disunity and fragmentation of efforts. This is illustrated in one of Tolkien's most touching myths of environmental disunity, that of the Ents and Entwives, which is discussed later. This book began with a citation from John Elder's lament concerning divisions between various subgroups in the environmental movement, especially between conservationists and preservationists. Maurice Telleen also writes about the need for cooperation, focusing on conservationists and agrarians. About the volume in which his essay appears, Telleen comments, "I would hope that this book might rekindle, or kindle in many cases, the partnership between farmers and conservationists. While our primary concerns are by no means identical, they are certainly kissing cousins. It is time they recognized their commonality and became better acquainted."[7]

The need for this sort of cooperation between agrarians and conservationists, between conservationists and preservationists, and among those concerned about healthy agriculture, horticulture, and feraculture—in short, the need for a deeper sense of community among those working for all forms of environmental restoration—is fundamental to success. The need for cooperation is illustrated metaphorically in many heroic endeavors in Tolkien's legendarium, particularly in the battle against Sauron. As Haldir tells the Company when they first arrive at Lothlórien in *The Fellowship of the Ring*, "Indeed in nothing is the power of the Dark Lord more clearly shown than in the estrangement that divides all those who still oppose him" (II/vi). This general call for cooperation among environmentally responsive citizens in our own world applies equally well to those who share Tolkien's basic belief system and those who do not.

Technology, Skill, and the Habit of Hard Work

Sam's answer to Robin Smallburrow adds yet another principle to the qualities of leadership evident in the scenes of the Shire's restoration: elbow grease. Knowing how much effort will be involved in repairing his damaged homeland makes Sam understandably gloomy, yet he goes forward undaunted. This is the same feeling one gets from Scott Sanders's essay describing how Aldo Leopold's work inspired him to restore his own property:

> With Leopold's help I can see the damage done by previous owners: the eroded gullies, the stumps from careless logging, the straightened creek, the rusted carcasses of refrigerators and trucks dumped along the road. The gullies can be mended, he assures me. The trash can be carted away. The creek can be slowed down and encouraged to wander. Here is a field we could replant to prairie. Here is a low spot that could be flooded for a marsh. Here is a snarl of grapevines that could be trained so as to make ideal cover for wildlife, and all the better if we plant some grain nearby and let it stand through the winter. Here is a sunny corner we could set aside for rare flowers. Here is a site for a bluebird house. With each glimpse of a wilder future for this land, I enter more deeply into the life of the place.[8]

Sanders's description of "damage done by previous owners" is akin to the damage done in both Isengard and the Shire during Saruman's tenancy. Although Sanders has hope for the land's restoration in the wake of this damage, he also details the hard work of mending, carting, slowing rivers, planting and replanting, flooding, training, and building.

Wendell Berry's account of repairing his farm at Lane's Landing in Port Royal, Kentucky, contains similar descriptions of hard, even toilsome labor.[9] Though neither Sanders nor Berry uses the specific phrase "hard work," it is evident in everything they say about their efforts.

The Ents' restoration of Isengard certainly gives us a good example of hard work. "All the day they were busy," Merry and Pippin tell the others, "digging great pits and trenches, and making great pools and dams." They are justifiably proud of their work, too, for it is difficult. When asked if they are growing tired, Treebeard replies, "Tired? Well no, not tired, but stiff. I need a good draught of Entwash. We have worked hard; we have done more stone-cracking and earth-gnawing today than we have done in many a long year before" (III/ix). Treebeard understands that such labor is necessary to accomplish what needs to be done.

Along with the rest of the hobbits, Sam also chooses to work hard. Tolkien describes this in the final chapter of *The Lord of the Rings*. Despite their penchant for food, drink, and leisurely comfort, we read, "Hobbits can work like bees when the mood and the need comes on them." Nor is this a job for one individual, and even if a cliché, the apian image is an apt natural metaphor for the collective effort the hobbits are called on to exert: "Now there were thousands of willing hands of all ages, from the small but nimble ones of the hobbit lads and lasses to the well-worn and horny ones of the gaffers and gammers." Although all this is described in less than a paragraph, we should not underestimate how much work is involved in this process or how many laborers take part in it. We might notice, too, that the hobbits' undertakings include a type of recycling: "Before Yule not a brick was left standing of the new Shirriff-houses or of anything that had been built by 'Sharkey's Men'; but the bricks were used to repair many an old hole, to make it snugger and drier" (VI/ix).

One nice thing about hard work, especially when it is directed toward a worthwhile endeavor, is that it can be habit-forming. Steven R. Covey's *The Seven Habits of Highly Effective People* makes this point. Writing specifically about the importance of what he calls "ecological virtues" in our care of the earth, Steven Bouma-Prediger summarizes an important aspect of Aristotle's notion of virtue: "Virtues, especially moral virtues, are formed by habitual behavior. We become just, says Aristotle, by doing just acts, and brave by doing brave acts."[10] This habit-forming behavior is yet another aspect of hard work that is well illustrated by the Hobbits, who practice habitual good stewardship toward the land in the small things, which carries over into bigger things. By showing this, as Bouma-Prediger leads us to understand, an important ecological virtue is communicated.

Such work habits have benefits not only for the long-term health and restoration of the Shire but also for the immediate well-being of its inhabitants. In the process of their labors, "Great stores of goods and food, and beer, were found that had been hidden away by the ruffians in sheds and barns and deserted holes, and especially in the tunnels at Michel Delving and in the old quarries at Scary; so that there was a great deal better cheer that Yule than anyone had hoped for" (VI/ix). Many hobbits get snugger and drier homes; all of them get more food that winter than they expected. And although he does not promote economic benefits as the best or the ultimate motivation for environmental restoration, Tolkien here acknowledges them as a worthwhile side effect.

This principle can be seen in our own world: local communities that do the difficult work of cleaning up their waterways benefit from the results; countries that enact stricter environmental laws enjoy legitimate boosts to their economies. To take a local example, dairy farmers in one county in Vermont recently did the hard work of adjusting their farming practices and outfitting their farms to produce milk that meets federal standards for certification as "organic." Such changes were costly initially. But the farmers found that abandoning the use of toxic herbicides, pesticides, and hormone supplements made their farmland generally healthier and the commercial value of their milk higher, meaning that the long-term financial viability of their farms is improved. Despite pressure from corporate agricultural entities and dairy conglomerates, whose industrywide controls pose a real threat to the survival of small farms, these farmers are able to keep farming. Most important, however, their milk is nutritious and free of toxins, and it tastes good.

Tolkien also makes it clear that technology is never a substitute for hard work, but hard work can and should be coupled with skill. In "The Farmer as Conservationist," Aldo Leopold writes, "Conservation, therefore, is a positive exercise of skill and insight, not merely a negative exercise of abstinence or caution."[11] Wendell Berry has written frequently about the need for skilled farmers and argues against dependence on technology to accomplish the exacting tasks involved in farming. Tolkien brings both these thoughts together. When Sam is trying to decide how to use the small box of soil given to him by Galadriel, Frodo offers the following advice: "Use all of the *wits and knowledge you have of your own*, Sam, and then use the gift to help your work and better it. And use it sparingly" (VI/ix, emphasis added). The first half of this command is straightforward: in his hard work, Sam must use skills that cannot be entrusted to or derived from artificial intervention. Galadriel's gift, interpretable as a sort of "magic," may supplement his wits and hard work, but it is not meant to replace them.

We can say more about Frodo's advice, but this requires an understanding of Tolkien's concept of magic in fantasy. In various personal letters, Tolkien suggests that "Magic" in his works is connected negatively with the "Machine"— technology—and often with the will to dominate others, which is always an evil motive in his narratives.

> By [Magic] I intend all use of external plans and devices (apparatus) instead of development of the inherent inner powers or talents—or even the use of these talents with the corrupted motive of dominating: bulldozing the real world, or coercing other wills. The Machine is our more obvious modern form though more closely related to Magic than is usually recognized. (*Letters*, 145–46)

Tolkien goes on to clarify that most Elvish magic is different—probably deserving of a different word—and associated more with Art than with the Machine. Certainly Galadriel does not *intend* for Sam to use the soil from her garden to dominate or enslave the other Hobbits in the Shire. Nevertheless, it is an "external device" available to Sam, not an "inherent inner power" of his own, and theoretically he could use it as a tool or as a weapon to gain control in the Shire. Galadriel's gift therefore constitutes a form of magic one might associate—though we believe mistakenly—with Tolkien's conception of technology.[12] Frodo's remark that Sam should use the magic soil sparingly and rely instead on his own skill and hard work in healing the Shire might be taken more accurately as an implicit comment on the inadequacy of purely technological solutions to environmental problems.

Tolkien expands on these points in a subsequent letter, using more precise terminology for the distinctions drawn earlier. Admitting that he has been "far too casual" about displays of magic and use of the word, he distinguishes between *magia,* characterized by "immediacy: speed, reduction of labor, and reduction . . . of the gap between the idea or desire and the result," and *goetia,* "witchcraft . . . performed by the invocation and employment of evil spirits."[13] The critical distinction, however, is the user's motivation. Aragorn's healing powers "might be regarded as 'magical,'" he says, and Gandalf and the Elves use *magia* sparingly "for specific beneficent purposes." The Enemy, he says—in terms similar to the earlier letter—uses *magia* "to bulldoze both people and things" and *goetia* "to terrify and subjugate." "Both sides live mainly by 'ordinary' means," however, which can be used just as easily, though less quickly, "to push mountains over, wreck forests, or build pyramids." But the Enemy and those like him use the accelerative power of magic "with destructive and evil effects," because they "have become chiefly concerned to use *magia* for their own power" (*Letters,* 199–200). Although Sam's use of the gift of Galadriel qualifies in this sense as an exercise of "magic," neither in intention nor in application or result is this the same thing as Saruman's wizardry at Isengard.

In this regard, we might consider the fact that Gandalf seldom works his wizardry through gratuitous displays of magic, power, or technology, and never for self-aggrandizement; instead, he achieves his purposes generally through vigilance, hard work, and—noted earlier—wise counsel. By contrast, Orcs and Goblins make use of both ordinary means—slave labor—and technology as substitutes for their own hard work; Sauron and Saruman use both forms of magic to enhance their own power. If dependence on or overuse of technology is the problem, then the use of more technology as a substitute for skill and hard work, particularly with selfish motives, is not the solution.

Ents and Entwives

The specific division between conservationism and preservationism and the devastating results of this divide are also represented directly in Tolkien's works. In earlier chapters, we presented the Ents as models of feraculture: preservation of the unspoiled character of wild nature in its original form. Entwives,[14] by contrast, are engaged in both horticulture (like Elves) and agriculture (like Hobbits)—both practices involving the intrusion into pristine wilderness and the imposition of a sometimes high degree of order on unordered nature. Treebeard summarizes the situation this way:

> The Ents gave their love to things that they met in the world, and the Entwives gave their thought to other things, for the Ents loved the great trees, and the wild woods, and the slopes of the high hills; and they drank of the mountain-streams, and ate only such fruit as the trees let fall in their path . . . but the Entwives gave their minds to the lesser trees, and to the meads in the sunshine beyond the feet of the forests; and they saw the sloe in the thicket, and the wild apple and the cherry blossoming in spring, and the green herbs in the waterlands in summer, and the seeding grasses in the autumn fields. They did not desire to speak with these things; but they wished them to hear and obey what was said to them. The Entwives ordered them to grow according to their wishes, and bear leaf and fruit to their liking; for the Entwives desired order, and plenty, and peace. . . . So the Entwives made gardens to live in. (III/iv)

It is a complex picture, and a sad one. The Ents are not interested in *sustainable* forestry, agriculture, or horticulture because they are not interested in forestry, agriculture, or horticulture of *any* kind. They want to preserve Fangorn as it is: wild. They do not plant trees for fruit, and they even refrain from eating cultivated and picked fruit, accepting only that which the trees let fall of their own accord. In contrast, the Entwives love their gardens. Like the Elves and Hobbits, they raise flowering plants; like the Hobbits, they cultivate corn. In fact, it is from the Entwives that Men are said to have learned the agricultural arts. From what little we are told, we can assume that the Entwives' agriculture and horticulture represent good environmental stewardship, just as the Ents' feraculture does. Nonetheless, in their environmental vision the Entwives differ from the male counterparts of their race: they desire order and structure, and they understand that some degree of soil cultivation is necessary for survival. In short, the Ents' policies can be seen as preservationist in character, whereas the Entwives are conservationists in their essential characteristics.

What makes the legend of the Ents and Entwives so tragic is that the two do not cooperate. Because their visions differ, they are said to have become estranged sometime in the distant past of Middle-earth's history. As a result of this estrangement, the Ents as a race are doomed for the lack of offspring. Toward the end of the trilogy, we read, "Treebeard's face became sad. 'Forests may grow,' he said. 'Woods may spread. But not Ents. There are no Entings'" (VI/vi). The message? Environmental positions should be held with conviction, but divergent views should not be adhered to so fiercely as to threaten one's very survival. Regardless of whether Tolkien was consciously aware of environmental disagreements over the policies of conservation and preservation, he had either the foresight or the intuition to create as part of his legendarium a moving and troubling myth that captures these issues in a persuasive way. The myth of the Ents and Entwives serves as a powerful warning.[15]

Self-Sacrifice and Celebratory Love

The Christian perspective on loving care for the earth that is central to Tolkien's environmental thought involves a natural progression from love for the creator who made the world and recognition that it was created to have meaning and purpose, to love of the world itself and the recognition that its goodness is grounded in the supreme goodness of its divine creator. And, as we indicated previously, the goodness of creation is worth celebrating. This idea is expressed often in the psalms. In a letter written in 1969, Tolkien notes that the chief purpose of life may be to be moved "to praise and thanks." He goes on, "And in moments of exaltation we may call on all created things to join in our chorus, speaking on their behalf, as is done in Psalm 148, and in The Song of the Three Children in Daniel II. PRAISE THE LORD . . . all mountains and hills, all orchards and forests, all things that creep and birds on the wing" (*Letters*, 400).

In the Christian perspective held by Tolkien, by virtue of its sacred origins, the earth is spiritually valuable not despite but because of its status as a physical reality. It is not to be despised an impediment to spiritual elevation, as in some Eastern philosophical traditions and some Christian heresies; nor is the physical realm to be regarded in materialist fashion as merely the product of blind chance, as in some modern philosophical systems. According to Lynn White Jr., one of the main reasons for our environmental and ecological problems is the loss of the perspective Tolkien typifies. Loss of the view of nature as sacred is one of the things leading to its exploitation. Philip Sherrard argues:

> The spiritual significance and understanding of the created world has been virtually banished from our minds, and we have come to look upon things and creatures as though they possessed no sacred or numinous quality. It is a process which has accustomed us to regard the created world as composed of so many blind forces, essentially devoid of meaning, personality and grace, which may be investigated, used, manipulated and consumed for our own scientific or economic interests.[16]

However, in seeing nature as sacred, Tolkien is not saying that any part of it—not even trees—ought to be worshipped. Nature was created by God for his own purpose, inscrutable as this may be—or seem—from the limited human perspective. An adequate appreciation of the world's inherent meaning and value cannot be attained—at least not as Tolkien would have us understand it—apart from this perspective.[17]

It must be admitted that a love of the earth does not necessarily proceed only from explicit acknowledgment of its transcendent purpose or goodness rooted in a divine creator. People with many different belief systems have nurtured a love of the world in a variety of ways. Countless readers who do not share Tolkien's Christian faith enjoy his books, and many share his love of the earth without reference to Catholic doctrines of creation or the Christian understanding of the goodness of the earth. However, like the other principles discussed in this chapter, the principle of sacrificial love, which is at the heart of Tolkien's environmentalism, may be appealing to all his readers, perhaps especially to those who share his religious views on these matters. Christianity is by no means the only religion that recognizes the spiritual significance of nature, but it certainly provides a plausible and consistent transcendent basis for understanding nature as sacred and worthy of loving care.

The characteristic displayed by the wiser characters of Middle-earth in situations of discussion, debate, and council can be identified as one of the deepest transcendent values with which the entire trilogy is imbued: self-sacrificial love. This principle—discussed at length in chapter 3—represents the idea that we ought not act for our own selfish ends but rather must sometimes be willing to give things up for the benefit of others. More than any other, this principle is the core belief of Tolkien's Christianity. A deeply biblical principle, sacrificial love is central to the life and teachings of Jesus and modeled in his death. One finds it throughout the gospels, and it is central to the Christian ethos developed and articulated in the epistles.[18] This principle runs through all of Tolkien's tales and has important implications for environmental stewardship. We have already discussed this briefly in relation to Frodo's willingness to undertake the quest for the sake of the Shire. He says, "I tried to save the Shire, and it has been saved, but not for me. It must often be so, Sam, when things are in danger: some one has to give them up, lose them, so that others may keep them." Frodo does not consider himself more important than other Hobbits or the Shire itself; in reflecting on the wounds he has received, he regards his mission as a sacrifice willingly made to save them. Similar actions can be seen elsewhere—Gandalf at Khazad-dûm, the Captains of the West at the Black Black Gate, the Ents at Isengard. As befits his character, when Treebeard laments that the march on Isengard may be their last, he uses imagery drawn from nature: "Songs like trees bear fruit in their own time and their own way; and sometimes they are withered untimely." Here he suggests that although the upcoming battle may accomplish a good purpose, members of his race may be withered in death. But he also states the purpose directly: "We may help the other peoples before we pass away" (III/iv). Even Boromir, whose motivations provide one of the worst examples of human fallibility, exhibits the virtue of self-sacrifice in his final moments. In Minas Tirith, recalling the scene of Boromir's fatal decision to defend Merry and Pippin from the Orcs, Pippin says to Denethor with allusive potency, "He died to save us" (V/i).

Scouring Enabled by Myths

As already discussed, in his film adaptation of *The Lord of the Rings,* Peter Jackson chose not to include material from "The Scouring of the Shire." Although this decision was certainly dictated in part by time constraints, it probably also reflected the director's view that this chapter is somehow anticlimactic and unnecessary. From a popular cinematic point of view, Jackson may well be right. Regarding Tolkien's ideas expressed in the books, however, readers may have a different opinion. The narrative of the hobbits' repair and restoration of the Shire should be seen not as an afterthought but as central to the whole tale. Viewed in terms of the novel's "applicability" and its portrayal of the author's environmental vision, the hobbits' return to the Shire is not an addendum tacked on at the end, a dispensable denouement; rather, it can be seen as fulfilling and completing ideas adumbrated in earlier chapters of the story, which serve as a prelude to what really matters.

Important evidence to this effect comes from Gandalf himself when he says good-bye to the four hobbits shortly after Butterbur hints that "all's not too well in the Shire" and just before they reenter their land:

> "I am with you at present," said Gandalf, "but soon I shall not be. I am not coming to the Shire. You must settle its affairs yourselves; that is what you have been trained for. Do you not yet understand? My time is over: it is no longer my task to set things to rights, nor to help folk to do so. And as for you, my dear friends, you will need no help. You are grown up now. Grown indeed very high; among the great you are, and I have no longer any fear at all for any of you." (VI/vii)

All the events of the great quest and the War of the Ring have trained the hobbits to deal with the troubles they find back home in the Shire. If the hobbits cannot apply what they have learned to help their own people, then their experiences have been wasted.

When Gandalf says this to the hobbits, we can hear Tolkien saying something similar to his readers. Like the hobbits, we must settle the affairs of the realms we live in, unaided in any direct way by Tolkien himself. If we cannot apply anything of what we have learned from *The Lord of the Rings,* then our reading of the books, though entertaining, is ultimately pointless. However, if, like the four hobbits, we have learned our lessons from the great tale, we should need no further help.

Can a work of fantasy really teach us this much? Tolkien thought so. At the beginning of this book we discussed the importance of myth in shaping people's imagination, including their capacity for imagining a better, healthier environment. Many environmental writers feel the same way: before we can change our habitual ways of interacting with the natural world, we need to change the way we think about it and ourselves in it. And one way—perhaps the best way—to do this is through the shaping of our narrative imagination. People often learn better from stories than from committee reports, government documents, charts, statistics, academic treatises, or pontification and sermonizing on matters of grave significance. In his stories, Tolkien suggests that the shaping of the imagination paradoxically involves both the development of maturity and the recapture of a childlike understanding of the world.

This is illustrated when Théoden first encounters Ents, a passage we touched on earlier. As Théoden and Gandalf make their way to Isengard after the Battle of Helm's Deep, three Ents come striding from the north toward them. In astonishment, Théoden asks Gandalf what they are. "'They are the shepherds of the trees,' answered Gandalf. 'Is it so long since you listened to tales by the fireside? There are children in your land who, out of the twisted threads of story, could pick the answer to the question. You have seen Ents, O King, Ents out of Fangorn Forest'" (III/viii). Gandalf here describes a form of knowledge often wrongly associated—both in Rohan's culture and in many cultures in our world—with children's tales. He suggests an approach to these tales that may be superior to the skeptical, supposedly "adult" understanding possessed by Théoden and matched by others in the story. In the debate at the Green Dragon Inn in "The Shadow of the Past," for example—a chapter in which the credibility of such stories is an important topic—Ted Sandyman says sarcastically, "I can hear fireside-tales and children's stories at home, if I want to." Sam's reply—"and I daresay there's more truth in some of them than you reckon" (I/ii)—bespeaks the valuation of childlike narrative understanding implied in Gandalf's remarks. Sandyman and Théoden (at least until Gandalf's discussion with him) both make the same mistake of regarding fairy stories as childish and untrue; like us, they have to be taught that profound truths can sometimes be found in genres scorned by supposedly sophisticated taste.

In sharing the importance of myth and story in shaping our imaginative view of life, Tolkien is making yet another comment about the world and our stewardship of it. As Gandalf goes on to tell King Théoden, "All the years from Eorl the Young to Théoden the Old are of little count to [Ents]; and all the deeds of your house but a small matter" (III/viii). Men in Middle-earth—like humans in our world—consider themselves to be quite important. But all the days of our lives are but a blink of an eye to an Ent or a giant California redwood. As Norman Wirzba says, we have to give up the "delusion that we live in a purely human world . . . the arrogant and naive belief that human ambition should be the sole measure of cultural success or failure."[19] We must preserve, acquire, or recapture the perspective that literature—perhaps especially fairy stories and fantasy—gives us. We also learn from Théoden's response and Gandalf's reply:

> The king was silent. "Ents!" he said at length. "Out of the shadows of legend I begin a little to understand the marvel of the trees, I think. I have lived to see strange days. Long we have tended our beasts and our fields, built our houses, wrought our tools, or ridden away to help in the wars of Minas Tirith. And that we called the life of Men, the way of the world. We cared little for what lay beyond the borders of our land. Songs we have that tell of these things, but we are forgetting them, teaching them only to children, as a careless custom. And now the songs have come down among us out of strange places, and walk visible in the Sun."
> "You should be glad, Théoden King," said Gandalf. "For not only the little life of Men is now endangered, but the life also of those things which you have deemed the matter of legend. You are not without allies, even if you know them not." (III/viii)

In Middle-earth, it is legend that helps Théoden better understand the "marvel of the trees" and the ways of the earth outside the confines of Rohan. So too in our world, the works of J. R. R. Tolkien help us better understand the nature of reality and the reality of nature in the wider world outside our own small domain. Concerning the development of his own imagination, Tolkien says, "It was in fairy-stories that I first divined the potency of the words, and the wonder of the things, such as stone, and wood, and iron; tree and grass; house and fire; bread and wine" (*TL*, 62). We trust and hope that Tolkien's legendarium can help people care more than just a little for what lies outside their own self-interest and beyond the borders of their own land. For Théoden, this involves the sort of maturing process alluded to in Gandalf's remarks concerning the hobbits' growing up. It is a process of maturation that recovers childlike wonder in the world.

Translated into terms applicable to the situation in our own world, Gandalf's words to Théoden give cause for concern but also reason for hope. Without hyperbole, it can be said that the environmental health of our world is more gravely endangered now than at any point in human history. On the success or failure of our environmental stewardship rests not only the "life of Men," as Gandalf puts it, but also the life of all that grows and is part of creation. Heedless pursuit of reckless environmental policies is tantamount to following the ways of Isengard and Mordor. Sanders writes: "[Aldo Leopold] recognized that we have to make a living from the land, that we all need shelter and clothes and food. But he also realized that we need a great deal more if we are to lead sane and honorable lives: we need beauty, community, and purpose; we need 'spiritual relationships to things of the land.'"[20]

J. R. R. Tolkien anchors his environmental principles similarly in a total imaginative vision of ecological harmony between the created world of Middle-earth, that world's creator, and the sentient creatures who populate it. In so doing, he offers us an inspiring, imaginative portrayal of how we might fulfill the responsibilities of environmental stewardship that are our burden and our privilege to bear. He illustrates the fundamental ethical perspective that energizes this vision, and, that if we succeed in applying it—each of us in our own community, each in our own small way—the impact on each individual and the total impact on the world we live in can be positive and profound.

Conclusion: Some Practical Matters

In the introduction to this book, we stated that in the strictest sense of the word, J. R. R. Tolkien was not an environmentalist. But after more than two years spent researching and writing, we are not nearly so sure of the unassailability of this position. As our project unfolded and we examined Tolkien's works in the light of books and articles by recent and contemporary environmental writers, our initial intuitions about Tolkien's environmental views were confirmed: concepts compatible with those of John Elder, Wendell Berry, Scott Russell Sanders, Aldo Leopold, Barbara Kingsolver, Wes Jackson, and a host of others appear in Tolkien's writings about Middle-earth. But we are now convinced that these ideas were expressed far more consciously on his part—and perhaps even deliberately—than we had initially suspected. It now appears to us that even the narrowest definitions of environmentalism and environmental literature would have to include Tolkien and his works.

Confirmation of this comes in part from Tolkien's nonfiction writing, especially his letters. For example, his affirmation that he chose consciously "in all [his] works" to "take the part of trees as against all their enemies" (*Letters*, 419) and his interpretation of Psalm 148 as a chorus on behalf of "all created things" (*Letters*, 400) suggest that Tolkien thought and wrote deliberately about the environment and environmental responsibility. In "On Fairy-stories," his expression of the "wonder" of nature inherent in such things as stone, wood, trees, and grass—part of his apologia for fantasy and other literary genres—fully justifies our claim that *The Lord of the Rings, The Silmarillion,* and most of the rest of his fiction belong to the category of environmental literature. But the justification for revising our earlier opinion came overwhelmingly from the narratives themselves, the true focus of this book.

We see more clearly now than we did at the outset how closely interwoven at the deepest level many of these issues were for Tolkien. The emphasis on consolation and recovery in the concluding sections of "On Fairy-stories," for example, makes it clear that literary concerns and environmental ideas were not merely cultural matters for Tolkien but fundamentally theological ones. His views of the environment grew out of his belief that the world originated as the good creation of a good God, that environmental responsibility is nothing more and nothing less than good stewardship, and that the failure to exercise such stewardship is a form of evil. We hope we have made this case convincingly not only by citing the nonfiction writing in which he addressed these issues but also, and more importantly, by examining the fictional narratives in which these ideas are exemplified.

Another position we took from the beginning is that these insights are applicable to us—to our readers and to ourselves. This also has been confirmed. Throughout the book we have offered incidental observations on how the essential virtues conducive to environmental stewardship might work out in the real world. Chapters 9 and 10, for example, discuss the character qualities necessary for the practical application of Tolkien's environmental perspective. Out of respect for his narratives as literary fiction, however, and to avoid treating them as environmental treatises, thinly veiled allegories, or sermons, we have not specified applications for our world in any detail.

Given everything we have said in earlier chapters, though, readers may now find themselves echoing Robin Smallburrow, a minor character discussed in chapter 10, who asks, "What can I do?" Our discussion emphasizes the fact that Robin's question is a rhetorical justification of his complicity in the Shire's problems. Tolkien's environmental vision is not offered to us as a merely rhetorical gesture, however; given the potency of his environmental imagination, and given the urgency of these issues in the world we live in, more specific answers to Robin's question seem to be in order. Readers are asked now to accept, or perhaps forgive, the rhetoric of advocacy that necessarily characterizes some of what follows. We would insist, though, that this is a natural outgrowth of the issues considered and the points raised in earlier chapters.

What We Can Do

Robin's question "What can I do?" is disingenuous; it is an evasive dodge that is all too familiar to many of us. But taken at face value, it can be read otherwise, as a way of asking how Tolkien's environmental vision might be applied to our personal behavior. Readers will remember that after Sam excoriates him for his complacency, suggesting that he give up his job "if it has stopped being a respectable [one]," Robin reveals that his deepest sympathies are not with Sharkey and his men at all but with Sam and the others. Lowering his voice, Robin says, "If we all got angry together something might be done" (VI/viii). Robin is not a *bad* character, after all, and although he does not appear in the narrative again by name, no doubt he is among the hobbits who take off their feathered shirriff hats, join the general uprising, and defeat the ruffians oppressing the Shire.

Many of us are probably something like Robin Smallburrow: uneasy about having compromised our principles along the way, but with our better selves committed to environmental responsibility; eager to participate in activities directed toward positive results and persuaded—despite estimates to the contrary—that we really can do something beneficial for the environment we share.[1] Throughout the earlier chapters, we have referred to many excellent books and articles touching on the subjects addressed here, and in the appendix we recommend some of the best of them, but for all of us there comes a time to stop reading books and start applying what we have read to what we do. As we said in chapter 10, each of us should (1) begin to take personal responsibility for ourselves, (2) exercise forms of leadership most appropriate to our place and purpose in the world, (3) participate in the hard work of environmental stewardship as opportunities arise, and (4) alter our habits and behavior in practical ways directed toward permanent, positive change. Personal responses such as these are less effective in isolation, however, and are best undertaken collaboratively in local communities; they depend on a collective recognition that in its natural state the world we have been given is a glorious, wondrous place. They also require communal acknowledgment that global warming; air, water, and land pollution; unsustainable agricultural practices; run-away technology; and exorbitant consumerism pose serious threats to our way of life and even to our survival.

If we all got angry together, something might be done. There are many local groups, national organizations, and public and private resources readers can consult for advice on how to participate in environmental preservation and conservation. Environmental groups such as the Nature Conservancy, Sierra Club, World Wildlife Federation, WILD Foundation, Wilderness Land Trust, Wilderness Society, Izaak Walton League, and many others are dedicated to the preservation and conservation of natural environments under feraculture and horticulture—the domains of the Ents and the Elves in our title. Such groups merit the consideration of Tolkien's readers, both those whose environmental conscience is informed by a religious perspective and those without such a perspective. There are growing signs that people of traditional religious faiths have begun to play a more prominent role in bringing a biblical perspective to bear on environmental issues.[2] Along with Wendell Berry, we hope people in churches who share these views will seek more opportunities for collaboration with groups like the ones cited above;[3] we hope those who view traditional religion skeptically can overcome their suspicion and welcome people of faith as fellow laborers. Farmer Cotton's remark, "There's got to be some fighting before this is settled" (VI/viii), is best perhaps avoided, however, as a warrant for more radical forms of environmental activism.

But the area of personal behavior most directly connected to our place in the environment, and the one most clearly relevant to the hallmark of the Hobbits' culture—referenced in the third domain of our title, Eriador—has to do with the food we eat and the agricultural practices that produce it. It is here, perhaps, that our individual patterns of daily behavior can be altered and, incrementally and in the aggregate, affect the larger patterns of our society and culture in the long term.

Eating Responsibly

In an essay entitled "The Pleasures of Eating," Berry has much to say that is of practical value for those of us who want to put Tolkien's environmental awareness to work in personal terms. "Many times," he begins, "after I have finished a lecture on the decline of American farming and rural life, someone in the audience has asked 'What can city people do?'" Berry's answer? "Eat responsibly."[4]

Among the many environmental writers mentioned in this book, Berry is perhaps the most successful in highlighting the fact that our most intimate and familiar connection to the physical environment is food. We all must eat; our physical survival depends on our ability to feed ourselves from the produce of the land. In all his books, the central figures in the total environmental economy by which we all subsist are—like Tolkien's Hobbits—the ones most intimately acquainted with the soil: farmers. Most of us, however, are largely if not totally ignorant of agricultural processes, and we probably consider the act of eating unrelated to environmental health. But as consumers of agricultural products, our actions are not neutral in their impact on the humblest, most easily taken for granted, and most important component in our natural environment: the soil. How we eat has environmental consequences. For the individual, Berry goes on to say, eating is more than "a purely appetitive transaction between him and his food" and far more than "a purely commercial transaction" between consumers and suppliers. "Eating is an agricultural act" and thus an environmental one, and members of urban and suburban societies who know little about the implications of their eating habits suffer from "a kind of cultural amnesia that is misleading and dangerous."[5]

Several of the books listed in the appendix address this issue; Barbara Kingsolver draws the links directly and dramatically. The environmental hazards posed by our dependence on fossil fuels for the transport of almost everything are obvious. But, she says, "Gas-guzzling area number two . . . is our diet." Americans have developed "a taste for food that's been seeded, fertilized, harvested, processed, and packaged in grossly energy-expensive ways and then shipped, often refrigerated, for so many miles it might as well be green cheese from the moon." She goes on, "Even if you walk or bike to the store, if you come home with bananas from Ecuador, tomatoes from Holland, cheese from France, and artichokes from California, you have guzzled some serious gas. This extravagance that most of us take for granted is a stunning energy boondoggle: Transporting 5 calories' worth of strawberry from California to New York costs 435 calories of fossil fuel."[6] Although vegetarianism does not appeal to everyone, a similar analysis of beef production provides some sobering data: the production, processing, and transport of each pound of hamburger served in a fast-food restaurant uses 100 gallons of water, 4.8 pounds of grain, and 4 cups of gasoline, emitting greenhouse gases equal to a 24-mile drive in the average automobile, and resulting in the loss of 5 pounds of topsoil, "every inch of which took five hundred years for the microbes and earthworms to build."[7] Berry's writings often note that industrial agriculture such as ours, in which the topsoil lost each year in the grain-producing states weighs more than the grain harvested, is not sustainable in the long term. Readers are advised to consult the *More-with-Less Cookbook* and others like it that provide practical suggestions for changing our cooking and eating habits to minimize pollution and waste while maximizing individual health benefits and equity for our economically disadvantaged neighbors elsewhere in the world.[8]

Berry concludes "The Pleasures of Eating" with seven recommendations for eating responsibly. In summary, they are: (1) participate in food production to the extent you can; (2) prepare your own food; (3) know the origins of the food you buy, and buy food produced close to your home; (4) deal directly with local farmers, gardeners, or orchardists whenever possible; (5) learn as much as possible about the economy and technology of industrial food production; (6) be aware of what is involved in the best farming and gardening practices; and (7) learn as much as you can about the life histories of food species. Berry believes eating should be "an *extensive* pleasure." People who "know the garden in which their vegetables have grown and know that the garden is healthy" will also "remember the beauty of the growing plants." He continues, "Eating with the fullest pleasure—pleasure, that is, that does not depend on ignorance—is perhaps the profoundest enactment of our connection with the world. In this pleasure we experience and celebrate our dependence and our gratitude, for we are living from mystery, from creatures we did not make and powers we cannot comprehend."[9] Berry's views here echo the highest principles defining the culture of the Shire; his recommendations suggest that another answer to the question "What can I do?" might be this: *eat like a Hobbit*, if not in quantity, at least in quality.

We would not want our recommendations to be mistaken for the facile or fashionable solutions of the "alfalfa sprouts and granola" crowd, and the pragmatic implications of Tolkien's environmental vision are more complicated than and go far beyond what and how we eat. Tolkien was not intellectually or culturally naïve, nor was he idealistic about these matters. "*Hobbits* are not a Utopian vision," he wrote, "or recommended as an ideal in their own or any age. They, as all peoples and their situations, are an historical accident—as the Elves point out to Frodo—and an impermanent one in the long view. I am not a reformer nor an 'embalmer'!" (*Letters*, 197). Despite all its admirable agrarian values, the Shire is no perfect model; Valinor has been removed permanently from the circle of the world. Just as the Elves' attempt to preserve the original form of creation in all its exquisite beauty is doomed to failure, the peaceable Shire cannot forever fence out the wider, darker world beyond Eriador. The peace and prosperity of their agrarian world depend on others' vigilance.

Even in extolling its environmental virtues, in retrospect we readily acknowledge that Tolkien's work is not perfect. His writings have much to contribute to a better vision of our relationship with the rest of creation, but the legendarium is not without flaws. We hope we have debunked the view of the Shire as a simplistic, romantic idyll. But there are other criticisms of his work that are harder to answer satisfactorily, and we want to address some of them briefly.

One of these touches on the wildlife of Middle-earth, which is so sparse as to be virtually absent. Eriador, for example, seems to be almost completely barren of wild fauna. Under Strider's guidance, after they leave Bree, the hobbits "saw no sign and heard no sound of any other living thing all that day: neither two-footed, except birds, nor four-footed, except one fox and a few squirrels" (I/xi). Shortly after, in "drier and more barren" lands farther east, they encounter no animals except "a few melancholy birds . . . piping and wailing." Where has all the wildlife gone? In the real world, these facts would point to some kind of widespread environmental devastation, but Tolkien does not offer an explanation.

Except perhaps for eagles, the wild creatures that do appear are almost always associated with the sources of evil in Middle-earth. Birds are in greatest evidence. As the Company of the Ring makes its way south from Rivendell, for example, flocks of "a kind of crow of large size" called *crebain* are seen "flying at great speed" and "wheeling and circling" above Frodo and his companions. Along with some hawks he has seen high above, Gandalf thinks they are "spying out the land," implying a connection with either Saruman or Sauron.

Similarly, the wolves that later attack the Company at night between Caradhras and Moria are characterized as "no ordinary wolves hunting for food in the wilderness" but as Wargs, malevolent phantoms in wolf shape, either evil themselves or servants of one of the Company's enemies. Just as in the Fell Winter, "when white wolves invaded the

Shire over the frozen Brandy-wine" (II/iii), wolves are vilified here and throughout the legendarium. In *The Silmarillion,* Carcharoth the wolf is a chief servant of Morgoth and the bane of the great hero Beren; in *The Hobbit,* wolves are on the side of the Goblins; in *The Lord of the Rings,* wolves again appear on the side of evil in the service of Saruman.

In our world, wolves have long been icons of wilderness, especially in Europe and North America. We may think, for example, of Jack London's *The Call of the Wild* or the 1983 movie *Never Cry Wolf.* In the real world, there have been no verifiable, documented reports of healthy adult wolves killing human beings. But in Tolkien's legendarium, they are always hostile. Why? The simple answer is that, as in other areas, Tolkien's characterization of wolves is based on old traditions in folklore, medieval legend, fairy tales, and Norse mythology. In the *Poetic Edda,* for example, Skoll and Hati appear as cosmic wolves that swallow the sun and moon at the end of time in Ragnarök, while Garm, the wolf-hound chained at the entrance to Niflheim, is released in the end to kill—and be killed by—the god Tyr. The offspring of Loki and the giantess Angrboda is Fenris-wolf, whose gaping jaws encompass earth and sky; he devours Odin in Ragnarök. In "Little Red Riding Hood" from the Brothers Grimm, a "big bad wolf" eats the grandmother and, in some versions, the title character herself. The list could go on.

Just as Tolkien drew from Norse mythology in his development of dragons and Dwarves, so he ladled soup from the same pot for his portrayal of wolves. Dan Stahler, a wolf biologist working with the Yellowstone Gray Wolf Restoration Program and an avid fan of Tolkien's works, admits that one of the biggest obstacles to good environmental policy regarding wolves is their negative popular image, drawn largely from the imaginative literary tradition of myth, fantasy, and fairy tale.[10] Works such as Tolkien's contribute to the perennially negative perception of wolves, thereby hindering wolf recovery efforts in the United States. Although support for certain kinds of environmental awareness can be found in Tolkien's works, for other ecological subjects, he may be a weak prop.

Despite our acknowledgment of this, we have the sense that the flaws in our book are not the result of taking our argument too far but rather of not taking it far enough. Taking our cue from Tolkien, the focus of our work here is largely on the biosphere—particularly the arboreal and vegetative life—of Middle-earth. Other facets of the total environment of Middle-earth no doubt deserve more extensive consideration: the alpine ecology of the White and the Misty Mountains; the wetlands of the Marish, the outflow of the Entwash, and (negatively) the Dead Marshes; the aquatic environments of Anduin, Isen, Gwathló, and Brandywine—Middle-earth's great rivers; the grasslands of Minhiriath, Enedwaith, and Rohan; the piedmonts of Rhudaur and the hill country of northern Eriador. We see now that we could have written much more. In any event, we hope that for visitors to that imaginary land, our book proves to be—like Niggle's Parish—at least a good introduction not only to the mountains but also to the whole environment of Middle-earth.

Afterword

It has been rightly said that the true hero of *The Lord of the Rings* is not Aragorn or Sam Gamgee or even Frodo but Middle-earth itself: Middle-earth, with its astonishing range of habitats, from the tilth of the Shire to the Riders' prairie, from the managed woodlands of Lórien to the deep dales of Fangorn, where the Huorns lurk in the hundreds. And the Great River; Tom Bombadil's willow-choked Withywindle; the Glittering Caves of Aglarond; Ithilien, with its "dishevelled dryad loveliness"; and Hollin in Wilderland, which still remembers the Elves, are all described with careful and loving attention. In a letter he wrote to his son Christopher in 1945, Tolkien remarked, "certainly there was an Eden on this very unhappy earth. We all long for it, and are constantly glimpsing it" (*Letters*, 110). He provided many glimpses of it himself.

But the critical word in the passage is "was," and in the same letter Tolkien notes the "many sad exiled generations" that have lived since the Fall. His fiction also shows again and again that the small bit of Eden left to us has been constantly betrayed and destroyed and is forever under threat. The wars of Middle-earth created the Dead Marshes, where the fair turns foul; Saruman's activities turn "singing groves" into a "waste of stump and bramble," all ending in the ghastly polluted plain of Gorgoroth, where nothing can live. In "The Scouring of the Shire" we are presented with the start of the Gorgoroth process in the most homely terms—trees cut down, filth poured into the river, black smoke spewing unchecked from chimneys—all backed by a vague (and unconvincing) ideology of progress. It is true that the process can be reversed, as it is in the Shire with the aid of Sam Gamgee and Galadriel's gift. And the recuperative powers of nature are also strongly present, especially in Ithilien, where Faramir and Éowyn are the counterparts of Sam and Galadriel: the wreath of stonecrop growing round the old king's brows, the "briar and eglantine and trailing clematis" that cover what was once a "place of dreadful feast and slaughter." Just the same, Tolkien leaves no doubt about the threat hanging over Middle-earth. It is not just the Elves and Ents and Hobbits that can vanish, but health and beauty as well.

Ents, Elves, and Eriador brings out this theme in a way that Tolkien himself surely would have approved of. The authors trace the diversity of Tolkienesque habitats: the Hobbits' agriculture (so strongly opposed to modern agribusiness), the managed horticulture of the Elves (again, markedly different from modern clear-cut forestry that has created so many gloomy, single-species woodlands in England and Scotland), and perhaps most fascinating of all, the feraculture of the Ents, to which we have no clear analogue. They probe the psychology that underlies different types of ecological management (or mismanagement), which perhaps goes back to the idea of ownership versus stewardship. A person who owns something can do what he or she likes with it, says Anglo-American law (though with increasing reservations). But can human beings own land, air, and water? Not entirely, not responsibly, and certainly not forever. As the old king in Tolkien's favorite poem, *Beowulf,* says, "another will take over." It is our duty, says Gandalf, to uproot the evil in the fields we know, "so that those who live after may have clean earth to till. What weather they shall have is not ours to rule."

In these words Tolkien gives his idea of stewardship. And Gandalf, both like and unlike Denethor, is well aware that he is a steward too. But Tolkien may have been wrong about the weather. It is possible that the weather our descendants have may indeed be ours to rule (or to misrule), in a way that Tolkien could not have known or predicted. To quote from his second-favorite poem, the *Elder Edda,* "much goes worse than one thinks." And that is why the warning sounded by Matthew Dickerson and Jonathan Evans in this book goes beyond even Tolkien's imagination in its earnestness, timeliness, and urgency. Tolkien, though he may not have known so himself, was a soothsayer, and soothsayers do many things: they resist conventional knowledge, they see things the way they are and not the way conventional knowledge would like them to be, they look far into the future, and they speak the true word even though they do not know it. Every Delphic oracle needs its interpreters, however, and in Dickerson and Evans, Tolkien has found two notable, clear-sighted, and passionate spokesmen. Not many writers have the chance to affect national culture, public policy, and private decisions, but Tolkien, wherever his spirit rests, would be delighted if *Ents, Elves, and Eriador* could bring to fruition the seeds that his work has sown.

Tom Shippey

Appendix: Further Reading

Any of the articles, essays, and books referenced throughout the text and in the notes would make for fruitful reading, and there are many others as well. Works we especially recommend, however, fall into the three broad groupings listed below.

Environmental Themes in Tolkien's Works

As indicated in our introduction, other writers have recognized the ecological and environmental dimensions of Tolkien's works. Our scholarly precursors include the following.

Curry, Patrick. "'Less Noise and More Green': Tolkien's Ideology for England." In *Proceedings of the J. R. R. Tolkien Centenary Conference*, edited by Patricia Reynolds and Glen GoodKnight, 126–38. Altadena, Calif., and Milton Keynes, England: Tolkien Society and Mythopoeic Press, 1995.
———. "Middle-earth: Nature and Ecology." In *Defending Middle-earth: Tolkien, Myth and Modernity*, 48–86. Boston: Houghton Mifflin, 2004.
Elgin, Don D. *The Comedy of the Fantastic: Ecological Perspectives on the Fantasy Novel*. Westport, Conn.: Greenwood Press, 1985.
Flieger, Verlyn. "Taking the Part of Trees: Eco-conflict in Middle-earth." In *J. R. R. Tolkien and His Literary Resonances: Views of Middle-earth*, edited by George Clark and Daniel Timmons, 147–58. Westport, Conn.: Greenwood Press, 2000.
Kocher, Paul H. *Master of Middle-earth: The Fiction of J. R. R. Tolkien*. Boston: Houghton Mifflin, 1972.
Pearce, Joseph. "Tolkien and His Critics: A Critique." In *Root and Branch—Approaches towards Understanding Tolkien*, edited by Thomas Honegger, 81–148. Zurich and Berne: Walking Tree, 1999.
———. "Tolkien as Hobbit: The Englishman behind the Myth." In *Tolkien: Man and Myth*. San Francisco: Ignatius, 1998.

Stücklin, Christina Ljungberg. "Re-enchanting Nature: Some Magic Links between Atwood and Tolkien." In *Root and Branch—Approaches towards Understanding Tolkien*, edited by Thomas Honegger, 151–62. Zurich and Berne: Walking Tree, 1999.

Tolkien Scholarship

General reference works on Tolkien and his books are legion, and the number is growing, with the *J. R. R. Tolkien Encyclopedia* (Routledge, forthcoming) a much-anticipated and important addition. Humphrey Carpenter's biography of Tolkien and his compilation of Tolkien's letters, cited throughout this book, are essential; we would also recommend anything written or edited by Tom Shippey. Among the more important popular and scholarly books, including specific studies relevant to our topic, we recommend the following.

Birzer, Bradley. *J. R. R. Tolkien's Sanctifying Myth: Understanding Middle-earth.* Wilmington, Del.: ISI Books, 2002.
Chance, Jane, ed. *Tolkien the Medievalist.* London: Routledge, 2003.
Clark, George, and Daniel Timmons, eds. *J. R. R. Tolkien and His Literary Resonances: Views of Middle-earth.* Westport, Conn.: Greenwood Press, 2000.
Curry, Patrick. *Defending Middle-earth: Tolkien, Myth and Modernity.* Boston: Houghton Mifflin, 2004.
Dickerson, Matthew. *Following Gandalf: Epic Battles and Moral Victory in* The Lord of the Rings. Grand Rapids, Mich.: Brazos Press, 2003.
Flieger, Verlyn. *Splintered Light: Logos and Language in Tolkien's World.* Rev. ed. Kent, Ohio: Kent State University Press, 2002.
Pearce, Joseph. *Tolkien: Man and Myth.* San Francisco: Ignatius, 1998.
Purtill, Richard. *Lord of Elves and Eldils: Fantasy and Philosophy in C. S. Lewis and J. R. R. Tolkien.* San Francisco: Ignatius, 2006.
Shippey, Tom. *J. R. R. Tolkien: Author of the Century.* Boston: Houghton Mifflin, 2000.
———. *The Road to Middle-earth.* Rev. and expanded ed. Boston: Houghton Mifflin, 2003.

Agrarianism, Environmentalism, and Environmental Literature

Since Aldo Leopold's *A Sand County Almanac* (1949) and Rachel Carson's *Silent Spring* (1962), the publication of books on ecology, the environment, and conservation has grown into a significant industry. New editions of these classic works have appeared in recent decades and are included in our list. Although we have omitted many wonderful books in the genre of nature writing, the University of Georgia Press is particularly distinguished in this area. The University Press of Kentucky's recently launched Culture of the Land series already includes a reissue of Sir Albert Howard's 1945 classic *The Soil and Health* and significant new contributions by Gary Holthaus and Paul K. Conkin. Much of our book follows Tolkien's lead in focusing on agriculture, and we urge readers to consult anything written by Wendell Berry, his friend Wes Jackson of the Land Institute, and Gene Logsdon.

Berry, Wendell. *A Continuous Harmony: Essays Cultural and Agricultural.* New York: Harcourt, Brace, Jovanovich, 1972.
———. *The Gift of Good Land: Further Essays, Cultural and Agricultural.* New York: North Point, 1981.
———. *The Unsettling of America: Culture and Agriculture.* 3rd ed. San Francisco: Sierra Club, 1996.
Callicott, J. Baird, and Michael P. Nelson, eds. *The Great New Wilderness Debate: An Expansive Collection of Writings Defining Wilderness from John Muir to Gary Snyder.* Athens: University of Georgia Press, 1998.
Carson, Rachel. *Silent Spring.* Boston: Houghton Mifflin, 1962. Reissued 1994; 40th anniversary edition, 2002.
Conkin, Paul K. *The State of the Earth: Environmental Challenges on the Road to 2100.* Lexington: University Press of Kentucky, 2006.
Elder, John. *Imagining the Earth: Poetry and the Vision of Nature.* 2nd ed. Athens: University of Georgia Press, 1996.
———. *Reading the Mountains of Home.* Cambridge, Mass.: Harvard University Press, 1998.
Glotfelty, Cheryl, and Harold Fromm, eds. *The Ecocriticism Reader: Landmarks in Literary Ecology.* Athens: University of Georgia Press, 1996.
Holthaus, Gary. *From the Farm to the Table: What All Americans Need to Know about Agriculture.* Lexington: University Press of Kentucky, 2006.
Howard, Sir Albert. *The Soil and Health: A Study of Organic Agriculture,* with an introduction by Wendell Berry. Lexington: University Press of Kentucky, forthcoming.
Jackson, Wes, Wendell Berry, and Bruce Colman, eds. *Meeting the Expectations of the Land: Essays in Sustainable Agriculture and Stewardship.* San Francisco: North Point, 1984.
Kingsolver, Barbara. *Small Wonder: Essays.* New York: HarperCollins, 2002.
Leopold, Aldo. *A Sand County Almanac: With Other Essays on Conservation from Round River.* New York: Oxford University Press, 1966. Reissued, New York: Ballantine, 1986.

Logsdon, Gene. *All Flesh Is Grass: The Pleasures and Promises of Pasture Farming.* Athens: Ohio University Press, 2004.

———. *The Contrary Farmer.* Post Mills, Vt.: Chelsea Green, 1993.

Oelschlaeger, Max. *The Idea of Wilderness: From Prehistory to the Age of Ecology.* New Haven, Conn.: Yale University Press, 1991.

———, ed. *The Wilderness Condition: Essays on Environment and Civilization.* San Francisco: Sierra Club, 1992.

Vitek, William, and Wes Jackson, eds. *Rooted in the Land: Essays on Community and Place.* New Haven, Conn.: Yale University Press, 1996.

Wirzba, Norman, ed. *The Art of the Commonplace: The Agrarian Essays of Wendell Berry.* Washington, D.C.: Counterpoint, 2002.

Wirzba, Norman, and Barbara Kingsolver, eds. *The Essential Agrarian Reader: The Future of Culture, Community, and the Land.* Washington, D.C.: Shoemaker and Hoard, 2004.

Notes

Introduction

1. John Elder, *The Frog Run: Words & Wildness in the Vermont Woods* (Minneapolis: Milkweed Editions, 2001), 32–34.

2. In letters written in 1954, Tolkien refers to the Middle-earth corpus as a "legendarium" (*Letters*, 189, 197), a term highlighted by Verlyn Flieger and Carl F. Hostetter in *Tolkien's Legendarium: Essays on "The History of Middle-earth"* (Westport, Conn.: Greenwood Press, 2000). We employ the term throughout this volume for the sake of convenience.

3. Paul H. Kocher, *Master of Middle Earth: The Fiction of J. R. R. Tolkien* (Boston: Houghton Mifflin, 1972), 26.

4. Readers are referred to our recommendations for further reading in the appendix.

5. Matthew Dickerson, *Following Gandalf: Epic Battles and Moral Victory in* The Lord of the Rings (Grand Rapids, Mich.: Brazos Press, 2003).

6. This includes strands of Protestant evangelicalism that emphasize eschatology—that is, the future, the end of the world, "last things"—rather than recognizing Christians' obligation to work to improve the present world.

Chapter 1. Varda, Yavanna, and the Value of Creation

1. Philip N. Joranson and Ken Butigan, eds., *Cry of the Environment: Rebuilding the Christian Creation Tradition* (Santa Fe, N.M.: Bear and Company, 1984), 277.

2. Norman Wirzba, "Introduction: The Challenge of Berry's Agrarian Vision," in *The Art of the Commonplace: The Agrarian Essays of Wendell Berry*, ed. Norman Wirzba (Washington, D.C.: Counterpoint, 2002).

3. Clyde S. Kilby, *Tolkien & the Silmarillion* (Wheaton, Ill.: Harold Shaw, 1976), 45.

4. In Tolkien's mythology, the Valar are powerful spirit beings of a quasi-angelic order known as the Ainur. The Valar choose to reside in the world they help create. From a narrative point of view, they function as gods or demigods—powerful demiurges who, though neither omnipotent nor omniscient, help to create

Middle-earth and govern its affairs. On rare occasions they appear before Men or Elves in physical form, taking on either male or female gender.

5. In Tolkien's mythology, *Arda* means "The Realm" in Elvish and refers to the realm of the Vala Manwë, which is the earth. The name *Eä*, which comes from the Elvish word for being and means "it is" or "let it be," refers to the entire created material and physical universe (*Silm*, 317, 325).

6. Jonathan Evans, "The Anthropology of Arda: Creation, Theology, and the Race of Men," in *Tolkien the Medievalist*, ed. Jane Chance (London: Routledge, 2003), 194.

7. In the essay "On Fairy-stories," Tolkien writes, "It was in fairy-stories that I first divined the potency of the words, and the wonder of the things, such as stone, and wood, and iron; *tree and grass;* house and fire; bread and wine" (*TL*, 55; emphasis added). Elsewhere in the essay, he uses the greenness of grass transposed onto an imagined "green sun" to illustrate the power of human mythopoeia in fairy tales and fantasy.

8. Humphrey Carpenter, *J. R. R. Tolkien: A Biography* (Boston: Houghton Mifflin, 1977), 172ff; Tom Shippey, *J. R. R. Tolkien: Author of the Century* (Boston: Houghton Mifflin, 2000), 1–5, 46–47.

9. We might contrast Hobbits with Elves, who, upon first awaking, behold "first of all things the stars of heaven" and ever after "loved the starlight" (*Silm*, 48), and with Dwarves, who are created "in a hall under the mountains" and remain ever after "a race apart . . . lovers of stone" rather than of Sun, Moon, stars, or "things that live by their own life" (App F).

10. There are exceptions, of course, such as the Sackville-Bagginses and the miller Ted Sandyman. But as we explore in later chapters, these hobbits are portrayed not as model citizens but as aberrant characters who bring harm to the Shire.

11. Colin Gunton, *The One, the Three, and the Many: God, Creation, and the Culture of Modernity* (Cambridge: Cambridge University Press, 1993), 76.

12. E. F. Schumacher, *Small Is Beautiful: A Study of Economics as if People Mattered* (1973; reprint, New York: Harper Perennial, 1989), 48.

13. In addition to his 1973 book, Schumacher's posthumous works *Guide for the Perplexed* (New York: Harper and Row, 1978) and *Good Work* (New York: Harper and Row, 1979) advance the same themes; as a social trend, the quest for simpler living is evidenced in many other books, including *Voluntary Simplicity* by Duane Elgin (New York: Harper and Row, 1982; revised 1998); *Less Is More* by Goldien VandenBroeck (Rochester, Vt.: Inner Traditions, 1996); and *Radical Simplicity* by Jim Merkel (Gabriola Island, B.C.: New Society, 2003).

14. Joseph Pearce, *Small Is Still Beautiful* (London: HarperCollins, 2001; new ed., 2002).

15. Joseph Pearce, *Tolkien: Man and Myth* (San Francisco: Ignatius, 1998), 159–60.

16. Richard Foster, *Celebration of Discipline* (San Francisco: Harper and Row, 1978), 70.

17. Ibid., 79–80.

18. Among the anachronisms in *The Hobbit*, Tom Shippey notes very few having to do with advanced modern technology or gadgetry, and they are no more complex than friction matches and umbrellas, the latter of which Tolkien regarded in retrospect as "a mistake" (*Letters*, 196). There is a reference to the sound of steam locomotives, but of course locomotives themselves do not exist in Middle-earth; the reference merely describes a sound. The Shire also has daily mail delivery, but the delivery system is not described as employing advanced technology. See Shippey, *Author of the Century*, 6, 23.

19. Foster, *Celebration of Discipline*, 79–81.

20. Ibid., 73.

21. This and other medieval sources of dragon lore are examined in detail by Jonathan Evans in "As Rare as They Are Dire: Old Norse Dragons, *Beowulf*, and the *Deutsche Mythologie*," in *The Shadow-Walkers*, ed. Tom Shippey (Tempe, Ariz.: MRTS, 2005), 207–69. See also Jonathan Evans, "The Dragon-lore of Middle-earth: Tolkien and Old English and Old Norse Tradition," in *J. R. R. Tolkien and His Literary Resonances: Views of Middle-earth*, ed. George Clark and Daniel Timmons (Westport, Conn.: Greenwood Press, 2000), 21–38.

22. Wendell Berry, "Conservation and Local Economy," in *Sex, Economy, Freedom and Community: Eight Essays* (New York: Pantheon Books, 1992), 4.

23. Wendell Berry, "Farming and the Global Economy," in *Another Turn of the Crank: Essays by Wendell Berry* (Washington, D.C.: Counterpoint, 1995), 3.

24. Shippey, *Author of the Century*, 9–11.

25. Jamie Williamson, lecture presented at the colloquium "Tolkien 2005," University of Vermont, Burlington, April 2, 2005. Williamson also suggests that the River God and hence Goldberry are Maiar (like Gandalf)—angelic beings akin to the Valar, though with less power.

26. Foster, *Celebration of Discipline*, 82.

27. It should be noted that when Gandalf returns from death, his power has increased. When he speaks a word of command and breaks Saruman's staff at their confrontation at Isengard (III/x), he is acting in a way closer to Tom Bombadil.

28. Foster, *Celebration of Discipline*, 69.

29. Berry, "Conservation and Local Economy," 3.

30. See, e.g., Patrick Curry, *Defending Middle-earth: Tolkien, Myth and Modernity* (Boston: Houghton Mifflin, 2004), esp. ch. 4, "Spirituality and Ethics"; Joseph Pearce, ed., *Tolkien: A Celebration* (London: HarperCollins,

1999); Pearce, *Tolkien: Man and Myth,* esp. ch. 6, "The Creation of Middle-earth: The Myth behind the Man," and ch. 7, "Orthodoxy in Middle-earth: The Truth behind the Myth"; Bradley Birzer, *J. R. R. Tolkien's Sanctifying Myth: Understanding Middle-earth* (Wilmington, Del.: ISI Books, 2002); and Matthew Dickerson, *Following Gandalf: Epic Battles and Moral Victory in* The Lord of the Rings (Grand Rapids, Mich.: Brazos Press, 2003), esp. chs. 8–10.

31. In the elided material, he says his faith "can be deduced" from his fictions. Some scholarship questions the orthodoxy of Tolkien's invented mythology. For example, Tadeusz Andrzej Olzański sees a tendency toward Manichaeism in the theodicy of Arda ("Evil and the Evil One in Tolkien's Theology," trans. Agnieszka Sylwanowicz, in *Proceedings of the J. R. R. Tolkien Centenary Conference,* ed. Patricia Reynolds and Glen GoodKnight [Altadena, Calif., and Milton Keynes, England: Tolkien Society and Mythopoeic Press, 1995], 298–301).

32. Steven Bouma-Prediger, "Creation Care and Character: The Nature and Necessity of the Ecological Virtues," *Perspectives on Science and Faith: Journal of the American Scientific Affiliation* 50, no. 1 (1998): 6–21.

33. Another important part of Tolkien's mythology is that even when Melkor rebels against Eru's will, Eru still accomplishes his purpose and uses Melkor's acts of rebellion to do so. "For he that attempteth [to alter the music] . . . shall prove but mine instrument in the devising of things more wonderful, which he himself hath not imagined" (*Silm,* 6). This idea is worked out in several places, and although it is important to Tolkien's mythology as a whole, it does not have direct, practical implications for the environmental ethic discussed here. Rebellion per se is not a virtue, and our moral calculus cannot justify evil acts in advance based on the expectation that they may be transformed to good results by some kind of divine alchemy. Good must still be pursued and evil opposed.

34. Wendell Berry, "God and Country," in *What Are People For?* (New York: North Point, 1990), 98, 100.

35. Ibid., 100.

Chapter 2. Gandalf, Stewardship, and Tomorrow's Weather

1. Tolkien uses OE to represent the language of Rohan. In OE, a *spell* is a "story" or "message," and *lath* (related to the modern *loathe*) means "hated" or "evil." A *láthspell* is thus "a hated message" or simply "bad news." Though not quite a coinage on Tolkien's part—the word occurs several times in surviving OE—it is in all likelihood a back-formation based on *gódspell,* which in turn is a calque of the Greek term *euangelion,* meaning "good news," or

"good message." We should not lose the significance of the insult, then, when Wormtongue associates Gandalf with the opposite of *gódspell* (or *gospel* in Modern English).

2. In OE, *wyrm* means "serpent" or "snake"; thus a *Wormtongue* is one with a snake's tongue—that is, a liar. In ON, there are many characters nicknamed *Ormstunga*. Interestingly, the ON word *gríma* means "mask," which has the connotation of deception (from hiding the face) and is used poetically for *serpent*. Cognates in OE include *grim-helm* and *here-gríma*, both of which appear in the poem *Beowulf*).

3. Although the realm of the Beornings is a significant community of Men, as are Long Lake and Esgaroth, and although they play a role in events at the end of the Third Age, none of them exists as a "kingdom" and none is significant to the narrative of *The Lord of the Rings*.

4. Wendell Berry, "Private Property and the Common Wealth," in *Another Turn of the Crank: Essays by Wendell Berry* (Washington, D.C.: Counterpoint, 1995), 51–57.

5. In many respects echoing Wendell Berry's "God and Country" in *What Are People For?* (New York: North Point, 1990), in "What Knowledge Is Required for Responsible Stewardship of Creation," *Christian Scholar's Review* 32 (2003): 365–80, Joseph K. Sheldon and David K. Foster give a persuasive indictment of Christians' failure in some circles to recognize the importance of the biblical view, calling such failure both "short-sighted" and "sinful." Their account also outlines broad categories of knowledge that they believe are essential for proper fulfillment of the stewardship mandate articulated in the Bible. In an exhaustively documented article in the same issue of that journal, H. Paul Santmire recognizes a healthy "first wave" of stewardship theology as an important recent response of churches to the environmental crisis. As a second wave, he proposes a "theology of partnership," which in his view is an even more effective implementation of the biblical environmental mandate.

6. Jim Ball, "The Use of Ecology in the Evangelical Protestant Response to the Ecological Crisis," *Perspectives on Science and Faith: Journal of the American Scientific Affiliation* 50, no. 1 (1998): 32–38.

7. The Greek root *oikos*, meaning "house," is the root of the modern word *ecology* and appears frequently in the New Testament in many forms. One such word is *oikonomos*, which is often translated as "steward," although "house manager" or even "economist" might also be accurate. It should be noted that many of these New Testament stewards were actually slaves. The Christian understanding of stewardship (as a translation of *oikonomos*) suggests servanthood and upward responsibility rather than lordship. Based on a study of the use of the root *oikos* in the New Testament and on examples of these household stewards or managers, Mark Stanton and Dennis Guernsey

draw the following conclusion: "Based on the etymology of the terms and the statements of scripture, it is possible to state our role in this manner: Christian = Steward = Ecologist" ("A Christian's Ecological Responsibility: A Theological Introduction and Challenge," *Perspectives on Science and Faith: Journal of the American Scientific Affiliation* 45, no. 1 [March 1993]: 2–7).

8. After the Norman Conquest, Anglo-Saxon landowners and aristocrats were reduced in many cases to the social status of peasants, farmworkers, or serfs, often on feudal estates they once owned. In this transition from a free, small-farm economy to an organized system of feudal obligation—a complex and rigid social hierarchy—the old comitatus system centering on the mead hall, the *dryht* (troop), and the *dryhten* (military leader) came to an end. In the accompanying linguistic transition toward Middle English, the formerly respectable *stig* was reduced and became pejorative in meaning, evolving toward its modern sense of *sty*, as in *pigsty*.

9. "Gondor has sufficient 'townlands' and fiefs with a good water and road approach to provide for its population" (*Letters*, 196).

10. Steven Bouma-Prediger, "Creation Care and Character: The Nature and Necessity of the Ecological Virtues," *Perspectives on Science and Faith: Journal of the American Scientific Affiliation* 50, no. 1 (1998): 6–21.

11. Actually, Gandalf also has a role in marshaling the defense of all Middle-earth. This includes the Ents—and through them the trees (Huorns) in their care—as well as the eagles that come to his aid more than once. But the reader is given only small glimpses of these efforts.

12. Likely objections concerning global warming are worth acknowledging here. Clearly, Tolkien could have had no scientific knowledge of ozone layer depletion, greenhouse gas buildup, and the resulting global changes in weather patterns such as we now witness. Perhaps it is best to interpret Gandalf's statement and Tolkien's deeper point in the more traditional terms suggested by the maxim: "Everyone complains about the weather, but no one does anything about it." Tolkien surely would grant the point that human behavior can have meteorological effects in both the present and the future—a further extension of his broader point about individual responsibility.

13. It should be noted that the race of Orcs (also called Goblins)—which in Tolkien's mythology are spawned from Elves who are twisted and corrupted by Morgoth—also represents some aspects of the human race, such as the potential for devious creativity and petty jealousy. However, they represent fallen and corrupted humans and illustrate little if anything of what humans in our world are *supposed* to be like.

14. Here and in subsequent passages we use the Douay-Rheims translation of the Bible, because this is the one that most early-twentieth-century English-speaking Catholics (including Tolkien) would have been most familiar with.

15. Lynn White Jr., "The Historical Roots of Our Ecological Crisis," *Science* 155 (March 1967): 1205.

16. William Deutsch and Bryan Duncan, "Everyone Lives Downstream," in *Creation-Care in Ministry: Down-to-Earth Christianity,* ed. W. D. Roberts and P. E. Pretiz (Wynnewood, Pa.: Aerdo, 2000).

17. Richard Foster, *Celebration of Discipline* (San Francisco: Harper and Row, 1978), 80–82.

18. White, "Historical Roots," 1206.

19. Calvin DeWitt, "Seeking to Image the Order and Beauty of God's 'House': A Scriptural Foundation for Creation-care," in Roberts and Pretiz, *Creation-Care in Ministry,* 9–24.

20. W. Dayton Roberts, "Icons at the Gates of History," in Roberts and Pretiz, *Creation-Care in Ministry,* 1–3.

21. White, "Historical Roots," 1206.

22. Humphrey Carpenter, *The Inklings* (Boston: Houghton Mifflin, 1979), 43–44, quoted from Alfred Siewers, "Tolkien's Christian Ecology: The Medieval Underpinnings," in *Tolkien's Modern Middle Ages,* ed. Jane Chance (forthcoming). Our thanks to Jane Chance for suggesting this passage in the context of Tolkien's environmental ethic.

23. White, "Historical Roots," 1203.

24. Notes from the editor Christopher Tolkien indicate that this passage held "authority" for his father, that it was complete, and that it was intended to be published in the appendix to *The Silmarillion* (*MR,* 303, 329).

25. The one known exception to this is Míriel, the mother of Fëanor. Much evil arises from the unwillingness of her *fëa* (spirit) to be reembodied, or reunited, with her *hröa* (*Letters,* 286).

26. Fred Van Dyke, "Ecology and the Christian Mind: Christians and the Environment in a New Decade," *Perspectives on Science and Faith: Journal of the American Scientific Affiliation* 43, no. 3 (1991): 174–84.

27. Ibid.

Chapter 3. Hobbits and the Agrarian Society of the Shire

1. Oddly enough, the few images we do get of agricultural work in *The Horse and His Boy* occur not in Narnia but in the realm of Calormen. Shasta and company pass through several farms on their journey northward, and outside of Tashbaan, Shasta raids private gardens for oranges, melons, figs, and pomegranates. Working agriculture is thus associated with the Calormenes, the traditional enemies of Narnia.

2. Like Lewis, Tolkien includes numerous hints and references by which

we can infer additional aspects of agriculture not explicitly presented. For example, the mention of bread and the widespread use of fermented beverages indicate the cultivation of grain, including wheat and barley, and, by further implication, malt works and at least small-scale breweries. We can also infer all the supporting activities of tool making, craftsmanship, and simple construction engineering required for the implements, vehicles, and storage structures necessary for plant and animal husbandry. The strength of Tolkien's writing is that there are also many explicit references to agrarian economy that lend greater verisimilitude to this dimension of Middle-earth.

3. Norman Wirzba, "Introduction: Why Agrarianism Matters—Even to Urbanites," in *The Essential Agrarian Reader: The Future of Culture, Community, and the Land*, ed. Norman Wirzba (Lexington: University Press of Kentucky, 1993), 8–9.

4. Brian Donahue, "The Resettling of America," in Wirzba, *The Essential Agrarian Reader*, 35.

5. Humphrey Carpenter, *Tolkien: A Biography* (Boston: Houghton Mifflin, 1977), 32–33.

6. David W. Orr, "The Uses of Prophecy," in Wirzba, *The Essential Agrarian Reader*, 172, quoting from Jacquetta Hawkes, *A Land* (Boston: Houghton-Mifflin, 1950), 202.

7. Carpenter, *Tolkien*, 50, 106.

8. Maurice Telleen, "The Mind-set of Agrarianism . . . New and Old," in Wirzba, *The Essential Agrarian Reader*, 56.

9. For comparative purposes, books by George Ewart Evans on rural English farm life up to the end of the nineteenth century give a more balanced, sometimes sobering view of the agrarian countryside that Tolkien memorializes. See *The Farm and the Village* (London: Faber, 1969); *Ask the Fellows Who Cut the Hay* (London: Faber, 1972); and *The Days That We Have Seen* (London: Faber, 1974).

10. Carpenter, *Tolkien*, 20.

11. Ibid.

12. BBC Radio interview, 1971.

13. Carpenter, *Tolkien*, 24.

14. "Beans on poles" with red blossoms glowing in the morning sunlight against green leaves, however, are mentioned growing not far from the Shire, in Tom Bombadil's kitchen garden (II/vii).

15. The county itself has had uncertain standing, and changes were underway even when Tolkien lived there as a boy. Historically located in the medieval county of Worcestershire, Yardley Parish was transferred to Warwickshire in 1857. In 1899, while the Tolkiens lived there, Yardley was transferred back to Worcestershire. The parish was incorporated into Warwickshire once and

for all with the general administrative reorganization that placed it within the newly remapped city of Birmingham twelve years later. Administratively speaking, for a time, Tolkien's beloved Worcestershire did not exist at all: in 1974, less than a year after his death, the county was combined with Herefordshire to form the short-lived administrative county of Hereford and Worcester, a situation that was reversed through local government reforms in 1998. See J. W. Willis-Bund, *The Victorian History of the County of Worcester*, vol. 3 (London: Constable, 1913; reprint, Folkstone, Kent: Dawsons, 1971), 238.

16. David Lloyd, *A History of Worcestershire* (Chichester: Phillimore, 1993), 107.

17. In *Defending Middle-earth: Tolkien, Myth and Modernity* (Boston: Houghton Mifflin, 2004), Patrick Curry writes: "the bucolic hobbits . . . clearly fall within the long tradition in English letters of nostalgic pastoralism," including Alfred, Lord Tennyson; William Morris; Rudyard Kipling; and others (28). Yet, although the image of the Shire "partakes of a national fantasy," Curry writes, "it does not follow that it has no reality." Readers all over the world "connect the hobbits with a rustic people of their own, relatively untouched by modernity—if not still actually existing, then from the alternative reality of folk- and fairy-tale" (27).

18. Arnor and Gondor, the "Realms in Exile," are founded by Isildur and Anárion, Men of Númenor, in the year 3320 of the Second Age, which ends in 3441.

19. Wendell Berry, *The Gift of Good Land: Further Essays Cultural and Agricultural by Wendell Berry* (New York: North Point, 1981), ix.

20. See, e.g., John T. Schlebecker, *The Many Names of Country People: A Historical Dictionary from the Twelfth Century Onward* (Westport, Conn.: Greenwood Press, 1989).

21. Tolkien also associates beer and beer brewing with women. For a long period in late medieval England, beer brewing, like bread baking, was exclusively a female occupation. See Judith M. Bennett, *Ale, Beer, and Brewsters in England: Women's Work in a Changing World, 1300–1600* (Oxford: Oxford University Press, 1999).

22. St. Paul writes, "Let nothing be done through contention: neither by vain glory. But in humility, let each esteem others better than themselves: Each one not considering the things that are his own, but those that are other men's. For let this mind be in you, which was also in Christ Jesus: Who being in the form of God, thought it not robbery to be equal with God: He humbled himself, becoming obedient unto death, even to the death of the cross" (Philippians 1:27–2:1).

23. C. S. Lewis writes of "this whole, huge pattern of descent, down, down, and then up again" as a fundamental one "imitated and echoed by the princi-

ples of the natural world." Further, its replication elsewhere in the natural environment and human culture argues for the universality and the essential truth of the story. "The principle is there in nature because it was first there in God Himself. Thus one is getting in behind the nature religions and behind nature to Someone Who is not explained by, but explains, not, indeed, the nature religions directly, but that whole characteristic behaviour of nature on which nature religions were based" ("The Grand Miracle," *Guardian*, April, 27, 1945, 161, 165; reprinted in Walter Hooper, ed., *God in the Dock* [Grand Rapids, Mich.: Eerdmans, 1970], 80–88).

24. Matthew Dickerson's *Following Gandalf: Epic Battles and Moral Victory in* The Lord of the Rings (Grand Rapids, Mich.: Brazos Press, 2003) demonstrates that although violence must sometimes be resisted with the same force used on its victims, Tolkien by no means promotes the use of violence for its own sake. An analogous point must be made here: The Hobbits are drawn to leave the Shire and join forces with those engaged in military action against their enemies *reluctantly*. In their own land, their response is both active—they forcibly eject their oppressors from the Shire—and negative—Frodo has to leave it not once but twice, the second time permanently.

25. Carpenter, *Tolkien*, 230.

26. Wendell Berry, "The Agricultural Crisis as a Crisis of Culture," in *The Unsettling of America*, 2nd ed. (San Francisco: Sierra Club, 1977), 39–48.

Chapter 4. Horticulture and the Aesthetic of the Elves

1. In certain passages in the legendarium, as well as in various letters, Tolkien describes in positive terms the Elves' worthwhile efforts at "the adornment of the earth," the "healing of its hurts," and the "preservation of beauty" (*Letters*, 151–52). Although this is generally portrayed as a positive trait, Tolkien also uses negative terms to describe the Elves' resistance to change, referring to it as "antiquarian" and "a kind of embalming." The real issue is their desire to avoid "the changes of time (the law of the world under the sun)" (*Letters*, 151).

2. Drawing once again on the etymology of words in which *-culture* is a formative element, it should be emphasized that although the Latin *hortus* ("garden") refers only generally to the cultivation of plants—and thus theoretically includes vegetable gardening of the kind practiced by the Gamgees—the English word *horticulture* almost exclusively describes botanical cultivation for aesthetic and ornamental purposes.

3. The goal of agricultural practices is usually understood to be the growth of products for consumption, whereas the focus of horticultural prac-

tices is the aesthetic qualities of the species under cultivation. Although it is certainly possible for horticultural practices to damage the earth, such selfish practices are less likely in horticulture than in agriculture.

4. We speak here of general racial characteristics; there are certainly examples of individual dwarves, such as Gimli, who show some Dwarfish characteristics but in other regards transcend the stereotype.

5. Many of the Noldor who return to Middle-earth learn Sindarin in order to communicate with the Elves who remain in Middle-earth, but they keep their own High Elvish tongue of Quenya for speech among themselves.

6. The name Nargothrond is sometimes used to refer to the whole realm of Finrod—the largest of the Realms of Beleriand—but it more often refers to the great underground fortress.

7. Melian is one of the Maiar, a race of angelic beings akin to the Valar but less powerful. In Tolkien's legendarium, Melian is the only one of her kind to marry one of the Children of Ilúvatar, Elwë Thingol, who is also unique. He is one of the two lords of the Teleri who visit Aman in the first voyage. However, when he returns to Middle-earth he meets and falls in love with Melian and chooses to remain. Many of his people, who have never been to Aman, stay with him. He is one of the Calaquendi, yet the Teleri he rules are Sindarin Moriquendi.

8. Tolkien was especially gifted at drawing trees but less talented at drawing people.

9. Robert Siegel, personal interview, August 28, 2004, quoting from *The Lord of the Rings* (II/vi).

10. The Elves as a race are also defined by their love of the stars and the sea; thus another aesthetic dimension emphasizing starlight and the sound of flowing water can be traced throughout the novels. But we believe the association of golden and silver light in green, sylvan environments is of even greater significance. At a profound level, it expresses for the Elves both their aesthetic appreciation—their love—for the natural environment and their highly developed ethical regard for its preservation.

11. Tolkien's language here seems to echo St. Paul's description of our world in Ephesians 6:12: *non est nobis conluctatio adversus carnem et sanguinem sed adversus . . . mundi rectores tenebrarum harum* ("our struggle is not against flesh and blood but against . . . the rulers of this world of darkness," sometimes translated in modern English as "this present darkness"). The Pauline context characterizes this world as the arena of a cosmic battle, interpreting physical adversities as manifestations of spiritual evil. Regardless of whether the echo is intentional, it is applicable to the suggestion that the Elves' protracted war against their enemy is waged in part in environmental-aesthetic terms.

Chapter 5. Woods, Wildness, and the Feraculture of the Ents

1. Steven Bouma-Prediger, "Creation Care and Character: The Nature and Necessity of the Ecological Virtues," *Perspectives on Science and Faith: Journal of the American Scientific Affiliation* 50, no. 1 (1998): 6–21.

2. For those unfamiliar with the hymn tradition of Christian worship, examples may not be familiar; for some readers, however, it should be obvious that in both Catholic and later Protestant liturgical tradition there are time-hallowed musical expressions of appreciation and respect for the world of nature. One classic example is "This Is My Father's World," written by Maltbie Babcock (1858–1901), Tolkien's immediate chronological predecessor. The title alone makes an important statement. The hymn proclaims, "All nature sings, and round me rings the music of the spheres"; it later adds, "The morning light, the lily white, declare their Maker's praise." Likewise, the popular hymn "Joyful, Joyful, We Adore Thee," by Henry van Dyke (1852–1933), notes not only that "Stars and angels sing around Thee" but also that "Field and forest, vale and mountain, flowery meadow, flashing sea, chanting bird and flowing fountain, call us to rejoice in Thee."

3. Translation by William H. Draper (1855–1933).

4. Bradley Birzer, *J. R. R. Tolkien's Sanctifying Myth: Understanding Middle-earth* (Wilmington, Del.: ISI Books, 2002), 129. In reference to the Czech figure of Radegast, Birzer cites Patrick Curry's *Defending Middle-earth: Tolkien, Myth and Modernity* (Boston: Houghton Mifflin, 2004), 413.

5. The Entwives' special interest in cultivated gardens and orchards is a significant problem, leading to the mythic rift separating them from their male counterparts. We discuss this in greater detail in chapter 10.

6. John Elder, *Reading the Mountains of Home* (Cambridge, Mass.: Harvard University Press, 1998), 18.

7. See the entry on "Ents" in *The J. R. R. Tolkien Encyclopedia: Scholarship and Critical Assessment* (Routledge, forthcoming).

8. This is called the agglutinative stage. Early-nineteenth-century philologists known to Tolkien saw European languages as proceeding from an early isolative stage, through an agglutinative stage, to an inflective stage. The particulars of this argument are of no consequence here, except insofar as Entish words appear to have been built by sticking many smaller words together.

9. T. A. Shippey, "Creation from Philology in *The Lord of the Rings*," in *J. R. R. Tolkien: Scholar and Storyteller*, ed. Mary Salu and Robert T. Farrell (Ithaca, N.Y.: Cornell University Press, 1979), 286–316; see also Shippey's "Philological Inquiries," in *The Road to Middle-earth* (Boston: Houghton Mifflin, 1982) and his *J. R. R. Tolkien: Author of the Century* (Boston: Houghton Mifflin, 2000).

10. Robert Siegel, personal correspondence, August 28, 2004.

11. In 1943 he wrote, "The poplars are now leafless except for one top spray; but it is still a green and leafy October-end down here. At no time do birches look so beautiful: their skin snow-white in the pale yellow sun, and their remaining leaves shining fallow-gold." Six months later, in the spring of 1944, he wrote of "the white-grey of the quince, the grey-green of young apple, the full green of hawthorn, the tassels of flower even on the sluggard poplars" (*Letters*, 50).

12. "*Aragorn* ... cannot contain a 'tree' word. ... 'Tree-King' would have no special fitness for him." However, what he takes away with one hand he offers with another: he adds, "and it was already used by an ancestor." Tolkien probably means Arathorn I, for whom his great-grandson Arathorn II—Aragorn's father—is named (*Letters*, 426).

13. Hugh T. Keenan, "The Appeal of *The Lord of the Rings*: A Struggle for Life," in *Modern Critical Interpretations:* The Lord of the Rings, ed. Harold Bloom (Philadelphia: Chelsea House Publishers, 2000), 3–15.

14. We use the word *sentient* here as it is normally used, to distinguish rational, animate, and self-aware beings such as humans from other living things such as plants. Of course, it could be argued that in Middle-earth some trees are sentient; Old Man Willow, for example, looks like a tree but certainly displays signs of awareness.

15. Tolkien here has a bit of linguistic fun. *Fangorn*, the name of both the forest and its chief Ent, in Sindarin Elvish, means "beard-tree"—hence the translated word *Treebeard*, a compound form something like an OE or ON kenning. The onomastic figure refers to this forest's shaggy "beards and whiskers of lichen."

Chapter 6. The Necessity of Margins in Middle-earth's Mingled Ecologies

1. John Elder, *Reading the Mountains of Home* (Cambridge, Mass.: Harvard University Press, 1998), 21.

2. Wendell Berry, "Margins," in *The Unsettling of America*, 2nd ed. (San Francisco: Sierra Club, 1977), 174, 178–79.

3. Arnold van Gennep, *Les Rites de Passage* (1909), trans. Monika B. Vizedom and Gabrielle I. Caffee as *The Rites of Passage* (Chicago: University of Chicago Press, 1960).

4. Victor Turner, *Blazing the Trail: Way Marks in the Exploration of Symbols*, new ed. (Tucson: University of Arizona Press, 1992), 132; emphasis added.

5. Thomas Pison, "Liminality in *The Canterbury Tales*," *Genre* 10 (1977):

157–71; Sara Higley, "Aldor on Ofre; or, the Reluctant Hart: A Study of Liminality in 'Beowulf,'" *Neuphilologische Mitteilungen* 87 (1986): 342–53.

6. Nicole LaRose, "Reading the Information on Martin Amis's London," *Critique: Studies in Contemporary Fiction* 46 (2005): 160–76; Jesse Oak Taylor-Ide, "Ritual and the Liminality of Sherlock Holmes in *The Sign of Four* and *The Hound of the Baskervilles*," *English Literature in Transition (1880–1920)* 48 (2005): 55–70; Katherine Hyunmi Lee, "The Poetics of Liminality and Misidentification: Winnifred Eaton's *Me* and Maxine Hong Kingston's *The Woman Warrior*," *Studies in the Literary Imagination* 37 (2004): 17–33; Christine Hoff Kraemer, "Between the Worlds: Liminality and Self-Sacrifice in Princess Mononoke," *Journal of Religion and Film* (April 8, 2004).

7. Lynne A. Searfoss, "Coordinates of Liminality: Emerson, Fuller, and the Landscape of Empire" (Ph.D. diss., Purdue University, 2002); Michelle M. Wilson, "Liminality and Exile Literature of Latin America's Southern Cone" (Ph.D. diss., Michigan State University, 2003); Kurt Russell Cline, "Legerdemain of God: Shamanic Praxis, Gnostic Speculation and the Poetics of Liminality" (Ph.D. diss., SUNY Binghamton, 2004).

8. Manuel C. Molles Jr., *Ecology: Concepts and Applications*, 2nd ed. (Boston: McGraw-Hill, 2002), 7.

9. "At last . . . they came to the eaves of the forest" (III/iii); "we are on the very edge of Fangorn"; "They were under the eaves of Fangorn" (III/ii).

10. Five pages later, Glorfindel also uses the term, expressing fear that Frodo and his companions might "become lost in the Wilderness."

11. J. Baird Callicott and Michael P. Nelson, eds., *The Great New Wilderness Debate* (Athens: University of Georgia Press, 1998), 121. See also Mark Woods, "Federal Wilderness Preservation in the United States (1998): The Preservation of Wilderness?" in ibid., 131–53.

12. After Rivendell, the story takes on an increasingly somber, serious tone. In summary, everything between the hobbits' entrance into the Old Forest and their departure from Rivendell—a section of narrative constituting more than 100 pages—is in some sense transitional or marginal. The terrain from Buckland to Rivendell is not quite the farmland of the Shire, but it is not quite wilderness either. On the one side of this lengthy zone of transition, the story reads like a continuation of *The Hobbit*, which was Tolkien's original intention. On the other side, the novel is more mature, shading ever more strikingly into the high heroic and chivalric mode that characterizes its central and climactic sections. In van Gennep's and Turner's terms, it is all a liminal space, an amazingly broad threshold in which the characters are introduced gradually to the wilder, more alien world before they reach actual wilderness in the wastelands of Eriador, the mines of Moria, and the River Anduin.

13. Natural, "relic" hedges surviving from primeval woodland include

various tree species, including elm and oak; planted hedges can include holly, privet, damson or cherry plum, crab apple, and hazel—several of these also providing fruit and nuts for various forms of wildlife and, of course, people. See Oliver Rackham, "Hedgerow Trees: Their History, Conservation, and Renewal," *Arboriculture Journal* 3 (1977): 169–77, and *Hedges and Hedgerow Trees in Britain: A Thousand Years of Agroforestry* (London: ODI Agricultural Administration Unit, 1989); M. H. P. Ward, "Hedgerow and Farm Timber," *Quarterly Journal of Forestry* 48 (1954): 145–46.

14. Christina Ljungberg Stücklin, "Re-enchanting Nature: Some Magic Links between Atwood and Tolkien," in *Root and Branch—Approaches Towards Understanding Tolkien*, ed. Thomas Honegger (Zurich: Walking Tree, 1999), 151–62.

15. In addition to its meaning with respect to literary concepts of liminality, *threshold* is, of course, a common noun describing the base of a doorway. Indeed, the specialized sense of the word derives from the more general meaning, and we must be careful not to invest too much meaning in its every use. However, Tolkien himself puts special emphasis on the threshold moment of entering the house of Tom and Goldberry. The final sentence of the chapter reads, "And with that song the hobbits stood upon the threshold, and a golden light was all about them" (I/vi).

16. Berry says, "any understanding of the Red River must consider how minute and manifold are its workings," how "its life and meaning are not merely local but are intricately involved in all life and all meaning" (Wendell Berry, "A Country of Edges," in *Recollected Essays 1965–1980* [San Francisco: North Point, 1981], 225).

Chapter 7. The Ecology of Ham, Niggle's Parish, and Wootton Major

1. Tom Shippey, *J. R. R. Tolkien: Author of the Century* (Boston: Houghton Mifflin, 2000), 289–92.

2. Ibid., 267.

3. Humphrey Carpenter, *Tolkien: A Biography* (Boston: Houghton Mifflin, 1977), 73–76; also cited in Shippey, *Author of the Century*, 289.

4. This contrast between farming and agribusiness, and criticism of the latter, can be seen throughout much of Wendell Berry's writing. See, for example, *The Art of the Commonplace: The Agrarian Essays of Wendell Berry*, ed. Norman Wirzba (Washington, D.C.: Counterpoint, 2002), and *The Gift of Good Land: Further Essays Cultural and Agricultural by Wendell Berry* (New York: North Point, 1981).

5. The OE *hām* is pronounced not as the Modern English *ham* but as *hom* (rhyming with *mom*).

6. The OE *hām* also appears in *The Lord of the Rings* in the name *Hamfast*, which means "one who is fast bound to home." Samwise Gamgee is the son of Hamfast Gamgee and also names his own son Hamfast. As the shared elements in their names suggest, the connections between Farmer Giles and Sam the gardener are quite strong. The name *Sam* is related to "semi," or "half"; thus *Samwise* suggests "half wise" or "dimwit." Further, Samwise son of Hamfast suggests a character who is a "dimwit" and the son of a "stay-at-home." Sam is, in short, another rustic. Of course, in *The Lord of the Rings*, Sam becomes an honored hero (like Farmer Giles) and even a local celebrity and authority. Probably the most important comparison, though, is that Sam is also a defender and cultivator of the land. It is the destruction of the trees and gardens of the Shire that most bothers him, and he uses his gifts—and especially his gift from the Lady Galadriel—to bring the land back from its Mordor-like blight.

7. Foreword to *The Gift of Good Land*, xi–xii.

8. Ibid., xvii.

9. Here, the term *vulgar* means the indigenous language of Ham and its surroundings, the "popular" language as opposed to the learned Latin (cf. Latin *vulgus*, "the common people").

10. Carpenter, *Tolkien*, 195–96.

11. See Shippey, *Author of the Century*, ch. 6.

12. Shippey (*Author of the Century*, 275–77) understands the workhouse as purgatory, two of the three disembodied voices who discuss Niggle's progress as Mercy and Justice—two of the traditional daughters of God in medieval drama—the verdant land around his tree as "the heavenly land," and the shepherd guide as an "obvious Christian suggestion" (we presume) of Christ.

13. Ibid., 108.

14. The 1964 and the 2001 editions have the word "wondered," while the version published in *Tales from the Perilous Realm* (London: HarperCollins, 1998) has the no doubt corrected "wandered," the reading offered here.

15. Interestingly, both John Elder and Wendell Berry look to, and provide in their abundant and varied writings, a similar union of art and agriculture. They both see, for example, imaginative literature as a necessity in a culture of sustainable agriculture.

16. See Shippey, *Author of the Century*, 8, 275–76.

17. The phrase is borrowed from C. S. Lewis's *The Last Battle*, which similarly represents spiritual progress from terrestrial to celestial states of being not as a process of increasing abstraction but, paradoxically, as one of increasing ascent and depth—a journey deeper into a land of ever-higher mountains.

18. Shippey suggests that these two voices may represent "daughters of God" (see note 12). They may also be suggestive of two of the three persons

of the divine Trinity, in whom mercy and justice are united. This reading is strengthened by the presence of a doctor in the workhouse who is explicitly related to the First and Second Voices when the two voices are identified as a "Medical Board" (*TL*, 84).

19. Shippey, *Author of the Century*, 116–19.
20. Ibid., 297.
21. Aldo Leopold, *A Sand County Almanac* (New York: Oxford University Press, 1987).

Chapter 8. Three Faces of Mordor

1. See also John Garth's account in *Tolkien and the Great War* (Boston: Houghton Mifflin, 2003). Douglas Anderson of the University of Georgia has commented in private communication that the vast weapons factories in the heavily industrialized Ruhr Valley may have inspired Tolkien's descriptions of Saruman's military manufacturing complex.
2. Wendell Berry, "Conservation and Local Economy," in *The Art of the Commonplace: The Agrarian Essays of Wendell Berry*, ed. Norman Wirzba (Washington, D.C.: Counterpoint, 2002), 195–96.
3. Charles Dickens, *Hard Times*, ed. Jeff Nunokawa and Gage C. McWeeny (New York: Longman, 2004), 23.
4. Tom Shippey, *J. R. R. Tolkien: Author of the Century* (Boston: Houghton Mifflin, 2000), 169–70.
5. Ibid., 171.
6. Norman Wirzba, "Introduction: Why Agrarianism Matters—Even to Urbanites," in *The Essential Agrarian Reader: The Future of Culture, Community, and the Land*, ed. Norman Wirzba (Lexington: University Press of Kentucky, 1993), 2.
7. David W. Orr, "The Uses of Prophecy," in Wirzba, *The Essential Agrarian Reader*, 177.
8. Shippey, *Author of the Century*, 75–76.
9. Wendell Berry, *The Gift of Good Land: Further Essays Cultural and Agricultural by Wendell Berry* (New York: North Point, 1981), xiv.
10. Michael Stanton, lecture presented at "Tolkien 2005," University of Vermont, Burlington, April 2, 2005.
11. Kathryn W. Crabbe, "The Quest as Legend: *The Lord of the Rings*," in *Modern Critical Interpretations:* The Lord of the Rings, ed. Harold Bloom (Philadelphia: Chelsea House Publishers, 2000), 156.
12. Shippey, *Author of the Century*, 6–7.
13. Scott Sanders, introduction to Aldo Leopold, *For the Health of the Land: Previously Unpublished Essays and Other Writings*, ed. J. Baird Callicott and Eric T. Freyfogle (Washington, D.C.: Island Press, 1999), xvi.

14. Orr, "The Uses of Prophecy," 179.

15. Sanders, introduction, xv.

16. Aldo Leopold, "Do We Want a Woodless Countryside?" in *For the Health of the Land*, 95.

Chapter 9. Rousing the Shire

1. "'Don't the great tales never end?' [said Sam]. 'No, they never end as tales,' said Frodo." "'What a tale we have been in, Mr. Frodo, haven't we?' [Sam said].... 'I wonder how it will go after our part'" (V/iv). "Probably every writer making a secondary world, a fantasy, ... hopes that he is drawing on reality: hopes that the peculiar quality of this secondary world (if not all the details) are derived from Reality or are flowing into it.... [I]n Fantasy he may actually assist in the effoliation and multiple enrichment of creation. All tales may come true" (*TL*, 64, 66). Also in this regard, in "Smith of Wootton Major," the boundary between the "real" world of Smith's village and the fantasy world of Faërie is transitional—*liminal,* in the terms developed in chapter 6 of this book. Smith journeys at will into that other, marvelous world through the woods of Outer Faërie and back again, and he obviously applies what he has learned in Faërie to his life in Wootton Major.

2. Unlike in Fangorn and the Shire, where the narrative gives considerable explicit attention to the land itself and the damage done to it by Saruman—the threats to feraculture and agriculture—in Rohan, the narrative emphasis is on human life and human habitation, with mention of the theft of horses by Sauron. Nonetheless, the reader can see how Saruman has attacked the natural world and the landscape in the Shire and Isengard and at the edge of Fangorn Forest. We can assume that the same would happen to Rohan under his rule. Our exploration of the rousing of people in all three of these realms is therefore instructive.

3. Norman Wirzba, "Introduction: Why Agrarianism Matters—Even to Urbanites," in *The Essential Agrarian Reader: The Future of Culture, Community, and the Land,* ed. Norman Wirzba (Lexington: University Press of Kentucky, 1993), 8.

4. "For our wrestling is not against flesh and blood; but against principalities and power, against the rulers of the world of this darkness, against the spirits of wickedness in the high places" (Ephesians 6:12). See Matthew Dickerson, *Following Gandalf: Epic Battles and Moral Victory in* The Lord of the Rings (Grand Rapids, Mich.: Brazos Press, 2003).

5. Maurice Telleen, "The Mind-set of Agrarianism ... New and Old," in Wirzba, *The Essential Agrarian Reader,* 53.

6. Aldo Leopold, *For the Health of the Land: Previously Unpublished Essays*

and Other Writings, ed. J. Baird Callicott and Eric T. Freyfogle (Washington, D.C.: Island Press, 1999), 166.

7. Ibid.

8. In chapter 12 of *The Hobbit,* Tolkien describes Dwarves as follows: "dwarves are not heroes, but calculating folk with a great idea of the value of money; some are tricky and treacherous and pretty bad lots; some are not, but are decent enough people like Thorin and Company, if you don't expect too much." The portrayal of Dwarves throughout the legendarium is consistent with this description.

9. Wirzba, "Introduction: Why Agrarianism Matters," 8.

10. Paul E. Lutz, "Interrelatedness: Ecological Pattern of the Creation," in *Cry of the Environment: Rebuilding the Christian Creation Tradition,* ed. Philip N. Joranson and Ken Butigan (Santa Fe, N.M.: Bear and Company, 1984), 254.

Chapter 10. Environmentalism, Transcendence, and Action

1. Or Rosie Cotton, Lobelia Took, Marigold Gamgee, or any of the other female hobbits. It should be noted that, upon her death, Lobelia Sackville-Baggins leaves all that remains of her family's money to Frodo, "for him to use in helping hobbits made homeless by the troubles" (VI/ix).

2. Of course, as noted earlier, Hobbits do belong to the race of Men in Middle-earth, and despite their small stature, they are meant to closely represent Tolkien's beloved Englishmen. As depicted, they provide wonderful role models for many aspects of good environmental stewardship. However, because Hobbits distinguish themselves from Men, we speak here specifically of the race known in Middle-earth as Men, not including the Hobbit branch.

3. Denethor remarks cynically that Aragorn comes "but of the line of Isildur"—that is, founder of Arnor, the Northern Kingdom of Westernesse in Exile, and not Anárion, founder of the Southern Kingdom of Gondor (V/vii). In "The Council of Elrond," however, Aragorn claims descent from Elendil, father of both Isildur and Anárion and cofounder, with his sons, of both realms. Aragorn's right to rule both kingdoms is legitimized, or perhaps symbolized, when Elrond brings the Scepter of Annúminas—the chief city of Arnor—to Aragorn's coronation (VI/v). Appendix A says, "There were fifteen Chieftains, before the sixteenth and last was born, Aragorn II, who became again King of both Gondor and Arnor." Many thanks to John Houghton for clarifying this tangle.

4. In S.R. 1427 King Elessar declares the Shire a Free Land; in 1434 he makes officials of the Shire "Counsellors of the North-kingdom"; in 1436

he gives Sam the Star of the Dúnedain, and Elanor is made one of Arwen's maids of honor; in 1452 the Shire's borders are expanded by Elessar's gift of the Westmarch.

5. Tom Shippey, *J. R. R. Tolkien: Author of the Century* (Boston: Houghton Mifflin, 2000), 68.

6. Judith Kollmann, "Elisions and Ellipses: Council and Counsel in Tolkien's and Jackson's *The Lord of the Rings*," presented at *Mythcon 35*, Ann Arbor, Mich., July 30–August 2, 2004.

7. Maurice Telleen, "The Mind-set of Agrarianism . . . New and Old," in *The Essential Agrarian Reader: The Future of Culture, Community, and the Land*, ed. Norman Wirzba (Lexington: University Press of Kentucky, 1993), 55.

8. Scott Sanders, introduction to Aldo Leopold, *For the Health of the Land: Previously Unpublished Essays and Other Writings*, ed. J. Baird Callicott and Eric T. Freyfogle (Washington, D.C.: Island Press, 1999), xviii.

9. Berry refers to these events throughout his essays, but see his meditations "Damage" and "Healing" in *What Are People For?* (New York: North Point, 1990), 7–13, and his lengthier account in the title piece in *The Long-Legged House* (New York: Harcourt, 1969; reprint, Washington, D.C.: Shoemaker and Hoard, 2004), 108–69.

10. Steven R. Covey, *The Seven Habits of Highly Effective People* (New York: Free Press, 1990); Steven Bouma-Prediger, "Creation Care and Character: The Nature and Necessity of the Ecological Virtues," *Perspectives on Science and Faith: Journal of the American Scientific Affiliation* 50, no. 1 (March 1998): 7.

11. Aldo Leopold, "The Farmer as Conservationist," in *For the Health of the Land*, 164.

12. A modern reader might see in this "soil additive" some sort of chemical fertilizer to enhance the soil's productivity.

13. The latter definition is supplied in a note by Humphrey Carpenter (*Letters*, 445) citing the *Oxford English Dictionary* definition of English *goety*.

14. Although Entwives do not actually appear in *The Lord of the Rings*, their absence is keenly felt, especially by the Ents, and the story of the Ents and Entwives carries considerable mythical and emotional weight in the second half of the tale. The longest story and song told and sung by Treebeard to the hobbits is his lament for the lost Entwives (III/iv). Likewise, both his final words to Aragorn and his final words to the hobbits Merry and Pippin are about the Entwives (VI/vi).

15. In personal correspondence dated June 3, 2004, John Elder suggests that Tolkien may have been aware of these issues. Elder points out that in the monastic tradition, Benedictines are associated with conservation and Franciscans with preservation. It is likely that, as a Roman Catholic, Tolkien

was indeed aware of these two approaches to the environment among the religious orders. Elder goes on to suggest that "the two [traditions] converge in a whole [Catholic and Christian] vision of the creation."

16. Philip Sherrard, *The Rape of Man and Nature* (Ipswich, England: Golgonooza Press, 1987), 90.

17. Interestingly, Sherrard connects the loss of our spiritual understanding of nature with our loss of a spiritual understanding of humankind: "Our understanding of man is intimately related to our understanding of nature. Indeed, so much is this the case that our failure to perceive the divine in man has gone hand in hand with a failure to perceive the divine in nature. As we have dehumanized man, so we have desanctified nature" (*The Rape of Man and Nature*, 90).

18. For example, "Greater love than this no man hath, that a man lay down his life for his friends" (John 15:13); "For let this mind be in you, which was also in Christ Jesus: Who being in the form of God, thought it not robbery to be equal with God: But emptied himself, taking the form of a servant" (Philippians 2:5–6).

19. Wirzba, *Essential Agrarian Reader*, 8.

20. Sanders, introduction, xix.

Conclusion

1. In April 2004, history professor James Farrell addressed Phi Beta Kappa graduates of St. Olaf College: "A few years ago, in an Environmental History course, a student started an environmental impact statement by saying, 'I believe that, given today's society, it is impossible for an American to have a positive impact on the environment.' What this student meant is that the ideas and institutions of this country, our social construction of common sense, virtually guarantees that a normal, 'good' American will live a life that is neither just nor sustainable. It is not just, because it is not possible for all people on earth to live this way. And it is not sustainable, because we are depleting resources at a rate that cannot last" ("Earth in Mind," http://www.stolaf.edu/academics/pbk/speeches/james_farrell.html). Our thanks to Heather Randazzo, a student in Jonathan Evans's spring 2006 Environmental Literature course at the University of Georgia, for this reference.

2. See, e.g., Laurie Goodstein, "Evangelical Leaders Join Global Warming Initiative," *New York Times*, February 8, 2006. Goodstein mentions prominent evangelicals including Rick Warren, Charles W. Colson, James C. Dobson, and Jim Ball (director of the Evangelical Environmental Network) among signatories of the Evangelical Climate Initiative. The Interfaith Stewardship Alliance, which opposes the initiative, is led by E. Calvin Beisner, whose principled

position is that the high costs of some of the solutions advocated in the initiative would fall most heavily on the poor.

3. Wendell Berry, "God and Country," in *What Are People For?* (New York: North Point, 1990), 95–102.

4. Wendell Berry, "The Pleasure of Eating," in ibid., 145.

5. Ibid., 146.

6. Barbara Kingsolver, *Small Wonder: Essays* (New York: HarperCollins, 2002), 114.

7. Ibid., 120. In her introduction to *The More-with-Less Cookbook* by Doris Janzen Longacre (Scottdale, Pa.: Herald Press, 1976), Mary Emma Showalter Eby cites similar statistics: An American uses on average "five times as much grain . . . yearly"—about 2,000 pounds—as one of the more than 2 billion people living in poor countries. "All but 150 pounds of this we consume indirectly in meat, milk, eggs, and alcoholic beverages," while poor persons in Asia eat "less than 400 pounds a year, most of it directly as rice or wheat" (13).

8. *The More-with-Less Cookbook* was commissioned by the Mennonite Central Committee and written "in response to world food needs." Longacre's preface refers to the book as part of the Mennonites' commitment to finding long-range solutions to the world food crisis by asking "each constituent household to look at its lifestyle, particularly food habits. Noting the relationship between North American overconsumption and world need, a goal has been set to eat and spend 10 percent less" (6). Efforts like this are thoughtful, practical, admirable, and easy to adopt.

9. Berry, "The Pleasures of Eating," 152.

10. Dan Stahler, personal interview, Yellowstone National Park, August 3, 2005. Stahler suggests that the problem goes beyond the vilification of wolves in literature and in our imagination; the fact that they are icons of wilderness, even when viewed in a positive light, can be problematic. When wolves are romanticized in the public eye, it is difficult to focus policy discussion on scientific issues.

Index

absolutism, 24, 34; language of, 48
accountability, 41–42, 66, 180
Adam and Eve, 51, 58
Aegidius, 167
aesthetics, 98, 100–101, 171
affluence, 15
Aglarond, 229–30, 269
agrarian culture and society, xxi, 48, 71, 72, 76, 77, 83, 84, 97
agrarian/agrarianism, xxi, 4, 17, 48, 71–94, 97–98, 103, 105, 145, 149–55, 165, 167, 168, 170, 173, 177–79, 199, 210, 216, 218, 221, 238, 245, 265, 284n2, 284n9. *See also* agriculture
agribusiness, 16, 71, 81, 100, 165, 167, 191, 201, 202, 270, 291n4
Agricola de Hammo, 167
agriculture, ix, xv, xxi, 16, 31, 32, 40, 45, 62, 71–94, 98, 99, 146, 155, 157, 164–70, 177, 178, 185, 191, 195, 207, 216, 223, 245, 248, 250, 251, 261–63, 270, 283n1, 287n3, 292n15, 294n2. *See also* agrarianism
Ainulindalë, 26, 28, 50, 143
Ainur, 11, 20, 26–29, 35, 50, 120, 143, 277n4
Akallabêth, 60, 62, 115, 187
Alf. *See* Prentice
Alfred, Lord Tennyson, ix, 285n17
allegory, xxi, 130, 163, 164, 167, 170, 174, 179, 219, 220, 235, 260
Aman, 101–2, 104, 107, 111, 113, 115, 116, 125, 287n7

ambition, 15, 226, 232, 257
Ambrosius, 169
American, 54, 263
Amis, Kingsley, 148
Amish, 74, 201
Amon Gwareth, 105
Anar, 10
Anárion, 285n18, 295n3
Anderson, Douglas, 293n1
Andes, 146, 160
Andor, 62
Andrzej Olzański, Tadeusz, 280n31
Anduin, 267, 290n12
Andvari, 16
angelic being and power, 26, 120, 122, 277n4, 279n25, 287n7
angel, 26, 120, 122, 288n2
Angrboda, 266
anthropocentrism, 42, 49, 54
anthropology, 50, 148
anti-ecology, 196
Aragorn, xi, xx, 7, 9, 33–34, 38, 46, 89, 101, 106, 114, 116, 126, 130, 132, 143, 148, 151–52, 156, 160, 194, 199, 208, 218–20, 225–27, 232, 237–42, 244, 250, 269, 289n12, 295n3, 296n14. *See also* Elessar; Elfstone; Estel
Aral Sea, 193
Arda, 8, 10, 23, 26–28, 33, 47, 50, 51, 54–56, 60, 61, 65–67, 99, 107, 110, 115, 120–23, 143, 196, 278n5, 280n31
Ar-Gimilzôr, 62

Aristotle, 66, 247
Arnor, 7, 48, 50, 82, 83, 239, 285n18, 195n3
Aros, 104, 133, 285, 295
Ar-Pharazôn, 62
art/artist, xxiii, 3, 4, 25, 31, 32, 104, 108, 113, 130, 164, 171, 173–78, 182, 218, 249, 292n15
Arthedain, 81, 82
Arthur, King, 148
Arwen Undómiel, 239
Assisi, St. Francis of, 122, 167
Atani, 49, 111
Atira, 120
Atkins, 176
Atlantis, 187
Auden, W. H., 219
Augustus Bonifacius, 169–70
Aulë, 8, 10, 27, 29, 49–52, 55, 56, 60, 110, 121, 123, 160, 163
Avallónë, 115
Avari, 101, 102
Avon, 78, 79

Babcock, Maltbie, 288n2
Bag End, 87, 90, 151, 153, 155–56, 204, 209, 211, 231
Baggins, Bilbo, 12–14, 16, 18, 46, 74, 81, 83, 87, 96, 99, 103, 105–6, 115–16, 136, 139, 155, 205, 224, 226, 231
Baggins, Frodo, xi, xii, xx, 5, 7, 18, 34, 45, 46, 47, 73, 74, 83–91, 95, 96, 99, 106–9, 112–16, 133, 137–38, 141–42, 144, 146, 148–50, 152, 155–56, 158–59, 161, 186, 188–91, 203–5, 208, 210–11, 215, 220, 224–25, 231, 236–37, 249, 254, 264–65, 269, 286n24, 290n10, 294n1, 295n1
Bagshot Row, 211–12
Balrog, 22
Bamfurlong, 72, 85, 154–55

Barad-dûr, 203
Barrow-downs, 148, 151–52
battle, xii, 34, 40, 44, 89, 169, 202, 211, 221, 224–26, 233, 242, 254, 287; against evil, 48, 168, 246, 287; in the Shire, 72. *See also* war
Battle of Helm's Deep, 125, 194, 200, 213, 225, 229, 256
Battle of the Pelennor Fields, 218, 221
Battle of the Somme, 187
Bay of Elvenhome, 111
beauty, xi, xii, 9, 11, 14, 16–17, 24, 27, 29, 31, 33, 35, 48, 50, 59, 77, 90–91, 98–117, 130, 142, 156–61, 171–81, 194, 216, 229, 231, 258, 264–65, 270, 286n1, 289n11
beer, x, 13, 71, 85–86, 92, 207, 229, 248, 285n21
being, 8, 51, 110; creature, 6, 8, 19, 26, 28–30, 32, 34, 50–51, 57, 64–65, 110, 120, 123–24, 128, 133, 138, 176, 277n4, 279n25, 287n7, 289n14; existence, 8, 20, 23, 26–28, 51, 63, 110–11, 120, 292n17; ontology, 23, 63, 65, 116, 125, 127–28, 278n5. *See also* Man/men
Beisner, E. Calvin, 297n2
Beleriand, 103–4, 109, 112, 133, 287n6
Bennett, Judith M., 285
Bent World, 115–16
Beorn/Beornings, 42–43, 76, 96, 281n3
Beowulf, 126, 147, 167–68, 270, 281n2
Beregond, 72
Beren, 5, 159, 266
Bergil, 72
Berkshire countryside, 20
Berry, Wendell, xvii, 4, 16, 23, 26, 31, 32, 39, 84, 93, 146, 160, 162, 165–67, 191–92, 201, 206, 247, 248, 259, 262–64, 291n16, 291n4, 292n15, 296n9
Bible, 31, 281n5, 282n14
Big Folk, 81, 143

Bilbo. *See* Baggins, Bilbo
Bindbole Woods, 157
biosphere, 8, 51, 266
Birmingham, x, 77, 79, 187, 191, 285n15
Birzer, Bradley, 122
Black Gate, 147, 186, 188, 243, 254
Black Land, 188, 190
Black Riders, 75, 91, 96, 151, 153
Blake, William, 193
Blessed Realm, 10, 111, 116
Bombadil, Tom, xx, 13, 18–24, 42, 84, 85, 115, 133, 138, 149–55, 158, 159, 219, 245, 269, 279n27, 284n14
Bouma-Prediger, Steven, 28, 44, 122, 247, 248
Brandybuck, Meriadoc "Merry," 13, 22, 73, 85, 108, 119, 137–40, 148, 150, 161, 193, 195, 205, 206, 217, 220–23, 236–38, 241, 244, 247, 254, 296n14
Brandywine River, 150, 152, 153, 190, 211, 212, 267
Bree, 12, 146, 151–53, 155, 265
Bregalad, 131–32
Brethil, 104
Bridge of Stonebows, 81
Bristol Cliffs, Vt., 145
Brookes-Smith family, 75
Bruchac, Joseph, ix
Bruinen River, fords of, 106, 141, 151
Buckland, 12, 74, 75, 149, 150, 290n12
Burma, 14
Bywater Road, 211

Calaquendi, 102, 103, 287n7
Calormen, 71, 283n1
Captains of the West, 48, 54, 254
Caradhras, 142, 244, 265
Caras Galadhon, 107
Carcharoth, 266
caring management, 42, 45, 48

Carpenter, Humphrey, 63, 73, 75, 77, 78, 92
Catholicism, xix, xxii, 24, 25, 54, 122, 167, 253, 288n2, 296–97n15
Celeborn, 107, 133, 144, 160, 199
celebrations, 15, 161, 229
Celtic sources, 3, 41
Cerin Amroth, 107
Cervantes, Miguel, x
Chetwood, 152
Children of Ilúvatar, 11, 27, 34, 35, 43, 44, 49–57, 60, 64–67, 104, 111, 112, 120, 122, 237, 252, 287n7
Christianity, xix–xxiii, 24–26, 28, 35, 39, 40, 42, 53, 54, 56, 63–66, 72, 89, 93, 116, 122, 131, 164, 224, 233, 252, 253, 254, 277n6, 281n7, 288n2, 292n12, 297n15
Chronicles of Narnia, 71, 72, 283n1
Cirith Ungol, 188, 190, 244
civilization, xxi, 32, 98, 136, 142, 152, 153, 221
Clean Air Act, ix
clean earth, 47, 48, 270
Coketown, 193
Colson, Charles W., 297n2
community, x–xii, 37, 39, 42, 47, 73, 74, 75, 76, 101–3, 105, 135, 142, 146, 166, 176, 181, 191, 192, 201, 206–9, 242, 243, 245, 248, 258, 261, 281n3
Company of the Ring, 141, 153, 244, 265
conservation, xi, xv, xvi, xxi, 23, 42, 95, 99, 124, 129, 144, 160, 172, 185, 191, 212, 227, 245, 248, 250, 251, 252, 262, 296n15
consumerism, 17, 201, 207, 261, 263
Cormallen, 116
Corollairë, 6, 7
cosmic enemy, 24
cosmology, 113, 116, 121
Cotton, Farmer, 18, 72, 73, 75, 84–87, 157, 160, 191, 208–11, 241, 262

Cotton, Rose "Rosie," 13, 86, 157, 160
council, 243, 244, 253
Council of Elrond, 20, 22, 133, 141, 153, 194, 198, 243
counsel, 37, 38, 48, 242, 243, 244, 250
Court of the Fountain, 132, 239
Crabbe, Kathryn W., 203
craft/craftsmanship, 29, 61, 180
created world, xx, 21, 23, 24, 28, 29, 34, 44, 56, 61, 65, 98, 109, 121, 145, 159, 161, 222, 225, 253, 258
creation, xx, xxii, 3–5, 8, 11, 14, 15, 23–36, 42–44, 49–52, 55–59, 61, 65–67, 78, 92, 95, 99, 109, 110, 113, 120, 122, 123, 132, 142, 159, 160, 163, 181, 190, 196, 225, 228, 233, 235, 237, 252, 253, 258, 260, 265, 294n1, 297n15
creation consciousness, 4
creation myth, 25–28, 32, 52, 58, 277n4, 278n5, 294n1; biblical, 28, 31, 51–52, 57
creativity, 4, 27, 29, 30, 35, 36, 74, 104, 120, 121, 128, 154, 158, 227, 252, 282n13
Creator, 59, 122
Crickhollow, 85, 152, 153, 155
Cuiviénen, 109, 111
cultivation, 12, 31, 32, 58, 59, 80, 95, 97, 99, 109, 112, 122, 123, 133, 142, 145, 151, 153, 157, 172, 174, 178, 251, 284n2, 286n2, 287n3, 288n5
culture, x, xv, xix, xxi, 3, 4, 14, 16, 18, 25, 30, 32, 39, 48, 74–76, 81–84, 88, 90, 95, 98, 166, 177, 185, 210, 228, 256, 262, 264, 286n23, 292n15
Culúrien, 7
Curry, Patrick, xviii, 285n17
Czech, 122

Dante Alighieri, x

Dark Lord, 19, 38, 101, 114, 159, 186, 192, 217, 246
Dead Marshes, 186, 267, 269
death, xxii, 6, 16, 34, 62, 63, 64, 73, 130, 147, 148, 161, 174, 188–91, 203, 218, 220, 237, 242, 254, 279n27, 285n22
Deep-elves, 103
Deeping Coomb, 217
deforestation, 132, 134, 136, 138, 196
Delphic oracle, 270
democratic institutions, xi
Denethor, xi, 34, 37, 38, 39, 40, 43, 55, 56, 237, 238, 241, 254, 270, 295n3
DeWitt, Calvin, 58, 59
Dickens, Charles, 193, 195
Dickerson, Matthew, 277n5, 280n30, 286n24
Dickinson, Emily, ix
Dillard, Annie, xvii
Dimrill Gate, 106
diversity, xi, xii, 30, 100, 145, 146, 154, 160, 200, 270
divine law, 35
Dobson, James C., 297n2
domination, xii, 22, 23, 29, 37, 45, 52, 177
dominion, 43, 51, 52, 55, 56, 57, 59, 60, 62, 113, 114, 120, 121, 132, 143, 231, 239, 240
Donahue, Brian, 73
Doors of Dúrin, 147
Doriath, 102–4, 133; Hidden Realm of, 103
Dorthonion, 101
Doyle, Sir Arthur Conan, 148
dragons, 15, 16, 163, 167, 168, 170, 266
dragon-sickness, 197
Dublin Review, 170
Duncan, Bryan, 53
Dúnedain, 116, 237, 296n4
Dunland, 134, 239
Durin, 230

Dwarves, 15, 16, 26, 27, 30, 33, 35, 44, 49, 50, 55, 60, 66, 76, 96, 101, 102, 120, 123, 136, 139, 140, 147, 159, 163, 219, 225–27, 230, 266, 278n9, 287n4, 295n8
Dyrness, William, 59

Eä, 27, 28, 50, 51, 99, 278n5
eagles, 123, 265, 282n11
Eärendil, 5, 7, 10, 12
Eärnur, 239
earth spirit, 19, 20
Eby, Mary Emma Showalter, 298n7
ecocriticism, ix, x, 145
ecological disaster, 200
ecological domain, xxi
ecological virtue, 76, 80, 83, 86, 89, 247, 248
ecology, xix, 8, 15, 24, 27, 31, 36, 39, 44, 45, 50, 53–55, 65, 69, 91, 92, 99, 100, 119, 124, 125, 145–51, 155, 157, 159–75, 177, 179, 185, 194–96, 200, 202, 206, 207, 210, 211, 216, 218, 232, 233, 240, 245, 266, 267, 281n7
economy, 4, 16, 23, 31, 38, 72, 77, 86, 90, 92, 93, 99, 100, 166, 169, 191,199, 201, 205, 207, 227–31, 263, 264, 282n8, 284n2
ecotone, x, xxi, 145–62, 172, 175
Edain, 125
Eden, 58, 116, 125, 269
efficiency, 17, 209
Elanor, 13, 157, 296n4
Elbereth, 95
Eldar, 101, 102, 115
Elder Days, 6, 7, 108, 110, 112, 158
Elder, John, xii, xv, xvii, 4, 124, 145, 245, 259, 292n15, 296–97n15
Elendil, 238, 295n3
Elessar, 237–39, 295–96n4. *See also* Aragorn
Elfstone, 237. *See also* Aragorn

Elgin, Don D., xviii
Elrond, 5, 20, 89, 103, 106, 114, 133, 134, 141, 153, 159, 194, 198, 199, 227, 243, 295n3
Elvenhome, 116
Elves, ix, xi, xxi, 8, 10, 11, 25, 26, 30, 32, 33, 35, 36, 42, 44, 49, 50, 51, 52, 54, 57, 60–66, 82, 95–119, 123–25, 132, 133, 134, 136, 140, 145, 147, 152, 154, 157, 159, 171, 198, 199, 215, 230, 232, 237, 239, 250, 251, 262, 264, 265, 269, 270, 271, 282n13, 286n1, 287n10–11
Elwë Thingol, 287n7
Emerson, Ralph Waldo, 148
Encircling Mountains, 103
Encyclopaedia Britannica, 127
Enedwaith, 135, 267
Ens, 128
Ent, Entia, 127–28
Enting, 143, 156, 252
Entish, 129, 196, 288n8
Entmoot, 222, 240, 243
Ents, ix, x, xxi, 19, 39, 110, 119, 123–34, 138–40, 142–45, 156, 160, 172, 195, 196, 197, 217, 218, 221–23, 226, 232, 237, 240, 242, 243, 245, 247, 250–52, 254, 256, 257, 262, 270, 271, 282n11, 296n14
Entwash, 247, 267, 288, 296
Entwives, xxi, 124, 144, 160, 218, 245, 250, 251, 252, 288n5, 296n14
Envinyatar, 237
environmental ethics, xxii, 24, 31, 33, 34, 35, 36, 40, 49, 66, 95, 119, 164, 180, 203, 235, 280n33
environmental justice, ix
Environmental Protection Agency, ix
Éomer, 9, 33, 34, 46, 89, 194, 225, 226, 232, 239, 240, 242
Eorl, 126, 256
Éowyn, 160, 218, 219, 237, 238, 240, 269

Ephel Dúath, 185, 188, 189
Ephesians, book of, 225, 287, 294
Eressëa, 115, 116
Eriador, ix, 48, 72, 82, 88, 95, 109, 135, 136, 156, 262, 265, 267, 270, 271
Eru Ilúvatar, xx, 11, 23, 26–36, 43, 44, 49, 50–52, 55–57, 60–63, 65, 67, 109, 111, 120–22, 127, 143, 187, 196, 224, 237, 280n33
Esgaroth, 281n3
Ettendales, 126
Ettenmoors, 126
eucatastrophe, 42, 89, 177
Eurydice, 41
Evangelical Climate Initiative, 297n2
Evangelical Environmental Network, 297n2
evangelicalism, 39
Evans, George Ewart, 284n9
Evans, Jonathan, ix, 270, 279n21
Eve. *See* Adam and Eve
Evesham, 75
evil, 15, 21, 22, 24, 34, 37, 44, 47–49, 56, 62, 66, 89, 100, 111–13, 136, 139, 148, 168, 170, 179, 183, 185–213, 218, 221, 224, 225, 227, 236, 238, 242, 249, 250, 260, 265, 266, 270, 280n33, 283n25, 287n11. *See also* morality
exploitation, xx, 24, 39, 45, 48, 52, 53, 54, 55, 64, 200, 230, 253
Ezellohar, 6, 7

factories, 187, 191, 194, 202, 206, 293n1
Faërie, 164, 167, 168, 177–81, 294n1
Fáfnir, 16
fairy-tales, 285n17
faith, xx, xxii, xxiii, 39, 54, 89, 116, 224, 225, 253, 262, 280n31
Fallohide, Marcho and Blanco, 81
Fangorn the Ent, 13, 19, 81, 107, 119, 123–29, 133, 134, 138–45, 152, 156, 161, 193–97, 208, 217, 218, 220–23, 226, 232, 233, 236, 240–45, 247, 251, 252, 254, 256, 289n15. *See also* Treebeard
Fangorn Forest, 34, 47, 119, 125, 126, 133, 134, 139, 140, 142–44, 148–51, 194, 195, 220–33, 236, 241, 243, 251, 256, 269, 289n15, 294n2
Far Easton, 178
Faramir, xx, 34, 89, 160, 188, 218, 219, 229, 237–40, 242, 269
Farmer Cotton. *See* Cotton, Farmer
Farmer Giles of Ham. *See* Giles, Farmer
Farmer Maggot. *See* Maggot, Farmer
farm/farmer/farming, 11, 16, 17, 18, 71, 72–75, 77, 80–90, 93, 97–100, 145, 146, 151, 155, 157, 162, 165–68, 171, 178, 187, 191, 201, 205, 207–9, 213, 223, 228, 245, 247, 248, 262–64, 284n9, 290n12, 291n4; industrial, 81, 191
Farrell, James 297n1
fate, 6, 62, 110
Fëanor, 10, 60, 61, 109
Fëanturi, 107
Felagund, Finrod. *See* Finrod
Fenris-wolf, 266
feraculture, xxi, 31, 32, 45, 119–44, 157, 164, 170, 172, 177, 185, 245, 250, 251, 262, 270, 294n2
Ferny, Bill, 227
fertility goddess, 120
feudal lord, 41
Finrod, 65, 104, 105
First Age, 5, 101, 103, 104, 125, 132, 159
First Voice, 176
Firstborn Children of Ilúvatar, 49. *See also* elves
Flieger, Verlyn, xviii
flowers, 6, 9, 10, 13, 21, 38, 44, 98, 104, 105–8, 111, 113, 123, 157, 159,

172, 173, 175, 176, 178, 179, 190, 230, 231, 239, 246
food, xx, 11, 12, 13, 14, 16, 17, 31, 71, 76, 84, 86, 92, 93, 95, 96, 97, 98, 99, 103, 106, 146, 152, 158, 169, 190, 191, 192, 201, 206, 207, 208, 247, 248, 258, 262, 263, 264, 265, 298n8
Forest of Arden, 79
Forest or Region, 104, 133
forestry 127, 130, 156, 231, 151, 270. *See also* trees: stewardship of
forests, xi–xii, xv, 8, 19, 21, 31, 43, 47–48, 63, 79, 103–6, 113, 119–20, 123–24, 129–30, 132–45, 148, 150–53, 155–57, 159, 161–62, 164, 171–72, 174, 194, 196, 200, 221–22, 232, 245, 250, 251–52
fossil fuel, xii, 100, 207, 212, 223, 263
Foster, David, 281n5
Foster, Richard, 15, 16, 22, 23, 54
freedom, xx, 23, 57, 61, 65, 88, 89, 100, 101, 113, 180, 215, 224, 239
Freya, 120
Frodo. *See* Baggins, Frodo
Frost, Robert, x
fruitfulness principle, 58

gadgets, 14, 15
Galadhrim, 107, 113
Galathea, 166
Galathilion, 132, 239
Gálmód, 37
Gamgee, Hamfast "Gaffer," 18, 72, 75, 156, 197, 292n6
Gamgee, Samwise "Sam," xi, xii, 5, 18, 72–74, 85, 88, 90, 91, 95–97, 112, 113, 150, 156, 157, 160, 161, 186–91, 197, 203–6, 210–12, 215, 220, 223–25, 231, 232, 236, 241, 242, 245–47, 249, 250, 254, 256, 261, 269, 292n6, 296n4
Gandalf, xi, xx, 7, 18, 19, 20, 22, 37, 38, 39, 40, 43–48, 54, 59, 78, 87, 89, 106, 115, 116, 125, 126, 128, 132, 141, 143, 144, 161, 194, 198–203, 208, 213, 219, 220, 222, 224–27, 232, 233, 237, 239, 241, 243, 244, 250, 254–58, 265, 270, 279n27, 281n1, 282n12
garden/gardener, x, xi, 12, 13, 18, 29, 43, 46, 58, 59, 72, 75, 87, 88, 90, 97, 98, 101, 104, 106, 107, 111, 112, 145, 153, 156, 160–62, 167, 172, 173, 175, 176, 204, 206, 212, 217, 218, 228, 231, 249, 251, 264, 286n2, 288n5
Gardner, John, 84
Garm, 266
Garth, John, 293n1
Genesis, book of, 31, 51, 52, 55, 57–60, 187, 239
Germanic language and culture, 40, 125
giants, 10, 126–28, 163, 166–70, 205, 256
gifts, 15, 31, 35, 36, 42, 45, 46, 60, 62, 130, 156, 169, 172, 173, 178–81, 237, 249, 250, 269, 296n6
Gildor, 83, 91, 95, 96, 109, 149, 154
Giles of Ham, Farmer, xxi, 87, 163, 164, 165–71, 177, 181, 292n6
Gil-galad, 135
Gimli, 43, 101, 148, 194, 219, 220, 225, 229–31, 287n4
Girdle of Melian, 103
Glittering Caves of Algarond, 229, 269
global warming, 261, 282n12
globalization, xi, xii
Glorfindel, 19
glory, 9–12, 27, 29–31, 57, 179, 237, 239
Gnostics/Gnosticism, 65
goetia, goety, 250, 296. *See also* magic, *magia*
gold/golden, 9, 16, 10, 33, 37, 96, 97,

104–13, 120, 131, 157–58, 231, 287n10, 289n11, 291n15; metal, 9, 16, 158, 230, 231
Goldberry, 20, 22, 149, 158, 159, 160, 161, 219, 245, 279n25
Golden Wood, 33
Gollum, 186, 188
Gondolin, 103, 105
Gondor, x–xii, 7, 37, 38, 41, 44, 47, 56, 72, 88, 132, 142, 143, 146, 147, 199, 218, 222, 236, 237, 238, 239, 240, 282n9, 285n18, 295n3
goodness of the earth, xx, 24, 253
Goodstein, Laurie, 297n2
Gorbag, 244
Gorgoroth, 185, 189, 190, 218, 269
Gospels, 88
government, 60, 76, 207, 256
grass, 6, 8, 9, 13, 15, 17, 19, 96, 104, 107, 108, 112, 150, 153, 154, 156, 190, 211, 212, 229, 231, 232, 257, 259, 278n7
grasslands, 47, 151, 154, 162, 212, 267
Great Fens, 135
Great Flood, 187
Great Music, 27, 28
Great River, 141, 269
Great Sea, 95, 109, 186
Greater Birmingham Act, 79
greed, 16, 61, 62, 170, 191
green, xii, 6–9, 33, 96, 104–8, 110–11, 113, 115, 120, 137, 141, 142, 158, 161, 173, 178, 186, 194, 195, 202, 217, 218, 251
Green Dragon Inn, 242, 256
Green-elves, 96, 102, 229
Green-Hill country, 151
Green movement, xxii, 14
Greenwood the Great "Mirkwood," 136, 140
Grey Havens, 88, 115, 215
Grey-elves, 102
Gríma, 37

Grimm, the Brothers, 266
Guernsey, Dennis, 281–82n7
Gunton, Colin, 14
Gwathló, 135, 136, 267

habitation, 50, 51, 54, 66, 67, 151, 177, 294n2
Haldir, 113, 114, 246
Halflings, 38, 225. *See also* Hobbits
Hall Green, 77
happiness, 5, 19, 41, 73, 177, 229. *See also* joy
Harad, 239
Hardy, Thomas, x
Harfoots, 82
harmony, xi, xv, 27, 28, 30, 36, 65, 85, 92, 122, 160, 161, 177, 181, 219, 237, 258
Harry Potter, 22
Harvard University, 185, 206
Hawkes, Jacquetta, 74
health, xi, xii, 17, 25, 37, 48, 62, 75, 76, 79, 80, 146, 149, 155, 157, 192, 199, 201, 207, 209, 213, 216–18, 228, 238, 245, 248, 258, 263, 264, 266, 270
heaven, 66, 109, 110, 116, 120, 121, 167, 177, 181, 224–28; the heavens, 5, 10, 51, 121 179, 224, 227, 292. *See also* Eden; heavens; paradise
hedges/hedgerows, 43, 90, 137, 149, 150, 153–55, 161, 171, 290–91n13
High Elves, 7, 91, 95, 97, 102
High Hay, 152, 155
Higley, Sara, 147
Hithlum, 101
hoarding, 15, 16, 17, 29, 61
Hobbit, The, xvi, 11–18, 26, 76, 82, 83, 96, 98, 102, 103, 105, 106, 136, 139, 152, 164, 165, 205, 226, 229, 266, 290n12
Hobbiton, x, 72, 74, 78, 85, 91, 151,

152, 155, 190, 204, 205, 211, 222, 231
Hobbits, xi, xii, xxi, 5, 11–19, 21, 22, 24, 26, 30, 44, 48, 49, 50, 66, 71–74, 76, 79–92, 95–99, 102, 103, 106, 111, 120, 123–61, 188–91, 195, 204, 206, 208, 210–23, 225, 236–38, 240–42, 247–51, 254, 255, 257, 261–65, 270, 278n9, 285n17, 295n2
Hollin, 147, 269
home, xi, xv, xxi, 14, 21, 46, 50, 54, 62, 78, 79, 83, 88–92, 104, 112, 139, 145, 150–53, 155, 159, 161, 165, 167, 170, 185, 204–6, 222, 224, 231, 248, 255–56, 263–64
hope, xii, xvii, xviii, xix, xxii, xxiii, 10, 36, 46, 47, 57, 136, 143, 187–88, 199, 200, 215–16, 218–19, 224–26, 235–38, 240, 244–46, 248, 257–58, 260, 262, 265, 267
horses, 33, 43, 44, 47, 168
horticulture, xxi, 31, 32, 42, 45, 95–117, 157, 164, 170, 172, 178, 185, 245, 250, 251, 262, 270, 286–87n3
Houghton, John, 295n3
humans/humanity, 4, 23, 26, 28, 31, 36, 42–44, 49–53, 55, 57–59, 63–66, 75, 81, 84, 114, 122, 124–27, 130, 141, 143, 146, 166, 168–70, 177, 178, 181, 212, 218, 227, 232, 233, 235, 253, 254, 256–58, 266, 270, 282n13, 294n2, 297n17. *See also* being; Man
humility, 35, 52, 88, 89, 285n22
Huorns, x, 140, 269, 282n11
Huxley, Aldous, 64, 65
hymns, 122, 288n2

Iarwain Ben-adar, 159. *See also* Bombadil, Tom
Illuin, 110
Ilúvatar. *See* Eru Ilúvatar

imaginary world, 25, 30, 50, 53, 56; history of, 76, 79, 92, 133, 146–47, 150; geography of, 164, 267, 278n5–9
imagination, 4, 78, 79, 80, 193, 205, 236, 255–57, 260, 270, 298n10
Imperishable Flame, 26, 27
Inari, 120
incantations, 22
Incánus, 7
incarnation, 19, 20, 23, 27, 89, 129
Indo-European, 129
industrialism, x, xxi, 4, 15, 71, 73, 79–81, 84, 92, 97, 99, 100, 147, 187, 191, 193–94, 196, 199–202, 205, 211, 227, 248, 263–64, 293n1
inherent value, 16, 24, 43, 43, 195, 227
Interfaith Stewardship Alliance, 297n2
Irmo, 104, 107
Isengard, xi, xii, xxi, 34, 47, 63, 134, 140, 143, 161, 170, 185, 192, 194–96, 198, 200, 202–5, 209, 211, 213, 215–18, 236, 242, 245–47, 250, 254, 256, 258, 294n2
Isil, 10
Isildur, 285n18, 295n3
Istari, 20, 27. *See also* wizard
Ithilien, 89, 188, 218, 229, 269
Izaak Walton League, 262

Jackson, Peter, x, xvii, xix, 78, 150, 194, 203, 254
Jackson, Wes, xvii, 93, 259
Japan, x, 120
Jesus, 88, 254, 285n22, 297n18
Joranson, Philip N., 277n1, 295n10
joy, 10, 23, 42, 98, 160, 161, 218, 229, 238
justice, ix, 168, 207, 292n12, 292–93n18

Keenan, Hugh T., 134
Kementári, 120, 123

Kentucky, 100, 162, 247
Khazad-dûm, 89, 254
Kheled-zâram, 229
Kilby, Clyde S., 6
Kingsolver, Barbara, xvii, 259, 263
Kingston, Maxine Hong, 148
Kipling, Rudyard, 285
knowledge, xx, 21–23, 87, 93, 127, 128, 159, 176, 195, 200, 230, 249, 256, 270, 281n5, 282n12
Kocher, Paul H., xviii
Kollmann, Judith, 244

labor, 10, 17, 18, 50, 98, 160, 186, 191, 207, 208, 231, 247, 250. *See also* work
Lancashire Fusiliers. *See* Nineteenth Lancashire Fusiliers
land, xii, 9, 16, 23, 35, 37, 39, 42, 44, 47, 48, 58, 62, 63, 72, 74–76, 79–93, 104, 107, 111–16, 125, 133, 134, 136, 141, 144, 146, 147, 152–55, 159–218, 224, 228, 238, 241, 242, 246, 248, 255–58, 261, 263, 265, 267, 270, 292n6; ethics, 47, 181
landscape, x, xi, xv, 12, 71, 73, 79, 80, 82, 100, 112, 124, 133, 136, 141, 155, 170, 171, 179, 187, 188, 189, 193, 195, 196, 205, 294n2
language, xxi, 28, 33, 48, 49, 61, 107, 127–29, 137, 199, 200, 210, 280n1, 288n8; of Elves, 102; of Men, 81, 125; of Rohan, 12, 125
Last Homely House, 141, 142, 153. *See also* Rivendell
Láthspell, 37, 222
Latin American, 54
Laurelin, xx, 7, 9, 10, 11, 61, 110, 111, 158
Laurelindórenan, 7, 108
leaves, 9, 15, 105, 106, 107, 110, 112, 116, 120, 126, 130, 131, 139, 142, 154, 157, 158, 171, 172, 174, 179, 237, 238, 239, 289n11
legend, 5, 9, 25, 41, 107, 159, 160, 167, 232, 251, 257, 266
Legolas, 101, 105, 106, 107, 109, 116, 148, 194, 220, 230, 231
leisure, 14
Lembas, 109
Leopold, Aldo, ix, xvii, 181, 209, 212, 213, 227, 228, 246, 248, 258, 259
Lewis, C. S. 63, 71–73, 130, 131, 285n23, 292n17
Lickey Hill, 73
Light-elves, 103
liminality, 147–51, 154, 158, 290n12
linguistics, xxii, 108, 128–29, 201, 289n15
Lion, the Witch, and the Wardrobe, The, 71
literature, ix, xvi, xix, xxii, 4, 32, 36, 41, 53, 60, 79, 89, 115, 147, 148, 163, 164, 168, 177, 180, 186–87, 193, 232, 238, 257, 259–60, 266, 292n15, 298n10; fantasy, xix, xxiii, 36, 46, 71, 72, 79, 161, 164, 180, 219, 220, 249, 255, 257, 259, 266, 278n7, 294n1; fiction, x, xvii, xxiii, 3, 78, 79, 92, 130, 163, 164, 192, 193, 195, 219, 220, 259, 260, 269. *See also* story; narrative
logging, xvi, 135, 227, 246
Logsdon, Gene, 93
Loki, 266
Lond Daer, 135
London, Jack, 266
Lonely Isle, 116
Longacre, Doris Janzen, 298n7–8
Lord of the Rings, The, x, xvi–xx, 5, 6, 9, 11, 12, 13, 18–21, 25, 26, 37, 42, 48, 49, 72, 75, 76, 77, 79, 80, 87, 88, 90, 92, 95, 98, 100, 103, 106, 108, 114–16, 119, 125, 126, 129, 131, 133, 134, 140, 143, 146,

147–49, 155, 164, 181, 185, 196, 198, 215, 219, 220, 223–27, 229, 232, 235, 236, 243, 244, 247, 254, 255, 259, 266, 269
Lórien, 104, 107, 112, 114, 269
Loth, 107
Lothlórien, 7, 97, 100–103, 106–14, 133, 143, 145, 159, 160, 171, 172, 199, 229, 231, 244, 246
love, xxi, 17–19, 21, 34, 35, 43, 52, 59, 61, 73, 76, 78, 80–82, 85, 88–90, 107, 113, 114, 115, 117, 119, 152, 159, 229, 230–32, 251–54, 269; of comforts, 14, 84 ; of earth and the created world, xx, xxi, 18, 19, 23, 24, 28, 29, 31, 55, 111, 190, 232, 235, 245, 287n10; of growing things, 8, 13, 110, 120, 129–30, 132, 139, 157, 218; of language, xxi, 129
Luke, gospel of, 41
Lumpkin, Fatty, 136
Lúthien, 5, 104, 159
Lutz, Paul E., 233

machines/machinery, 13, 14, 17, 81, 179, 191–93, 195, 201, 249
magia, 250
magic, 13, 16, 22, 71, 72, 87, 112, 249, 250
Maiar, 27, 29, 120, 279n25, 287n7
Malinalda, 7
Man/men, 4, 8, 16, 23, 25, 26, 28, 31, 36, 42–44, 49–54, 57–59, 63–66, 75, 81, 84, 114, 122, 124–27, 130, 131, 141, 143, 146, 148, 162, 165–66, 168–69, 173, 178, 180–81, 187, 212, 218, 225, 227, 232–33, 235, 253–54, 256–58, 266, 270, 278n4, 297nn17–18
managed forests, xv
Manichaeism, 280n31
Manwë, 8, 10, 28–30, 51, 56, 60, 63, 110, 120–23, 125, 225, 278n5

maps, xi, 152, 157, 212
Marish, 72, 267
Marmon Silko, Leslie, ix
Marring of Arda, 65
Master Cook, 180
Master of Laketown, 197, 227
materialism, 18, 64, 252
meals, 71, 85, 96. *See also* food
Meduseld, 37, 46, 96, 222
Melkor, 10, 26, 29, 30, 32, 33, 35, 56, 65, 110, 111, 121, 225, 280n33. *See also* Morgoth
Men, of Middle-earth, 7–8, 11, 26, 30, 33–37, 49–52, 54, 60–62, 64–66, 81–83, 102, 106, 111, 114–15, 117, 120, 123–24, 132, 136, 140, 143–44, 159, 192, 196, 198–202, 212, 215, 219, 226, 230, 232, 236–37, 239–40, 242, 247, 251, 256–58, 261, 278n4, 278n6, 281n3, 285n18, 295n2
Menegroth, 104
Meneltarma, 62
Mennonites, 298n8
Mercian, 196
Mere of Dead Faces, 186
Merry. *See* Brandybuck, Meriadoc
Middle English, 41, 282n8
Middle Kingdom, 165
Middle-earth: creation of, 5, 26, 28, 142; ecology environment of, 27, 48, 54, 99, 143, 145, 149, 151, 157–58, 161, 163, 185, 200, 216–17, 221, 232, 235, 265–67; history of, 5–7, 11, 19, 34, 41, 50, 76, 80, 82–83, 101–5, 114, 125, 132–33, 138, 159, 187; kingdoms of, 7, 8; landscapes, regions of, x–xi, 62, 72, 76, 84, 88, 95, 98, 102, 109, 111, 119, 129, 133–34, 136, 138, 141–42, 144, 153, 159, 185, 233; mythology of, 5, 8, 10–11, 20, 25, 30, 36, 121, 123, 132, 196, 257; nature of, 23,

123; races of, 49–52, 83, 95, 97–98, 100–101, 113–14, 117, 119, 125, 127, 138, 237, 240, 256, 295n2
Midgewater Marshes, 151, 152
Midlands (English), 13
Milton, John, ix
Minas Morgul, 147
Minas Tirith, 72, 101, 142, 237, 254, 257
Mindeb, 104
mines/mining, 32, 99–101, 187, 191, 192, 194, 227, 230
mines of Moria. *See* Moria
Minhiriath, 135, 267
Míriel, 283n25
Mirkwood, 96, 98, 102, 103, 105, 133, 136, 139, 140, 229, 239
Mirror of Galadriel, 231
Misty Mountains, 37, 141, 267
Mithlond, 115
Mithrandir, 7
modern/modernity, 14–15, 17, 30, 45, 74, 76, 81, 84, 99, 165, 187, 191, 198, 204, 241, 249, 252, 270, 279n18, 285n17
monsters, 122, 167–70
moon, 10, 11, 12, 122, 159, 190, 263, 266
Moore, Marianne, x
moral truth, xxiii
morality, 33, 34, 48. *See also* good; evil
Mordor, x, xi, xii, xxi, 5, 37, 38, 48, 63, 87, 114, 146, 147, 170, 185–94, 196, 202–6, 210, 211, 213, 215, 216, 218, 219, 221, 224, 225, 239, 258. *See also* Udûn
More-with-Less Cookbook, 264, 298n8
Morgai, 185, 189, 190
Morgoth, 5, 32, 63, 65, 100, 103, 109, 126, 139, 140, 187, 196, 266, 282. *See also* Melkor
Moria, 22, 106, 147, 155, 230, 244, 265, 290n12

Moriquendi, 102, 103, 287n7
Morning Star, 5, 10, 12
Mountains of Lune, 134
Mount Doom, 5, 88, 190, 191, 243
Muir, John, ix
music, xx, 27, 28, 32, 33, 35, 36, 50, 103, 122, 143, 229, 288n2
myth/mythology, xx, xxii, xxiii, 3–11, 45, 49–52, 57–64, 66, 81, 86, 95, 98, 99, 109, 110, 120–27, 132, 140, 158–61, 163–68, 179, 185, 187, 196, 218, 225–39, 252–56, 266, 277n4, 278n5, 278n7, 280n31, 280n33, 282n13, 288n5, 296n14

names/naming, 5, 7, 10–13, 26, 62, 78, 85, 86, 90, 92, 105, 107, 108, 125, 126, 128–30, 134, 157, 159, 165, 167, 169, 175–77, 196–98, 217, 237, 278n5, 281n2, 289n15, 292n6
Nandor, 102
Nargothrond, 103, 104, 133, 287n6
Narnia, 71, 72, 283n1
Narog, 105, 133
narrative, and importance of nature, xviii, 3, 5, 41, 95–98, 108, 133, 136, 139, 141, 149, 151, 153, 160–62, 164, 168, 254–56, 259–61, 277n4, 290n12, 294n2. *See also* story
natural science, 21, 23
nature, ix, x, xvi, xxi, 8, 11, 12, 13, 17, 19–23, 26, 39, 42, 44, 45, 50–66, 81, 83- 84, 87–88, 98, 105, 107–11, 114, 119–23, 129, 139–40, 146, 152, 158–59, 161, 166, 171, 173, 175, 176–79, 189, 190, 195, 200, 229–33, 250–53, 254, 257, 259, 262, 269, 286n23, 288n2, 297n17
Nature Conservancy, 262
nature writing, ix, xvi, 131, 132, 163
Nazgûl, 148, 218
Neldoreth, 104, 133
Never Cry Wolf, 266

New Testament, 56, 281n7
Nienna, 6
Niggle, xxi, 130, 163, 164, 170–81, 267, 292n12
Nimloth, 62, 63, 132, 143, 239
Nineteenth Lancashire Fusiliers, 187
Ninquelótë, 7
Noah, 187
Nokomis, 120
Noldor, 10, 61, 91, 102, 103, 109, 114, 159, 287n5
Nonent, 127
Norns, 127
Norse. *See* Old Norse
Norse mythology, 120, 266
North Farthing, 157
Northern Kingdom, 50, 82, 83, 295n3
Northfield, 79
nostalgia, x, 74, 112, 198, 205, 285
Númenor, 37, 60–63, 115, 134–36, 187, 199, 194, 285n18

objective morality, 34, 48
objectivity, xxii, 24, 25, 33–35, 48, 49, 60, 91, 146, 151
Odin, 266
Old English, 12, 40, 125, 126, 165, 197
Old Entish, 129
Old Forest, 43, 109, 133, 136–40, 142, 144, 145, 150–52, 155, 158, 160, 161, 290n12
Old Man Willow, 43, 133, 138, 139, 140, 151, 152
Old Norse, 3, 16, 52, 120, 126, 279
Oliver, Mary, x
Olórin, 7
One Ring, 45, 87, 90, 114, 202, 210, 217, 244
Onodrim, 119, 127, 128
ontology, 50, 51, 127. *See also* being, ontology
oppression, 22, 101, 137, 231
Orald, 159

Orcs, xii, 17, 18, 34, 89, 124, 131, 132, 134, 140, 192, 195, 196, 211, 220, 226, 244, 250, 254, 282n13
Ormal, 110
Ormstunga, 281n2
Orodruin, 188, 217
Orr, David W., 74, 200, 210
Orthanc, 114, 142, 143, 161, 195, 202, 203, 217
Outer Faery, 178
Oxford English Dictionary, 127
ozone, 282n12

paganism, 53, 54
pantheism, 54
Paradise, 198
Parish, 77, 163, 164, 170, 172–73, 175–77, 179, 181, 267
Party Field, 157, 231
Party Tree, 157, 213, 229, 231
pastoralism, 285n17
Pawnee, 120
Pearce, Joseph, 14, 15
Pelóri, 111
Perkins, 176
personal preference, 24, 25, 34, 48, 49
personification, 19, 20, 23
Phial of Galadriel, 7
Pillars of Argonath, 147
Pimple. *See* Sackville-Baggins, Lotho
Pippin. *See* Took, Peregrin
Pison, Thomas, 147, 289
Platonism, 65, 128
Poetic Edda, 266
politics, xi, xvii, xxii, 4, 38, 39, 42, 82, 119, 124, 200
pollution, 17, 53, 189, 195, 198, 211, 212, 224, 225, 227, 261, 264, 269
possessiveness, 61
poverty, 53–54, 170, 298
power, xii, xx, 6, 10, 13, 17, 20–26, 27, 29–31, 38, 60, 92, 100, 107, 114, 135, 136, 161, 168, 179–81,

194, 195, 197–200, 202, 203, 209, 223–25, 240, 246, 249, 250, 279nn25–26
Powers of Arda, 120
Prancing Pony Inn, 153
Prentice "Alf," 180, 181
preservation, xi, xv, xvi, xxi, 44, 82, 88, 100, 107, 109, 113, 119, 129, 133, 134, 142, 144, 172, 185, 228, 229, 232, 240, 245, 250, 252, 262, 286n1, 287n10, 296n15
pride, 62, 63, 72
primary world, 30
Prince Caspian, 71, 72
progress, xii, 81, 84, 91, 173, 176, 194, 199–201, 203, 205, 206, 269
propaganda, xxiii, 209
Protestantism, xxiii, 39, 122, 277n6, 288n2
provincialism, xi, 73, 74, 75, 92
Psalm 104, 28, 122
Psalm 148, 31, 122, 252, 259
purpose, of existence, xvi, xvii, 22, 24, 28–38, 43, 44, 50, 51, 56, 66, 67, 89, 113, 122, 161, 164, 180, 196, 198, 200, 211, 225, 229, 252–54, 258, 261, 280n33

Queen of Faërie, 178, 180
Quendi, 35, 49, 101, 111
Quenta Silmarillion, 5, 8, 33, 61, 143, 187
Quenya, 102, 125, 287

race, xii, 24, 36, 49, 50, 55, 62, 64, 83, 88, 90, 91, 95, 97, 101, 103, 111, 114, 227, 229, 230–32, 235, 237, 240, 242, 251, 252, 254, 278n9, 282n13, 287n7, 287n10, 295n2
Rackham, Oliver, 291
Radagast, 122
Ragnarök, 266
Rangers, 244

realism, 4, 75, 185
recovery, 125, 152, 236, 241, 260, 266
Rednal Cottage, 73
redwoods, 63, 256
Region, Middle Earth, 104, 133
resources, xii, xx, 4, 30, 46, 53, 54, 80, 100, 128, 205, 212, 261, 297n1
responsibility, xvii, 35, 40–42, 46, 48, 52, 54, 60, 61, 64, 67, 116, 145, 210, 221–23, 226, 229, 232, 235, 236, 240, 241, 242, 259–61, 281n7, 282n12
restoration, xii, 24, 35, 143, 149, 156, 157, 172, 176, 187, 215–19, 225, 228, 229, 235, 236, 238–40, 245–48, 254
Revelation, book of, 31
rhetoric, 39, 43, 54, 198–203, 208–10, 260
Rhudaur, 267
Rivendell, 7, 87, 89, 95, 96, 101, 103, 106, 109, 112, 113, 133, 141, 142, 145, 151–53, 199, 243, 244, 265, 290. *See also* Last Homely House
River Cole, 77, 78
Roberts, W. Dayton, 59
Rohan, x, 9, 12, 33, 34, 37, 47, 88, 89, 125, 142, 146, 148, 149, 194, 196, 218, 220, 223, 232, 233, 239, 240, 244, 256, 257, 267, 280n1, 294n2
Roman Catholicism. *See* Catholicism
Romania, 207, 208
Romans, book of, 56, 65
romanticism, 73–75, 79, 85, 92, 165, 265, 298n10
ruffians, 87, 207, 210, 211, 223, 236, 241, 242, 248, 261
rulers, 37, 38, 41–43, 60, 107

Sackville-Baggins, Lotho, 86, 206, 208–10
sacrifice, 81, 87–91, 253, 254
Sanders, Scott Russell, 209, 212, 213, 246, 247, 258, 259

Sandyman, Ted, 72, 78, 209, 210, 231, 256, 278n10
Santmire, H. Paul, 281n5
saplings, 6, 156, 231
Sarehole, 77–79, 197
Sarn Ford, 207
Saruman, xi, xii, 18, 53, 63, 77, 81, 87, 89, 91, 113, 124, 134, 140, 142, 170, 185, 192, 194–211, 215, 217, 220–23, 226, 231, 241–46, 250, 265, 266, 269, 279n27, 293n1, 294n2
Sauron, 37, 38, 43, 44, 46, 47, 48, 49, 63, 89, 100, 113, 114, 134–36, 139, 140, 142, 170, 185, 186, 188, 190–94, 196, 198, 201, 202, 210, 212, 213, 217–20, 222, 224–27, 244, 246, 250, 265, 294n2
Scandinavia, 127
Schumacher, E. F., 14, 15, 278n13
science/scientists, 21, 22, 298n10
sea-elves, 103
seasons, 20, 82, 187
Second Age, 6, 115, 133, 134
Second Children of Ilúvatar, 132
Second Voice, 171, 176, 177, 292–93n18
Secret Fire, 26
servanthood, stewardship, 43, 45
Shadowfax, 43, 44
Shagrat, 244
Shakespeare, William, ix
Sharkey, xi, 185, 203, 208–12, 236, 247, 261. *See also* Saruman
Sheldon, Joseph K., 281n5
Shelob, 188
shepherds of the trees, 119, 123, 125–27, 128, 144, 156, 256. *See also* Ents
Sherrard, Philip, 253, 297
Shippey, T. A. "Tom," 18, 129, 163, 173, 177, 196–201, 204, 243, 271, 279n18, 292n12, 292n18

Shire, x, xi, xxi, 11, 13, 15, 18, 48, 53, 71–92, 95, 97–98, 103, 106, 109, 111, 134, 137–61, 170–72, 179, 185, 190, 191, 203–23, 231–32, 236, 238, 241, 242, 245–49, 254–55, 260–61, 264–66, 269, 278n10, 279n18, 284n14, 285n17, 286n24, 290n12, 292n6, 294n2, 295–96n4
Siegel, Robert, 108, 129, 287n9, 289n10
Sierra Club, 262
Siewers, Alfred, 283n22
Silmarillion, The, xvi, 5, 6, 11, 24, 26, 35, 36, 42, 49, 50, 55, 56, 65, 98, 103, 107, 109, 110, 115, 116, 122, 125, 132, 133, 179, 225, 259, 266, 283n24
Silmarils, 5, 7, 10, 61, 109
Silpion, 7
silver (color), 9, 10, 96, 105, 106, 107, 110, 111, 113, 115, 122, 132, 157, 231, 238, 239, 287n10; metal, 63, 104, 105
Silverlode, 107, 112
simplicity, xx, 11, 13–15, 17, 22–24, 278n13
Sindar, 102
Sindarin, 102–4, 107, 125, 287n5, 287n7, 289n15
Sir Gawain and the Green Knight, 41
Sir Orfeo, 41
Sirion, 104
Skuld, 127
Smallburrow, Robin, 223, 236, 241, 242, 246, 260, 261
Smaug, 15, 16
"Smith of Wootton Major," xxi, 163, 164, 177, 179, 180, 294n1
Snaga, 244
Snyder, Gary, x
soil, xi, xx, 13, 17, 30, 32, 48, 49, 53, 75, 76, 79–82, 84, 90, 92, 95, 97, 99, 100, 156, 170, 189, 200, 201, 207, 212, 213, 231, 249, 251, 263, 296n12

soul, 23, 65, 66
Southfarthing, 207, 208
spells, magical, 22, 148, 161
spiders, 10
Spring of Arda, 110, 132
St. Giles of Assisi. *See* Aegidius
St. Isidore the Farmer. *See* Isidore
Stahler, Dan, 266, 298N10
Stanton, Michael, 202, 281n7, 293n10
Stevens, Wallace, x
stewardship, x–xii, xx, xxi, 31, 37–50, 52, 54, 56, 58–60, 64, 66, 76, 83, 88, 89, 91, 93, 110, 133, 143, 145, 160, 164, 180–82, 191, 192, 196, 207, 210, 213, 216–19, 223, 225, 227, 228, 235, 237–39, 241, 245, 248, 251, 254, 256, 258, 260, 261, 270, 281n5, 281n7, 295n2
Stockbrook, 152
stone, 8, 13, 20, 78, 104, 105, 120, 142, 144, 148, 161, 188, 189, 190, 202, 216, 217, 230, 257, 259, 278n7, 278n9
Stoors, 82
Stormcrow, 37, 222
story/storytelling, xvi, xvii, xx, xxi, 3–7, 16, 19, 21, 25, 28, 29, 41, 42, 47, 52, 77, 80–86, 88, 89, 95, 103, 110, 115, 116, 119, 125, 126, 129, 130, 134, 139, 141, 146, 149–52, 156, 159, 163–81, 185, 187, 199, 204, 213, 215, 217, 219, 220, 224, 227, 228, 232–36, 254–56, 266, 280n1, 286n23, 290n12, 294n1, 296n14. *See also* narrative
Straight Road, 115
Strider, 265. *See also* Aragorn
subcreation, 26, 50
subjectivity, 3, 33
Súlimo, 60
sun, 10–12, 19, 106, 108, 110, 113, 120, 122, 126, 131, 139, 142, 159, 179, 238, 257, 266
Sussex, 75

sustainability, x, xii, xv, xvi, xxi, 16, 76, 84, 90, 92, 98–100, 146, 223, 251, 264, 297n1
Sylwanowicz, Agnieszka, 280
symbolism, 6–8, 10, 25, 41, 61–63, 132, 134, 147, 154, 168, 178, 179, 194, 212, 217, 229, 238, 239; biblical, 41

Tar-Aldarion, 135
Taur-en-Faroth, 133
Taur-im-Duinath, 133
Taur-na-Neldor, 133
technology, x, 13, 14, 17, 18, 21, 30, 63, 72, 77, 81, 84, 99, 121, 123, 124, 144, 197–200, 246, 248–50, 261, 264, 279n18
Teleri, 102, 103, 287n7
Telleen, Maurice, 75, 226, 227, 245
Telperion, xx, 7, 9–11, 61, 62, 110, 111, 132, 158, 239
Thain, 82
Tharkûn, 7
Théoden, 37, 44, 46, 47, 96, 125, 126, 194, 200, 213, 219–22, 226, 232, 233, 240, 242, 244, 256, 257
theology, 58, 281
Thingol, 102, 104, 105
Third Age, 5, 7, 34, 41, 46, 80–82, 105, 114, 132, 133, 136, 138, 143, 159, 199, 239, 281
Thomas, the apostle, 176
Thoreau, Henry David, ix
Thorin, 16, 105, 295
Thranduil, 96, 98, 102, 103, 105
Timmons, Daniel, 279
Tirion upon Túna, 105, 111
Tolkien, Christopher, 41, 130, 269, 283
Tolkien, Hilary, 75, 77
Tolkien, J. R. R.: artistic illustrations, 108; life of, 7, 13, 20, 73, 75, 77–79, 187, 191; love for trees, 130–32, 170; perceived failures, 163, 173; wartime experiences, 187

Tompkins, 176
tools, 17, 38, 72, 81, 178, 179, 257
toxic waste, 64, 187
transcendence, xxii, 24–26, 33, 34, 49, 50, 53, 55, 57, 58, 63, 65, 66, 115, 116, 119, 122, 161, 164, 171, 174, 175, 178, 181, 182, 224, 228, 229, 233, 253
Treebeard, 13, 19, 81, 107, 119, 123–29, 133, 134, 138–40, 143, 144, 152, 156, 161, 193, 195–97, 208, 217, 218, 220–23, 226, 232, 233, 236, 240–43, 245, 247, 251, 252, 254, 289n15, 296n14. *See also* Fangorn
Treegarth, 143, 217
trees, xx, xxi, 13, 19, 21–22, 28, 34, 78, 90, 96, 98, 101–40, 142, 145, 153–59, 211–12, 228–32, 239, 241, 253–54, 257, 259, 269, 291–92n13; destruction of or harm to, 55, 63, 185, 188–90, 193–96, 204–6, 215, 217, 220–21; sentient, 151, 289n14; stewardship of, 39, 251; symbolism of, 63–64, 170–79. *See also* forests, Hourns; Two Trees of Valinor; White Tree of Númenor; woods
trolls, 126
True West, 101
Tulcea, 207
Turgon, 105
Turner, Victor, 147, 148, 290n12
Two Lamps, 110
Two Trees of Valinor, 6–12, 23, 35, 61, 62, 102, 104–6, 110–13, 120, 158, 179
Tyr, 266
Tyrannus, 169

Udûn, 191, 192, 194, 218
Ulmo, 8, 28–30, 33, 35, 42, 51, 57, 120
underworld, 41

Undying Lands, 112
Unfinished Tales, 122, 134
Ungoliant, 10
Urð, 127
Uruk-hai, xii, 148
Utopia, 198

Vala, Valar, 6, 8–11, 20, 27, 29, 30, 33, 35, 49, 60, 62, 63, 101, 104, 107, 109–11, 115–16, 120–21, 123, 159, 187, 225, 277n4, 278n5, 279n25, 287n7
Valaquenta, 111
Vale of Evermorn, 178
Valinor, 6, 7, 9–12, 35, 42, 57, 60, 61, 63, 95, 101, 104, 105, 108–10, 111–17, 121, 132, 159, 171, 238, 265
Valmar, 6, 7
Van Dyke, Fred, 65, 66
van Gennep, Arnold, 147, 148, 290n12
Vanyar, 102, 103
Venus, 120
Verðandi, 127
Vermont, xv, 100, 145, 248
victim mentality, 45, 241
Vingilot, 5
virtue, xx, 7, 14, 15, 17, 34, 44, 76, 80, 83, 86, 89, 206, 240, 247, 248, 252, 254, 260, 265, 280n33

Waldman, Milton, 49
war, xii, 17, 29, 32, 33, 37, 41, 43, 44, 47, 48, 50, 60, 61, 75, 82, 83, 89, 102, 103, 109, 114, 130, 134–36, 142, 155, 168, 187, 191, 192, 196, 199, 202, 213, 216–18, 220, 221, 226, 239, 255, 257, 269. *See also* battle
Warren, Rick, 297n2
Warwickshire, 77, 284n15
water, 9, 20, 57, 72, 77, 78, 115, 120, 144, 156, 158, 169, 187–91, 204,

217, 218, 229, 238, 263, 270; importance of, 30, 122; pollution, 17, 53, 99, 211–13, 227, 261; quality, 13, 30, 81, 100
Water, The, 190, 212
weather, 47, 48, 75, 270, 282n12
well-being, 48, 59, 86, 177, 236, 258
Well of Being, 127
West Marches of Rohan, 76
West Midlands, 77
West Saxon, 196
Westernesse, 106, 112, 295
Westwood, 178
white, 105, 107, 108, 111, 115, 186, 230, 238, 239, 265
White, Lynn, Jr., 53, 54, 63–66, 122, 252
White Havens, xi
White Lady, 218
White Mountains, 142, 267
White Tree of Númenor, 62
White Wizard, 194–95. *See also* Saruman
Whitewell, 72
Whitman, Walt, ix
WILD Foundation, 262
Wilderland, 141, 152, 269
wilderness, ix–xii, xv, xvi, xxi, 32, 39, 83, 99, 100, 123, 127, 130, 140–61, 172–79, 187, 194, 195, 227, 228, 241, 250, 262, 265, 266, 298n10; areas in Middle-earth, 132, 133, 290n12; ethics, 124; value of, 119, 124, 129, 134, 232
Wilderness Act of 1964, ix
Wilderness Land Trust, 262
Wilderness Society, 262
Williams, Raymond, x
Williamson, Jamie, 20, 279n25

Wirzba, Norman, 4, 5, 73, 74, 198, 199, 221, 229, 232, 233, 256
Withywindle, 138, 269
wizard, 37, 39, 122, 124, 194–95, 197, 242, 250
wolves, 112, 202, 265, 266, 298n10
Wood-elves, 105
Woodhall, 95, 96, 109, 110, 154
woods, x, 13, 43, 96, 104–7, 119, 136, 137, 139, 143, 144, 148, 152–54, 156, 220, 228, 251, 252, 269, 270; as symbol of wilderness, 124, 127, 132–34; love of, 130; in the Shire, 82, 83, 87, 91, 157, 190. *See also* trees; forests
Woody End, 95, 153, 155, 157, 190
Woolf, Virginia, x
Wootton Major, 163, 164, 177–79, 180, 291, 294
Worcestershire, x, 76, 77, 78, 79, 284, 285
work, 10, 17–18, 23–24, 28–29, 36, 43, 50, 57–58, 71–72, 75, 84, 86, 92, 98, 101, 110, 116, 127, 156, 165, 169, 174–77, 192, 225, 230–31, 236, 240, 243–50, 261–62, 283n1. *See also* labor
Workhouse Infirmary, 174
World Ash, 127
World Wildlife Federation, 262
Wormtongue, 37, 47, 125, 222

Yardley Parish, 77, 79, 284n15
Yavanna, 8, 10, 11, 23, 55, 56, 62, 104, 111, 120–23, 127, 158, 160, 218, 239; creation of Two Trees, 6–8, 35, 62, 110, 179; song of, 6, 8
Yellowstone Gray Wolf Restoration Program, 266
Yggdrásil, 127

4/09

DATE DUE

9/15			
MAR 1 1 '10			
1/6/11			
75758275			
OCT 1 5 '12 4/25/14			

Library Store #47-0108 Peel Off Pressure Sensitive